GLIMPSES OF ETERNITY

THE JOURNEY OF MY SOUL TO CONSCIOUSNESS

RA HETER

Imprint Universal Consciousness Publications

Imprint Universal Consciousness Publications

Nuvo Development, Inc.
Decatur, GA 30034
Copyright © 2020

ISBN 979-85393749-7-6

To Anna Mae & Genie Dixon
For Whom I am Eternally Grateful

When I am dancing with my shadow,
because it seems much older than me, even ancient,
I am afraid that it might start dancing on its own.

CONTENTS

PART I JOURNEY TO BLACK CONSCIOUSNESS

PART II SPIRITUAL AWAKEINING

PART III UNVEILING CHRISTIANITY

PART IV JOURNEY TO CONSCIOUSNESS

PART I
JOURNEY TO BLACK CONSCIOUSNESS

1
SOUL YEARNINGS

I don't know when my soul's journey began, where it had been, or why it was here. All I know is that some years ago, I came to Earth; a place that is magnificently awesome, but at the same time, can exact what seems like indifferent and incredible pain and suffering. I do not know how many times my soul has passed through here, or other places it has lived. I have no memory of these places when I am awake. But the places I travel to when I am asleep tell me that my soul is much older than I am, and at one time may have even danced among the gods.

What is a life? It is a mystery of the unfolding of the self on a journey that will eventually lead to somewhere. As one journeys on Earth, one will find that every second that one is here, every minute of every hour, is an expression of a reality that is preparing one for a journey once this one ends. How one goes through this journey will determine whether one will come back here, or somewhere else.

The ancients say that there are seven states of consciousness. The first three—deep sleep, dreaming, and waking—most of us are familiar with. However, many of us exist in a dreamy state, even while we are awake. The other four states of consciousness that we are not so familiar with are "*soul* consciousness, where the soul is aware of and observes itself; *cosmic* consciousness, where the soul is awake in deep sleep, dream and waking; *divine* consciousness, where the soul is aware of the universal in the particular; and *unity*, where the soul is aware that the personal and universe are one."[1] I believe in what the ancients say because they lived thousands of years before our time, and therefore, were as close to the gods as we can get. And this may be because they were birthed by them and may have even lived among them.

The ancients also say that the state of awakening that one enters the earthly realm depends on what one did in previous lifetimes. However, I believe that one's state of awakening may also have to do with what happens at birth. The events surrounding one's birth or even one's child-hood are so shocking, even if one wanted to live in a dreamy, waking state, one was so shaken it awakened one to a higher state of conscious-ness. And when this happens, one—or rather, one's soul—spends the rest of life watching. I think that was the case with me.

~~~~~~~~~~

My soul's journey began—this time—when I was birthed by my teenage mother and left in a maternity home. I believe the wound of that experience was so shocking, I was awakened to soul consciousness because, since I can remember, I have felt like I was on the outside looking in. When one does not know their origins, the question that will haunt one, as one goes through life is *Who am I?* This becomes even more complex when you discover that you are the descendant of a people whose history was purposely erased so that you would not know who you are. The question then becomes *Who are we?*

But as you ponder this question, it will lead to even more questions; age-old ones of why do we come here anyway, why there is so much suffering, and where do we go after death? Since Western science, being entrenched in a materialistic paradigm, offers pitiful answers to some of these questions—the Big Bang, evolution, and no answers to some of the other questions—one may feel compelled to turn to religion. But when one struggles with religion, at least the one was raised with, it raises even more questions, forcing you to look further.

Although these questions remain ever-present in your consciousness and rise from time to time, they pale little against the forces that you are up against as are trying to figure out what you will do with your life; and once you figure that out, as you struggle to make it through this life. You, therefore, go on with the business of living, wandering through life, stumbling into bits of information here, pieces of information there, leading you to become more awakened; more conscious. But then some-thing happens that is so life-changing, it compels you to search until you find answers.

~~~~~~~~~~

Life is hard. But it can be really hard for Black people living in America. And it was no less so for the family who took me in as a foster child and eventually adopted me. Being born during the height of the Civil Rights and Black Power movements and being raised in a working-class Black family in the 1960s and 1970s, a lot of things can happen that can profoundly affect one and how one sees the world. However, a few of these experiences will stand out, some that drive your life-giving it a profound sense of purpose; others raising even more questions that cause you to spend the rest of your life searching for something that even you didn't know what it was until you found it.

By the time I reached the age of nine, both Malcolm X and Martin Luther King, Jr. had been murdered, and the Civil Rights Movement was waning to the rising Black Power Movement. My family, it seemed, however, was on the periphery of the Black movements. Although my mother (like most Black people) had pictures of Martin Luther King, Jr., John F. Kennedy, and white, blond, and blue-eyed Jesus on the mantle in the living room and had to be conscious of being a Black woman in America simply because she lived as one, it seemed she was estranged from the movement, and my father even more so. I believe this to be the case because as nosey as I was, tuning my ears to everything they talked about, I hardly ever heard them talk about anything related to the Black movements. It could have been a function of living in Albany (the Capital of New York State), a quaint and predominantly white city, encircled by mountains, and approximately two-and-one-half hours from New York City. Or, it could have been that by the time I would be able to comprehend what they were talking about, the Civil Rights Bill of 1964 and Voting Rights Act of 1965 had been signed in law, followed by the ushering in of affirmative action programs, giving Black people hope.

I do remember a little about the riots that gripped American cities in the mid-to-late-1960s. There was turmoil in Albany High School, but I do not know if the students were just fighting, or whether it had to do with the movements. What I do remember is negative comments made by my mother, particularly her saying that the students would be too full to do work, in response to demands that were being made for free meals in schools. I would pass a house that was a Black Panther office on Clinton Avenue on my daily walk to school. Although, news coverage and my mother's negative comments made me confused about who they were, for some reason I admired the Black Panthers, without really understanding why I did. I didn't know anything about the Nation of Islam but would see *Muhammad Speaks* newspapers laying around the house. Either my father (who was an avid reader of newspapers and stacked them in his room, causing much strife between him and my mother) must have been purchasing them, or they could have been purchased by my mother, just because somebody asked her to. I do not remember anything about Malcolm X being shot—at least in the news that my father watched, which he watched without fail. It could have been because I was too young at the age of six to remember; it could have been that I did watch it, and knew about it, and was it somewhere deep in my consciousness.

When John F. Kennedy got shot, I do remember feeling hurt that my mother was crying about it, as I would feel the few occasions I would see her cry, but I could not understand why she was crying over him. Being about four or five years of age and not understanding that he was the president of the United States who had introduced the Civil Rights Bill, all I could think of was how awfully mean white people were to Black people. I somehow gathered that John F. Kennedy being shot to death meant that things were going to remain hard for Black people.

The only thing that I recall vividly about the movements is the news coverage of Black people being sprayed with water hoses, beaten by white cops, and attacked by dogs. Martin Luther King, Jr. got shot when I was in the third grade. Many of the Black kids at school, I suppose, feeling the pain of their parents, were hurt and angry. I do not think they really understood the gravity of him getting shot, nor did I. All we knew is that Martin Luther King, Jr., a Black man, a hero for Black people, had been shot by hateful whites, and it caused a lot of tension in school that day. The Black kids were angry at the white kids, and so was I. Besides the news coverage of Black people being treated badly by whites that affected me profoundly, the news footage of Blacks being brutalized by white cops and the murder of Martin Luther King, Jr. may have been the beginning of an awakening of Black consciousness for me.

~~~~~~~~~~

Although my mother and father seemed estranged from the movements, they carried over the helping tradition, a legacy stemming from both our

African roots and our experiences in slavery and after emancipation. During slavery, free Blacks, putting their own lives at risk to harbor those who had escaped slavery and looking for refuge in northern cities, provided escaped slaves food, shelter in hidden places in their homes, clothing that Black women made in their sewing circles, and other necessities to help them survive and protect them from being captured by slave catchers and sold back into the horrors of slavery. Even free Blacks could meet the fate of being be kidnapped and sold into slavery as was the case with Solomon Northrop, who spent twelve years in slavery (the subject of the film; *Twelve Years a Slave*).

After slavery was abolished, many Blacks provided housing and similar help for those who were escaping from sharecropping (neo-slavery) terrorization, segregation, and other forms of oppression in the South. Decade after decade, millions of African Americans came to the North in search of better opportunities. My mother, Anna Mae, who left Greenville, North Carolina, looking for better opportunities in the North, and my father, Genie James, who left St. Louis, Missouri, I believe were among those people. Once they settled in Albany, New York, some of their family members followed them, making our house a haven for not only extended family members but also for whoever needed a place to stay, including homeless men and children. I was among those children.

My mother and father were hardworking, working-class people who held middle-class values of get an education, working hard, saving your money, and helping people (which they drilled in us) who managed to purchase their own brownstone, Victorian-style home on Ten Broeck Street in the 1960s. It was a herculean feat, considering that my mother only had a third-grade education and my father, a self-proclaimed genius, whose level education we did not know, but was more educated than my mother, some of which he attained through informal self-education. The house was in an integrated community consisting of poor, working, and middle-class Blacks, Whites, and a few Latinos.

Being raised as a foster child in a family with five sisters and a brother (all of whom would eventually be adopted), numerous other foster children, aunts and uncles, cousins, homeless men (whom my father housed in our basement), and even a three-generation white family; who came and left throughout my childhood a lot can happen and did happen.

At first, our lives seemed like a TV version of a middle-class family that my father—and especially, my mother—dreamed of, aspired to, and worked hard to achieve. My father went to work in a factory and my mother was primarily a homemaker, although she worked occasionally as a dietary aid and cleaned houses (which I went with her to help on a few occasions). When my father would come home, dinner would be prepared, and we would eat around the big antique dining room table, with a matching buffet with glass doors and a sideboard. My father would then put on his pajamas, bathrobe, and house shoes that my mother laid out for him and retire to the recliner to watch the evening news with Walter Cronkite. When he would return home from part-time work as a painter, his bathwater would be drawn, and my mother would help him remove the paint from his hands with paint thinner. We loved the Jell-O fruit cocktail and rice pudding desserts that my mother made in her special dishes. My father would catch us when he could, saying "Give me those sugar toes!" when we were barefoot and put our feet in his mouth. We would awake in the morning with candy under our pillows that he'd put there before going to work, and when we would lose a tooth, we would also find money, which he'd tell us was put there by the tooth fairy. I am sure that my father had a special relationship with every one of us, but the relationships we shared, evolved around books. I was the one he would pull out of play to teach me something from the books he had in his library that he was extremely proud of. It was these experiences that would instill in me a love for books and learning.

Things changed after my father retired from full-time to part-time work and drinking with the alcoholics or "drunken bums" (what my mother called them) that would sit on our steps, while my mother went to work full-time. Although things seemed to get worse, I am assuming because my father's income dropped, they continued to take in foster children (including a sibling group addicted to heroin), provide care for children of family members and friends, and provide housing for family members, and it seems, anybody who needed a place to stay. Along with the turmoil that came from my mother nagging my father about his drinking, his poor eating habits, homeless men and women hanging out on our doorsteps, and all the things that happened from day-to-day, the dream they had worked hard to achieve seemed to slip into a hellish nightmare. Every day, it seemed like if it wasn't one thing, it was another.

Of all that happened what left an indelible mark on my soul, was our house being struck by lightning and catching on fire, virtually charring the bedroom that three of my sisters and the children who stayed with us slept in.

It had rained earlier that day. After the rain, my sisters, brother, and I went next door to play with the three cute Ford boys that we loved. My mother, Uncle James, (who stayed in the den downstairs), father, and one of my younger sisters were in the house napping. Suddenly, I heard Uncle James yell out the door, "Patty! Patty! Call the fire department!"

Time seemed to stand still as I watched the events after that moment unfold. My mother dragging my father and younger sister out of that burning house. My mother going back in to get my nephew (who was an infant during that time) and the fishing box with her money in it. The firefighters going in with the axes. Our house being drowned in water. My younger sister's (who was asleep in the room) burnt hand. My father's singed white hair. The ambulances carrying my father and sister off. Out of all that happened during and after, what became etched on my consciousness was not only the damage caused by the fire, but also the damage caused by firefighters, the water, and the smoke.

The night of the fire, we moved in with a woman, Loretta across the street, who remarkably allowed eight people to move into her house with her new husband and two daughters. My father moved back to our house the next day. Interestingly, it was the so-called "drunken bums," my mother said, that came to her and offered to give her their last dollar. A lesson for her, and especially for me that I would carry with me for the rest of my life. No matter the road that people travel that leads to circumstances like alcoholism and homelessness, it does not mean that they are not decent human beings and they should be treated humanely.

During the next few weeks that we stayed with Loretta's family, we would go back to the house to retrieve things that we needed. One night, as I was walking through the house in awe of the damage caused by the firefighters and the water, I looked down and saw that some of my favorite records laying on the dining room floor. I knelt and picked one up and stared at it for a long time in wonderment, asking, "How could the smoke from the fire from all the way in the back room upstairs, melt these records down here?"

We moved back into that house in the horrible conditions it was in because my mother used some of the insurance money for entrepreneur endeavors and had to use jackleg contractors to fix up the house, leaving it incomplete. After two years of living in those conditions, our house caught on fire a second time, causing us to have to move from Ten Broeck Street. After a stay on Clinton Avenue, for about a year, my mother and father purchased a six-bedroom, big white house on First Street with in-wall stainless steel appliances (in the 1970s), hardwood floors, thick crown molding, high ceilings, and plush carpet. It was the biggest house on the block, with upper and lower-level front porches and a large backyard, in a predominantly white community.

However, a year after moving into our new home, my father died. I believe the Camel cigarettes that he smoked led to throat cancer, the cause of his death, and the fact that his diet consisted primarily of coffee and doughnuts did not help matters. Before my father's death, Aunt Liz (Uncle James's wife, and my favorite aunt), who suffered from alcoholism and had seizures quite often, causing much chaos in our household (interestingly, ammonia was used under her nose to bring her back) was sent home after visiting the hospital to die. A few days later she did die of Cirrhosis of the liver on the couch in our abandoned, burnt-up, dilapidated house that she had moved into after we moved out of it. Then, suddenly, Sister McCoy, who was like a grandmother, died of constipation.

The Black movements, and the many things I witnessed and experienced in my family and community, including the compassion and humanitarianism of my mother and father; even in the face of their own hardships, would profoundly shape how I would see the world. However, our house catching on fire, and the deaths of those I loved dearly by the time I was fifteen years of age, would reveal to me not only the powerful forces of water and fire but also the force of the hand of death. More importantly, they revealed to me, very early in my life, the temporality of it all.

~~~~~~~~~~

My struggle with religion—Christianity, specifically—began with the Sunday school lessons that we would have in our basement when Elder McCoy would come and conduct church around the dining room table with the adults on the first floor. Although we loved Elder McCoy and his wife Sister McCoy, who we loved going to the country to visit, we hated seeing him come. This is because my mother I believe trying to impress upon him that she was a good Christian would become sterner, and we had to sit in boring Sunday school classes. Since Elder McCoy came to our house, I have very few memories of attending church during my early childhood, aside from going to church with my older sister, Lonnell, on Easter, who took us to the museum and let us walk down the long stairwell along the pathway to and from the church.

Other than these few early experiences, I do not remember much about religion, until adolescence, when I was about fourteen years of age. I believe that my mother must have taken me to the storefront Pentecostal Church of God in Christ (COGIC) that she attended from time to time after we moved to First Street because that is what I remember the most. And probably because it was the time that I began to form a strong opinion about religion. Although I did believe and accepted some of the teachings, other teachings, like Jesus being the only pathway to God, I did not believe and could not accept. And I believed even less in the preacher that some of the teachings were coming from. I did not feel that some of his spirit-filled sermons where he was shouting and jumping about were genuine.

The total congregation consisted of probably fewer than twenty people, and most, if not all, were women. I was suspicious that the women were being taken advantage of, as I always watched whose hands my mother (with her soft heart) put her money into. Although she could not have been making much money cleaning offices, she put money into the hands of a lot of people who were struggling to make ends meet. And considering how hard our lives seemed to be at times, she seemed to put too much money into the preacher's hands. I would sit in church, watching congregation members get filled with the Holy Ghost and shout, making sure that whatever got in them did not get in me, because it would be too embarrassing to let myself go like that.

At times, I wondered if all the shouting and jumping around was genuine. Other times, I did not doubt that it was when women would be stretched out on the floor, with their bodies contorted in unusual ways, and especially when they would be foaming at the mouth. My doubts were completely dispelled when one day, I was sitting next to my mother, who was quiet and shy, got possessed by something. I am not sure if it was the Holy Ghost because she started howling as if something else had taken over her body.

Although, as time went on, I was the only one in the household getting up and going to church; I was beginning to be torn about religion. I knew that people were being possessed by something. I knew there was a power, a force because I could feel it—I could see it in everything around me. I felt, however, that my understanding was different from what I was learning in church. And there was just something suspicious about it all, something that just did not sit well with me. I think I went to the church less and less and at some point, stopped going altogether.

I would encounter Christianity again in my senior year in high school with one of my high school boyfriends, Sam, a nineteen-year-old who was frustrated with being under his mother's tyranny and going to her sanctified church. As frustrated as he was, he frustrated me because he wanted me to conform to being a churchgoing "saved" girl who wore ugly, boring dresses. I was in theater and dance and wanted to dress like dancers on *Soul Train*. So, I started going to his COGIC with a female minister who ministered to a small congregation. Like the church I attended before, this tall, dark-skinned, ragged-looking woman, who wore a matted wig, gave high-spirited sermons where she would get "happy" and jump about and shout. Her theology, for the most part, was about getting saved, as evidenced according to her by speaking in tongues, which she did quite often and got filled with the Holy Ghost.

Since I was still too shy to let myself go while in church, I had conversations with God in private. At home, I would pray until I would start speaking in tongues—at least, I thought I was. One day, I went to my mother and said,

"I'm saved."

"How do you know?" she asked.

"I can speak in tongues. Look!" I then got down on my knees beside her bed and started praying. The faster I prayed, the more what I was saying sounded like another language. My mother looked at me oddly and did not say much of anything, something she did quite often throughout my childhood. My guess is that she was thinking, "Odd child."

At some point, I joined Sam's church, and one day I told the minister I was saved. She said, "No, you are not because you have not been filled with the Holy Ghost." I was not only shocked that she said that I was not saved but what was more disturbing was the suggestion that I was not saved because I did not shout and jump about at church. "How can she tell me what my relationship with God is?" I asked myself.

Becoming more and more frustrated, feeling that her theology was stifling, feeling that I knew I had a personal relationship with God—and I knew God—that discontent feeling I had before about Christianity reared its head again. I eventually left Sam and that church, and it was the beginning of my leaving Christianity behind, or at least I thought it was when I left Albany to attend college.

~~~~~~~~~~

I was probably the first or second generation of Blacks to take advantage of affirmative action programs that came about from the Civil Rights Movement. Going to college was a way out of my mother's house (who was strict) and a way out of Albany for me. Since I spent my entire adolescent years in gymnastics, dance, and theater (all three of which I loved more than life itself), I thought I might pursue a career in acting. Following in the footsteps of Charlyne Woodard, who had studied at the State University of New York, (SUNY) at New Paltz, a college about an hour and a half from Albany, (and who later landed roles in *Ain't Misbehavin'* on Broadway and the *Fresh Prince of Belair*), I enrolled in its theater department.

There are several things however, that would end this pursuit and my stay at New Paltz. The first is that because the plays were typically about white reality, which meant that white actors were necessary to portray white life (unless the directors were willing to do something radical like my high school theater director John Velie did: cast a white woman with a Black man in Shakespeare's *Midsummer Night's Dream*, in which I played the role of Puck). Second, we were told that we needed to be able to act, sing, and dance. Since I could not sing (at least well), I did not feel confident that I would make it in show business. Third, was the superficiality of it all. Some of the students were acting like they were superstars on Broadway. "This is only New Paltz," I would think when I would see them carrying on like that.

And last, was how difficult living and working in New York City was for me, where I had moved to with my cousin, Freda after my first year of college. Feeling like I was roasting while being sandwiched between people on New York's filthy and overcrowded subways was grueling as I made my way to my job at HUD and the part-time work as a telephone operator, an odd job which Freda got me and was also doing while she was trying to make it as an actress. It was a meeting that Freda had with some of her artist friends, however, that put the nail in the coffin that would end my pursuit of becoming an actress. One of the men who attended the meeting was a self-claimed playwright. However, because of the way he was dressed and how poor he looked, if I did not already know that he was a playwright, I would have thought that he was a hobo.

"I don't want to be poor. I don't want to do odd jobs until I make it," I thought to myself. "I need a profession that is going to pay me enough to make a decent living." Since there was a shortage of Black engineers during that time, I decided I would pursue a career in engineering.

While at New Paltz, I also felt that I was not having the full experience that the white students seemed to be having, with their beer blasts and parties. "How can I have the kind of experience the white students seem to be having?" "I asked myself."

I recalled while in high school, a guidance counselor asking a student, who was one of the most promising Black girls in Albany High School, what college she wanted to attend. Her response was Howard University. Although at that time, I did not know that Howard was a Black college, nor did I even know that historically black colleges and universities (HBCUs) even existed, something clicked: "That's the college you will go to." I decided that if I was to have the complete college experience, I needed to attend a Black university, and left New Paltz.

Not having the resources, however, to get to Howard, I first attended SUNY Stony Brook, where I started my engineering major. Although I had received honors for having the highest scores in math and science in junior high school and graduated in the top ten percent of my class in high school, I was below average in math and science in college. I struggled with physics because the constructs expressed in the mathematical equations seemed to not be connected to anything concrete, and because I could not understand how it was all connected, it created a stumbling block for me, making it difficult to do the math (this type of pedagogy is difficult many Black children, I would later learn). But although I had difficulty with the math, this does not mean that some of the constructs expressed by the mathematical equations, did not become deeply etched in my consciousness. Especially those of Einstein (who's larger than life exhibit I discovered while there); his $E=mc2$ which essentially says that it is all energy; that mass and energy are one and the same thing, and his theories on relativity were captivating.

Stony Brook was the first time I was struggling in my classes and I was homesick because I could not go home as often as I could while in New Paltz. Although I spent a lot of time with friends, Tanya (who was from Albany and who left New Paltz with me) and Steve and Gary, who were engineering majors I met while there, I still felt extremely isolated at Stony Brook, and I was crying almost every day. I was determined to get to Howard University.

2
THE DEATH OF ADAM

When I first got to Washington, DC, I was struck by how on one block you would see nice well-kept homes, and in the next block or one street over, it looked and felt like you were right in the middle of the ghetto. It didn't matter though I guess because I was surrounded by Black people at Howard, and living in Washington, DC, which was called Chocolate City at the time, I didn't feel lonely or the disconnect I felt at New Paltz and Stony Brook; it felt like I was home.

Howard, however, had a housing shortage. So, in my first semester, I was unstable. Howard's housing department referred me to a woman who was renting a room, where I met a young woman who would become my roommate. The woman, however, discovering how difficult it was to board two young adults (who were acting like teenagers, especially me) kicked us out, leaving us without a place to live. Homeless and with nowhere to go, we stayed briefly at the YWCA (which was a virtual slum) for a moment until I found a large one-bedroom apartment in a five-garden apartment complex, right in LeDroit Park, which was within walking distance from Howard University. The Black man who owned it (we learned had given generously to Howard University) had just died, and a dear man named Jerry (who I will never forget because he treated us like we were his daughters) who managed it rented it to us.

I continued the major in engineering but still struggled with physics and calculus. In my first year, I bought an old piano, painted it white, enrolled in piano and dance courses, and auditioned for a Howard play. I, however, had to drop the courses and drop out of the play because I could not balance it with the math and science courses.

Because I was not doing well in my classes, after a few semesters, I decided, "If you do not change this major, you are never going to graduate." A young man I met while studying engineering, Neil, who had changed his major, eventually convinced me to major in geology.

It made sense to me because I had come to love earth science through my seventh-grade teacher, Ms. Bressler, who I also loved. But I did not love her enough to become an atheist, which she was. Burdened by the fact that I wanted to believe what she believed when she said that she did not believe in God, I went to my father. He pulled out his Bible and showed me a passage, which I do not recall. After that, the burden was lifted, and I no longer questioned whether God existed; I knew God existed. With how connected I felt to Earth, the moon, and the stars, there was just too much evidence of the existence of God, and regardless of my shaky journey with religion throughout the rest of my life, there would be nothing that could shake this belief.

While still trying to decide what I would do with my life, I met a professor with long, white, curly, neatly brushed hair, who looked like the Black version of Einstein (and my father). He tried to convince me to major in astronomy. "Come on over astronomy!" he would say every time he would see me on campus. "Majoring in geology you are limited to the earth. With astronomy, you have the whole universe." My thinking at the time was the universe is so vast, how can we possibly come to know it? It seemed like it would be a virtual waste of time.

While enrolled in a paleontology course, I had a Black female professor who was working on her doctorate in paleontology. If she got her doctoral degree, she would be the first Black woman to earn one in paleontology. She, like other professors who tried to help me, suggested that I might consider paleontology as a career. In her class, I learned how ancient life was on Earth, how radioactive dating could tell us how old life was, and the vastness of life in the ocean. Applying Einstein's law of relativity, I imagined the coral reefs as big apartment complexes that housed the life that lived in them.

In my last semester, we had to go on field trips in the geology major. The only other Black female (from England, who was also a geology major) and I went on our first trip in high-heeled shoes. The professors and the other students (who were all male), looked down at our shoes, with facial expressions like, "How in the hell do you think you can walk in the field in those shoes?" During our numerous field trips, we had to climb mountains and walk in waterbeds, which was hard for me. On our final field trip, we stayed in a cabin where we slept in bunk beds. I determined then that fieldwork was not for me and that I would not be pursuing a career in geology. But I was in my sixth year in undergraduate school and decided I just needed to finish this major so I could graduate.

~~~~~~~~~~

One day, I was in Howard University's reading room, sitting in one of the chairs across from a collection of books on a shelf. As I sat there admiring the antique architecture and furniture, something I did quite often, I glanced at the books and saw one entitled *The Death of Adam* by John Greene. I had always been interested in religion, so a book with such a title piqued my interest.

I walked over, took the book off the shelf, and began browsing through the pages. As I continued to read, I became more and more shocked by what I was reading. I checked the book out of the library and took it home. The more I read, the more infuriated I became.

Although the goal of *The Death of Adam* was to provide a detailed account of the evolution of Western thought, from ideals about creation in the late 1600s to ideas about evolution in the late 1800s (and more specifically, to trace the leading ideas that lead to Charles Darwin's works *Origin of the Species* and the *Descent of Man*), it was revealing in terms of how early scientists thought about people of color, particularly people of African descent. At first, they attempted to conform scientific thought in the newly emerging fields in science to Judeo-Christian ideas of providence, the idea that man and nature are static and perfect creations of God, with man falling from grace. As new discoveries were being made, however, and travelers were encountering different species that were not much different from humans in their anatomy and their behaviors, scientists began to question previous thought. They began to see man as being closer to other species among what is now referred to as *hominoid* (family of apes and man) that had evolved from a common ancestor, rather than the other way around, toppling the very notion of Adamic man, a perfect creation of God, who had fallen from grace.

From these two prevailing ideas, humanity had either degenerated from Adam into savages and barbarians (as people of color, specifically African peoples) or he had evolved from savages and barbarians to become a superior man (as Europeans had), the latter view eventually becoming generally accepted by Western scientists. Such thought also revealed the role the scientific community played in perpetuating white supremacy.

With regard to creation, it was thought that although something may have set things in motion, all existence was but matter in motion, with laws dictating how it would exist. Nature was no longer a static creation of God, but it was constantly changing and brutal in force, extinguishing entire species, and because of this, nature needed to be controlled. Under this theory of creation, the world is ever-changing and species either adapt in a way that the strongest and fittest survive, through a process of natural selection, or they die, potentially becoming extinct altogether.

Interestingly, as this view of the world was becoming more accepted, the brutal institute of slavery was well underway, and to support it were studies in which African people were being compared to apes. Encountering different types of species and being extremely perplexed by the fact that apes and humans looked a lot alike and behaved similarly, scientists began classifying apes and man in the same order. It, however, was not just man and ape. It was African man and ape. One species that was particularly perplexing was the orangutan. John Greene wrote:

An ape as tall and strong as man and equally ardent...[He] knows how to bear arms, to attack his enemies with stones, and to defend himself with clubs...[H]e resembles man more than the pygmy...for independent of his having no tail, of his flat face, of the resemblance of his arms, hands, toes and nails to ours and of his walking constantly on end, he has a kind of visage with features which approach to those of the human countenance, a beard on his chin, and no more hair on his body than men have, when in a state of nature...This orangutan or pongo is only a brute, but a brute of a kind so singular, that man cannot behold it without contemplating himself, and without being thoroughly convinced that his body is not the most essential part of his nature.[2]

In fact, one scientist found that the pygmy resembled man more than monkeys and apes in forty-eight aspects and monkeys and apes more than man in thirty-four aspects, and he went as far as to suggest that the pygmy was not even a man, but a link between man and ape.[3] In another account, it was suggested that apes resemble men not only by their physical appearance but also in their behaviors:

> They often go erect and on their hinder feet alone: they pick their food and carry it in their mouths with their hands; they drink liquids from cocoanuts scooped out, and when short of water, dig wells with their feet. They are omnivorous like us...they are always hunting after lice; they remove dirt from their bodies, they are fond of games as boys, they are capital rope-dances, always clever gesticulators, at whom you can never laugh enough. They are malicious by nature, ready for every mischief, given to theft, very salacious even when pregnant. Very mindful of injuries, and difficult to be appeased; anxious, but at the same time very timid hunters; imitators of every folly; difficult to castrate; both fathers and mothers are very fond of their children, even after having had as many as nine. They run away from crocodiles and serpents, and what you would be surprised at, even from those who are ill of contagious fevers.[4]

Some scientists focused on the jaw structure and the shape of the head and face, finding the African's to be closer to the ape, making him closer to the animal kingdom than to the human kingdom, as one scientist describes below.

> Upon placing beside the heads of the Negro and the Calmuck those of the European and the ape, I perceived that a line drawn from the forehead to the upper lip indicates a difference in the physiognomy of these peoples and makes apparent a marked analogy between the head of the Negro and that of the ape... Among human beings, the angle formed by the face line and a line drawn through the base of the nose to the auditory opening varied between eighty and seventy degrees. Everything above eighty degrees belonged to the realm of art, everything below seventy degrees to the animal kingdom.[5]

Greene also notes that this same scientist "himself noted uneasily that comparisons of the Negro and the ape had led some philosophers to imagine that the Negro might be a hybrid produced by intercourse between white men and apes."[6] In addition, he states "the Caucasian was seen to have the most beautiful and symmetrical form... In a like manner, the white color of the Caucasian skin was the norm from which degeneration toward darker shades had taken place."[7]

With Linnaeus's (1758) work and the eventual classification of species, all these ideas culminated into there being primarily three races of men (Caucasian, Mongolian, and Negro), with those of European stock being held to be the highest and most evolved, and Africans being the most degenerate and lowest on the scale of humanity. Summed up in the words of one scientist of the day: "The Caucasian is 'the most beautiful, the most enterprising and the most cultured," while "the Negroes... constitute[s] 'the most degraded race among men, whose forms approach nearest to those of the inferior animal and whose intellect has not arrived at the establishment of any regular form of government, nor at anything which as the least appearance of systematic knowledge.'"[8]

In *The Death of Adam*, Greene explains how as the ideal of evolution was evolving, so was the idea of progress. And there was nothing more indicative of the strongest and fittest surviving than the progress that Caucasians, who were viewed as the most evolved people, evidenced by advances they were making in industry, science, and technology. Thus, as Western nations were attaining a stronger foothold into the lands of peoples of colors, people of color were increasingly being viewed as savages on the lower scale of humanity who needed to be subdued, and if they did not acquiesce, they needed to be *exterminated* in the name of progress. And it was scientific discoveries that were now being merged with emergent social science that sought to model its methods on natural science, with the primary scientist being Herbert Spencer, who is considered the father of Western sociology who supported this notion. One can see this idea in an excerpt from Darwin's *The Descent of Man*, where the extermination of indigenous people by Europeans was compared to the extermination of native rats by European rats:

The New Zealander seems conscious of this parallelism, for he compares his future fate with that of the native rat now almost exterminated by the European rat... If we wish to ascertain the precise causes and their manner of action it ought not be so to our reason, as long as we keep steadily in mind that the increase of each species and each race is constantly checked in various ways; so that if any new check, even a slight one, be superadded, the race will surely decrease in number; and decreasing numbers will sooner or later lead to extinction; the end, in most cases, being promptly determined by the inroads of conquering tribes.[9]

Greene noted that scientists believed "the decline of savage nations was a somber theme, but there was consolation in the reflection that their extinction signified the upward progress of mankind as a whole through the triumph of the higher over the lower varieties of the human species." Darwin, reflecting on how the British had bought about major change in a few decades in Australia, wrote in his diary, "My first feeling... was to congratulate myself that I was born an Englishman."[10]

Reading *The Death of Adam*, made me more conscious of how such ideologies had led to the most brutal form of slavery and genocide of millions of people not only in Africa but all over the world. But what was more disturbing is that some of the very scientists that I may have revered may have been white supremacist racists. I knew that whites were awful to Black people from the footage I saw during the Civil Rights and Black Power movements when I was a child. I knew racism all too well because I could feel it. But *The Death of Adam* awakened me to how deeply rooted it was.

Sometime after that, while going through Howard's course schedule, I stumbled into an African American Studies course. Before that, I did not even know that such courses existed. I took an African American History course and wrote a paper in response to *The Death of Adam*. From that point on, whenever I had to do a research paper throughout both my undergraduate and graduate studies, I would focus on African Americans.

~~~~~~~~~~

During my first years at Howard, I found a book by an Indian author (whom I do not recall), who said it took him forty years to reach the state of nirvana, and I was moved by the work. I was also introduced to Islam through my roommate, who had started seeing a Muslim guy, converted, and started wearing Muslim clothes, including a headcloth. Since she seemed to had fallen under his spell (and under his control), based on my observations of her experiences, I did not find Islam particularly appealing; although, I was moved by the sheer truth of the messages by the Honorable Minister Louis Farrakhan and some of the Black nationalistic tenets in the theology of the Nation of Islam.

What I did find more appealing was the theology of Elizabeth Clare Prophet, the founder of Church Universal and Triumphant (CUT), Summit University, Summit Press, who came to Howard to speak. I found CUT's approach to religion particularly appealing because it seemed to draw from both Western and Eastern religions, which made more sense to me. To me, God was everywhere, and all the religions seemed to be referring to the same thing.

I, however, continued to go to Christian churches from time to time simply because living in DC, they were more accessible; I could walk a block and be at a church. But I still struggled with Christianity. There was just something suspicious about it, and I did not believe that Jesus was the only way to God. Although I prayed, especially when I would get myself into something that I could not easily get out of, I eventually abandoned Christianity throughout the rest of the ten years that I lived in DC.

Over the course of those ten years, aside from completing a bachelor's degree in geology and a master's degree in business administration, I had the best time of my life because three of my childhood friends from Albany (Marcy, Mel, and Darlene) had moved to DC, and I met two other women in school who became friends (Tammy and Antionette). I also met Renee, who was from Albany, while in Stony Brook. After graduating from undergrad, I moved in with Joe, who was my boyfriend at the time. He and my friends from Albany were like one big family,

I went on to earn a Master of Business Administration (MBA) degree during that time because I decided I was not going to do anything with geology, and I needed a degree that would make me more marketable in the job market. However, finding it hard to land a job with an MBA and no experience, since I always liked houses, I got a real estate license and tried selling real estate during my first year out of graduate school. I worked for one of the largest real estate companies in DC, during that time, Shannon and Luchs (and others throughout my time in DC). I did not make one cent, ever. I, however, did get a chance to see a lot of real estate in DC, and it was during that time that I would learn how racially, and economically segregated DC was. Sixteenth Street, considered the Gold Coast, was the dividing line. Most Black people lived on one side, and a few affluent Black people and mostly white people lived on the other side, with it becoming whiter and ultra-rich the closer you got to Georgetown.

Neil, the young man who had talked me into geology, met a man, Ray Carlise, one day when he picked him in in his taxicab. When he said he was looking for someone with a real estate background, Neil spoke so highly of me that he wanted to interview me. After we met, I landed my first job out of graduate school with the National Association of Real Estate Brokers (NAREB). Founded in 1947, NAREB, where members refer to themselves as Realtists, is one of the oldest (if not the oldest) African American professional real estate associations in the country. It was established because African Americans were not allowed to join the National Association of Realtors. Working with NAREB was an eye-opener in terms of discrimination in housing and the real estate industry. Working with Ray Carlisle, I would learn a lot about managing grants, HUD's housing programs, real estate, the mortgage industry, and quasi-governmental agencies like Fannie Mae and Freddie Mac.

However, after working for NAREB for three years (two years in their national office in the Booker T. Washington building on Georgia Avenue, managing their membership association), I felt I had stopped growing. I had also ended my six-year relationship with Joe and was back out in the dating market. Because of the difficulty I was having landing a committed relationship, I began to believe the stories I had heard since moving to DC about the high number of women to men. While I was at Howard, I had no problem with suitors, and therefore did not pay much attention to it. However, after graduating and being in the marriage market, I began to experience what I had been hearing about. And from what I could see, men would not commit to a relationship because they were so outnumbered by women, they simply did not have to.

One day, while sitting on the couch feeling lonely, I looked around the apartment and thought, "I have no husband, nor any prospects of one. If I stay in DC, I might not ever get married or have children. And even if I get married and have children, there is no guarantee they will be with me when I grow old. You need to focus on something that can sustain you for the rest of your life; focus on your life's work." Throughout the time I was in graduate school in business, I remembered I contemplated a career as a professor for two reasons: I found the independence that my professors seemed to have appealing, and I love learning. So, there was probably no profession better suited for me than one which allowed me to earn a living while learning.

After completing my MBA, and before working for NAREB, I had left DC for a semester to pursue a doctorate in marketing at the University of California at Berkeley. During that time, there was a shortage of Blacks with doctorate degrees in business. However, sitting in class one day while at UC Berkeley, and seeing an equation that was about as long as the chalkboard itself describing consumer behavior (and how ridiculous it seemed to me), I decided that a doctorate in marketing would not be for me. Especially since I knew I would focus on Black people in some way or other, and I could not see myself helping big corporations market products to them that they probably did not need. But after returning to DC and spending two years in the workforce, not sure what I wanted to do, I thought about a doctoral degree in marketing again. I found that Temple University in Philadelphia, only two-and-a-half hours away from DC, had a doctorate in business, so I ordered one of its catalogs.

When I got the catalog and opened it, a page opened to African American Studies. "There is a doctorate in African American Studies?" I asked, surprised. As I sat there gazing at the page, I remembered that when I was a child, somewhere between seven and ten years old, staring out of a window feeling anguish about the state of the world, a voice came to me and said that I would write about it. I also remembered that I met a young woman while at UC Berkeley who was getting a doctorate in ethnic studies, and how passionate she was about it, making me feel that is how I wanted to feel about what I do. When I saw the African American Studies program I thought, "Maybe this is what I am supposed to write about. But what can I do with a degree in African American Studies, other than be a professor?" I asked myself. I asked everybody what they thought about it, already knowing I was going to apply for the program regardless of what they said. I was just seeking affirmation. "Hell, you only live once, you may as well do something you really like," said Marcy (my childhood friend since the second grade). "You love African American Studies." I applied for the doctorate program at Temple.

I continued to work with NAREB that year and was feeling more stifled by the day. I was also still grieving the loss of my relationship with Joe and was crying at the drop of a pin. And although I was still having a lot of fun, I had grown sick of the job at NAREB and I was sick of Washington, DC. One day after work, I came home and got down on my knees and prayed, "God, please get me out of here. Please let me get into Temple." A few days later, the acceptance letter from Temple came in the mail.

~~~~~~~~~~

Wanting to start preparing for my courses at Temple, I bought one of my books early, *Afrocentricity*, by Molefi Kete Asante, the founding Chair of the Department of African American Studies at Temple, and took it with me to the bus stop on the way to work one day. Being someone who has difficulty sitting for a minute without having something to do, while waiting for the bus, I opened the book and read:

> The psychology of the African without Afrocentricity has become a matter of great concern. Instead of looking out from one's own center, the non-Afrocentric person operates in a manner that is negatively predictable. The person's images, symbols, lifestyles, and manners are contradictory and thereby destructive to personal growth. Unable to call upon the power of ancestors, because one does not know them; without an ideology of heritage, because one does not respect one's own prophets, the person is like an ant trying to move a piece of garbage only to find that it will not move.[11]

After reading that one paragraph alone, I had a paradigm shift. As I continued to read, I felt a profound sense of connection I had not felt at this point in my life. Before that, I often felt like I was dangling and not connected to anything. At times, I felt I had nothing in common with my family, which made me feel disconnected from them, and I was still questioning religion. I could not identify with the value of materialism undergirded by notions of the "good life" that had gripped some of my friends, who, if they were not already, up-and-coming buppies (middle-class Black Americans). My flighty, artistic side had been grounded by my studies in business administration. So when I saw two people standing in the hall, having what I considered a useless, seemingly going-nowhere intellectual debate while I was visiting Temple for an interview with the Graduate Director, Dr. Keto, I wondered whether I was making the right decision.

As I continued to read Asante's work, I not only learned a lot, but I felt excited and looked forward to entering the program. "Wow," I asked, "Black people made contributions to the world?" It gave me a newfound sense of empowerment. Knowing how unstable my life might be, as I attempted to land a position in academe once I finished the program, I did not want to be dragging furniture around the country. I sold my bedroom set to Tammy, sublet my apartment to Toni, and left for Philadelphia.

3
AFROCENTRIC STRIVINGS

What I would learn at Temple and what I would observe about Black life while living in Philadelphia would change my life and how I would see the world dramatically and forever. When I first got to Philadelphia, I rented an apartment in a mixed-use building on Broad Street, a few blocks from Temple because I wanted to live close to the university. Living in North Philadelphia was an eye-opener to the reality of Black life in urban cities and the crime that gripped some communities. Once I moved into the building, I discovered that it was a virtual slum. My bedroom window faced a roof that had trash on it and somewhere in the building, some people, when having sex, it sounded as if they were in the same room with me. Within the month or two of staying there, my car got broken into several times. The window got smashed, and it got hit while parked on the street. I had lived in DC for ten years, and it was not until the year before I left that things seemed to be getting worse and my car got broken into.

I would later discover that it was because of the new drug, crack cocaine, which I had learned about while living in DC. A friend from DC, who traveled to Philadelphia weekly for a temporary job, stayed with me and his truck got broken into every time he visited. What was too much was to wake up one morning and find, was his truck sitting up on a jack, with not one, but two tires stolen. After that, I decided that living close to the university was not worth it. Discovering that another student in the department was looking for housing, we found a huge two-bedroom apartment in West Philadelphia and moved in.

Because I became so engulfed in my studies and was trying to hold down two part-time jobs, for the most part, it was like I was under water. The only time I would come up for air is when I would leave to travel to DC to visit my friends. I, therefore, reserved my social life for those visits. I did not make any female friends but made some male friends. I dated one, and I would discuss what we were learning with others, who were students when we worked together in the homeless shelter. This pattern would continue throughout my academic career. I thought I might be considered un-collegiate, and this would follow me as well.

The readings, specifically in the proseminar course taught by the late Dr. Keto, not only changed my life, but saved it. Temple's African American Studies program made sure we not only challenge Eurocentric hegemony in all its forms, but also that we were steeped in knowing the contributions African people made to the world. In the course, we had to read about a book (some over four hundred pages) a week. And I, not knowing the almost impossibility of doing this, with two jobs and the other classes, attempted to do so.

Afrocentricity, which essentially means an African-centered perspective, is revolutionary. It is the greatest intellectual challenge to Western-world hegemony that I know of. And I believe if critics of Afrocentricity really understood it and were honest with themselves, they would agree. Although there have been other challenges to Western hegemony (particularly research methods in fields like ethnomethodology, which shares some of the tenets with Afrocentricity), ethnomethodology is still steeped in Western particular ways of knowing, even while it attempts to step outside itself. In *Afrocentricity, Kemet, and Knowledge*, Asante asks:

> What is ethnomethodology conceptually but the white Western Eurocentric researcher saying to other white Western Eurocentric researchers that 'we ought to study these people from their own contexts'? 'Ethno' is derived from 'ethic which is derived from the medieval English 'ethnik' and the late Latin 'ethica' which means 'heathen.'[12]

C. Tsehloane Keto's *the Africa Centered Perspective of History* is particularly insightful because it raises critical questions about hegemony in

Western scholarship, especially as it pertains to history, and the book provides a few examples of how hegemony reveals itself. First, Keto notes that although only 20 percent of the population lives in Europe, North, and Middle America, Western scholarship, "indiscriminately imposes the parochial and non-parochial aspects of the European experience on the rest of the world."[13] And although Western scholarship poses itself as objective, it is sort of a subjective-objective approach, where theories and paradigms are based on Western ideas, values, and principles, parading in the world as the universal source of authority. When this happens, "the rest of the world are overly influenced and often distorted by theories and conclusions drawn from studies based on a minority of the world's families, a minority of the world's women, a minority of the worlds' social structures and a minority of the world's cultures."[14]

Keto provides a few examples of ways in which the West has colonized the world and its psyche. One is geography. He notes that "Lines of longitude to map out international time are most convenient for Western Europe. The phrase 'Greenwich Meantime' is one indicator of this centeredness."[15] He also points out that the names given to the various regions of the world—'Middle East,' 'Southeast Asia,' and 'Far East'— are reference points derived from where they are relative to Europe. Similarly, in the United States, the 'Midwest' and the 'Far West' reflect the patterns of human settlement by America's immigrants of Anglo-European descent who came to dominate the continent after the Mexican war of 1846-1848."[16]

Another way in which European scholarship is Europe-centered is with the use of language. Keto notes that "English, the international language of science in the contemporary world, being a Western European language, automatically carries within its internal construction, the Europe-centered geographical bias."[17] Thus, using language as the organizing principle to communicate about Africa and African descendants in other places in the world "has profound implications," and when we study Africans and other peoples throughout the world in European languages "we are consciously selecting a European centered perspective of the people we are studying."[18]

There is no other place in which the use of language and geography is hegemonic than in the scholarship of "third world" or developing countries. Keto points out that the use of the phrase "third world" began as a positive and affirmative action when "a group of African and Asians who did not view themselves as ideological appendages to either the East or the West, but saw themselves as a 'Third Force' in world affairs."[19] It, however, evolved to be a "dependent concept, predicated on poverty, low economic performance, low per capita income and unfavorable health statistics."[20] Further, "the terms describe a peripheral relationship of dependence and the status of a supplicant state."[21] From this emerged an academic industry of "Third World" studies outside the "Third World." He notes that the use of such a dependent term is problematic for several reasons:

> First, it is a peripheralizing concept which focuses the definition of parts of the world on their economic subservience to the 'industrial countries. It smothers the positive affirmation of the people in culturally diverse regions of the world. Second, it oversimplifies by placing over 80% of the world's people on one side as a counterpoint to 20% of the world's people who live in industrialized countries... Many institutions of higher learning in developed countries believe that one specialist can cover everything from sociology, anthropology, literature, politics, economics and history about all of Africa, Latin American and Asia, while six to eight specialists are necessary to study one century of 'history' for North America or Europe alone. The change of terminology to international studies does not alter this basic built-in conceptual distortion.[22]

There have been challenges to Afrocentricity as a theoretical framework, some of which include its origins and its tenets, more specifically the notion of Egypt being a "classical civilization." But regardless of its origins and some of its shortcomings, one cannot deny its basic premise, which is simply that there are different epistemologies (that is, the way people come to know and view the world), and the West has imposed its way of knowing and how it views the world onto other people. While doing this, Western scholarship has suggested that other people's ways of knowing are inferior and that African and other peoples of color are inferior peoples. In addition, to justify the murder and enslavement of African peoples, the West (with the help of scholarship), had to erase the contributions that African people made to the world, specifically to Greek civilization, where Western education typically begins. Furthermore, what is considered scholarship, beginning with the Greeks, came to full form in the positivist movement in the early 1920s and 1930, is entrenched in a materialistic conception of reality (under the guise of being scientific) and it says that this is a superior way of knowing.

In *Kemet, Afrocentricity and Knowledge*, Molefi Kete Asante, a leading scholar in shaping the field of Africalogy, lays out the basis of the Afrocentric enterprises, stating very specifically that "it is intended to be anything more or less than one person's earnest attempt to provide a sense of clarity around the field that is now being called Africalogy."[23] With this said, it was understood that the field of Africalogy or Africana Studies was a work in progress, so it would take years to shape the discipline.

Besides challenging hegemonic Eurocentrism, two primary tenets of Africology are starting the study of African phenomena with Kemet and reclaiming the legacies of African peoples. According to Asante, when studying African phenomena (no matter where it is in the world), one must start with Kemet, which he refers to as Africa's "high" classical civilization. Opponents argue that Asante is doing what the West has done when it refers to Greek as its classical civilization; he valorizes one civilization over the other. Although arguments can be made for and against doing this, scholars doing work on Egypt not only show the tremendous contributions that Black Egyptians made to the world, they also show the measures white supremacist Eurocentric scholars went to deceive the world about these contributions, including taking Egypt out of Africa and annexing it to the "Orient," and ultimately suggesting that the people who were phenotypically African people were not the builders of the civilization. Thus, while Western scholars made Greek civilization the foundation upon which Western civilization was founded, they attempted to deceive the world by erasing the fact that much of what Greek civilization was founded upon was what they learned from African civilizations built and ruled by Black people, which extended back some ten thousand years or more.

In his extensive work *Black Athena*, Martin Bethal, under his "overthrow of the ancient [Egyptian] model and rise of the Aryan model" thesis makes a well-documented case for African origins of Greek civilization. He uses numerous documents from Greek philosophers including Isokrates, Plato, and Aristotle where they themselves indicate the influence Egyptians had on their philosophies, and that they were Black people. It was only when attempting to justify the enslavement and colonization of African peoples under the "new racism" that seventeenth through nineteenth-century scholars became hostile to the African origin of Egyptian civilization and attempted to replace it with the European model. For example, according to Bernal, "Isokrates and Plato maintained that the great lawgivers and philosophers like Lykourgos, Solon and Pythagoras had all brought back Egyptian knowledge."[24] Aristotle indicated that Egyptian "priests had invented the *mathematical technai* (mathematical arts) which included geometry, arithmetic and astronomy, which the Greeks were beginning to possess."[25] Recognizing that Egypt, in that era, was what the United States is to the world today (a world power) Asante shows the tremendous influence that Egypt had on Greece.

> Indeed, the Greeks saw Egypt, an African country, as the cradle of wisdom and knowledge. The most famous of the Hellenes crossed the sea to be initiated, if they could, at the temples of Egypt. Such was the attraction of this center of information and culture for the Greeks, Sicilians and Persians. Even the most quintessential Greek figures such as Orpheus, and Homer, are said to have traveled to Egypt. Both Salon and Plato crossed the Mediterranean to pay their homage to ancient Egypt. Thales, Pythagoras, Oenopidus and Eudous are only a few of the early Greek thinkers who found it necessary to study in Africa... Thales learned his astronomy and geometry from Egyptian priests. We also know from the Greeks that Pythagoras spent twenty-two years in the temples of Egypt... Plato spent thirteen years in Egypt learning geometry and theology. The celebrated writers of Greece became more popular if they could proclaim, they had been educated by the priests in Africa"[26]

With regard to who the Egyptians were; their phenotype, Cheikh Anta Diop, in his work *African Origin of Civilization: Myth or Reality* notes that the Greek historian, Herodotus, after his eyewitness account of the Egyptians, said "They are black-skinned and have wooly hair..."[27]and "that Greece borrowed from Egypt all the elements of their civilization, even the cult of the gods, and that Egypt was the cradle of civilization."[28] Yosef A.A. Ben-Jochannan in *African Origins of the Major Western Religions* provides substantial evidence to indicate that even the Hebrews were phenotypically indigenous African people. Both Ben-Jochannan and Diop even provide evidence to show the great influence that Egypt had on Judaism. Diop notes specifically that the Hebrews went into Egypt as seventy shepherds, during a time when they were faced with famine, and "left there 400 years later 600,000 strong, after acquiring from it all the elements of its future tradition, including monotheism."[29] Even the biblical story itself tells us that Moses was raised by Egyptian aristocracy and that Joseph, one of the sons of Abraham, was sold into Egypt by his brothers and rose in the ranks before Abraham and the rest of their family settled there.

Egypt is thought to be the source of not only monotheism but also other ideas and concepts that were transported into Judaism, and later Christianity, such as the individual soul, the judgment, eternal life, balance, justice, and other universal moral principles. Even the Mosaic Commandments are speculated to have been derived from the "*Negative Confessions*" or "*Declarations of Innocence*," which are a list of forty-two sins which the soul of the deceased says he has not committed when he is being judged in the afterlife. Diop and Ben-Jochannan point out that even ancient writers on the Egyptians understood that they were derived from the Ethiopians, civilizations older than the Egyptians.

According to Asante, there were cities "in the region of the Nubian desert in Northern Sudan and Southeastern Egypt around 20,000 BC. Data first recorded by the U.S. shuttle in 1978 pointed to buried cities under the desert"[30] Diop notes: "The opinion of all the ancient writers on the Egyptian race is more or less summed up by Gaston Maspero (1846-1916): 'By the almost unanimous testimony of ancient historians, they [the Egyptians] belonged to an African race [read: Negro] which first settled in Ethiopia, on the Middle Nile; following the course of the river, they gradually reached the sea....'"[31]

Stolen Legacy, the title of George James's work (discussed later) might be what to call the 500 years of theft of African treasures and "falsification of history" as Diop puts it. Asante notes how such a tragedy was able to occur:

As African people were colonized and enslaved both on the continent and in the Americas, there were few voices raised against the appropriation of African history as there were few voices raised against the appropriation of our land and labor. Just as we had to throw off the yoke of oppression from our bodies and our lands, we had to liberate the study of the classical civilizations, because the European colonization of geography, that is land, went hand-in-hand with the colonization of information and knowledge. Visit any museum of any major European city and there you will see the treasures of Africa, taken over a five-hundred-year period. Read any African book on African people and you will see the robbing of African civilization, history, and culture. This is why it seems in most European works that African people had no culture, no history, no dynamism prior to European domination and exploitation. A people's classical history is important for the reason that it forms a part of the grand continuity of concepts, values, experiences, visions, and possibilities.[32]

And while African peoples were being enslaved and colonized, their land, labor, material resources, and treasures were being stolen, and their histories falsified and appropriated, a scholar of "good faith," according to Diop, Count Constantin de Volley, who visited Egypt between 1783 and 1785, was astonished by what he found stated:

> Just think that this race of Black men, today our slaves and the object of our scorn, is the very race to which we owe our arts, sciences and even the use of speech. Just imagine, finally, that it is in the midst of peoples who call themselves the greatest friends of liberty and humanity that one has approved the most barbarous slavery and question whether Black men have the same kind of intelligence as whites.[33]

4

THE AUDACITY

While in Temple's doctoral program, I would learn that Egypt was not the only great African civilization of antiquity. It is predated by Ethiopia, where some of the oldest human remains were found with estimates dating between 130,000 and 195,000 years old (older remains were found in Morocco, dating approximately 300,000 years old). Other kingdoms in East Africa include the Nubian states of Kerma, Kush, and Monroe, and later the Aksumite Empire. "In West Africa, there were numerous kingdoms with great wealth, advanced technology, educational institutions, and militarism, the most known in modern history being the states of Ghana, Mali, and Songhai. There were also numerous smaller states throughout Africa, including but not limited to the Mossi states, the states of Kano, Zaria, and Katsina of the Hausa people, Benin, Bornu, the Kongo, Zimbabwe, the Zulus, Oyo, Nri, etc. Today, there are still an estimated 3000 people who speak over 2,000 languages in Africa."[34]

The history of Africa and its people would take a dramatic turn when their nations came under siege by Western nations, their people were captured, and an estimated 40 to 100 million people over a period of three hundred years were sold into slavery through the transatlantic slave trade described as Maafa, which means in Kiswahili "disaster or great misfortune.[35] Barbarous might be an understatement to describe the atrocities that African people experienced under the brutal system of slavery. "Starting with their capture, to the sometimes hundreds of miles' walk from the interior of Africa to the coast—where they would be held in slave pens —to the voyage overseas, to the scramble—where they were sold as human cargo—to life on the plantation, African people experienced one horror after another."[36] I don't think there is anything more powerful in telling what these experiences were like than the voices of the people themselves. Through slave narratives, autobiographies, biographies, and other documents, one discovers just how horrifying some of these experiences were. A few brief excerpts are illustrative, although they do no justice to the horrors that generations of Africa Americans experienced over a period of three hundred years or more.

In *The Destruction of African Civilization*, Chancellor Williams explains what the experience was like during the journey from the interior of Africa to the coastline. It was so horrendous, that many did not survive it. For every 2 million that made it, another million died. Below is an excerpt from a written document that may have been intended for other purposes but is quite revealing about the experience.

There are many problems in this business. The captains, taking it easy on the coast, are always complaining about our slow movement and the many weeks it takes on the march. They never take into account how much we are slowed down by the trampling and stumbling over the skeletons and rottening of dead bodies of slaves that went along these trails before us, sometimes years before us. The stench of those who died recently is unbearable, yet we bear it. We also lose much time trying to find routes free of the dead and dying. ... Another problem was the large number of suicides during the two-hundred-mile trek to the slave pens. The greatest number died from poison which hundreds of women would conceal on their bodies for the purpose, passing it to friends and kinsmen in the darkness of night before giving it to their children and finally taking it themselves. ... The dead and dying had to have their chains chopped off from the living. Many babies were deliberately smothered to death by their dying mothers.[37]

The voyage overseas—the middle passage, was no less horrifying. The following is an account of the middle passage from Olaudah Equiano who was kidnapped along with his sister when he was eleven years old.

I was immediately handled, and tossed up to see if I were sound, by some of the crew; and I was now persuaded that I had gotten into a world of bad spirits, and that they were going to kill me. ... I asked them if I were not to be eaten by those White men with horrible looks, red faces and long hair. ... I was soon put down under the decks, and there I received such a salutation in my nostrils as I had never experienced in my life ... the closeness of the place, and the heat of the climate, added to the number in the ship which was so crowded that each had scarcely room to turn himself almost suffocated us ... the air soon became unfit for respiration, from a variety of loathsome smells and brought on sickness among the slaves of which many died. ... This wretched situation was again aggravated by the galling of the chains ... the shrieks of the women, and the groans of the dying, rendered the whole scene of horror almost inconceivable.[38]

Equiano also describes some of the brutalities that many experienced during the middle passage.

> One White man in particular I saw, when we were permitted to be on deck, flogged so unmercifully with a large rope near the foremast, that he died in consequence of it; and they tossed him over the side as they would have done a brute. ... One day ... two of my wearied countrymen who were chained together ... preferring death to such a life of misery, somehow made it through the nettings and jumped into the sea; immediately another ... also followed their example ... two of the wretches were drowned, but they got the other and afterwards flogged him unmercifully for attempting to prefer death to slavery.[39]

Once Africans made it to North America, they were subjected to the "shout" or "scramble" where they were stripped, greased, branded, examined, and touched all over, including in their genital areas. Again, Equiano describes the experience:

> On a signal given (as the beat of a drum), the buyers rush at once into the yard where the slaves are confined and make a choice of that parcel, they like best. The noise and clamor with which this is attended and the eagerness visible in the countenances of the buyers, serve not little to increase the apprehension of terrified Africans.[40]

After they reached the United States, they were usually sold and scattered, some onto small plantations. This was done to erase historical and cultural memory and to make communication difficult. Although experiences on plantations varied, and some slaveholders were described as kind, African Americans experienced insufferable horrors. In *The Slave Community* John Blassingame summarizes plantation realities:

> On the plantations ... strong Black men suffered from overwork, abuse, and starvation; the overseer's horn usually sounded before sleep could chase the fatigue of the last day's labor ... mothers cried for the infants torn cruelly from their arms, and whimpering

Black women fought vainly to preserve their virtue in the face of the lash or pleaded for mercy while blood flowed from their bare buttocks. A cacophony of horrendous sounds constantly reverberated through such plantations: nauseated Black men vomited while strung up over slowly burning tobacco leaves, vicious dogs tore Black flesh, Black men moaned as they were hung up by their thumbs with the whip raising deep welts on their backs and as they were bent over barrels or tied down to stakes while paddles with holes in them broke blisters on their rump. ...Floggings of 50 to 75 lashes were not uncommon. On numerous occasions, planters branded, stabbed, tarred and feathered, burned, shackled, tortured, maimed, crippled, mutilated, and castrated their slaves. Thousands of slaves were flogged so severely that they were permanently scarred[41]

After the Civil War and emancipation, reconstruction plans were put into place in 1865 under the Andrew Johnson administration (who assumed office after President Lincoln was assassinated) to readmit the states that had succeeded back into the Union in 1865. The Freedmen's Bureau was also established to integrate four million newly freed African Americans into U.S. society and address the inequalities stemming from the legacy of slavery. However, under his administration, the land that was given to the African Americans by the union army was given back to previous owners, southern states were given free rein, and Black codes were established throughout the south to restrict their activities and keep them in a system of labor as close to slavery as possible. In response to this, the south was split into five military districts, and the Freedmen's Bureau Act was passed in 1867 (extending its existence). The south remained under the control of the federal government until a Democrat, Samuel J. Tilden, and a Republican, Rutherford B. Hayes, both claimed the presidential election. In 1877, a compromise was struck between representatives on both sides that Hayes would be president if the federal troops were withdrawn from the South.

Without the support of the federal government, Black codes were reenacted, and many of the programs that had been established during the reconstruction period were dismantled. Jim Crow Segregation was sanctioned in all areas of life, and African Americans continued to be terrorized by white supremacy groups such as the Ku, Klux Klan, Red

Shirts, regulators, Jayhawkers, and others, that were established to keep them from participating in social and political life but ultimately to keep them in their "place."

By the last quarter of the nineteenth century, 3,284 lynchings were reported.[42]

~~~~~~~~~~

We learn very little about these horrific experiences in the American education system (although it lasted for 260 or so years in American history), but even less about the hundreds of years of resistance in Africa, the Caribbean, and the Americas. It took no less than 300 years for European nations to eventually gain control of Africa (except for Ethiopia and Liberia). During slavery, the types of resistance included cultural resistance, day-to-day resistance, abolitionism, emigration, and armed resistance.

One of the most significant forms of cultural resistance was building and maintaining their families against all odds. Blassingame notes that although it had no legal existence in slavery, the family was one of the most important survival mechanisms; it was the one place that African Americans could find refuge. Other forms of cultural resistance were cultural retention, synthesis, and creation, in African American spiritual-religious beliefs and practices, moral narratives, dance, music, art, etc.

Day-today-resistance included "breaking tools, destroying crops, shamming illness or weakness, taking property, spontaneous and planned strikes and work slowdowns, self-mutilation, arson, attacks, poisoning of slaveholders and their families," suicide, infanticide and escaping.[43]

Armed resistance included ship mutinies; guerilla warfare (by members of Maroon societies—at least fifty—offered asylum for fugitives), Afro-Mexican alliances, Afro-Native American alliances, and revolts, where over 250 are recorded in the U.S.[44]

The Abolitionist Movement was another form of resistance. By 1830 free Africans had organized fifty anti-enslavement societies dedicated to the abolition of slavery and to aid enslaved Africans who had escaped or were purchased out of slavery (some purchased themselves) or were freed by other means. It also included the underground railroad.[45]

Emigrationism, the push to emigrate back to Africa or go some-where else, was another form of resistance. Petitions to emigrate back to Africa began as early as 1773 with a group of enslaved Africans who petitioned colonial officials, and in 1787 eighty Blacks in Boston peti-tioned the state legislature to assist them in getting to Africa. The most known Emigration effort was that by Paul Cuffe, a Quaker who used his own money to repatriate 38 Africans to Sierra Leone in 1815. Also was the 1817 Negro Convention Movement, which advocated emigration.[46] Unfortunately, the American Colonization Society (ACS) tried to get in-volved, for racist reasons. According to Charshee McIntyre in *Criminal-izing a Race*, the ACS became interested in sending Blacks to Africa be-cause its creators thought slavery would be a scar on America forever, and that African Americans would never forget it (or let America forget it).

From the end of slavery to today the most known efforts against discrimination and injustice include the 19th Century Club Woman's Movement, the Niagara Movement, the National Association for the Ad-vancement of Colored People (NAACP), the Urban League, the Black Nationalist Movement, the United Negro Improvement Association (UNIA), the Southern Christian Leadership Conference, the Nation of Islam, the Civil Rights Movement, Congress for Racial Equality (CORE), the Student Non-violent Coordinating Committee (SNCC), the Black Student Movement, the Black Power Movement, the People United to Save Humanity (PUSH), the Rainbow Coalition and of recent, the Black Lives Matter Movement, among numerous others.

~~~~~~~~~~

Learning about horrors that African Americans experienced during and after slavery and the various forms of resistance is one thing. However, it is the sheer audacity of a few who led or participated in these struggles to rise, some, out of the depths of hell on earth, their herculean feats, and their voices that I found to be empowering. And it was not just the big things that some of our great Black liberators are known for, but it was learning things about their childhoods, the process of coming to do what they did, and other small things that were revealing and extraordi-narily inspiring. Although one can learn a lot from reading their stories and what life was like for Black people when they lived; bits and pieces of their stories will rise above the rest stirring one's soul. I will briefly describe a few that stirred mine.

In Sarah Bradford's *Harriet Tubman*, it was is not so much that she dared to escape from slavery (two of her brothers left with her but turned around) and made nineteen or more trips to the south (with the largest bounty in the history of the U.S. during that time, $40,000 for her dead or alive), to deliver her people from the brutal grips of slavery (literally carrying her elderly father on her back) earning her the title of "Moses of her people," but it was her deep spirituality and connection with nature that resonated with me the most. It was said that Tubman was as strong as any man; her strength may have been acquired after being put to work in the fields when she proved to be inept as a nursemaid.

It was how she relied on the North star and voice within to guide her through the woods, telling her which path to take and which path to avoid. Tubman had learned how to communicate with plants from her father, giving her the ability to know which plants were eatable and which ones were poisonous. As the greatest conductor of the underground railroad, she instructed those who dared to follow her, to sleep in or near water or in swamps by day to kill their scent so that dogs could not find them and to travel by night. She knew which plants to give to babies to put them to sleep. Interestingly, Tubman did all this while suffering from a brain injury that she sustained, (from being hit in the head by a slaveholder who had thrown an object at another slave) causing her to have severe headaches and narcolepsy where she would fall asleep suddenly.

The audacity of David Walker in his *Appeal to the Colored Citizens of the World,* to call America a mockery, call out White Christians about their treatment of African Americans, and to warn America of a day of reckoning when enslaved African Americans would fight for their freedom.

Frederick Douglas dared to learn to read (in secret), escape from slavery, and rise to become a great orator and a leading figure in the Abolitionist Movement. When Douglas was called upon to speak at a fourth of July celebration, he called America's democracy a hypocrisy and asked: "What to me is your fourth of July?

It was not only that Sojourner Truth was an advocate and charismatic orator for the abolitionist and women's rights movements, but it is also that she dared to walk away from the cruel reality of living as a slave (where she was repeatedly raped by her owner) in a cold basement in

West Park, New York (to a nearby abolitionist family in New Paltz, who purchased her freedom). It was also her bold act of changing her name from Isabella Baumfree to Sojourner Truth because God ordained that she would "sojourn" the land and tell the people "truth." And that she did. Her "Ain't I a Woman" speech is a resounding voice in Black feminism today.

The audacity of Ida B. Wells to lead a crusade against lynching. Her crusade began after three Black men were dragged from jail cells and shot to death. One of them, Thomas Moss, an upstanding citizen and a friend of hers, owned and operated the People's Grocery that competed with a white-owned grocery store across the street. Because she believes this is the reason that the men were killed, she wrote an editorial in *The Free Press* (a black-owned newspaper), urging Blacks to leave Memphis stating, "There is, therefore, only one thing left to do; save our money and leave a town which will neither protect our lives and property, nor give us a fair trial in the courts, but takes us out and murders us in cold blood when accused by white persons."[47]

After the incident, Wells began investigating lynching and published another editorial stating, "Nobody in this section believes the old thread-bare lie that Negro men assault white women. If southern white men are not careful, a conclusion will be reached which will be very damaging to the moral reputation of their women."[48] The suggestion that White women were attracted to Black men and claimed rape only after their relations are discovered, to avoid damage to the reputations (and in some cases their lives) lead to *The Free Press* office being ransacked, its building and contents being destroyed, and Wells being exiled from the south. Her research was published in "Southern Horrors: Lynch Law, in all its Phases," and was later expanded in "The Red Record," in which she asserted that the rape of white women was an excuse for lynching Black men who were making economic progress.

In *Up From Slavery*, it was not only that Booker T. Washington, rose out of slavery to become *the* bold and audacious leader in Black education and Black business; it was not that he raised millions of dollars from philanthropists for Black education (unfortunately, his accommodation stance led to a bitter divide between him and other Black leaders), but it is that under his leadership, the first students who attended Tuskegee Institute, built it themselves, brick-by-brick, with their own hands, that was moving. It was also the support the Tuskegee Institute received from

African Americans in the local community; it was the small contributions that they made that were truly inspiring. One woman donated six eggs.

Marcus Garvey came to America from Jamaica and built the largest and most influential mass movement in the history of America (in the early 1920s), organizing six million African Americans under the United Negro Improvement Association (UNIA). Considered by some to be the father of Black nationalism (Martin Delaney preceded him); Garvey taught Africans racial pride, racial solidarity, and financial independence, and raised $800,000, selling stock for five dollars a share, to purchase a fleet of ships, the Black Star Line. His early life experiences and observations (that Black people were on the bottom of the socio-economics strata everywhere) shaped his thinking, his practices, and subsequently his skill-set (he practiced being an orator at a young age, carried a dictionary in his pocket, learning new words daily and he worked at a printing press where he learned the power of mass communication). He was inspired by Booker T. Washington's messages of economic self-sufficiency and came to America to meet him but arrived in 1916 a year after his death in 1915. Garvey's success showed just how powerful pooling our financial resources can be.

A. Phillip Randolph (and many others with him) struggled unceasingly to eliminate discrimination in employment practices and the armed forces. He unionized Pullman porters, establishing the first predominantly Black union, the Brotherhood of Sleeping Car Porters. Randolph along with other Black leaders (including Bayard Rustin and Walter White) organized a March on Washington in 1941 to challenge discrimination in employment and the armed forces. The threat of 10,0000-50,000 Black ascending on Washington, DC (Eleanor Roosevelt asked him to call it off the 1941 March) led Franklin D. Roosevelt to issue Executive Order 8802, which prohibited discrimination in employment in the defense industries. This order also established the Fair Employment Practices Committee to investigate incidents of discrimination. Direct mass action through non-violent civil disobedience would lay the foundation for the 1963 Civil Rights March on Washington (which he helped to organize. Bayard Rustin, who spent three years in India learning Mahatma Gandhi's techniques was the primary organizer). At one point when "a senator raised the question of treason, Randolph replied, 'we are serving a higher law, than the law which applies to the act of treason.'"[49]

Fannie Lou Hamer not only dared to vote in the face of terror but worked unceasingly to register thousands of disenfranchised African Americans to vote. She co-founded (with Ella Baker and Bob Moses) the Mississippi Freedom Democratic Party ((MFDP), to challenge the all-white Mississippi Democratic Party (where Black people were excluded from becoming delegates to vote for the presidential candidate) and appeared as an MFDC delegate at the Democratic National Convention (DNC) credential committee where she stated in her moving and painfully powerful voice, ". . . if the Freedom Democratic Party is not seated now, I question America. Is this America, the land of the free and the home of the brave, where we have to sleep with our telephones off of the hooks. Our lives be threatened daily, because we want to live as decent human beings, in America?"[50] She co-founded MFDP and attended DNC after she was brutally beaten (with a Billy Club by two Black inmates who were made to beat her and then a white man pulled her dress) after returning home in Mississippi from a voter registration workshop (others were also brutally beat). The beating caused her to sustain physical injuries, specifically to internal organs that led to illness that lasted for the remainder of her life (not to mention the deep psychic injury).

Charles Hamilton Houston and his protégé Thurgood Marshall and other lawyers and workers of the NAACP kept *strategically* pushing court cases that challenged segregation, specifically those in education until it eventually led to the 1954 supreme court case, *Brown vs. the Board of Education* decision that overrode the 1896 *Plessy vs. Ferguson* supreme court decision that sanctioned segregation. This victory served to eventually rid America of the "legal" sanction of her awful segregation.

Martin Luther King, Jr. Ella Baker, and numerous other leaders of the Southern Christian Leadership Conference (SCLC), and thousands of Black people from all walks of life (and their children, who some sent to participate because being jailed prevented them from going to work. Their children were jailed as well) who organized and participated in the Civil Rights Movement, boycotted and used mass non-violent civil disobedience to embarrass America on the international stage into passing the Civil Rights Act of 1964 and the Voting Rights Act of 1965.

Elijah Muhammad of the Nation of Islam (NOI), taught Black people "to know yourself (and your kind), protect yourself (and your kind), and to do for yourself (and your kind)."[51] He taught African Americans that God was Black, and the Devil was White, and to not carry weapons so that those who would do so could justify killing you. Elijah Muhammad rose from the fields of sharecropping (neo-slavery) to lead the NOI (after the disappearance of Master Wali Fard Muhammad, its founder) and spent four years in prison because he refused to be drafted into the military, where he continued to build the organization. Through the creed of self-determination and economic self-sufficiency, between 1934 and 1975, the NOI and some of its members established numerous business enterprises including grocery stores, restaurants, bakeries, a meat-packers plant, a clothing factory, dress shops, dry cleaners, etc. In the mid-1960s, the NOI purchased and developed thousands of acres of farmland in Michigan, Alabama, and Georgia that provided fresh meat and vegetables for its growing number of urban supermarkets.[52]

In the *Autobiography of Malcolm X*, Malcolm X stated that when Elijah Muhammad reached out to him while he was in prison, he sent him five dollars. Not only was this a humanitarian act, but pure genius. Having been a prisoner himself, Muhammad understood firsthand, what it was like to descend into the depths of hell in American prisons and to be a dearth of financial resources. If helping someone when they are in the depths of hell does not gain their loyalty, I don't know what else would.

The bold, fearless and uncompromising way in which Malcolm X spoke truth to power, telling America just how wrong she was in her treatment of Black people; his telling other Black leaders that it was criminal to teach Black people to not defend themselves in the face of violence and that they had the God-given right to fight for freedom "by any means necessary" was soul-stirring, to say the least. But was even more moving is that he came to recognize that the oppression of Black people in America was not just a national civil rights issue, but an international human rights issue that should be taken to the world court.

The audacity of students of the Student Nonviolent Coordinating Committee (SNCC) to sit at lunch counters, while they got spat on, and brutalized to end segregation in the south and to dare to register thousands of Black people to vote and organize and participate in other efforts in the face of terror. Seeing that despite their "non-violent" efforts

African Americans were still subjected to vicious violent attacks and getting nowhere, Kwame Nkrumah (Stokely Carmichael) shifted SNCC's stance from civil disobedience to Black power.

The audacity of Huey P. Newton and Bobby Seale to form the Black Panther Party for Self Defense, and the numerous others who joined them to defend Black people against police brutality. Some members of the Black Panther Party (who turned revolutionary) decided that after 300 years of trying we still cannot seem to reform America (or at least some in America), then perhaps revolution was the answer. They were incarcerated and murdered.

The founders of the Black Lives Movement, numerous other, social, civil, and human rights organizations, and the thousands of protestors, continue a struggle that has been going on for over 400 years.

There are thousands upon thousands of named and unnamed; sung and unsung Black heroes, (and heroines), who have (and continue) to sacrifice themselves (and their families) some even laying down their lives so that we not just live, but can do so—equally, freely, justly and humanely, in this American land. If every Black person in America knew, *intimately*, the stories of these great Black liberators, if they knew well our legacy of struggle, how empowered we might all be.

~~~~~~~~~~

In one of the courses while at Temple, we were required to read *African Culture: The Rhythms of Unity*, coedited by Molefi Kete Asante and Kariamu Welsh Asante. When I came upon the chapter "The Implications of African Spirituality" by Donna Richards (whose name is now Marimba Ani), it was the beginning of finding what I had been searching for. In this chapter, Richards discussed several things, including how to understand culture from the perspectives of ethos and worldview, differences between Western "materialistic" and African "spiritual" cultures, how the former is forced on the world, how African Americans and those throughout the diaspora are confronted with how to reconcile the two, how we continue to practice African spirituality (although we may not be consciously aware of it), and how our spirituality has helped us sustain in the face of Western domination and oppression.

What captivated me the most is what I began to learn about African spirituality. It was the first time in my life that I found someone who articulated what I had felt my entire life: God is everywhere, in everything. Richards states, "the essence of the African cosmos is spiritual reality; that is its fundamental nature, its primary essence....spirit is not separate from matter."[53] Throughout my life, I would find myself gazing at the moon, the stars, and the mountains that lined New York State, and the Hudson River, feeling so profoundly connected to it all. I knew I could see God. For me, it was not just about a savior, as I had been taught in Christianity, who had come to save me from my sins. It was more to it than that. Sometimes after attending church, I would look out the window, especially at night, at the moonlit trees and try to understand how people could not see what I saw. "How can they not see it?" I would ask over and over.

As I continued to read Richard's chapter, I began to feel so grateful to her for the work, I let the tears that began to well in my eyes flow. Since I had a roommate and did not want her to hear me crying, I let them flow in silence, saying repeatedly, "Thank you, God, for letting me find this."

After reading some of the chapters in the text, it made me realize that if I were to learn the Afrocentric perspective, then I needed to know more about African culture. This led me to look for books on the subject. I picked up *African Religions and Philosophy* by John S. Mbiti, the only one that I could find during that time that seemed to provide a comprehensive overview of African culture (this was when you had to go to bookstores to find books; before you could easily find them on Amazon). While in my room one day, I began browsing through it, and the more I read, the more engulfed I became.

After reading some of it, I began to think about how I had not been accepted into the program at Temple, I may have missed this. I thought about how unfortunate it would have been to have gone to my grave not having found this information. I felt saddened by the fact that although African Americans may practice some of what Mbiti details in the work, how unfortunate it is that they would never know what I had come to know, nor would they feel the connection I had made.

I later found *African Spirituality: On Becoming Ancestors* by Anthony Ephirim-Donkor. It gave me an even deeper understanding of African spirituality among the Akan people of Ghana. While reading it, I thought about how wholesome and natural the African way of life seemed, how much sense it made. And although Black people (at least those whom I was surrounded by in my childhood) were deeply spiritual and practiced African culture in many ways, I thought about how much healthier we would be if we knew it and practiced it *consciously*.

5
THE BROTHERS AT RIDGE AVENUE

When I first got to Temple, I met with Sakai (the department's administrative assistant) and expressed my interest in receiving financial assistance. I believe because I was persistent, when the time came to get one of the limited assistantships, she made a point to make sure I would receive one. It takes sometimes a lifetime to recognize the earth guardians and angels that come into our lives, and she surely was one, because I really needed that assistantship.

Sometime after that, I saw a flyer from the Psychology Department, advertising for graduate assistants to work on a grant interviewing African American men in a homeless shelter. "Is this real?" I asked. "This is exactly what I want to do!" I rushed to respond to the flyer.

When I was called for an interview, in response to the question of why I was interested in the assistantship, I told one of the co-principal investigators on the project, "I want to know what happens to African American men. What happens in our upbringing that makes the lives of African American men and women turn out so differently?" I think he was impressed by my passion, and I got the assistantship. Other students from the African American studies department also got the assistantship. Our job consisted of interviewing the men in a homeless shelter on Ridge Avenue, a few blocks down from Temple, and entering the data at the administrative office in South Philadelphia, near the Delaware River.

We later learned that the project was one of several demonstration grants that were being conducted throughout the United States to explore the effectiveness of drug rehabilitation programs (which we would later learn would be used for support to stop funding them). The project was based on an experimental design, with two control groups. Some men were being treated in an intense rehabilitation program, others in a less controlled one, and others were not treated at all. We were trained on the Addiction Severity Index and began interviewing the men.

I believe it was my second interview that the man I was interviewing broke down and started crying. A lot of his pain stemmed from his childhood experiences with being in a family of Jehovah's Witnesses. When he started crying, it must have tapped into the pain of my childhood, and I started crying with him. The interviews and working in the shelter began the process of not only awakening my pain, but also awakening me to the pain of our people, and the devastating toll that crack cocaine was having on the lives of Black people and in our communities. Although Philadelphia is considered the city of brotherly love and one can feel the warmth of love in the air, there is no love for Black people, because from what I could see, they were suffering terribly.

Living in Philadelphia and working at the shelter opened my eyes to how hard life was for Black people. Throughout conducting the interviews and based on what I was finding in the stories of the men, I would find myself asking over and over, "Is this America? Are people really living like this?" When I would visit some of the communities, especially in North Philadelphia, and go down some of the side streets that are not easily visible, I would see places that were like so-called "Third World" countries.

I began to make the connections between the experiences of the men, being in a shelter, and slavery. "Are these the descendants of the slaves?" I would ask myself time and time again. "Are we still suffering from the aftermath of slavery?" I think as I continued to research, I'd learn that too many Black people were on the fringes of U.S. society, and too many were simply not surviving—at least at a level that would be expected in the wealthiest country in the world.

While living in DC, from what I could see, many Black people worked in the federal and state governments. This was how they were able to feed themselves and their families, making it to the middle-class. But not in Philadelphia; there was not much industry there, and too many Black people were not being hired in whatever industry was there in the early 1990s.

There are so many things that were life-changing for me in terms of how I would see the world and the one which Black people inhabited. The introduction of crack cocaine in the mid-1980s, the underground economy (the only means that many African Americans see as a way to make a living), and the drug wars that came along with it only exacerbated the conditions of the broken lives that many inner-city African Americans lived. It was so bad that we had to be concerned about where we parked our cars for fear of them being broken into while we were in class. One author compared the effect of crack cocaine on the Black community to it being hit by a nuclear bomb: crack cocaine made mothers do something even slavery could not make them do—walk away from their children.

Although I sincerely believe that the researchers had good intentions, there was so much wrong with how the men were treated in the study. First, was the degradation that is a part of the culture in some homeless shelters, and the men were being treated badly by some of the staff. Many of the men may have made poor choices that landed them in the shelter, however, there were many more who were there because of what happened to them while they were children. Becoming addicted and finding themselves in a homeless shelter it seemed was the natural course, and considering what some of them had been through, things could have turned out a lot worse.

When I searched the literature on homelessness during that time, it was hard to find any research about homelessness among African Americans. It had been considered a white man's problem, and the cause was alcoholism. But one knows that given the history of Blacks in America, particularly when they were migrating to urban cities, there must have been homelessness, something I would discover later in E. Franklin Frazier's *The Negro Family in the United States*. I guess homelessness among African Americans was not important enough to study.

It could have also been because Black families still sheltered family members addicted to alcohol. I was around alcoholism throughout my childhood, and from what I could see, many alcoholics were still able to live with their families. Even some families were able to provide housing for family members who were addicted to heroin (at least my family did) when it was an epidemic in Black communities. However, when family members are addicted to crack, many Black families do not have the resources to insulate them when they steal from them.

Although addiction to crack cocaine led to homelessness, what seemed to be a salient factor in their addiction for some of the men was unresolved grief. Many of them it seemed, were not able to overcome the pain from some of their experiences. No matter the various theories about addiction, I was convinced that drugs helped many of the men (at least the ones I interviewed) medicate the pain.

As time went on, some of their stories began to weigh heavily on me and raised some questions. How does one get past witnessing their step-father come into their house (while his mother, who he believes left town because she thought he would kill her), shooting all his brothers and sisters, killing one of them? That brother wept so—it was soul-shattering. How does one recover from the pain of his favorite uncle (who, incidentally, was one of two who introduced him to the drug trade) slipping on train tracks while drunk, being electrocuted to death? How does one get over his father (whom he felt close to) having his throat slit by his stepmother while he was in the bathtub? How does one recover from watching his mother (a single parent) he cared for when he was fourteen having her hands and lower arms were amputated ("finger after finger, from nubs up to her elbows") after she got a disease from being a seam-stress before she eventually died? Some were suffering from not just the deaths of significant family members. It was how these loved ones died.

In many instances, these incidents happened while they were still children or adolescents. And after the death of that significant family member, their family fell apart. With nowhere to go, some found refuge in the streets. For others, the adult members in their families were so distraught themselves, they could not help them get through the loss. When adults are grieving themselves, they often forget about the children. Because they do not know how to get through grief themselves, they cannot help the children.

These kinds of experiences put some of these men on the trajectory of drug addiction and their unfortunate encounter with crack cocaine. There was a young man I will never forget because I will never forget his smile. When I complimented him on his smile, he said, "My whole family has it. If we stop smiling, something is really wrong." My thoughts were, "Here I am sitting in front of a man who is homeless, in a shelter, one of the worst things that can happen to almost anybody and could wipe the smile right off anybody's face. But he was still smiling because "it could be worse." Later, as I reflected on this, I thought, "If some Black people are not living Hell on Earth, I don't know what you would call it."

~~~~~~~~~~

Although the graduate students were grateful for the opportunity to work on the project, especially me, we were suspicious as to why researchers from the Psychology Department sought assistants from the African American Studies Department. Why did they not choose assistants from the Psychology Department, which we assumed was predominantly white? Were we being used to draw the men in? And how and what was the research going to be used for; really? Two articles that we were required to read in our Black Psychology course were "The Death of White Research in the Black Community" by Reginald Williams, and "Science and Oppression" by Jacob Carruthers.

Carruthers made us aware that science has been used as a tool of oppression, and Williams made us aware of how science has been used on people of color. Carruthers pointed out that although science is posed as objective and value-free, it is founded on the experiment, and is about control, for whatever purpose that suits the scientist or controller. It is far from value-free and is entrenched in a particular view and approach to the world.[54] Williams pointed out how communities become laboratories for social scientists to build their careers and promote their self-interests, with little or no benefits to Black communities.

A lot of the research that came out of the sixties and seventies found Black personality and social behavior to be deviant and pathological, all of which supported a Black-inferiority paradigm. Black students were sought out by white researchers and used to gain entrance into Black communities because white professors were afraid to enter or negotiate with them. This set the stage for Black students to become agents in exploiting their own people. Williams suggested that Black students obtain a commitment from university officials that Black students, faculty, and administrators be represented on review boards. If this is not possible, students should use other means to block research that has a racist agenda, even if it means that they become infiltrators and saboteurs.[55]

With this level of awareness, we could not participate in the project without feeling some level of discomfort. We also had issues with the research instrument that was being used because it was not tapping into what was really going on with the men, and we were concerned that whatever they were going to do with the research, it would not give an accurate depiction of what the men were really experiencing.

What was most disturbing is that the men were being put into the groups based on random selection. This means that those who needed more intense help would not get the help they needed, while others would receive no help at all. "How wrong is that?" we asked. How can people who clearly need help be denied the help they need? "For the sake of research" was the answer. This is one of the most significant disadvantages of the experimental method—the ethics of randomizing people into groups and denying them the treatment they need. This research project reeked of the highly unethical Tuskegee experiment, where hundreds of Black men were denied treatment for syphilis when it was available—all "in the name of research." Tragically, such a travesty occurred at Tuskegee University, a black university.

We later learned the researchers had incorporated an ethnographic component into the study. They planned for the research assistants to conduct long interviews, to gain more insight into what the men were experiencing. Since I decided that I would make the life stories of the men the topic of my dissertation, I had already started delving deeper into their stories on my own.

Some of my colleagues, it seemed, however, did not give a damn. Not that they did anything intentionally. I think some did not feel comfortable with presenting what we were finding in some of the life stories of the men, to white people. So was I. But I aimed to help the researchers understand the relationship between these stories and African American experiences in slavery, segregation, and ongoing racial oppression.

We asked the researchers for a meeting, and I took on the task of presenting the information. It, however, was an unsuccessful attempt to provide a historical backdrop of the African American family in the United States. The consultant, who I surmised suffered from low self-esteem, sat there twirling her hair around in her fingers, looking uninterested. She looked at me and asked, "What does this have to do with the research.?" I was stunned. I left the meeting feeling disappointed and surmised that were too removed and unempathetic to give a damn. "Why am I even wasting my time?" I asked myself.

As time went on, the researchers began to slowly bring in white graduate students. Because we were challenging them at every turn, I believe the Black research graduate students were becoming too difficult. They just needed to do their research. Later, in the study, I had asked the principal investigator to allow me to administer the African Self-Consciousness Scale, (ASC) which was designed to ascertain ones' level of awareness of African history and culture among other things. I knew they that would be put off by it because of some of the questions, particularly those pertaining to white people. The principal investigator said he would consider it; however, I believe he was just hoping it would just go away because he kept putting it off. Later, we discovered that there were plans to administer an antisocial disorder questionnaire and that the researchers were going to have the white graduate students do it. I was outraged and I challenged it.

But the fact is I liked the researchers. I especially liked the principal investigator, who had snow-white hair, who struggled with what seemed like Parkinson's disease because he shook terribly and was kind. It is in these moments when you realize that race really does not matter; it is just about people. I even took a psychology course he taught and learned a lot from him.

I had taken Black Psychology and learned that one of my professors, Dr. Daudi Azibo (whom I worked on a project with) had devised the Azibo Nosology, a list of psychological disorders that Black people suffer from, stemming from racial oppression. I went to him and expressed concerns about administering such an instrument to a population of Black men, who were homeless and addicted to crack cocaine. I asked, "How can you not be anti-a society that is anti-you? It is only natural." However, most of these guys had an addiction problem, but that did not make them antisocial.

I don't think it was stated explicitly, but somehow a deal was struck; they would allow me to administer the ASC questionnaire if I would stop harassing them about theirs. I figured regardless of whether they administered the instrument or not, there was still going to be white research in Black communities. Why not take advantage of the opportunity to present research that might challenge what they find?

6

THE BLACK MADONNA

No matter how much I learned in books, it was not until traveling to the lands that I was studying about that I really began to get it. My first international trip overseas was to Italy. Until I got to Italy, I don't think I even realized that the Romans were among one of the tribes of the Italics and that they had dominated the Italians. Nor had I realized the reality of the impact that Rome has had on the modern world. More importantly, I did not get a full understanding of the big deal being made about African influence on the Greco-Roman world until I got to Italy. I, however, did not go to Italy because it would enhance what I was studying. I visited Italy simply because the opportunity presented itself. The ex-boyfriend (Larry) of my friend Tammy, whom I met at Howard, was playing basketball in Italy, and it provided an opportunity for us to travel there.

When we got to Fabriano, where Larry was residing, I marveled at the cobblestone streets, and the marble buildings and bathrooms, an indication to me of how wealthy the country was (or at least had once been). But I was disturbed by how rude the people seemed. While in line at stores, people would just get right in front of you, as if you were invisible. "This is where Americas get their rudeness from," I thought. "They inherited it from their ancestors."

What bothered me more was how the people stared at us. At first, we thought that they were staring at us because Tammy is tall. "Maybe they think you are a model," I said to Tammy. One woman sat right in front of us on the train and stared at us while we were on our way to Rome. After we had been in Italy for a while and had seen a lot of Africans, who were darker-skinned, we thought it may have been because we were light-skinned Black people; maybe they had never seen light-skinned Blacks, we speculated.

We also encountered a convention in which the men were dressed like Peter Pan and looked just like whites looked in America. What was disturbing was that they were saying things to us in Italian that we had no idea of what they were saying. Interestingly, we met a group of young Black women who were living in Italy, and ironically, a couple was from Albany—one from First Street, the street I lived on. They knew how to speak Italian and based on how they were responding to the men, I knew that they were saying derogatory things to us.

We visited Milan—I was not impressed at all. It seemed like a typical American city, and even less so when I saw McDonalds. At some point, Larry rented a room in a hotel for us, for which he paid a hefty amount of money. Although the hotel was nice and in an upscale area, we were appalled and afraid when an Italian guy came toward us with his penis pulled out. Tammy said, "Oh my God, Patty—his penis is out. I don't believe it!" as she pulled me close to her and we crossed the street. "I don't care how much money Larry spent on this hotel. We're being disrespected by these Italian men because they see Black women as whores," I said to Tammy.

Tammy and I spent a great deal of time goofing off and drinking wine after we discovered that wine was more accessible and cheaper than water. Tammy would wake up every morning that we were there, happy, and start the day off with "It's time for vino." A few days before we were to leave Italy, I realized that time was running out and we must get down to Rome, a place I had dreamed about going to since I was a child.

When we got to Rome and began touring its cathedrals and monuments, I was absolutely moved to tears because of the immensity of their sizes, the detail of the architecture, and the statues they contained. "How could human hands have constructed these?" I asked. They were, to me; a true indication of what humanity does to honor the ancestors and the gods. When we went to the Coliseum, "This is where the Romans used to feed the Christians to the lions," I said to Tammy. "Rome is also where Christianity was invented," I said in one of the numerous conversations as I was sharing my newfound knowledge.

When we went to St. Peter's Basilica, I was surprised to find that Vatican City was an independent state, and that it looked like it was no more than a few blocks (although it is about 102 acres or about 0.2 miles). I inquired about seeing the Black Madonna, to which the response was that it had been hidden away, and they were not showing it for now. Although I did not see it, the response confirmed to me that it existed; it was real and not just made up. We, therefore, did not get to see the Black Madonna, nor did we get to see the Sistine Chapel because it had closed early that day, due to siesta time (which is shocking for those of us who live in a country where things are typically open during times that they say they are going to be open).

I cannot recall if, by then, I had read Ivan Van Sertima's book *Black Women in Antiquity*, with the essay written by Eloise McKinney-Johnson, "The Black Madonnas." McKinney-Johnson's essay details how the story of Mother Mary and Jesus was a Europeanized or "whitenized" version of the story of the African Goddess Isis and her child Horus,

(Auset and Heru their African names before the Greeks changed them) who was conceived by immaculate conception.

"Wow talk about a stolen legacy," I thought. "If only Black people knew that the very concepts that have not only moved the world, but also moved it to create some of the most awe-inspiring churches and cathedrals, to their honor, comes from African people. If they knew that when bowing down to Mother Mary and Jesus, the world is bowing down to a Black woman and Black child, how different we might see ourselves, how different the world might see us, and how different our lives might be."

7

TOUCHING MALCOLM

Out of the mass mailing I did when I began to search for a job, I got three job interviews and two offers. One offer was from Eastern Michigan University, and the other was U-Mass, Boston. I did not think Michigan would work for me for several reasons: Michigan was cold and had too much snow and although I liked the chair, I felt I would go insane if I had to work under him. He had an extraordinary memory (which I have found to be the case with historians), and almost every time he spoke about something, it turned into a long story with an incredible amount of mundane detail (which I have also found to be something some historians do). Also, when we went around the university and drove around the city, I saw no Black people. My feelings were "I'd be awfully cold and lonely here."

When I got to Boston for the interview, I was met by a bubbly young man named Mark, who did everything he could to make sure I was comfortable the day before my interview. And little did I know that when I was asked what classes I could teach, and I responded with, "I can teach anything in Black Studies," that is exactly what they would have me do. I loved the field so much that I sincerely felt I could teach anything in African American Studies. I felt that if I did not know a topic area, all I had to do was do the research, because I love learning, especially about anything in Black Studies. Although the job offer from U-Mass, Boston went from a tenure-track position (which can lead to a permanent more secure job) to a visiting lecturer, I, however, was willing to take my chances and declined the offer from Eastern Michigan University. Although Boston is probably as cold as Michigan, at least it was only three hours away from Albany and I could visit home.

I, however, came to Boston amid controversy. There had been a student protest in support of Dr. Clinton Jean, a professor in the Black Studies Department, whose job I was being hired to replace. Because of student protests, he was kept on. I surmised that that was probably the reason that the offer had been changed from tenure-track to visiting lecturer. When I saw this very strikingly tall, thin, very dark-skinned, stately looking man, I looked forward to meeting and getting to know him. However, this never happened because he died the week I got there. Mark believed that the stress of trying to hold on to his job killed Dr. Jean. I could feel the pain the students were experiencing, who loved him as they talked about him, especially Mark, who assisted me at every phase of my experience while in Boston, from the first time I got there for the interview until I left.

While at U-Mass Boston, a conference was held in Jean's honor, entitled *Behind the Eurocentric Veils* after a book he had authored, and I was charged with the task of coordinating it. Since it was named after his book, I picked up a copy of it, with hopes of getting some insight into his work for the conference. It is not so much of what Jean argued about the limitations of liberal sociology and Marxism for understanding "Third World" cultures in general and African peoples in particular, and the need for an Afrocentric view of history that stood out to me. It is what Jean said about war that was eye-opening.

Using the works by Richard L. Rubenstein, *The Cunning of History* and Philip Slater's *The Pursuit of Loneliness*, Jean highlighted the profound atrocities that occurred because of technologies of mega violence, including elaborate technologies of extermination from a distance; the strange fruit of twentieth-century science. He noted, 'No century in human history can match the twentieth century in sheer numbers of human beings slaughtered by the great states; an estimated one hundred million.'[56] In the First World War, six thousand people were killed per day for fifteen hundred days, and the death toll estimates range from twenty to forty million. For the Second World War, there were an estimated eighty-five million casualties. Jean also brought to light the unrestrained use of such technology used in Vietnam. Todd Gitlin, who wrote in the introduction in Slater's latest edition, indicated that 'between 1965 and

1973 the government of the United States dropped on Indochina, including Laos and Cambodia more than four times the bomb tonnage it dropped on Europe and Asia during World War II!"[57]

"How can this happen?" I asked. "What kind of world do we live in?"

~~~~~~~~~~

One day, the chair called me in and told me he was looking for people to work on a project for a series of books on African culture.

"We need someone to do Namibia," he said. "Would you be interested in doing that volume?"

"Let me do some research on it and I will let you know."

I was teaching three courses a semester and was working on my dissertation, in addition to coordinating the Clinton Jean conference. I did not know whether I would have time to do it. But I saw it as an opportunity to be a part of a book project. When I started the research, I first found that information was scant on the Namibian people, and all I could find at first was information about the Herero people and how they were known for their distinguished clothing. I then found out that their population was reduced from about fifty thousand to twenty thousand by the Germans.

I went to the library to seek out additional information and discovered what looked like a journal written by a German author. As I browsed through the pages, I found that the Germans had set in motion a program of extermination for the Namibian people. According to the author, because the Namibian people rebelled against German colonization, a German official said (in so many words), "We have to exterminate them." Adding that bit of information to the pain I was already struggling with from learning about the atrocities that Black people experienced, I closed the book immediately, and said, "I can't do this." Because I was also finding it difficult to find information on the Herero people, I went back to the chair and said, "There is not enough information, so I won't be able to do it."

Living in Boston was one of the most inspirational periods in my life for several reasons. It was an international city, it was a hub of intellectual life (particularly at Harvard University at Harvard Square, which I frequented the summer after my academic year ended), I lived by the water, and my office was off the bay.

However, it was one of the most difficult times in my life, and I really struggled. During the winter, it seemed that every time I looked out of my window, it was snowing. It snowed so much that year in Boston, it was unbelievable. I just did not remember that much snow in Albany. I looked out of the window one day and wondered, "Is the world coming to an end? How do people live like this?"

I also felt terribly lonely, teaching three preps a semester while working on my dissertation was overwhelming, and I was stressed out and depressed.

That winter, MIT hosted a conference called *Black Women in the Academy, Defending Our Name 1854–1994*. I went to the conference and could not believe it I was sitting in the same room with Angela Davis, a childhood icon, who was one of the speakers.

I was a kid when Angela Davis made it to the FBI's ten most wanted fugitives list for kidnapping and first-degree murder for an incident in which Jonathan Jackson, then seventeen years old, took as hostage judge Harold Haley, a prosecutor and three jurors with a sawed-off shotgun that allegedly had been purchased by her. Three African American men (Jonathan Jackson, James McClain, a prisoner who was on trial for an attempted stabbing of a guard, and another prisoner, William Christmas) were killed when the police shot up the van, they attempted to escape in. Although Davis fled California, she was eventually caught and jailed. This sparked a movement where she was supported by thousands of people, and a group of writers from New York formed a committee called the Black People's Defense of Angela. When all of this was occurring, I was about eleven or twelve years of age and had not a clue about what was going on. Angela Davis was popular because she had a big Afro, which was symbolic of the Black struggle, and we wanted to emulate her, which we tried to do with our big Afros.

Although Davis (who since then has a remarkable record of scholar-activism, and achievements) discussed her research on prisons, what stood out more to me was what she said about Black women in academe. She said a lot of the sisters were not getting the support they needed and that there was a session earlier in the conference where they were crying and falling apart. That is exactly what I was going through.

I purchased the two-volume encyclopedia *Black Women in America* by Darlene Clark Hines, went home, and spent the rest of the weekend reflecting on one of the most inspirational moments in my life at the time: I had met an icon and I was in a room with some of the brightest sisters in the world.

The name of the conference was taken from a statement by Fannie Barrier Williams (a major player in the nineteenth-century club women's movement) when she made a speech to a group of white women at the World Columbian Exposition. Because Black women did not have a national organization, they were pretty much excluded from speaking. When Williams (one of the few Black women allowed to speak) spoke, she said, "The morality of our home life was been commented on so disparagingly, that we are placed in the unfortunate position of being *defenders of our name.*"[58] Such a statement was in response to stereotypes that were being printed in newspapers and magazines that Black women were sexually licentious and morally degenerative, as in the following commentary made by a white woman in a national magazine:

> Degeneracy is apt to show more in the weaker individual of any race; so, Negro women evidence more nearly the popular idea of total depravity than the men do. They are so nearly lacking in virtue that the color of a woman's skin is generally taken (and quite correctly) as a guarantee of her immorality. On the whole, I think they are the greatest menace possible to the moral life of any community where they live. And they are evidently the chief instruments of the degradation of the men of their race...I sometimes read of virtuous women, hear of them, but the idea is absolutely inconceivable to me...I cannot imagine such a creation as a virtuous Black woman.[59]

I felt the pain of the women even before Angela Davis spoke about it because I was in pain myself. There was a moment while living in Boston that I felt so alone that I just wanted to end it all. I called Barry (a friend and mentor I had met when he helped me the time my car broke down right in the middle of Connecticut Avenue in DC) to tell him I was going to check myself into a hospital because I was afraid I was going to hurt myself.

"I need to call 911 because I am afraid to drive," I said to him, thinking that in the state I was in, while driving I might hurt someone else.

"Don't do it!" he responded. "Don't do it! They will put you in a straitjacket and put you under seventy-two-hour observation." He then went on to explain how a friend of his went to St. Elizabeth Hospital in Washington, DC to check himself in. He sat on a bench all day, and people just walked by him as if he were not there, which was typical of the service you get from Black-managed government agencies in DC during that time. Seeing that nobody paid attention to him, he eventually got up and walked out.

After the conversation, I felt better. I began to think about what would happen if I did not show up to work, what my life would look like if I lost a job that was so hard to come by. I thought about Ntozake Shange's work *for colored girls who have considered suicide when the rainbow is enuf.* I had been moved by the work as an adolescent, especially because the play made it to Broadway, and I thought suicide was an option. I did what I always did, however, when the "rainbow"—the changes—were too much: I got on my knees and prayed. This time I put on Mariah Carey's song "There's a Hero Inside of You," and played it over and over the entire weekend, while I prayed until I could do it again.

~~~~~~~~~~

Things got better during the summer and after I started dating Mark. We spent a lot of time visiting shops and bookstores in Harvard Square and Cape Cod. While teaching African American History that summer, a few things stood out to me. One is that a descendant of Marcus Garvey, who enrolled in the course, brought a letter written by him to class. Touching a letter that Marcus Garvey wrote made me feel as if I had touched him.

The effect the course was having on the students was also revealing. Toward the end of the course, I asked them to form a circle so that they could express what they were "feeling" rather than what they were "thinking" about what they were learning about African American history. Although the class consisted primarily of African American students, I was more surprised by the responses from the white students. Some of the women started crying and expressed how surprised they were, how hurt they felt, and how embarrassed they were that their ancestors had been so awful to Black people. A Japanese student who enrolled in the course indicated that he had been warned before coming to

America by his family and community, "Stay away from the Black community." He, however, being brave and curious, wanted to find out for himself about the Black community and decided to take the course. I used this to point out how negative images and stereotypes shape not only national but also global opinions of Black people in America.

Of all the great experiences I had while living in Boston, there was none more inspiring than spending a day with Malcolm "Shorty" Jarvis, Malcolm X's friend.

At the time, he was seventy years of age, and it was about a year and a half after Spike Lee's production of *Malcolm X*. Mark and I found out that a friend of his knew Jarvis and we asked that he arrange for us to meet him. As a new and excited scholar during those days, I carried my tape recorder with me pretty much everywhere I went. After we got to Jarvis's house and he started talking, it occurred to me to ask him if I could record him, which he allowed me to do.

Jarvis talked a lot about Malcolm's autobiography. He said that there were a lot of things in it that were incorrect. He believes that Malcolm's coauthor and a journalist, Alex Haley, probably improvised because Malcolm X was traveling a lot and busy. Because of some of the things that were incorrect, he believed that Malcolm must not have read it. Specifically, he pointed out that he "never smoked a joint" (let alone used cocaine), and that although Malcolm did smoke marijuana, he never used hard drugs or cocaine; (he may have not known of his use of other drugs). Jarvis indicated that he was not from Lansing, Michigan, but was from Massachusetts and that he plays the trumpet, not the saxophone (which Malcolm X knew). In addition, he, Malcolm, and the three white girls had robbed six houses over a two-week period, for fun and excitement, suggesting that the depiction of him and Malcolm leading lives of crime was not true.

Jarvis believes that he and Malcolm went to prison for their involvement with white women because of a remark that was made to them by the District Attorney while they were in Middlesex County Jail in Boston: "You niggers had no business being involved with white women." He and Malcolm got eight to ten years (which he thought they should have received probation for a first offense), while the white women were given suspended sentences.

Jarvis said that while in prison he and Malcolm "argued profoundly most of the time," but were friends. However, he could not understand why Malcolm would not listen to him while they were in prison. Jarvis described Malcolm as "hot-headed," "strong," "electrifying," "rambunctious," and "ready and rearing to go." He also described him as "mean...who would tell a white boy in a minute... [who tried to mess with him] "Man, I'll cut your throat." Jarvis said he knew that one day Malcolm was going to do something that would cost him his life. He would tell him, "Man, you better slow down."

To our surprise, Jarvis had not been interviewed for the *Malcolm X* movie, which was done about six months before he met Spike Lee. He speculated that he was not contacted because it was thought that he was dead, which he believes came from Betty Shabazz, Malcolm's wife. A niece of Jarvis was enrolled in a filmmaking course taught by Spike Lee at Harvard, and when he bought up Jarvis's name in class, she told him that he was still alive and lived in Roxbury; she would bring him to meet him. When they met, Spike Lee, excited about meeting him, "grabbed and hugged" him, "was friendly," "but did not know what to say." Spike sent him a copy of the *Malcolm X* movie and an invitation to come to the premiere of it.

Of all the things Jarvis talked about, what I found most intriguing was the spiritual transformation that he said both he and Malcolm had while in prison. He pointed out that although the intent of incarceration is to destroy people, for about one-tenth of one percent of them, it has the opposite effect. He explained that being in a cell with nothing—no books, nothing but a bucket of water and cot for 90 days, 18 hours a day—your conscious mind slips away from you, and you go into the realms of the subconscious mind. It is like being in a monastery: it takes the external world away from you and makes you go inside yourself. Jarvis reiterated several times:

Incarceration bought about isolation; isolation bought about meditation; meditation bought about purification, and Malcolm and I went into the forbidden door in the realms of the unknown of our own minds and what we saw, no man can take from us.[60]

And there is no shortcut, according to Jarvis: you must pay your dues to get in the door (I am assuming that he meant to higher levels of consciousness). After Malcolm went through the transformation, according to Jarvis "It changed him. ...When he came out of prison, couldn't nobody tangle with him." He would go to "Harvard and Yale; they could put the best legal brains up against him and he could whip them to death with the bare truth."

Jarvis showed us a letter he received from Malcolm. I held the letter in utter awe; touching it, I felt I had touched Malcolm. Jarvis said that Malcolm had the ability to mass hypnotize and that he and Malcolm were "in transmission" with their minds. Because of this and because of the frequency at which he, himself was operating, he caught Malcolm's murder conspiracy a week or two before it happened. According to him, the only way somebody could see it is if their mind traveled to the frequency that it came through the atmosphere. He believes Malcolm was upset and in turmoil, and that is why he missed it. He said, "I saw a vision a week before he got killed. I was at my house in Connecticut the week before. I had not seen Malcolm in a year; I [wanted] to tell Malcolm whatever he is doing next Sunday, drop it and bring your family up to Connecticut and spend the day with us." However, he attempted to call him about five or six times, but his messages were not being given to him.

Jarvis said that twenty years after Malcolm's death, he was going to a funeral of an aunt who lived in New York, and it was suggested that he visit Malcolm's grave, which he had not done yet. He was supposed to get the information on where Malcolm was buried but had not done so. Ironically, and to his surprise, while at his aunt's grave, the undertaker came back to him and said Malcolm X's grave was twenty feet away. He described what happened once he got there.

> I knelt down on the ground, and put my hand on top of the [plate], and it was like a bolt of electricity came out of the ground and he [Malcolm X] said, "Jarvis, it is about time you got here to see me. Carry on as best you can," and the voice faded away.[61]

After that, his hand came up. He picked up a stone and two beads off the ground, bought them home, and put them in a piece of plastic that said: "from the grave of Malcolm X." It wasn't a week later that Jarvis got a call from CBS, requesting him to do a documentary on

Malcolm X. His "phone jumped off the hook for the next six months," which he believes happened because he touched Malcolm X's grave.

8

THE IVORY TOWERS

While in Boston, I applied for jobs and got callbacks to be interviewed from the University of Montana, Xavier University, and Georgia State University. When I arrived for an interview for the position in Montana, I discovered that the only Blacks on the campus were pretty much the sports team with a few other students, and the university had only one other Black professor who was female. Also, because it was so cold, I wondered whether it would be realistic to think I could live out there.

Since my research was on a drug-addicted urban population, the committee took me to visit the drug rehabilitation center on campus. To my surprise, it was filled not with African Americans as I had seen in Philadelphia, but with Native Americans. I was told I was not offered the job because I would not be able to continue my research on urban African Americans in Montana. They probably also knew I would not stay there had I got a better offer.

I interviewed for the tenure-track position at U-Mass Boston, which I did not get, either I believe simply because the committee liked who I was competing with better. I don't recall what happened with Xavier University. But I do recall that a colleague from Temple was working there and really wanted me to take the job there. Although it was a black university, it was a small private Catholic university, and I did not find it appealing.

When the chair of African American studies at Georgia State University (GSU) called me about interviewing for the position there, based on how the conversation went, I sensed I was not his number one candidate. He said, "I called Temple and asked for their best and brightest, and you were among those who were recommended," something he would say every time he would introduce me to an audience. The fact that I was recommended was surprising to me, considering that I was pretty much a recluse with tunnel vision while at Temple. I guess because I was not very social and very focused, the professors thought I was serious, which I was.

When I got to Georgia, I was met by the chair, a tall, chocolate brother, whom, I described when one time someone asked me about him, as being "good-intentioned." Since it was in Atlanta, I knew if I got that job, I would take it. Atlanta was considered the place to be, giving it the name "Hotlanta." I had already seen too many Black Studies jobs in cities in states like Idaho, Iowa, and the one I interviewed for in Montana, places that were not ideal places for African Americans to live, especially me. A job in academe is a privilege. A job in African American Studies in Atlanta is a gift from the gods.

Since the program at Temple was founded by Molefi Asante three years before I got there, I would be among Temple's second or third group of graduates. I knew that the more people who graduated with doctoral degrees in African American Studies, the tougher the competition would get. I thought I had better land a job now, if I can, in a city where Black people live and with a warmer climate.

Once I got to GSU, I discovered that the department was created because of the demands of a student sit-in in 1992. Students had occupied a building in protest to growing frustration with racism at GSU in general, and an incident of a racial slur written on a trash can. During the sit-in, students occupied the president's office until their demands were met, one of which was the establishment of a Department of African American Studies. "Oh, my God! They're still having sit-ins in the 1990s?" I asked.

Many Black Studies programs were born out of the student movement which was rooted in the Civil Rights and Black Power Movements during the 1960s. Students began to view the university as a microcosm of the racist, exploitive, and oppressive larger society, that excluded Black people and other people of color, and perpetuated a white supremacist paradigm, that was designed to perpetuate the established order. They organized sit-ins and demanded that education be moved from the "ivory towers" and that it be relevant to the lived experiences of Black people. They demanded an education that not only emphasized excellence in academics but one that teaches students the responsibility they have to use their knowledge, talent, and skills for the betterment of Black communities. The fact that GSU was founded as early as 1913, was in a predominantly Black urban city but did not have a Black Studies program spoke volumes about the South to me.

When I was being led to the department's main location on campus, I saw a flyer that had the names of all three candidates, including mine. One of the names sounded familiar. "I know that name," I kept saying to myself. The feeling that I knew the person continued to nag me. It finally came to me who it was. "Oh, my God. That's Jeff!" Without even knowing who the third person was, I knew that he was the number one candidate.

I had met Jeff at Temple when we enrolled in some of the same courses. We even became friends for a while, after another colleague put us on a blind date without me even knowing I was on a date. I had just forgotten his last name. Jeff was certainly one of the best and brightest in the department and he was articulate.

The presentation I did during the interview at GSU was on the research I had conducted at the shelter. It focused on unresolved grief among the men I had interviewed. The chair was impressed with my research, and I believe because he was grieving over the death of his wife. Because he believed both Jeff and I were outstanding candidates, he went to the dean and asked if he could make two hires and hired both of us.

Atlanta is Tammy's hometown, so I went to Atlanta for a visit in the summer before I began the job in the fall to find an apartment. On that visit, I discovered that Georgia is a big state and has a lot of land and wooded areas. Although I thought it was pretty, seeing the trees made me think of what I had learned about the terrorization and lynching that Blacks experienced in the South.

In terms of the number of lynchings that occurred between 1882 and 1968, Georgia was second to Mississippi (531 and 581, respectively). And there was a riot in September 1901 in downtown Atlanta, where twenty-five to forty African Americans were murdered. Numerous others were injured, and considerable damage was inflicted on their property through mob violence.[62]

"Do I really want to go south?" I kept asking myself over and over, feeling terrified about moving to Georgia. Resolving that I needed to get over it, I stored the rest of my furniture that I had left in DC, let my nephew whom I had turned my apartment in DC over to know that it was now his, packed my belongings in a small trailer that I pulled with my car and with help from Mark, drove to Atlanta. He then went on to Ohio State University to work on a master's degree in Black Studies and we continued a long-distance relationship.

~~~~~~~~~~

There was a lot to be desired for a new department with almost everybody except for Jeff—the chair, the support staff, and me—being new at our jobs. During the very first month I was there, I was already starting to harbor negative feelings toward the department, academe, and the university.

Although I thought I could teach anything and had already taught seven different courses at U-Mass Boston, now I was teaching three new courses in my first quarter and seven new courses the first year I was there and I was struggling. Not only was I teaching a heavy course load, but I was also feeling the pressure to finish my dissertation and to publish it.

In addition to teaching seven different preps (courses we had to prepare to teach) on a quarter-system, what made my experience particularly difficult is the cross-disciplinary nature of Black Studies. While I was teaching the courses, I began to understand the reality of African American Studies being an interdisciplinary discipline. For example, if one taught a course about women (which I was asked to do, I believe because there was an assumption that because I was a woman, I'd be interested in doing so), one had to be abreast not only of the literature in woman's studies, including feminist theory but also African American women. The course was cross-listed with Women Studies, and women who were steeped in feminist theory, and women's research would be taking the course. If one were to teach African American Female Activism, African American Relationships, African American Family, Issues in the Community (which included a number of issues like health, poverty, incarceration, drug addiction, and policy)—courses that I taught—one needed to be familiar with the bodies of knowledge in these respective areas to be effective. The same principle applies to those who teach in other areas like economics, political thought, psychology, etc. Teaching that many courses was grueling, and it was taking a toll, especially considering that the chair required that I be in the department four days a week.

One day, attempting to mentor me, the chair asked, "So, what do you want to do?"

I looked at him in utter disbelief that he was asking such a question. "What do I want to do?" I asked myself. "I am about to earn a doctorate.

I am already doing what I want to do. Are you telling me I have to do more?"

"What do you mean?" I asked.

"What do you want to focus your research on?"

That is when the reality of publishing hit me. I had heard the "publish or perish" mantra while at UC Berkeley and Temple. "Don't get caught up in service," I had heard. "It's a trap. To survive academe, you have to publish." I heard that over and over and loud and clear, especially at UC Berkeley.

When the chair said, "I need you to develop a course on African American male-female relationships," my thoughts were, "This man has bumped his head." I had already done the research and realized that the literature was scant on the subject matter, which I discovered while living in DC. The only work I had found was by Nathan Hare and Julia Hare, *Crisis in Black Sexual Politics*. The lack of literature on this subject was one of the reasons that I decided to pursue a doctoral degree in Black Studies. After being at UC Berkeley, I realized that I did not know the literature in the field nor did I know the literature on African American relationships, marriages, and families.

Then he said, "I need you to be in the office at least four days a week, so the department can have a presence on campus."

"Are you saying that? Are you really telling me that I have to be in the office four days a week?" I asked angrily, in silence while holding back the tears. "One of the reasons I chose this profession was to be independent, which means having control over my time."

What made being in the office difficult was that I don't work well around people; I need quiet to read and write, and I need to know that I can do so without being interrupted, which is difficult to do in an office environment without seeming un-collegiate and unavailable to students. What made that first semester even more difficult was that the administrative assistant had a gregarious personality, and as nice and sweet as she was, she was in my office what seemed like every five minutes waving her hand, saying, "Hiiiiiiii!" And once she got my attention, she would start talking, and I could not get anything done. So, I had to spend Friday and the weekend making up for what I could not get done at the office.

When Jeff came the next semester, I complained about the four-day week.

"How can he tell me I have to be here four days a week?" I asked. "I have to teach all these courses and I have to write, and I cannot focus in this office—it's too distracting."

Jeff started developing issues of his own. Faculty were also being asked to help answer the telephone. "Are you kidding me?" Jeff would ask. I tried to reason with him.

"I don't see a reason why we can't pitch in. The department is new, and it needs all the help it can get while it is building."

"How can I do my job when I am being asked to do somebody else's job? This is utterly ridiculous," he'd complain.

As time went on, Jeff became more unhappy about how things were being done. "Be patient," I'd plead with him, "We are all new at our jobs. Give us a chance. You're the only one who has been doing what you do for a long time. The rest of us are learning."

He'd respond, "What! Are you kidding me? The university administrators did this on purpose. It's a setup. They want us to fail!" he would say over and over, sometimes frantically.

One time when Jeff was flipping out about how the department was operating, I responded saying, "That's how Black people do stuff."

"Oh, that is antidotal," he retorted. "You have absolutely no evidence of that."

"But I do," I responded.

In Albany (a predominantly white city) and the two colleges in New York's state's university system, you are treated with the attitude, "I am here to serve you." But at Howard, when I was standing in the line with other students on my very first day, the clerk acted like we were not there, and did not even look up for a very long time. My mouth dropped open in utter disbelief. That kind of service never changed the entire time I was at Howard, although in one-on-one sessions with the staff you were treated with care and kindness, something I discovered when I really needed assistance. At times, trying to get things done at Howard was a virtual nightmare.

I didn't experience this just at Howard. I found this to be the case with almost every establishment operated and managed by Black people, including in DC government and business establishments, even fast-food restaurants. You'd be standing in line, and the customer service representative would look at you like, "Why are you here or what do you want? You are bothering me."

In departmental meetings, the arguments would get heated, especially between Jeff and the chair. Because it seemed we were getting nowhere with some of our concerns with the chair (particularly with the number of courses we had to prepare for and teach), Jeff and I requested a meeting with the associate dean. After we laid out our concerns, she looked at us, without even flinching, and said, "You should not be here."

Perplexed by her response, we looked at her waiting for her to explain further. She continued, "You are under contract and do not have tenure yet."

Without saying it directly, what she was saying is that by being at odds with the chair or university administrators, we were putting our jobs at risk, and that our contracts could very easily not be renewed.

I was very clear about what she had just said. "Oh!" I responded silently. But I went on to attempt to explain to her the interdisciplinary nature of Black Studies, and she started with that same old response that she had when we brought it to her attention during a meeting that the department had with the dean's office, about how she likes preps. I explained that teaching different courses in psychology is different from teaching different courses in Black Studies. When you teach a course in psychology you are still teaching psychology. When you teach Black Psychology, you must know the theories and research in psychology, and the theories and research in Black Psychology, as well as the socio-historical experiences of Blacks in America. I gave her more examples. Finally, I saw the "ah-ha" moment; "I see," she said.

"She got it." I thought to myself. "I'm done with this," I concluded, without saying so, as we walked out of the office.

I think there was silence as Jeff as I walked back to the office as we went to our inner worlds about what had just happened, whether we did the right thing; whether it was worth it, and whether any progress had been made. I am sure we had some discussion about it. Regardless of what we said, I had heard loud and clear what the associate dean said about our jobs. Nevertheless, I received what I needed to survive the job: release from the four-day requirement, Jeff had gotten the chair to back off and we got the associate dean to understand our concerns about the preps. Finding that the teaching load of the African American Studies Department faculty was higher than other faculty at the university, the number of preps was reduced, and I moved on. In retrospect, I believe they knew our course load was higher; they were just exploiting us because they thought we did not know any better.

Jeff, on the other hand, continued to struggle with the chair's leadership style and continued to agitate. Some of his personality quirks, (being a perfectionist, having extremely high expectations of people, and being prone to gossip) did not help matters. He struggled so much that he started getting therapy. The therapist suggested that it had to do with unresolved issues with his father. He even purchased the book *Don't Sweat the Small Stuff*, doing everything in his power, to deal with it.

Regardless of his struggles, he never stopped making me laugh. One time, we were sitting in his small and dingy office and he looked around and asked, facetiously, "Does this mean we made it?"

"I guess it does," I responded.

"Pat, we made it," he said.

We laughed and laughed.

Jeff loved his job, was extremely proud of it, and was so happy to be in Atlanta. I guess having a tenure-track professor job in Atlanta was a far cry from having a tenured position in Shippensburg, Pennsylvania, which he risked giving up to move to Atlanta. We would be walking down the street from lunch, and he would look up and point to the building and say, "Look, we work there." And I would look up and we would crack up.

Although I was having my own issues, I still cared about him (because he felt like a big brother) and had a lot of respect for the chair because I saw somebody who worked as hard as I did, somebody who was committed, somebody who cared about the department, and somebody who went to battle against the good ole boy (and girl) network at GSU.

Fighting against the good ole boy network was hard, but what was worse was that it was the *Southern* ole boy network. Working in the white male power structure in academe, where there are power and turf wars, must be as challenging as working in corporate America. I know for sure that if I had to fight through that, I would not be successful.

Because there were no doctoral programs in African American Studies before the one established at Temple University, in 1987, chairs would come from other disciplines. Therefore, some of the people who were chairing departments were not be trained in the discipline nor familiar with the politics surrounding Black Studies departments, much of which centered around whether it was a discipline. If Black Studies was established as a discipline, it would have the autonomy to operate as an independent department with its own budget, a chairperson, and faculty who would control it, rather than be a program or other entity within the university that is controlled by outsiders. Significant in making the case for Black Studies being a discipline was whether it has its own theories and paradigms, whether it has a particular research method, and whether it has a body of accumulated knowledge, which raised the question of when the discipline began. Did it begin in the sixties with the new departments that emerged out of the Civil Rights, Black Power, and student movements or did it begin with early scholarship by scholars such as W.E.B. Du Bois and Carter G. Woodson?

In addition, chairs and scholars that were coming from other disciplines may have conducted research on African phenomena, but it did not necessarily mean that the paradigms were African-centered. Much of the scholarship done by white scholars was entrenched in a deficit paradigm, and some of the early scholarship by Black scholars was as well, for example, that of E. Franklin Frazier and W.E.B. Du Bois. It was thought that chairs and professors were seeking positions and being hired in Black Studies departments because they were not being hired in traditional white departments in disciplines that they had done their studies in because of racism and that these departments did not value their research, particularly when it was Black-focused.

The chair at GSU, however, fought the fight about how to value our work, which had to do primarily with acceptable venues to publish it. Because some whites who serve on tenure committees do not value Black journals or Black presses, it would make getting tenure difficult for Black Studies professors. His efforts helped me tremendously, because my work was published in Black journals and a Black press.

Despite the challenges of the department in the early years, how blessed I was to be there continued to reveal itself. I got to meet significant people in the Black Power Movement, like Kathleen Cleaver (I met Bobby Seale at Temple University). Dr. Maulana Karenga and other renowned professors came to speak and visit the department. I also had the opportunity to meet community activists like Dick Gregory.

I went to a conference at Morehouse, and Jeff and I looked at each other in utter disbelief as he asked, "Do you believe we are sitting in the same room with the descendants of Ida B. Wells and Martin Luther King (there is a third person I do not remember)?" "It's unbelievable," I responded. Although King's daughter Bernice is well known in Atlanta, seeing her at the conference was the first time for us to hear from and see her directly. Sounding almost like Dr. Martin Luther King, Jr. herself, when she started doing her speech, which focused on women, I was a little nervous for her, because she was addressing an audience of academicians, some of who I am sure were feminists with that sexist Christian theology. I would see King's youngest son, Dexter, at nightclubs in Atlanta. I had the good fortune of sitting in a small group in conversation with King's oldest son, Marty.

Meeting people who had played a role in the Black struggle, in some way or other, including academics, continued throughout my entire career in African American Studies at GSU.

9

A CALL FROM THE ANCESTORS

Understanding how the uneven ratio of women to men made it difficult for Black women to land a committed relationship (let alone get married) while living in DC and feeling so alone at times while living in Philadelphia that I did not know what to do with myself, I began to look at polygyny as an option.

When I began to explore research in the area while at Temple, I found a book entitled *Man Sharing: Dilemma or Choice* by Audrey Chapman. I was inspired by the work, started bringing up the idea in my classes, and did a presentation on polygyny at a forum. When I began to do more extensive research, I found that polygyny had been practiced all over the world, and specifically that it had been universally accepted and practiced in Africa. The more I researched the topic, the more I began to see how it might be a viable option for Black women in the United States.

When I began to seek out African American communities that were practicing polygyny, I found that a colleague and his wife were contemplating bringing another wife into their family. Upon hearing about my interest in polygyny he invited me to interview his wife. I interviewed her, and when I heard her story of how her family tried to make her give her child up for adoption when she was a teenager, something clicked. I made an immediate connection with her because I heard the story surrounding my birth (I would later learn that my mother was led to put me in foster care by an aunt). I then interviewed the woman they were considering bringing into their family.

I was moved by the perspectives of these women, but the fact that the first wife was openhearted enough to accept sharing her husband with another woman in her own house because she wanted "to help a sister in need" was consciousness-raising, to say the least. The woman they were considering bringing in was in her forties (they were in their twenties and thirties) with no children, which meant they would be providing an opportunity for a middle-aged woman to get married and be a part of a family. Because the interviews went so well, I asked him to introduce me to other families in Ausar Auset Society, the organization that he was a member of.

Becoming my informant, my colleague not only introduced me, but drove me to interview families in Philadelphia, New York, and Washington, DC. While interviewing the families, I would find that their practice of polygyny was established to ensure that all women would have the opportunity to marry, and to ensure that no one would be without the support of a family and community. The more I learned, the more it made sense to me. The fact that women cared enough about other women to share their husbands was revolutionary to me (at least in America; I would learn that it has been practiced all over the world for those very reasons). The more I learned from these families, the more real polygyny came to me, and the more I began to see the possibility of it being a viable option for African American women.

But there was more to it than that. Being introduced to Ausar Auset, I would stumble onto an organization that was based on the African way of life, where African Americans were *consciously* practicing African spirituality based on the principles of one of the oldest African civilizations in the world: ancient Egypt.

What was even more impressive is what the organization had accomplished over a twenty-year period. Ausar Auset Society was founded by Ra Un Nefer Amen in 1973, right after the Civil Rights and Black Power movements. By the time I discovered Ausar Auset (in the early-1990s), the organization had managed to establish fifty chapters throughout the world in North America, the United Kingdom, West Africa, and the Caribbean. Major chapters in the United States were in New York, Philadelphia, Chicago, Washington, DC, Atlanta, and Milwaukee. Each community was independently owned and operated, with some having a social center, school, restaurant, and grocery store. At that time, the Atlanta community had a grocery store and a center where one could take classes on Kemetic (Egyptian) spirituality and how to read the oracles, get counseling and readings, and participate in meditations. I got a copy of the *Medu Neter Vol. I: The Great Oracle of Tehuti and the Egyptian System of Spiritual Cultivation* by Ra Un Nefer Amen, and thought, at the time, that I must have been one of the most divinely favored people on the planet to have come upon the knowledge contained in that work.

~~~~~~~~~~

During my early years at GSU, although Jeff and I had cultivated a friendship, we primarily saw each other at work, and I spent my weekends alone. I had a moment, that I felt so lonely, in my first year, I seriously considered packing my bags and moving back home to Albany. At the end of the semester, Mark, however, graduated from Ohio State and moved to Georgia. We moved in together but broke up a few years later and I was back out in the dating market.

During this time, I was also tossing around the idea of continuing the research I had already begun on polygyny, so I wrote an article about it that was published in a magazine called *RAW*. Someone from the African Hebrew Israelite community saw the article, and one of its members reached out to me, and eventually visited my office at GSU. He invited me to meet the community's leader, who was visiting America from Israel.

When I got to Soul Vegetarian (the restaurant owned and operated by their community in the West End in Southwest Atlanta), I was escorted up some steps into a room with men sitting around a table. When I walked into the room, they all stood up. Someone began introducing them. "This is Ben Amin Ben-Israel" (the community leader who, sadly passed in 2014). "This is Prince Asiel." "This is Prince so-and-so. "This is minister of so-and-so." If I did not stumble, it felt like I had; I was taken aback because it was the first time in my life that I had met African

American men who referred to themselves as princes and other dignitaries.

I believe the community orchestrated my meeting with Ben Amin Ben-Israel because he wanted to feel me out and hear my perspective on polygyny. He asked me a few questions. There was one I do not recall exactly, but it was something about how to get more people interested in the practice.

I naively responded, "It has to be popularized. People seem to want to do what is popular."

"Hmm," he responded, as if I said something that got his attention.

The meeting ended with him inviting me to visit Israel to study polygyny in their community. After receiving a grant that was specifically set aside for new African American Studies faculty, I decided I would use the money to continue my work on polygyny in African American communities.

Because they were still dealing with being treated as outsiders by the Israeli government, a member of the African Hebrew Israelite community, Yafah, the community's spokesperson at the time who helped me every step of the way, prepared me for the trip. She told me that when the airport agents ask me why I am coming to Israel to tell them "I'm coming to see the holy land." Because I had no attachment to Judaism or Christianity at that point, I had not even thought of seeing the holy land.

When I got to Israel, I was a bit disappointed because it seemed like just another American city. When I got to the African Hebrew Israelite community in Dimona, I saw a woman out at night by herself and became alarmed and asked, "What's she is doing out by herself at night?" The people who met me at the airport and who were driving assured me that the community was safe and that I need not worry about her.

Throughout the visit, the members of the community took good care of me, providing me housing and meals and taking me on tours of the land. The housing in the community is comparable to substandard housing in the United States, but there was not the kind of substandard values that typically goes along with it in the United States. I think it was the first time I realized that although people are materially poor, it does not mean that they have to be poor in their values and behaviors. People are poor in America; however, the individualistic, materialistic, survival of the fittest, rat race values make many poor communities dangerous to live in.

Members of the African Hebrew Israelite community took me to their soy factory in Israel where they produce soy ice cream that is distributed throughout Israel. It was the first time I had seen a factory at all, and one that was owned and operated by African Americans. Although I had heard that African Americans had factories in the United States (especially those that manufacture hair care products), I had never seen one. What made this phenomenal was that Black people established a factory in a foreign country within twenty-five years after leaving America, and during that time, there were only a few in the United States, even after 260 years of our living here. Members of the community also took me on a tour of the land, including the four quarters of the Old City in Jerusalem, which consisted of Jewish, Christian, Muslim, and Armenian sections that are right next to each other, divided by walls.

When we went behind one of the walls, I was so glad to finally see people of African descent who were residents of Israel other than the African Hebrew Israelites. They looked just like African Americans because of their different complexions and hair textures—I felt like I was home. They said that they had been there a thousand years before the various invasions and wars and the wall that was built relegating them to that small piece of land. They were literally living behind the wall. It reminded me a lot of what I had seen in Montana with the Native Americans. I also saw other very dark-skinned people who lived between Dimona and Tel Aviv, who said that had been in the land for thousands of years.

I was taken on a tour of the holy land by Prince Nasik Rahm and other tour guides to some of the places of Yeshua's (Jesus's) ministry including Tiberius, Mount of Arbel, the Galilee Sea, the location of the Sermon on the Mount teachings, and the Jordan River. While at the Jordan River, three of the men who had taken me on the tour stood in a line like a singing group and started singing a song. The song was referring to the woman in Samaria (John 4), telling me (as Jesus told her) to submit. I took this to mean that they were asking me to join their community.

The African Hebrew Israelites had learned both Aramaic and Hebrew languages and thus had interpreted many of the Hebrew texts themselves. This meant that their interpretation of the Hebrew tradition was different from the Christian interpretations based on the King James Version of the Bible, which was based on Greek translations. Although I believe I was converted on some level, as being in the land was transforming, I still could not get past the seemingly patriarchal and nationalistic undercurrents of their theology.

While in Israel, I got so sick that I thought I might die there, especially since the community practiced a natural way of life, had a vegan diet, and did not use antibiotics. "Don't tell me I am going to die in Israel," I thought. The women said I needed to heal naturally. Although I believe in natural healing, I was concerned that my body might not be able to handle a bug in Israel and thought, "Somebody please give me some American medicine to knock this thing out!" Conducting the interviews was hard because I had to do most of them while I was sick.

As for their practice of polygyny, it confirmed my belief that it was something that African American women might consider. Although I learned a lot about the way the community practiced polygyny, a lot of which I discuss in my book *We Want for Our Sisters What We Want for Ourselves*, some of the most significant things that stood out to me had little to do with polygyny, but more with the community and the women who resided there.

The women loved and respected the men and held them in the highest regard. They also really cared about each other and had each other's best interest at heart, or in the words of some of the sisters, "we have each other's backs." The sisterhood among the women reminded me of the women of my childhood. I loved women simply because I had been surrounded by them all my life. It was women—whether sisters, cousins, aunts, or friends—who had always taught me and who had given me comfort and support.

In one family, a sister-wife had died. I could feel the love her sister-wife had for her and the sadness she felt over losing her. In another family, four women were married to the same man. In that same family, the sisters had invited the fourth sister-wife into the family because she was a good sister who had been in the community for seventeen years, and they wanted her to be married and have a family. Each sister I interviewed alone talked so highly of their husband that I wanted to meet him myself, which I eventually did later when he was visiting the United States.

I was impressed by how confident and empowered the women seemed. Typically, people think of women in polygyny as being oppressed. Just like you see in African societies and in some African American families and communities in their organizations and churches, there are male spheres and female spheres, and the sexes dominate in their respective spheres; you saw the same thing in the African Hebrew Israelite community. Also, like what you see in Black American families, women were running things. They taught in the schools, operated their birthing center, and had a sewing center where clothes were made for the community. The women were also business owners. And some of them traveled internationally. They made their food from scratch, including their mayonnaise and ketchup.

I did informal interviews throughout the community and began to develop a close relationship with one woman. I was impressed when I saw her with her husband and nine children with matching outfits that she made herself. Large families were common with some having as many as fifteen children.

The gender roles, however, I thought were rather rigid, as women did most of the work in the domestic sphere, no matter what else they did. And during that time, only the men were able to participate at the highest level of the political-spiritual hierarchy.

I seriously considered joining the community but was more invested in my new career in academe. Although I had a lot of respect for the community and the women, I thought if I were to eventually join a family, I could not see myself putting that much of my life force in the domestic sphere like a majority of the women did. Although I did not join the community, I felt they were family and it was an option when and if I decided to let go of all I had invested in, especially my career in academe, in the United States.

~~~~~~~~~~

Since I was already in Israel and Egypt was only a two-hour flight away, I asked the community to assist me in making a trip to Egypt. They obliged me and had one of their members escort me to Cairo, where he took me on a tour.

When we got there, I was surprised by how many of the Arabs looked like light-skinned Black people in America, with frizzy hair. Many of them did not look like the images you see on television. Most of the women were fully clothed in black and many were veiled. As we walked by some of the Arabs, would say, "Hey, cousin." Because many of the people looked extremely poor, it seemed that Egypt would be considered a "Second World" country.

Cairo looked developed, but the people looked poorer than you see in America. I was struck by Cairo's City of the Dead, a cemetery that is about four miles long, where recent estimates indicate that a half million people live. When you ride by on the bus, you see people walking around, in the graveyard just like any other place. "People are so poor they live in a cemetery?" I asked myself. I was absolutely astounded by the poverty.

I began to understand the fascination with Egypt when I visited the Egyptian Museum, which houses over 120,000 ancient artifacts, especially considering the beautiful pieces of furniture, some of which were trimmed in gold. The reality that some of the kings were buried in solid gold caskets was mind-blowing. "Black people being drawn to gold is as old as time," I thought as I began thinking about the big and gaudy gold chains and the gold teeth that were popularized by hip-hop rappers in the United States during the 1990s. I began to see the wealth that Europeans and Arabs have been robbing from Egyptian tombs. As we were going through the city, I could see the paradise that may have once been. "Black people had all this land and cannot even get a piece of land in the U.S.," I thought. "How crazy is this?"

Although my understanding of Hebraism deepened, I was transformed in Egypt. I had been fascinated by the pyramids all my life. However, when we got to the Great Pyramid at Giza, I did not get what the big deal was, and even less so as I began climbing up into its chamber. Before I began my ascent up, I stood at the bottom looking up, hesitating, and started to turn around when I realized I was climbing into a tomb (at least this is what some of the archeologists thought it was at the time).

"Do I really want to do this?" I kept asking myself. "I do not feel like climbing up this ladder to go into a tomb; it is too hot, and I am claustrophobic. People make such a big deal out of everything." I climbed up anyway and found an empty room, which was uneventful. It was when I got to the light show that I begin to get it. I learned that when the sun hits the pyramid at noon, it represents Perfect Light. This is what Egyptians were striving for: Perfect Light.

~~~~~~~~~~

Before traveling to Israel, while in my office one day at GSU, I got a call from a young man named Trenyaae Bondoja. I believe the ancestors sent him to me to open my eyes to what I was engaging in, with the research on polygyny. When I answered the phone, I listened for a few minutes and told him I had to go and would speak with him another time. He called me a few more times after that at GSU. Being stressed out and overwhelmed, when he would call, I either did not talk with him or talked to him briefly. I thought he was a college student who just wanted to talk about polygyny and did not take him seriously.

I must have given him my home phone number because he caught me at home after my return from Israel. Since I was having some down-time, I had a conversation with him and began to listen more intently. I am glad I did because he put a whole new spin on the practice of polygyny, especially regarding the politics around it.

We continued to have a lot of conversations after that. Out of all the things I learned from Trenyaae, two things stood out to me: First, he made it clear to me that suppressing polygyny was a means of population control, particularly of people of color. Under social Darwinism, whites are losing the race in terms of the survival of the fittest since Blacks have a higher fertility rate. Second, was the Mormon practice of polygyny.

I already knew that the Mormons practiced polygyny in the United States, but something told me not to study it, at that time, so that I would not be influenced by what I would learn. However, after speaking with Trenyaae, I began to investigate the Mormon community and was not only shocked by their struggles but would learn that it was more about political and economic dominance and that their practice of polygyny was used to bring them down.

The Church of the Latter-Day Saints (also called the Mormons) was founded by Joseph Smith in 1830. He and some of his followers, however, were vying for economic and political power in local politics in various communities in Ohio and Missouri and were promoting a theocratic form of government. Smith was also considering running for president of the United States. Conflicting with those who were avid supporters of a democratic government, he and his followers were forced to leave these communities and eventually settled in Nauvoo, Illinois. Encountering conflict there as well, Joseph Smith and his brother Hyrum were eventually jailed and murdered by a mob (which was heartbreaking to read).

The Mormon communities eventually moved to Utah. Because they had established political control with its theocratic form of government on U.S. territory that had not acquired statehood yet, the Mormon community posed a threat to the entire U.S. government. To get rid of the threat, the U.S. government invaded Utah, passed laws that criminalized the practice of polygyny, restricted the church's ownership of property, forced leaders who continued to practice polygyny underground, incarcerated members of the Mormon community, and split up their families. In fact, the two major items on the agenda of the first Republican Party's convention in 1854 (when it was founded) were to eliminate the "twin relics of barbarism," slavery and polygamy. Being forced to comply caused a split in the Mormon community and the Mormon fundamentalists who wanted to continue to practice polygyny left the Mormon Church. After that, the conflict shifted from the Mormons against the United States to the Mormon Church against the Mormon fundamentalists.

After learning about the Mormon's struggles, particularly their conflict with the U.S. government, I was glad I had not started the polygyny research with the Mormon community. Had I been aware of how hard the U.S. government had come down on them, I may have not pursued the research.

~~~~~~~~~~

While searching for African American communities that practiced polygyny, I would discover that some African American Muslim communities practiced it. The study of polygyny among African American Muslims would take me down the road of Islam. I began my study of polygyny in the Islamic community by searching out mosques and decided I would explore one in the West End in Atlanta and one on the east side in Decatur. Someone referred me to Jamil Al-Amin, who was an imam in the West end with a store that produced and distributed incense throughout the Atlanta area. He also had a following.

According to Aminah McCloud in *African American Islam*, "There [were] at least thirty communities in the United States and the Caribbean who [had] pledged their allegiance to Imam Jamil Al-Amin.[63] Jamil Abdullah Al-Amin, then known as H. Rap Brown, served as chair of the Student Non-Violence Coordinating Committee in 1967, and served as the Minister of Justice for the Black Panther Party for a moment.

His autobiography *Die Nigger Die* describes his experiences in the Civil Rights Movement. Also, if one views the revolutionary thought of this beautiful man when he was in his youth in the YouTube video "Violence is as American as Cherry Pie," one might surmise that his conviction and life sentence at a federal prison after being convicted of shooting two Fulton County Deputy Sheriffs is suspicious, and might have been a setup to finally put down another revolutionary.[64] Convicting and sentencing Al-Amin in 2002, led to the dismantlement of the store he operated, which many African American Muslims had depended on for their livelihood.

When I met Imam Al-Amin in the Malcolm X Park and interviewed him, I think two of the most significant things he said as it pertains to polygyny is that it is unhealthy for women to go years without a sexual relationship, and that the prophet Muhammed prophesied that because of war, there would come a time where there will be seventy women for every man. I asked him to refer me to members of his community. He told me to come to the masjid and he would introduce me to a member who could help me with my research.

When I went to the mosque, I noticed a man who seemed to be surrounded by so much light, it looked as if he had a halo over his head. He turned out to be the man that Imam Jamil Al-Amin would introduce me to. I interviewed him, and he then introduced me to his first wife, who after interviewing her, put me in touch with his second wife, and they introduced me to other women.

When I interviewed the imam in the East Atlanta mosque, he provided me with more information about the practice of Islam, particularly its laws and their applicability to African Americans. I began reading the Koran and doing research into Islam. I would learn that there are sects in African American Muslim communities. There are the Moorish Science Temple communities. There is the Nation of Islam (which primarily follows the teachings of Elijah Muhammad under the leadership of

Minister Louis Farrakhan, who focuses on racial oppression and economic empowerment). And there is the American Muslim Mission, founded by Elijah Muhammad's son Wallace Deen Muhammad (who has passed since then), which focuses on the traditional teachings of the Prophet Muhammad.

As I continued to interview women in the two Atlanta communities, I learned that the Islamic communities were having a lot of issues with polygyny. Although it was a part of the religious creed of Islam (the prophet Muhammad declared that men could have up to seven wives), most of the women were conditioned in U.S. society and did not accept it. Some went along with it for the sake of being with the man, but there was heart-wrenching and perpetual conflict because, as one woman put it, their "husband was their God."

What exacerbated the problems in the Muslim communities was the way men were practicing polygyny. Some of the women claim that men were becoming Muslim just so that they could have multiple wives. Some men did not have a good sense of fairness and were neglectful. Some were abusive, lacked the skills for having multiple wives, and essentially did not know or follow Islamic law.

Before I began to learn anything about Islam, when I would see African American women dressed in Islamic clothing, I would secretly admire them. After interviewing some of the women, I learned that clothing is all it is for many of them. Their understanding of Islam is as about as deep as that of the average Christian's understanding of Christianity. They miss the essential principles, which are brotherly (and sisterly) love. However, I only interviewed a few women (and men) who were or had been in polygyny (some willingly because they saw the value in it); so, their experiences and perspectives might not be representative of women who practice Islam in general.

In ethnographic research, there is a phenomenon referred to as going "native." This is when the researcher becomes so immersed in the experience, they become a part of the phenomena. When I was interviewing members in each of the communities, I seriously considered joining every one of them because I was deeply moved, especially by their spirituality. I was inspired by the sisterhood and the sense of community in the families and I found truth in all the spiritual-religious systems. However, to remain objective, I decided not to join either community so that if I did present polygyny as an option for African American communities, it would not appear that I am promoting any one religion or any one community's agenda.

Interestingly, although I intended to explore polygyny, I had no idea that it would lead me into a deeper understanding of three major world religions: Judaism, Islam, as well as an ancient Egyptian spiritual system.

~~~~~~~~~~

When I finished writing *We Want for Our Sisters What We Want for Ourselves*, I had to figure out how to get it published. I thought about doing a mailing to university presses but did not think any of them would publish it. The chair called Paul Coates, the owner of Black Classic Press. Paul came to a presentation I did at a conference in DC on polygyny. Although he had helped me find an editor and I think he considered publishing the book, we did not come to anything conclusive.

While working on the book, there were three deaths within two years: my nephew, (who was like a little brother), one of my younger sisters, and a guy I had dated but was a friend. My sister and friend died suddenly. After I came from under the cloud of grief and feeling that one does know when one's life will end, I felt that since this was my destiny work, I could not wait for anyone to publish it—I had to do it myself.

I told the chair about my intentions. He warned, "Don't do it. You will not be given credit for it," which meant that the university would not recognize it. It would be like I had never written the book. I, however, felt an urgency to publish it anyway. Throughout doing the polygyny work, at times I felt like it was a call from the ancestors to tell the world about the truth of their ancient practice. Still unsure about whether I was making the right decision, that little voice came: "Go on and publish it, and things will work out."

Although he was strongly against me publishing the book myself, the chair put me in touch with a friend of his who was a manager of a printing company that was transitioning into the print-on-demand self-publishing arena. The issue with publishing your work yourself has to do with whether it is reviewed by other scholars. Since scholars are expected to adhere to certain scientific standards when conducting research, critical review by other scholars not only helps you to see what you might not be able to see, or may have missed, but also ensures that scientific standards are met. Also, having one's work published by a university press is considered the top of the echelon in terms of meeting academic standards. Reputable commercial presses are also highly valued in academe.

I met the chair's friend in the Los Angeles area. He gave me a tour of their printing company as well as Hollywood. I tried to work with his company. However, because the technology was still new and his company could not get the printing right, I decided to pursue other avenues to do it myself. I published the book and started selling it through my own website and through a new company that was selling primarily books at the time, Amazon, and shipped the books to purchasers myself.

10
KISS THE GROUND

Being a person of African descent, I felt it was necessary to visit West Africa since according to researchers, the majority of African Americans are descendants of West Africa. For me, it would be like returning home. My first trip to West Africa was to Ghana. However, it also included a more extensive African-centered tour of Egypt which I felt I needed and was looking forward to.

On this trip, I met some of the members of Future America Basic Research Institute founded by Nkosi Ajanaku, a lawyer, in 1973, to research "Humaculture" to bring to fruition the dream of Dr. Martin Luther King, Jr. There are a few brothers I have met in my life who were so deeply in tune with the rhythms of the universe, so deeply spiritual, they seemed like they were from another planet. I would refer to them as "brothas from another planet," after the film *Brother from Another Planet*. Nkosi Ajanaku, (who I had the opportunity to meet and learn his philosophy) was one of them, and so were some of the sisters and brothers who were members of his organization, who were on the tour.

Visiting Ghana was absolutely eye-opening. Every moment I was there, I was so stunned, that I believe my mouth was open the entire time. When we first got to Ghana, I was struck by how Black American some Ghanaians seemed. When I looked at some of the people, I could see some who resembled people I knew. No one could not have told me that a family that lives in my neighborhood were not the descendants of the Ghanaian people.

The cities we visited in Ghana were like American cities, in some respects but different in others. It reminded me of when I first visited DC. On one street you would see some of the most beautiful homes. The next block up or over, you could find yourself in a virtual ghetto. In Ghana you would see development, similar to modern U.S cities; then a little ways away, there would be little or no development at all, and people would be sleeping in the makeshift stands they were using to sell or barter whatever it seemed they could muster up.

I was utterly amazed at how many people were in some of the cities that we visited. At times, I would see more people than I had ever seen before other than in New York City; some places were like New York City —with huts. It seemed that everywhere we went on the bus, people stood with their hands out and that never stopped. "Did the West do such a job on Africa that it turned its peoples into countries of beggars," I asked? Or is this just something that people who follow tourists do? It was unbelievable.

One of the men on the tour said he was looking to move to Ghana because he did not want to grow old in America. I thought that a person certainly would not have to worry about being alone because there were so many people, at least in Accra. Just being there, you would not have a choice but to become attached to somebody's family.

When we went to rural areas, we saw places that seemed like people were living the way they lived a thousand years ago. In some areas, it seemed as if they did not know anything about modern life, like television, let alone a computer with the Internet. In the rural areas, there were outhouses, and for some, plumbing or irrigation was a line in the dirt where the urine runs into the woods.

In America, we get up and go to work. In some parts of Africa (and I imagine in other places untouched by the modern world), they get up and go fishing or barter something. When we went to Cape Coast, a city with a fishing port where Cape Coast Castle is, I had never seen so many people in my life, bartering items as small as a grapefruit for fish. In America, we make a big deal over low-wage jobs because we struggle to take care of our families on such low incomes. In some places in Africa (at least when I visited in the early 2000s), it seemed like there was no place to go to earn a wage—period.

~~~~~~~~~~

I had seen the independent film *Sankofa* produced by Haile Gerima that came out in the 1990s while living in Boston. The film is about Mona, a young African American model on a film shoot at Cape Coast in Ghana. She visits Cape Coast Castle dungeons that were used to store Africans before they were transported overseas. While there, she goes into a trance and becomes Shona, a house servant on a plantation. While going through this experience she finds herself in a relationship with a field hand and participates in an uprising. After going through the process of "remembering," the African American woman is transformed.

I think what the writer and producers were trying to do in *Sankofa* was to reveal the transforming effect that visiting the African dungeons can have on visitors. It is believed that the spirits of some of those who went through some of the horrific experiences still reside there; some people get possessed by them because the spirits want us to know what they went through.

I had heard stories of students visiting the dungeons and some getting possessed, and of people having deeply spiritual life-transforming experiences. As I had done in the church all my life—not allowing anything to possess me—I was determined I was not going to let that happen to me in Ghana and I was also not going to let what I would learn about the atrocities that occurred get me upset. By all means, I reasoned, this happened over a hundred years ago and the people who committed the crimes are dead.

As we drove up the palm-tree-lined street to the castle, I could see the beauty of the land. Because the Cape Coast Castle faces the Atlantic Ocean (the Gulf of Guinea), it makes it even more beautiful. While we were being guided by the tour guide, he said a lot of things that were quite disturbing. "How could such atrocities happen amid all this beauty?" I asked. After seeing the dungeons, I thought about how dark they were and how Africans were crowded in them for long periods in the heat, in conditions I'm sure were as worse as they were during the Middle Passage: stool, vomit, and blood from being beaten, and the stench from not being able to take care of their hygiene and from those who died.

Some of the members on our tour were shocked by what they were learning, started getting worked up; and started talking loud, shouting, "They are animals!" in front of other tourists, most of whom were white.

I was surprised that members of Ajanaku did not already know a lot about what we were finding out. I felt a little uneasy, not only because I sensed they were directing their anger at people who had nothing to do with this but also because I get like this when people start getting worked up. You do not know what might happen next and I really did not want to find out. I even said what I was thinking. "Come on y'all. This happened a long time ago," to cool them down. I believe it worked.

I later realized that although I had still had moments of rage, I had already gone through the process: the hurt and the pain of learning of some of the atrocities that Black people experienced during the slave trade; they needed to go through theirs.

Of all I learned, what was appalling is that some of the European countries that were involved in the wholesale sell of Africans had planned to breed a class of Africans through whom they could gain control of Africa. Just as slaveholders on U.S. plantations had set aside some African women to breed light-skinned women who could demand more on the market (to be purchased by wealthy bachelors to serve as their mistresses), the controllers of the dungeons had attempted to breed a class of Africans who would become puppets through which to rule Africa. Some of the women were bought to the top to provide sex services for the men who resided there.

It is like what has occurred all over the world under the practice of concubinage. When captured in war, women become sex and domestic slaves, forming complex relationships with their captors because of their attachment to them through the children they bear. Likewise, the children form complex relationships with the captors because they are their fathers. This same thing happened in America on plantations as well and explains why after slavery ended, the Black middle-class consisted predominantly of lighter-skinned Blacks. They had been afforded greater opportunities not only because they looked more like whites but also because many of them were the children of slaveholders.

I was surprised to find that besides focusing on Ghanaian history in the museum gallery in the castle, there was also information on the diaspora. The gallery contained some of the same pictures of slavery that we have in the United States. It also contained pictures of African American freedom fighters like Fredrick Douglas, Sojourner Truth, Harriet Tubman, W.E.B. Du Bois, Martin Luther King, Jr., Malcolm X, and others.

Although I was determined not to get worked up while on the tour, that would change after visiting the memorials of W.E.B. Du Bois and Kwame Nkrumah.

While at Temple, I had enrolled in a course on W.E.B. Du Bois and was moved by his scholar-activism and the tremendous contributions he made to the global struggle for the liberation of African people. While most people are aware of his classic work, *The Souls of Black Folk* (which I believe every American, not just Black Americans, should read), fewer people are familiar with his astounding work, *The Philadelphia Negro*, one of the most extensive and first sociological studies done in the United States, in 1899, and the first one done almost single-handedly by an African American scholar.

In this study, Du Bois collected data on nine thousand residents in the Seventh Ward in Philadelphia, thousands of whom he interviewed himself. He also visited African American schools, churches, and institutions, and attended social, political, and business gatherings, to collect data on every aspect of the lives of African Americans living in Philadelphia.[65] I was moved by the sheer fearlessness in the work: Du Bois urged America to recognize the humanity of Black Americans and to be humane toward them. In his chapter the "Final Word," although he outlined "the Duty of the Negro" (what African Americans needed to do be accountable), he also outlined the "Duty of the Whites," stating:

If in the hey-day of the greatest of the world's civilizations it is possible for one people ruthlessly to steal another, drag them helpless across the water, enslave them, debauch them and then slowly murder them by economic and social exclusion until they disappear from the face of the earth—if the consummation of such a crime be possible in the twentieth century, then our civilization is vain and the republic a mockery and a farce.[66]

In response to questions of what is the greatest cause of the so-called "Negro problem," Dubois essentially indicated that it was discrimination in employment stating that, "Such discrimination is morally wrong, politically dangerous, industrially wasteful, and socially silly [and] it is the duty of whites to stop it."[67]

Du Bois contributed a lot to the Black struggle in his long life of ninety-five years, and as a scholar-activist, never stopped agitating for social justice for Black people throughout the world. Some of his most significant achievements and contributions include being the first African American to earn a doctorate at Harvard University, becoming a founding member of the Niagara Movement in 1905, being a founding member, board member, and director of publicity and research of the NAACP, and serving as an editor of its magazine, *The Crisis*. He was a leading figure in racial protest for anti-lynching legislation, consultant to the United Nations, and author of the famous "An Appeal to the World." Du Bois held positions twice at Atlanta University, was co-chair of the Council of African Affairs, chaired, organized, served on, wrote speeches for, and presented at numerous national and international conferences, including peace conferences held in Paris and Moscow, the first Pan African Conference held in London in 1900, and the seven Pan African Congresses that followed. Du Bois authored twenty-one books, edited fifteen others, published over one hundred essays and articles, and traveled extensively throughout the world, including Russia and China.

Despite all that he accomplished and the contributions he made to the liberation of Black people and the liberation of America from her ridiculous prejudice, he also faced many challenges throughout his life. He was accused of being an elitist, particularly because of his talented tenth thesis. He struggled with the NAACP when he changed his integrationist stance to Black nationalism. He lost his job at Atlanta University. He experienced the death of his firstborn son (because white doctors would not treat him) and the death of his first wife. And he got into ugly and bitter public brawls with other leaders like Booker T. Washington and Marcus Garvey, where they called each other out of their names, because of their opposing ideas and views regarding the Black struggle. Du Bois was also accused of being a foreign agent by the federal government and was arrested and indicted at the age of eighty-six (he was later acquitted).

After his arrest, however, he lost his passport for eight years, and this prevented him from being able to continue his work abroad. With his American citizenship hanging in the wind, upon the invitation of Kwame Nkrumah, president of Ghana, Du Bois became a citizen of Ghana in 1961. He began his work as director of the *Africana Encyclopedia,* but before he was able to complete it, Du Bois died at the age of ninety-five on the eve of the 1963 March on Washington. Knowing about his life, I felt it was a privilege to visit the W.E.B. Du Bois center with his tomb, where the ashes of his second wife sit on top of his casket. But even more of a privilege was the opportunity to visit his home with its library. I could not believe I was in W.E.B. Du Bois's home, let alone his library with his books.

Visiting W.E.B. DuBois's home was mind-blowing, but it was not until coming to Kwame Nkruma's mausoleum in Accra that I was shaken to the core. After we went to his tomb, we went to the museum in a room with a wall lined with pictures of Kwame Nkruma and other heads of state of African countries. It was the first time I had seen Black presidents and heads of state. And it was the first time I saw them visiting other countries, shaking hands with the white heads of states in white countries. "A Black president?" I asked myself. This is when a Black president was a foreign concept to most Black Americans, and way before Barack Obama ran for and became president of the United States.

"Black people governing their own countries?" "Black people with power?" were questions that whirled around in my head. I guess I knew so little about Africa (other than the scant material that I read while at Temple), it never occurred to me that the heads of state and leaders were Black. I had to have known that they were Black, I had just never paid attention to it. I knew that Kwame Nkrumah was the first to lead an African country to independence from colonial rule (Britain), but I did not get it until I got to the mausoleum. I did not know that he was Ghana's first president.

What shook me the most is when I got to the picture of the woman who birthed him. He was the only child she had given birth to. Because of the significance of large families in Africa, it is almost as unusual for an African woman to have only one child as it is for a woman to not have a child at all. It was the birth of this one child, Kwame Nkrumah, that would change the course of African history. His work and those who worked with him inspired other leaders in African countries to follow in their footsteps and pursue independence from European colonial rule. "What would Africa look like had Kwame Nkrumah not been born?" I asked myself. As the tears began to well in my eyes, I did everything I could do to keep from falling apart in front of the other tourists.

One of the Ajanaku women, who seemed like a sista from another planet, had dreadlocks that were wrapped high on her head with a head wrap that was high as well. I did not realize that a person's hair could be as long as hers was until one day, while she was getting on the bus, one of her dreadlocks fell out and she stepped on it. I also did not realize at that time how powerful she was or how powerful words are. She kept saying throughout the entire time we were in Accra, "I want to see the president."

"This woman has lost her mind," I thought every time she would say it. "Who does she think she is that she can just ask to see the president of a country? We cannot do that in the U.S. What makes her think she can do it here? What is wrong with this woman?"

However, one day, while we were eating lunch, we discovered that a conference was being held at the auditorium in a building right next to where we were eating and that the current president of Ghana, Jerry Rawlings, would be speaking. I was absolutely flabbergasted. My questions changed to "Who is this woman that by her mere words she summoned the president of Ghana?"

Since we were there early, after we finished lunch, we walked right into the auditorium and were pretty much the only people there. I sat five rows from the front, waiting to see the president of Ghana. It was unbelievable to me. There was some entertainment before he came, and it was surprising how American it seemed. I thought about how the West had colonized African people and the type of music they were playing; I would not go to see it even in America. Others, as we did, walked in off the street and sat down.

When Rawlings came in, he did have a small entourage, but there seemed to be no security, at least not to the level we are accustomed to in the United States. He started a speech using a script, but later put it down, and started speaking from his heart.

He said, in so many words, "I need to talk to you straight. We need you to come back to Africa and lend your talents and skills to help us build. When the colonial governments came in, they did some development, and when they left, they left things where they were, half-developed. We need your help."

Exactly what he said is what I had seen. In some of the areas, there was some development, but in some areas, the sewage systems were exposed, and people were urinating in them. His sincerity made you want to do just as he had asked: come back to Africa to help. But it looked as impossible as it would be to revitalize some ghetto areas in the United

States. While living in D.C. my thinking was it would take nothing short of a bomb to revitalize some areas on Georgia Avenue. He also talked about how Ghana had set in motion dual citizenship; African Americans could have citizenship in America as well as in Ghana.

After Rawlings's talk, we went outside to see an event where Africans were staging the slave trade. I was able to stand not more than two feet from the president of Ghana. I later learned that an African American conference is held in Ghana every year, and we just happened to be there during that time.

~~~~~~~~~~

After the tour of Ghana, we took a flight to Egypt. I chose this tour of Egypt because it was supposed to be led by an African-centered tour guide and included tours of monuments in Luxor and Aswan. However, the tour guide got sick and did not make it to Egypt and these tours were canceled. To keep the trip going, the tour company contacted an Arab tourist company. The Arab guide gave the tour from an Arab-centered perspective as if the Arabs were the people who created all the ancient monuments that we were seeing. He also treated us like we are often treated in the United States, like second-class citizens (or second-class tourists, I suppose).

When we found out that the other tours were canceled, I told the other tourists (in so many words) that we were not getting what we paid for because the monuments in Aswan and Luxor were just as significant if not more so than what we were seeing in Cairo. Some of the other tourists became angry and began to challenge the tour guide, telling him to stop lying. They then began to take their anger out on each other, making me regret that I had bought it to their attention.

After we got over the shock of the tours being canceled, things got better. One night, while having dinner at an outside restaurant, the weather was so perfect, it seemed like a virtual paradise. Diop in *the African Origin of Civilization: Myth or Reality* suggested that Arabs and Europeans kept coming into Africa trying to get a piece of paradise. "Maybe Diop was right," I thought. The sentiment that Egypt had been a virtual paradise seemed even more real when we took a boat ride down the Nile River in the evening with the perfect weather under the starlit sky. Since we did not get to visit Luxor or Aswan, I decided that I would have to make another trip to Egypt.

While on my return to the United States, I reflected on what I had experienced while in Africa. I thought about the many things that those of us who live in the United States, with all the conveniences of the modern world, take for granted. The average American lives like a king by comparison to people throughout the world. We have the convenience of running water and electricity, which gives us light so that we can stay active far past when the sun sets. I thought about how important it is for me to shower in the privacy of my own home, in my bathroom, so that I can feel clean and feel good about myself. In many places, there is no such thing as a shower. There are only public baths, and in some places, no privacy anywhere.

I thought about how white men had bullied the world and taken their stuff, leaving people the world over in desperation. Before Western-world domination (and robbery), many peoples throughout the world worked their farms and were self-sufficient, but lost control of their land once their farms were turned into cash crops to feed Western countries.

"What does it mean that because of slavery I was born on this side of the Atlantic Ocean?" I asked. Had my ancestors not been born in slavery, I might still be living somewhere in Africa in, to me, horrible conditions. I thought about how many people I had met who would give anything to get out of Africa, all the people who had begged me to help them get out. How glad I was to be returning to America. I had heard people say that when they get to Africa, the first thing they were going to do is kiss the ground. The first thing I wanted to do when I got back to America was to kiss the ground.

Some white people say that they experience white guilt. I think what I was experiencing was American or Western guilt. It has been almost twenty years since I traveled to Ghana, but every time I take an international trip to places inhabited by people of color who live in poverty, I experience guilt. I know that I was able to travel to Africa because Western nations have bullied and robbed countries of color, making it possible for us (depending upon where we are in the race and class hierarchy) to live a privileged life by comparison to the way they live. When I think of those granite countertops, stainless steel appliances, hardwood floors, and crown molding that we are all clamoring to get so we can say to our friends "Look at me! I am living the good life!" I question, "Whose country did it come from?" "Did we pay a fair price for it?" "Was somebody's labor exploited?" and "What is the lifestyle of those who labored so that we could have these things?"

11
THE DEBT

I don't know how it happened to be that I would be reading Randall Robinson's (founder of the TransAfrica, an advocacy organization for global justice throughout the African world) *The Debt: What America Owes to Blacks* while taking a European tour in the early 2000s. I was excited about taking a tour of Europe because I had dreamed of visiting some of the cities that were a part of the tour when I was a child. Before traveling, however, I had not made the connection between what I would be seeing in the various countries and the exploitation of Africa. I guess somehow the ancestors and whom or whatever else is guiding me made me pick up that book to take on the tour for me to get it. What Robinson wrote in the first pages of *The Debt* shifted my paradigm and shaped the lens through which I would go through the European tour.

In the first chapter, Robinson makes it clear the role that Black slave labor played in the construction of not only the Capitol and the White House, but also Charles L'Enfant's grand design for Washington, DC. And despite that Blacks did much of the work for DC's architecture and monuments, aside from a bust of Martin Luther King, Jr. and a few representations of Native Americans in their frieze figures, frescoes, oil paintings, and statues, inside of the Capitol, one will see: "No Douglass. No Tubman. No slavery. No Blacks period."[68] Because of the lack of Black presence, every minute of the arduous work of lifting and hauling large sandstone blocks, firing and stacking bricks, mixing mortar, being nearly buried alive in sawdust, and the casting and loading of the 7.5-ton Statute of Freedom (which Phillip Reed, an enslaved African American was responsible for), is not recognized, as tourists the world over stand spellbound by the majesty of the dome; and the dwarfing effect of everything in the room that inspires awe.[69]

In this work, Robinson makes a poignant and provocative argument for reparations, why Blacks ought to be paid what is owed to them, and how the pay ought to match the crime. He points out why solutions like affirmative action (which was hotly debated in the 1990s), although needed and served those who were poised to take advantage of the opportunities, were *a* solution, but was not *the* solution. He argued:

> [Affirmative action programs] do little for the millions of African Americans bottom-mired in urban hells by the savage time-released social debilitations of American slavery. They do little for Americans, disproportionately Black, which inherit grinding poverty, poor nutrition, bad schools, unsafe neighborhoods, low expectation, and overburdened mothers. Lamentably, there will always be poverty. But African Americans are overrepresented in that economic class for one reason and one reason only: American slavery and the vicious climate that followed it. Affirmative action, should it survive, will never come anywhere near to balancing the books here. ... Let not the vision of blacks... fail to see the staggering breadth of America's crime against us.[70]

Interestingly, since Robinson's work, nine states have abandoned affirmative action policies, and although demands for reparations have been made in the UK, Africa, and the Caribbean, the one major bill for reparations, H.R. 40, the "Commission to Study Reparation Proposals for African Americans Act, proposed by Representative John Conyers, has been unsuccessful every year from 1989 until his resignation in 2017 (Conyers is the longest-serving African American in Congressional history. He passed on October 27, 2019).

Despite the failure of the Reparations bill to pass, the struggle continues for Black Americans to get what is owed to them. H.R. 40 was reintroduced in January 2019 by Representative Sheila Jackson Lee, and in April 2019, S.1083 was introduced by Senator Cory Booker. Some states, colleges, universities, banks, and other businesses and organizations have apologized and established reparations programs. Also, in response to protests led by the Black Lives Movement and other community and civil and human rights organizations, in response to the murders of George Floyd, Ahmaud Arbery, Breona Taylor (and numerous others before 2020), the California General Assembly passed a bill to study how reparations could be implemented. Asheville, North Carolina approved a resolution to make investments in areas where Black residents face disparities, and numerous businesses and organizations, including the

National Football League (NFL) and National Basketball Association (NBA), are establishing programs to donate hundreds of millions of dollars to combat systemic racism.

~~~~~~~~~~

But it seems that not only does America owe a debt to Black Americans, but that Europe also owes a debt to Africa. I had read bits and pieces of *How Europe Underdeveloped Africa*, by Walter Rodney, *The Destruction of African Civilizations* by Chancellor Williams, and had seen the films, *Africa: A Voyage of Discovery*, *The Bible and the Gun*, and *The Magnificent Piece of Cake* by Basil Davidson, which details not only how long (three-hundred years) it took for European nations to finally bring Africa down (they fought until they could no more), but the gruesomeness by which they did it. On the European tour, I would find that many of the things that European countries boast about, things that sets them apart from other countries (and in some instances fuel their economies), things they are most proud of, are based on theft from Africa and other countries with people of color.

The tour of England included tours of Windsor Castle, Hampton Court Palace, and the Tower of London. All three of them stood out to me, not for the reasons one might think, but because of the sheer gaudiness of the rooms and the things contained in some of them. I imagine the bigger and the gaudier, the more it gives the illusion of power—things that make those who possess them feel if not better than other people then at least special. In a room of one of the castles, the walls were lined with all types of firearms. The question that came to me when seeing this was, "Why would people glorify firearms?" I answered my question. "People who are always at war, bullying and killing other people, and taking their stuff."

The Tower of London included a tour of the crown jewels, which are crowns with gems in them worn by monarchs, such as the Imperial State Crown with 2,901 precious stones, including a diamond (Cullinan II) cut from another diamond (the Cullinan), the largest gem-quality diamond ever found (3,106 carats), from South Africa. There is also the Black Prince's ruby, one of the world's largest red spinels. Interestingly, a woman from India who was on the tour vowed that she would not see the crown jewels because one of them (Queen Elizabeth's) contains a diamond from India called the Koh-i-Noor.

The Koh-i-Noor diamond, whose Persian name means "mountain of light," was found three to five thousand years ago in Southern India. Once 793 carats, and eventually cut to 105 carats (making it one of the world's largest cut diamonds) to fit the European style, the Koh-i-Noor has passed through many hands over the years, through conquest, pillage, looting, and seizure, and eventually came into the possession (more than likely by theft) of the British East Indian Company and eventually to the collection of crown jewels in England. India, as well as Pakistan and Afghanistan (whose leadership also claims it), have requested that it be returned. Returning it, however, could open the door to claims being made to all the gems that were stolen. The woman became somewhat withdrawn when we got to that part of the tour, and I surmised that for her, it was too much of a reminder of the outright theft and subjugation that India experienced under British colonial rule.

I had always dreamed of going to Paris. However, when we got there, I was reminded again of the crimes committed against African people when I saw the lion statues at the entrance of the Eiffel Tower, and the obelisk at Place de la Concorde, at the entrance of the Bridge over the Seine. "Did they get the symbols of the lions and the obelisk from Egypt?" I asked myself. "Of course, they did," I answered.

I found out later that the obelisk, originally located at the Luxor Temple in Thebes, was given to Muhammad Ali Pasha (a ruler of Ottoman Egypt) in exchange for a French mechanical clock. Eight obelisks from ancient Egypt and one from Ethiopia (which was cut into pieces and returned in 2005) were taken out of Egypt and put in Rome. Others taken out of Egypt are in New York, London, and Istanbul.

"What is the big deal about the Eiffel Tower?" I asked the tour guide.

"Nothing," he responded, "other than at one time, it was the tallest building in France."

What was most surprising to find was that the people who were drug-addicted and hanging out in the park were primarily men of African descent. "How is it," I asked myself, "that I come all the way to Paris only to find what I see at Woodruff Park at GSU, and what one will see pretty much anywhere they visit in urban cities across the U.S.? Black men, outside of the opportunity structure, sitting around on park benches, addicted or homeless." The drug might be different; it was heroin in Paris, but crack in the U.S. during that time. "How can this be?" I asked myself.

Upon discovering that I had artistic ability when I was a child, my mother and father were looking into putting me in an art class. However, after overhearing how much it was going to cost them ($250, which was a lot of money back then, especially for a child), I told my mother that I did not want to take the class. So, my father, who was an artist himself, taught me how to draw. I also took an art course in high school that introduced me to some of Europe's and American's greatest artists. So, I had somewhat of an appreciation for art.

However, when I visited one of the art museums in Paris, although appreciating the detail and the enormous amount of work it must have taken to produce some of the pieces, I responded the way I typically do when a big deal is made about art and the costs to purchase it are exorbitant: "What's the big deal? It's just paint (or whatever other medium was used) on canvas. Am I missing something here?"

I had also been told when I was a child, "You will love Amsterdam. You must go." As a young adult, I heard people say, "You can't leave Amsterdam without going to the Red-Light District," and while on the tour, the tour guides and some of the tourists kept making a big deal about it. Some of them also made a big deal out of the fact that marijuana was legal in Amsterdam; this is way before it became legal in some states in the United States.

I must admit, I did like Amsterdam; it reminded me a lot of Boston. How enchanting were the tall narrow buildings, which seemed to be constructed to save space, with the door-sized windows on the houses that lined the canals. How badly I wanted to go into one of the houses. I have always loved Victorian-style houses with high ceilings, and as an adult, I longed for one like the one of my childhood.

I could not wait to visit the diamond factory. Although I am sure I had learned somewhere that the Netherlands was the home of the Dutch, I do not think I got it until I got there. But what I did not get was that it was the home of the Boors, who were the originators and promulgators of apartheid in South Africa, and the exploiters of African labor in the mines, where they essentially stole the diamonds and literally worked the people to death. The more the other tourists made a big deal out of the factory and the diamonds, the more infuriated I became.

My anger would grow as we strolled down the Red-Light District, one of the largest tourist attractions in Amsterdam, to see women barely dressed on display, in parlors as if they were mannequins, waiting for suitors to pay for sex services. Seeing a Black woman in the window, who looked African, made me wonder what happened in her life that she would find herself a prostitute, selling sex in Amsterdam.

While in Amsterdam, a Jewish woman made a big deal about her and her children seeing the Anne Frank Museum. As tragic as the story is of two families who lived for two years in hiding in a secret room behind a bookcase while Anne Frank wrote in her diary about her day-to-day experiences before she and her family were caught by the Hitler regime, my thoughts were, "Oh, lucky for you. It is a happy trip, where you can take your children on a European vacation and to a museum to remind them of the tragedy of the Jewish Holocaust." Although there are several local African American museums in the United States, many African Americans do not even know that they exist, let alone visit them. And the opportunity to take their children on vacation to Africa, to see the tragedy of the Great Maafa (i.e., the Great Disaster, the slave trade) is not a reality for the majority. Nor do most even know about, let alone will ever see, the monuments throughout Africa that provide a glimpse of the greatness of African people.

Seeing pictures of Brussels in magazines as a child, I had also dreamed of going there. The tour included visits to stores that sold chocolate, and at first, I was excited because I really like chocolate. Once we got to the chocolate shops, it occurred to me: "Where does Brussels get its chocolate?" I speculated that it came from somewhere in Africa but was not sure.

I would later find that it comes from cocoa, which was first imported from the Congo during the Spanish occupation in the seventeenth century. Although I do not know for sure, one might speculate that early exportation of cocoa to Belgium left the Congolese people on the losing end of the deal, as it has throughout Africa and that the deal between the Democratic Republic of the Congo (which it became after its independence from Belgium in 1960) accrues more benefit to Belgium's economy than to Congo's economy, even today. What was more interesting to find were the atrocities that the Congolese people experienced under King Leopold II of Belgium between 1885 and 1908.

Under his regime, Leopold established the only "privately-owned" colony—the Congo Free State (although it was far from free)—after being permitted to do so at the Berlin Conference of 1884–1885. European nations met at this conference (without a single African nation being present) to address conflicts they were having as they scrambled for pieces of Africa. After the conference, the continent was divided among European nations, giving them free rein in Africa. There are not even words that can describe the atrocities that the Congolese people experienced under Leopold, as Belgium attempted to extract ivory, diamonds, and other natural resources, and specifically rubber for Western nations' growing demand for tires and belts for the machinery of the industrial revolution.

The mercenary Force Publique went from village to village, raping the women and taking them and children hostage, while forcing the men deep into the jungle to tap the rubber trees. Those who resisted were mowed down with machine guns, beheaded, or had their feet, hands, and who knows what else was cut off. Concerned that munition (which was costly to export from Europe) would be used for hunting, personnel had to show proof of how they were used by the number of cut-off hands. To avoid the penalty of death for not meeting rubber quotas, they were partly paid off in chopped-off hands. Because the quota demands were unrealistic (and probably to terrorize those who failed to meet them), the hands of hostage women and children were also chopped off. Tragically, when a hand was cut off, the victim was left to die. However, some survived; one can find pictures of victims with chopped-off hands by searching the Internet. In addition to the atrocities and not being able to hunt for game or grow food, the Congolese social infrastructure fell apart, leading to widespread starvation and disease. Approximately half of the Congo's population died—an estimated ten million people between 1880 and 1920—under Leopold's reign of rubber terror. This kind of genocide occurred not only in the Congo but all over Africa.[71]

Interestingly, Belgian chocolate hands, called *Antwerpse Handjes*, are supposed to symbolize the mythical hand of a terrorizing giant named Druon Antigoon, who terrorized laborers by chopping off their hands and throwing them in the Scheldt River if they were unable to pay him undeserved tolls. The giant's hand was eventually cut off in battle and thrown into the river by a brave soldier named Silvius Brabo. Ironically, Antwerpse's chocolate hands also symbolize the atrocities that the

Congolese people experienced at the terrorizing hands of Leopold II. They are still sold in Antwerp.

While on the train touring the Rhineland, on the outskirts of Western Germany, one of the tour guides pointed out that during World War II, there was a movement to preserve the castles that lined some of the mountains. "Oh, bomb and kill people, but preserve the buildings. What is wrong with these people?" I asked. The place that I was least interested in visiting but was the one I liked the most was Lucerne, Switzerland; it was enchanting and felt familiar, reminding me of the quiet and quaintness of Albany, New York. The snow-capped mountain was captivating, and I had never seen water as clear and fresh-looking as the water in Lucerne.

Taking the tour, I was now not only mad at Europe because of the crimes committed against African people, but I was also mad because of all the things its nations stole from Africa and passes off as their own. Robinson's *The Debt* made me realize that people tell the world of their contributions and their greatness through the things they produce and their monuments and museums. I realized that when people visit Washington, DC, they will see the Lincoln Memorial, they will see the Washington Memorial, they will see other memorials of America's great leaders, and they will see a memorial for all the lives lost in the Vietnam War.

But they will not see a memorial for the millions of Black people who slaved and died so that not only America, but Europe also could get ahead in the "race" toward so-called "progress." When they visit the mall in Washington, DC, they will see the obelisk, but most people will never know that this symbol comes from Black people in Egypt. They will visit the museums to see some of the most significant discoveries made by humanity and the most significant contributions that humanity has made to mankind, but these museums will feature discoveries mostly made by white people. No one will ever know that many of the ideas that inspired some of the great contributions first came from Black people.

Interestingly, unbeknownst to me, two years later in 2003, a law was passed to establish the National Museum of African American History and Culture.

12
VISIONS OF 911

I was running frantically as a ball of fire was following me. My heart was pounding so fast, I thought I might have a heart attack after I awakened. "You can do it; you can do it," I kept saying to myself to calm my heart down. It was this dream that made me realize why people die in their sleep. The experiences are so traumatic, it causes them to have a cardiac arrest.

I laid awake longer than I usually do after having a bad dream, thinking about what I had just dreamed: two large disks hitting the Twin Towers in New York City. When this happened in the dream, I looked up and said, "Oh my God, it is the end of the world!" and began running and kept running and running, which is why my heart was beating so fast. "Maybe it won't happen in my lifetime," I eventually convinced myself, so that I could go back to sleep.

About six months later, I turned on the television (something I never do in the morning) to see a plane crashing into one of the Twin Towers in New York City. "Oh my God! I don't believe it! I don't believe it!" I screamed. "It's the end of the world!" I was merely repeating what I had said when I saw the disks hit the towers in the dream. My subconscious in my dream state knew that if anyone attacked America because the nation has weapons that could essentially annihilate the world as we know it, that is exactly what would happen. And some of us believe that the small number of individuals who really hold the power will blow up the world and everything and everybody in it before they give it up.

Although I was afraid to go into downtown Atlanta after the planes crashed into the Twin Towers on September 11, 2001, I had a class to teach and did not want to just not show up. I was going to go and tell the students they could go home because I was not going to stay. As I was driving, I thought about all the possibilities of what might happen in downtown Atlanta. I thought about the Centers for Disease Control and Prevention (CDC), biological weapons, and all the possibilities.

As I was walking up the street, I saw the department chair and started walking beside him. Since he seemed so calm, I wondered if he knew that the planes had crashed into the towers, whether he knew the dangers we were in. Because based on what I had read about some of the crimes committed the world over, I know there will be retribution. You cannot have the kind of disregard that the West has for humanity and nature and think there are not going to be some consequences. A whole lot of innocent people are going to be casualties as they were in New York, and all we can do is to do our best to get out of the way.

When I got to the class, some of the students showed up, but they just started walking out; I did not have to tell them to leave. When I got home, the television networks kept playing over and over the footage of the building collapsing and all the things that were going on in New York. I could not help but feel a heavy burden and deeply sad. Later, Joe (my ex) called me and said, "This is symbolic of war."

"This is not symbolic of war," I responded, "This is war."

Later that evening, the news showed members of Congress standing on the stairs of the Capitol, singing. What stood out to me was not just how vulnerable they looked, but that there were few African Americans and few women standing there with them; a handful of white men, most of whom have no idea about how the majority of us live, were making decisions for the rest of us.

Since then, I have had several more of those frightening dreams, or shall I say visions. In one recurring dream, planes are flying over the skies in DC. I look up and try to determine whether we are at war as I am running for cover. In other dreams, something is happening in the sky. I look up trying to figure out whether it has to do with something of our doing, like war or something from the cosmos, penetrating the atmosphere, like objects or visitors from outer space. In one dream or vision, the sky got black with smoke and we were running trying to get away from it. As I do in all the dreams, I was looking back as I was running, trying to figure out the source of it. Then a form raised from the dark smoke, looking like a black cloud with a big head and with an earth-shattering, rumbling voice said "Praaaaaaaayyyyyyy!"

13

ENTREPRENEUR STRIVINGS

"Hello," said a voice over the telephone. "My name is Khalil... I saw your résumé and..."

I don't recall what he said after that, but I do recall that he revealed to me within the first few minutes of the conversation that he had done twenty years in the penitentiary and that he would like to meet me so that we could explore the possibility of working together.

In our numerous telephone conversations, I found Khalil to be one of the most brilliant minds I had gotten to know on a personal level at this point in my life. Khalil said he had read the Bible in its entirety and had read the Koran back-to-back three times, although he never claimed Christianity or Islam to be his religion. It bought back the pain of knowing that some of our most brilliant and gifted men are in shelters, on the streets, or wasting away in prison, while too many Black women are without husbands.

I finally met Khalil on one of his visits to Atlanta. Having known intimately the life and work of many of our Black activists and leaders, I think we both longed to make a contribution to Black people that could even light a match to the contributions as significant that some of them had made. Khalil would brag, "I did time in the prison Malcolm X did time in, and I got a degree at the university that Dr. Martin Luther King got his degree from." Since we were exploring how to work together, I expressed my interest in bringing the information from the relationships course I was teaching at GSU to the broader African American community. Khalil and I co-authored *TLC: Talking and Listening with Care* and co-founded the National African American Relationships Institute (NAARI).

Through Khalil, I had the privilege of meeting and getting to know Elaine Brown, the first and only woman to chair the Black Panther Party. She is also the author of *A Taste of Power*, a story about her experiences in the Black Panther Party. Khalil was fascinated by the fact that he had not only met and was developing a friendship with one of his childhood icons, but that they also shared similar ideas around political ideology and desired to do work with ex-convicts and around prison reform. He was in the process of co-authoring *The Psychology of Incarceration* and she had authored *The Condemnation of Little B.*, which addressed the issue of children being tried as adults.

After about a year of meeting Khalil, I would meet the man who would become my husband, Tim. After Mark and I broke up, I started dating in Atlanta and had been in a couple of serious relationships, but up until that point, I had not met anyone where there was mutual interest in marrying. After my classes ended for the semester, feeling down about not having a partner to celebrate with, I reached out to Scotty, a friend I had met when he was bartending at A Taste, a bar, and restaurant in Atlanta. During the time I was hanging out with Scotty, although I was not in a serious relationship, I was having a lot of fun. I would meet Scotty and other friends whom I referred to as the "crew," who were entrepreneurs in the mortgage and real estate industries. I met the crew through Mike, someone I had dated a couple of years after Mark and I broke up.

That night, Scotty was with Derek, one of the crew members, and others renovating the space to open another restaurant, that A Taste had been in before it closed. When I reached out to him, Scotty he said that he was just hanging out on the balcony but had a gig later that evening (he is a drummer). My thoughts were, "Is your life that bad that you have to go and stand around on a balcony?" After I got there, while I was sitting at the bar, a tall guy came out from the back. When I got up to leave so that Scotty could go play, our eyes met, and we spoke. When we got in the car, I asked,

"Who was that guy?"

"Oh, that's Tim. He's a really good brother. That is a good brother. You want me to call him? I'll call him."

Scotty then continued to go on and on about how good of a brother Tim was. Because it was unusual for him to say anything positive about another man, let alone speak that highly of one, my thoughts were "Oh, why not? You're not doing anything else." "Yeah," I responded.

"Hey, Tim. My sister wants to meet you." He then went on and on, totally exaggerating my interest in meeting him, and invited him to come to the club that he was playing at.

When Tim came into the nightclub, I was indifferent as he sat down next to me. His arm touched my arm, and my thoughts were, "Why is this brother touching me?" Then I looked at his arm and hand and thought, "Hmmm, he has nice arms and hands." Then he looked at me and said something that I do not recall. He got my attention not because he said anything deep. It was his energy. I looked at him and thought, "Wow, this brother has really good energy." We talked, parted, talked a few times on the telephone after that, then about a month later we started dating. I would later meet his two adult sons, teenage daughter, and other members of his family, including his mother and brother who lived in Atlanta.

Before meeting Tim, I had looked at where I was financially and could clearly see that at my salary level, I would not be prepared to retire comfortably. I remembered that although I had not made any money selling real estate, I did make money when I worked briefly in the mortgage industry. I had also seen how successful Derek seemed to be in the mortgage business. When I first met him through Mike, Derek had a medium-sized office in downtown Atlanta. The next time I visited his office shortly after that, he had expanded into a much larger office. A few years later I heard he had expanded to a whole floor in the building with the peach on it in Buckhead. I had already started working with a mortgage company, and in fact, the day I closed my first loan, Tim called, and we started dating that night.

I had already enrolled in a mortgage broker course and wanted to get into real estate investing. Tim had worked with Derek in his mortgage company and they had bought, renovated, and sold real estate. When they ran out of money before they could complete the restaurant, Derek, Tim, and I decided to start a mortgage company. We purchased a small house in East Point and opened Georgia Residential Mortgage.

~~~~~~~~~~~

Because we now had an office to work out of, in that same year, NAARI held its first national conference, where Elaine Brown and Iyanla Vanzant, and numerous other scholars and community activists, participated. Khalil and I began to be invited to make presentations for both the state and federal government and I was invited to serve as a consultant for some organizations that provided technical assistance and marriage education.

Before NAARI's conference, the federal government gave us a grant to support the effort. However, the woman who worked for the Department of Children and Family Services in Atlanta met with us when we first got started and questioned me about my work on polygyny. She indicated then that she did not know if she would be able to support us.

While I was in New York for a healthy marriage consulting assignment, she called me and said, "Somebody has sent the federal government material and said that you are telling people to practice polygyny."

I said, "Well I did research on it, but that does not necessarily mean that I am telling people to practice it." I began to think quickly about what I had done recently where someone would find my material and send it to the federal government. I recalled seeing a white woman in an audience when I did a presentation for the National Black Herstory Task Force conference, co-founded by Mozella Calloway Ross. I got a funny feeling about her. I believe I had seen her in other audiences at conferences I presented at after that. I also recalled a Black woman who was really upset with me about polygyny.

This is something I have found when I make presentations on polygyny: there will be at least one African American woman who will be really angry. I surmised that for many, the only experience with anything remotely resembling polygyny is how their fathers treated their mothers or their own experiences with men who cheated on them, causing them a great deal of pain. Because what they are hearing is being filtered through a lens of pain, they are not able to hear what I am saying.

"Well, we need to know your position on it," she said. "What is your position on polygyny?"

I contemplated saying, "Since doing the work, I changed my view on it," and my friends thought I should have said that. But needing to be true to what I believe, I said, "Well, I think that it should be an option for those who choose to practice it."

"Okay," she said. "We are going to ask the bank to return the check."

I was shocked that the federal government would send a check and turn around and take it back. After that, I realized that since I did not know where my life was going, it might be best to back away from polygyny for a while. "Besides," I rationalized, "most people don't know how to practice monogamy, let alone polygyny."

~~~~~~~~~~

Before meeting Tim and going down the entrepreneur road, I woke up one day to find that someone from Philadelphia had purchased six copies of my polygyny book that I was selling on my website. His name was Theodore Pendergrass. When I responded to the email, I asked, "Is this *the* Teddy Pendergrass?" to which he responded that he was. We talked and he invited me to visit him at his home in Philadelphia to do a presentation on polygyny.

When I got to his home, I noticed the big portrait of him on the wall, and I was greeted by a woman who took me to his room to meet him. He was in bed, completely covered with the blanket going all the way up to the bottom of his chin, which I thought was unusual. I loved Teddy Pendergrass's music and played it all the time, mostly in the fall. When I saw him the next day, although he was in a wheelchair, he was still as good-looking as he was in pictures, if not more so. Because I could see the spirit of the man, and as I got to know him, I found him to be as good a human being as he was good-looking.

Over the few days I spent at Teddy Pendergrass's home, I learned that he ran his house like a business, and people who were in and out were walking on eggshells. He explained that he ran his household as he did because he had care professionals in his house around the clock and he had to be careful so that they would not forget they were at work. He had to be concerned about what he did around them lest they put his business out.

He talked about the public versus private persona, articulating something I had experienced but at that time did not know how to articulate: what people present in the public sphere (particularly, famous people) may not be who they are in private. This resonated with me because while I lived in Boston, a young man I met accused me of "fronting."

"What do you mean?" I asked, "I'm being who I am."

"You be acting like you are one person on campus, but you are someone else."

He apparently mistook how I carried myself in my professional life with how I was in my private life, which was someone who was struggling with a new job as a visiting lecturer, extremely lonely, stressed-out, anxiety-ridden, depressed, and without an emotional support system.

Through the numerous conversations I had with Teddy Pendergrass and his partner, I would also learn that although he was suffering from a spinal cord injury (the same thing that Christopher Reeve had), the Teddy Pendergrass Foundation was not getting the large sums of money from donors that the Christopher Reeve Paralysis Foundation was getting. He was disgruntled about this. This indicated to me that no matter how rich and famous you are, if you are Black in America, there are certain circles you may not be able to run in, and you may still experience racism.

~~~~~~~~~~

A few years after publishing my work on polygyny, I revisited the idea of getting a publisher to publish it so that I could get academic credit. I sent it to Third World Press (one of three major Black presses at the time). Haki Madhubuti, its founder, called me personally and talked to me about it, but did not publish it. I sent it to African World Press. They turned it down. I turned again to Paul Coates at Black Classic Press. He read the book and called and told me that it was great work. But had I included a chapter of the impact of polygyny on children, "it would be a greater work," and that he would publish it. Since the chair had already fought the battle with the university administration for Black Classic Press to be recognized, especially since his book had been published by the press, this means I would get academic credit.

Some time afterward, a Jewish woman who worked at ABC's *20/20* called me for an interview about my work on polygyny. She said she had some friends who were not married, and she thought that polygyny might be an option. I called Barry to ask him what he thought I should do.

"Don't do it," he warned. "You will be viewed as being on the left, and this might cause you to miss mainstream opportunities."

"I am probably already perceived as being on the left. At least with this, I have something that may help people when I am dead and gone."

"What do you really think about polygyny? Do you really think it is an option?" he asked.

"Yes," and I went on to explain why. I decided to do the interview. When the woman from 20/20 called again to ask me to refer her to people I had interviewed, I told her I would try.

I called the African Hebrew Israelite community and talked to the same sister, Yafah, who had coordinated my trip to Israel. She said she was skeptical.

"We have agreed to interview with people in the past, and they twisted what we said and made us look bad," she said.

"I don't think she will do that," I responded. "She seems to be in support of polygyny, and I think she will be true to what you say."

After that, I began to reflect on how whites had gone into communities of people of color the world over, acting friendly, bringing them much harm. "I know when someone is genuine," I said to myself. "I just don't think she will do that."

When I called Ausar Auset Society and asked whether members of their community were interested in being interviewed, the woman seemed unaware that interviews had been conducted in their community and that a book had been published. I went on to explain myself more. The woman said she would get back to me.

I began to wonder, "Did the leader not know that members of their community had been interviewed? How could they not know that a book had been published that included their community?" I began to reflect on it and remembered that a colleague had introduced me to the community and helped me set up the interviews. I did get permission from local leaders and had even interviewed them. Did they not get permission from the leader and did they not tell him? The next time I spoke with the woman she gave me a flat-out "No!" It was like I had done something I should have not done.

The interview with *20/20* was uneventful. I imagined that the experience would be more glamorous and that we might be picked up from the airport in a limousine. The car was black, but it was far from a limousine. I got the charge I always get when I visit New York because of the fast pace and lights, and it was something I needed badly. The hotel was nice, and although it was not right in the middle of downtown Manhattan, it was close to it.

What took away from the joy I might have experienced was the anxiety I felt about the interview—it was one of the most stressful days of my life. "Will I be articulate today?" I worried. This is what I go through every time I have to speak because sometimes, I am articulate and on point, and sometimes, I just am not. Although I acted and danced in front of audiences early in my life, I was usually someone else, acting someone's script; when speaking, you are yourself, speaking your own script. This is what has made teaching difficult. And although I typically am not so anxiety-ridden with interviewing because I like conversation, this was national television and I would be interviewing with a national personality, John Stossel.

We were told to flag down a taxi and come to ABC's building. I left early something I always do when I have a speaking engagement or an interview. This is something I would also go through with teaching; every time I teach a class, it is like a major performance. I imagined I would be going to a building with a glamorous large studio—with lights, camera, action!

However, when we arrived at the building and caught the elevator up to the floor that I would be interviewed on, we discovered that it was just a plain office, and the actual room that the interview took take place in was a small dingy office with lights and cameras. The fact that the cameramen made me look good with no makeup on, in the dark, with dim lighting, because they knew what they were doing was an eye-opener.

Although I was stressed at the beginning of the interview, what made me snap out of it is that Stossel was extremely tired, I am assuming because he had been interviewing all day. Throughout the entire interview, it looked as if he was falling asleep. I figured if this was going to go well, I had better step it up.

I left feeling like I said what I needed to say to clarify misunderstandings, and why I thought polygyny might be an option for African Americans. With my family and friends all over the United States anticipating to see me when the show aired, the entire session with all the other people they had interviewed probably lasted fewer than five minutes, and the thirty-minute interview with me lasted fewer than thirty seconds.

Some years later, Ra Un Nefer Amen came to speak at GSU. I attended the event, not to just hear him speak, but to meet him. At the end, I walked in front of him and said, "Hi, I just want to introduce myself to you. I am Pat, the author of the polygyny book." I gave him a copy. After taking classes in the Ausar Auset community more recently, and getting to know some of its members more intimately, and knowing how polygynist communities have been persecuted by the U.S. government, I realized I may have put their community in harm's way. Maybe, I thought, I should have used a fictitious name when describing their community.

14
SHINING, BLESSED ONE WHO BENDS

Not only did Barack Hussein Obama, as many before him, (as far back as Frederick Douglas), dare to run for the presidency of the United States of America, but he had the audacity to win. I do not think anyone who is Black in America, and who is minimally conscious, did not think about race when Obama won the bid for the presidency. Especially those of us who may have thought it was impossible.

I first began to pay attention to Obama when I was home, visiting my mother one summer. There was a Democratic debate that both he and Hilary Clinton were participating in, and Hilary kept saying something to the effect of "We Democrats are on the same side. It's us against them," the Democrats against the Republicans. During that time, I did not follow American politics, simply because I was not interested in it. And I was not interested in it because I had absolutely no faith or trust in it. Once one learns how the electoral college works, it can be even more discouraging.

I had not been able to get past what I learned about Black experiences with American politics. I saw terrorists of the old—the Democrats—and I saw the users of the past—the Republicans. I could not forget the reports of the terrorization that Black people experienced at the hands of terrorist groups like the KKK, Red Shirts, White League, Loyal League, Redeemers, etc., terrorist arms of the Democratic Party whose aim was to keep Blacks from voting or to force them to vote Democrat in the Reconstruction South. When a joint congressional committee was created in 1871, consisting of twenty-one members of both houses to hold hearings to "inquire into the condition of the late insurrectionary states," also known as the "Klan Hearings," this collection of thirteen hardbound volumes of roughly seven hundred pages each reveals testimonies—with graphic details—of the terror and violence that African Americans experienced.

There were numerous accounts of men being beaten and threatened to be killed if they dared to vote "radical" (republican and if they did not vote Democrat). Since women could not vote yet, when men were not at home (some left to avoid being killed), their houses were raided by white terrorists who would terrorize their wives by eating their food and taking their money. Some would then drag them and their daughters to the street and beat them and (in their words) make "connexion" and "ravish" (gang rape) them. In some instances, they would shoot up their houses or burn them down, or both.[72]

Because the Republicans' campaign when Lincoln ran for president was to rid America of the "twin relics of barbarism" (slavery and polygamy), most Blacks were Republicans until the New Deal under Franklin D. Roosevelt. The Republican Party established policies to help the newly freedmen during reconstruction. One of its most significant achievements was the establishment of the Freedmen's Bureau. However, the way I saw it when these policies were put in place in the Reconstruction South, Blacks were simply pawns in a tug-of-war between one group of elite white men against the others. This revealed itself in the 1876 election with the Tilden-Hayes compromise, when both Samuel J. Tilden, a Democrat, and Rutherford B. Hayes, a Republican claimed the presidential election. In 1877, a compromise was struck: Hayes would be president if federal troops withdrew from the South. This left African Americans at the whim of the terrorist South, which led to their disenfranchisement, the establishment of Jim Crow apartheid, and terror and violence against them.

Interestingly, in the tug-of-war between the parties, African Americans are the benefactors of some of the social programs that are designed to help lower-income Americans, and sometimes they are not. For example, when the programs under Franklin D. Roosevelt's administration that were designed to pull America out of the Great Depression were created (e.g., the Social Security Act, which includes old age and unemployment insurance), Black people left the Republican Party in droves. Unfortunately, many of the New Deal programs did not support many Blacks during that time because many were agricultural workers and domestic servants. Consequently, under the Social Security Act (or rather, under this "new deal"), the majority of employed African Americans were left with no protection for unemployment or old age.

Knowing this history, I had no trust in American politics but felt compelled to vote because of the numerous African Americans who lost their lives so that we could exercise this right. Black people would be outright murdered during elections, and in one election, as many as fifty people lost their lives. Although I vote, I see it as the lesser of the two evils, and still could not see the United States, the so-called free world as nothing more than a country ruled primarily by elite white men. I felt that although the political machine is designed to be fair, it is not. Those who run for national office and win are typically white, wealthy, and powerful. This gives them unequal access to resources and people with affluence, and that does not look fair to me at all. So, when someone from the other side—who is non-white, not-rich, and not powerful—wins, it almost looks like the political machine works.

Although the debate with Hilary and Obama sounded like the same old story, I needed to hear the brother. "What was he really saying? Was he really a voice of change?" I asked myself, and I began to tune in a little. But, because I was so involved in my own life, and still was not convinced that American politics is fair, I did not pay much attention to Obama until I saw Michelle doing a speech during the Christmas holidays, the year before he won.

I think it was her passion and how hard she was working for her husband that really got my attention. I was drawn in by how genuine, articulate, serious, and intelligent she seemed, and I connected with her. This is not to mention that she was dark-skinned with "kinky," permed hair; she did not look like a trophy wife, which for some Black people means "light, bright, and damned near white."

Intraracial conflict around color and class put a divide between Black people that has been going on since slavery. Lighter-skinned Blacks and house servants were closer to the slaveholders, which means they had more access to their language and other privileges simply because some of them were their descendants. Had Michelle had lighter skin, Obama may have not been taken as seriously by some Black people, especially because many may have seen them as privileged light-skinned Black folk; although, they may have voted for them anyway, not just because they were Black because they were articulate and highly intelligent, and exemplified integrity, high moral character, and grace, among other attributes. I also wondered had Michelle worn her hair natural, whether Obama would have won the bid for the presidency. Because there is just as much politics around hair texture as there is around skin color for both Blacks and Whites.

When some whites suggested that Blacks voted for Obama because he was Black, my answer was "You damn right." But not only was he Black, but he was also the most intelligent and articulate candidate of them all; he had the gift of gab—that brother could talk, something that

Black people respect. It may be a retention from Africa. Being able to talk well was considered a gift, which is why our greatest political and spiritual leaders usually have great oratorical skills. As it got closer to election day, I, as I am sure others, began to think that he might just win.

After Obama won the election, it made you rethink American politics, or at least, I did. "Maybe the political system is fair; maybe it really does work. I mean, a Black man won the bid for the president of the United States." It made you think maybe we are living in a post-racial society, as some naive people have suggested.

It also made you think about your own choices. I asked myself, "Had I put myself in a race box?" I had grown extremely frustrated with living in the Black community for numerous reasons: the dull, dirty, downtrodden, uncared-for look in surrounding commercial areas, the low-quality amenities (particularly restaurants), and not to mention the high levels of crime. As I was walking down the street one day to Family Dollar, I asked myself, "How in the hell did I end up in Decatur, Georgia?"

One day while giving a lecture on race, ethnicity, and culture in my African American Family course, I was surprised to find that although I was teaching an African American Studies course, and many of the students looked African American (and I assumed they were), many did not identify as African American; some identified as Puerto Rican, Caribbean, African, etc. It was absolutely eye-opening. I was also shocked to recently meet a biracial family member that had I not known she was a relative, I would have thought she was Latino (my biological uncle is her father). When I went to her Facebook page, I would discover a multiracial group of friends, some of whom one could not tell their race, ethnicity, or culture; I wanted to say "Hallelujah!" Maybe this messy, awful race thing that is only a few hundred years old might one day just go away.

Being in African American Studies, I had already begun to wonder about its relevance as the world continues toward globalization. Is African American Studies dated? Are we living in a post-racial society? But the events that led to the Black Lives Matters movement (i.e., the outright murder of Black people, that has been going on since slavery, but is just coming to light because of cell phones and social media) and knowing about the disparities between Blacks and Whites in all areas of life—housing, education, employment, income, health, mortality rates, incarceration rates, etc.—it's clear that a post-racial society is still far off.

When Obama came out on the stage the night he won the election to make his victory speech, I sensed how uncomfortable it was for him and Michelle to have their children with them. I also noticed how quickly they were whisked off the stage. Although I (as many Black Americans) also worried that Obama might be assassinated as he and Michelle strolled down Pennsylvania Avenue on the day of his inauguration, I don't think we ever felt so proud. I picked up a copy of *Time* magazine and gazed down at the picture of him and began to reflect on what life might be like to have the kind of access they would have, not only to power and affluence in the United States but to the world. Their children would be able to go to the best schools and Michelle (unlike many Black mothers) never has to worry about whether her children will get the best—they will.

Before he won the election, I listened to Obama's autobiography, *Dreams from My Father,* and thought of how he was not even above average in high school and how his mother stayed on him to get motivated. I imagine that with his cool, Type B personality, she may have been flipping out the way I do when I encounter Black youth with this personality type. I fear that they will miss out on opportunities because they are too laid back. After winning the election, when we would see Obama strut, almost bopping, in the Black man's cool style of walking, with dapper and swagger, Tim and I would say, "Damn, he's cool." Over and over, we would say, "He's so cool. We got a cool president. He must be the coolest president we have ever had."

I gathered from Obama's autobiography, that his father was pained by knowing that he, himself was born for greatness. For many like him who are not able to bring their greatness to fruition, it burdens them, causing them to resort to alcoholism or other kinds of unhealthy behaviors to quell the fire burning in them. But what some may not know is that their greatness is in their loins, (something I learned from African spirituality) and it may come to fruition through their descendants.

During a Martin Luther King, Jr. celebration at GSU, Dick Gregory was a speaker. When he said, "They treat Obama like a mangy dog." he bought to light the utter lack of respect that Obama got from other politicians. Regardless of how they wanted to make it appear, we know that some of it was because he was Black, and they were just jealous, plain jealous. Anybody with any understanding of power knows that "real" power comes from within. And that is what his white peers were jealous of. They wished they could exude his intelligence and his cool. The way Obama handled it, however, with his calm and cool demeanor and sheer grace, when they treated him badly only made us prouder of him.

I am sure many whites were as shocked as Blacks were, that Obama won the bid for president. But as some whites slept, many of their sons and daughters woke up. It was young whites who went to school with Blacks and were ultimately able to see past the racist lens of their parents that helped to vote Obama into office; although, many young whites de-racialize Blacks they accept, something I learned from students in my courses. Some of the white students said they did not see Obama as Black; they said they did not see race. They also saw Obama as "their" president, not "our" Black people's president.

In African spirituality, words have power. A person's name takes on special significance because it can determine their destiny. When one's name is called, it reminds them of their purpose. With this understanding, I looked up the meaning of Barack Hussein Obama. Barack has Hebrew origins, which means "lightning" and "to shine." Its Arabic meaning is "blessing," or "blessed." Hussein is an Arabic name that means "good," "handsome," or "beautiful." Obama is a surname derived from the Luo people of ancient Kenya and means "to lean or bend." Barack Obama's ancestors, from the Nyanza area in Kenya, had a specific walk where they were "bent over" or "limping," earning them this name. Interestingly, Obama's cool stride, may not be indicative of his name. However, Barack Hussein Obama—this shining, blessed, handsome one—seemed to have an uncanny ability to graciously lean away from and bend a lot of the negativity that was hurled his way.

One day, after Obama won the bid for the presidency, I went into a federal building and saw pictures of him and the attorney general Eric Holder on the wall, and I thought to myself, "How amazing is this? Two Black men—the faces of the most powerful country in the world. Did this really happen in my lifetime?"

When I saw Antionette, my friend I met in graduate school at Howard, we jumped as we slapped hands, almost in the way men do when they jump chest-to-chest, and said, "Did you see the pictures of those two brothers on the wall? You see that! You see that!" "Yeah! Yeah!"

PART II
SPIRITUAL AWAKENING

15
THE AWAKENING

It is interesting how people come into your life to help you with your destiny and they don't even know it.

Dr. Marimba Ani was my first link to African spirituality when I read her chapter, "African Spirituality" in *The Cultural Unity of Africa* by Molefi Asante and Kariamu Welsh Asante. The first time I met Dr. Ani was at a job interview at Hunter College in New York City. I went on the interview, knowing full well that with the competition in New York, getting the assistant professor job right out of college was slim to none. I felt that Hunter already knew who they wanted for the position; they were just following university protocol. In addition, I was not sure I wanted to live in New York City; I had already been down that road. I went on the job interview because I wanted to meet the woman whose work had changed my life, spiritually.

Years later, Dr. Ani came to visit the African American Studies Department at GSU. I told her that I was teaching a course on African American relationships. She introduced me to Sonbonfu Somé's critical works, *Spirit of Intimacy*, and *Welcoming Spirit Home*, which I incorporated into my relationships and family courses. Both readings deepened my understanding of African spirituality, specifically, spirituality among the Dagara people of West Africa.

Since I used Somé's work, when I found out that she would be presenting a workshop at GSU, there was no way I could not attend it. During the break, I went to her and said, "I need a spiritual teacher." I am not sure whether I was asking her to be that person or asking her to refer me to someone, but she said, in so many words, that she would be returning to Africa, and directed me to a couple of women in the room.

The women were associated with Spelman and the Interdenominational Theological Center (ITC) in the Black university area in Atlanta. I had considered enrolling in ITC myself but realized that it would be focused on Christianity. I spoke with them briefly and they gave me a phone number to contact them later.

When the workshop resumed, I asked, "What does one do when they have knowledge about different religions, but don't practice any?" I do not recall her answer, but after the workshop, a young man came to me and said, "I understand what you are going through." He talked briefly about some associations that he could refer me to and gave me his phone number.

About six months after the workshop, I was feeling so spiritually low, I was starting to feel sick. I knew religion in theory but did not know it in practice. I prayed and I had private conversation with God. I occasionally went to church when I got spiritually low or needed an answer to something. However, I still found it difficult to completely embrace Christianity because of how it has been used to hurt people. I also found medieval European and Roman cultural symbols in the church challenging and weeding out the truth in the theology was too difficult at times. So, although attending church helped me from time to time (and still does), I would go until I was no longer getting anything out of it, then I would stop going.

I went through my book, seeking the phone number the woman gave me, but could not find it. I kept seeing an unfamiliar name, Cazembé, with a phone number. I thought it might be the phone number of one of the women because I did not remember meeting him or taking his.

I called the number. He reminded me of who he was. "Oh, well, I'm looking for a spiritual teacher. Can you refer me to someone?"

He first referred me to Dr. Daniel Black, who he said does initiations. I knew Danny from Temple, and at the time, I was thinking he was talking about rites of passage.

"No, that's not what I am looking for," I said. "I am looking for someone like Kung Fu."

I was referring to the early-seventies television series in which the main character, Kwai Chang Caine had fled China to the United States after killing someone in retaliation for his spiritual teacher being killed. When he was faced with an obstacle, he would have flashbacks and reflect on the teachings from his spiritual teacher, Master Po, who called him "Grasshopper." I liked the show as a child. There was something about having a spiritual teacher that I found intriguing.

"Okay, I think you would like Kaia. He has healing sessions on Fridays, around 5–7 p.m., so maybe you can go to a healing tonight." He gave me the address. I got myself together and rushed out of the house.

~~~~~~~~~~

"Is this the house? It looks kind of dreary. Should I drive up in there?"

I had driven up to a house that was sitting way back off the road, and I was feeling somewhat intimidated about going to the house. As I was driving up the long driveway to the house, it appeared more and more like I was going into another time, a place where time stood still. It was like a country back-road in Lithonia, Georgia, a reminder that I was actually living in the South.

As I got out of my car and approached the house, I noticed how old the house was. On the far corners on each side of the porch of the house sat two statutes of heads. Seeing the two heads just sitting there by themselves, "Interesting," I thought, "but spooky." There is something about heads just sitting alone; they can either bring up images of something deeply spiritual or the opposite—something deeply dark.

I was greeted by a Chinese-looking Black man dressed in white clothing. I stepped off the porch into the house. He directed me into a room off to the side.

"Have a seat."

I looked down and sat on a little white table-stool in front of him as he sat in a chair facing it.

"What's your name?" he asked softly.

"Pat," I answered.

"How can I help you?"

"I am here for healing, and I need to get on my spiritual path," I responded.

"What does that mean to you?"

"Well African spirituality is what I need," I responded.

"Why African spirituality?" he asked?

"Well, it's the only spirituality that makes sense to me," I said.

"Well, the only thing I want to do is move energy," he responded. "Pat, ask for what you want."

I do not remember what I asked for. I have always been very shy about expressing myself before God in front of people. It has always been a private affair for me. He took my hands, turned them up, and laid them on my lap. "Close your eyes," he said. I then felt him moving around me, saying what I suspected to be prayers.

As he was doing this, I began to realize that I was sitting in a strange man's house, and he was doing God knows what around me. I then realized that I had rushed out of the house to see him without telling Tim. He had no idea where I was. Nor did my sister know. I was so desperate that I did not even think to tell anybody. "What if he is a murderer? What if he kills me? You dummy!" I thought to myself again. "Here you are, sitting in a strange man's house. Nobody knows you are here, and you have no idea what he is doing." As he continued to work around me, I began to relax a little and decided to let go of such notions and go with it.

About twenty minutes later, he said "Pat, you can open your eyes now." I opened my eyes and looked at him. "Did you feel anything?" he asked.

"Yeah, I felt a surge of energy."

"Okay," he said softly. I put a donation in a jar and then he escorted me out of the house.

I left his house and went to visit my sister Gina, who lives not far from where I had just visited. As I was driving, I began to feel good. By the time I got to her house, a feeling of euphoria had come over me. "I can't believe what I am feeling," I said to her. "I have never felt this good." I went on to explain to her what I had just done. Although I had lived over two-thirds of my life (if I live until the age of life expectancy for Black women, which is about seventy-eight), this would begin the journey of what I have searching for my entire life.

~~~~~~~~~~

Having taught Black religion while at U-Mass Boston I recognized that all peoples all over the world practiced some form of religion or spirituality. Although I knew about different religions or spiritual practices and knew there was truth in all of them, I could not embrace nor practice any of them completely. Hebraism, Christianity, and Islam felt too limiting, and although African spirituality felt more natural, I was still not clear, because I did not understand the science of it.

I had been introduced to Yoruba while at Temple. A couple of Temple students were Yoruba Priests, a colleague did a paper on Yoruba, which I read, and I bought a couple of books on it. I also went to a ritual, that my colleague invited me to. While I was there a woman who was a medium got possessed by one of the orishas. She walked up to me, looked at me, and then licked my hand. I think this left a lasting, but conflicted impression on me.

After being at GSU for a few years, I thought I might pursue the Yoruba priesthood, and I think because it was the only African spiritual practice that seemed accessible at the time. I bought some cowrie shells (and a book to learn how to divine using them), the *Odu Ifá*, by Maulana Karenga, and went to get a reading from a Yoruba priest. The Babaláwo (also Baba, which means "priest of the Ifá oracle") gave me a task to fulfill to begin priesthood training. However, what he asked me to do was overwhelming for me at the time, so I decided it must not be the right time for me. When I was ready to try it again, I inquired about him and found out that he was sick. The colleague who referred me to him referred me to his son, saying that although he was young, he was good and that he was doing readings. I went to get a reading from the Baba's son, taking Tim with me.

"I'm lost," I said. "It's like I knew my way. But now, it is like I'm in the woods and I've lost my way, and I need to find my way back."

His son said I was a descendant of the Akan people of Ghana and that I needed to start with a shrine. He told me how to create one. "Let the ancestors help you find your way back," he instructed.

What was particularly interesting was how he responded to Tim. He said, in so many words, that Tim was at the top of the spiritual hierarchy, and that he ought to build a shrine for the ancestors and do daily practice; I needed to do it only once a week.

When I first met Tim, I felt that I had met a rare find. He had spent most of his adult life as a husband (he was divorced) and was an outstanding father, son, and brother. I found him to possess a lot of attributes that were important to me at that point in my life. He was kind, compassionate, and he cared about people, among numerous other attributes. But there was something else special about him, and when people would ask about him, I would describe him as a giant. Although I knew it had something to do with spirituality, I was not clear what I really meant.

Tim would say things and then say, "You don't understand," or "Nobody understands what I see."

"But I do," I would respond. "It's just African spirituality; it's not strange to me."

Tim took the instruction seriously and built an ancestor shrine, which he said he turns to every day. I, on the other hand, could not get it together because I could not figure out where to put it in the house. I moved it all over the place. A year later, when I reached out to the Yoruba priest again to inquire about learning under him, I discovered that he had moved out of the Atlanta area.

~~~~~~~~~~

Right after the healing session with Kaia, I had a dream that Kaia was in and Tim was standing by, looking at him. He eventually approached Kaia and told him to leave. I did not tell Tim about the dream until later. He told me he knew and confirmed everything that happened in my dream. I asked him to go to a healing session, so he and I went the next week.

Kaia took him into the room, just as he had done with me. I was concerned about whether Tim would feel the energy because I believed that would be what he needed to get him interested in taking classes with me. When he came out of the room, I felt he had felt the energy, based on how he looked. He looked around the room and said to Kaia, "Interesting." We left.

After that, I began taking a class with Kaia. At first, Tim did not take the class with me. However, after a few weeks of me coming home looking discombobulated (which I thought was from the driving because I do not see well at night), he said it was from what was going on in the class. He was concerned, and he started taking the class with me. This would begin our true spiritual journey together.

In the first class, Kaia gave me some literature about Reiki. Because I was so moved by the experiences I was having in class (and I needed to know what I was involving myself in), I began to explore Reiki on the Internet.

What I would find is that Reiki is Japanese for "universal life force." It is the energy that surrounds everything in the universe and because of this has been around since the beginning. However, as a healing modality, Reiki energy was first channeled by a Japanese teacher, Mikao Usui, in 1922 (although I am sure it was channeled thousands of years before that, it is just how we understand it in the West). To explore how other great healers used healing energy, according to legend, Usui went to Mount Kurama-Yama in Japan to fast, pray, and meditate. After about twenty-one days, he channeled the Reiki energy. The practice was bought to the West from Japan by Hawayo Takata, who had been healed by a life-threatening disease herself. She became the first Reiki Master in the United States in 1938, and in 1976 began training practitioners. To become a Reiki healer, one is typically attuned to the energy and/or trained by a Reiki Master on how to use it as a healing modality on others.

I was amazed by how I could walk into the house and feel the energy in the room that Kaia had literally put there. "What is this? How can somebody just put energy in me or a room?" I kept asking myself. I wanted to know what kind of energy he had given me in the first energy session because whatever it was, I needed to keep that going.

I found that it was Sekhem and began to dig on the Internet to find out what that was as well. It took me to Egypt. Although it has many different spellings—Seichim/Seichem/Sekhem/Skhm—it is considered a form of Reiki and is referred to as living, light, and love energies and essentially means "spiritual power." I would later find that the term was used extensively in some of the translations of *The Pyramid Texts* by Samuel A. Mercer and E.A. Wallis Budge, which are texts inscribed on the walls of the pyramids of Egyptian kings of the fifth and sixth dynasties between 2350-2170 BC (believed to go back as far a 3000 BC) found in the ancient necropolis of Memphis.

At the beginning of taking the energy healing course with Kaia, I would only feel the energy when he would pass it to me. But when I would try it, I could not make it happen on my own. After about a month or two, I was sitting at my computer, and I called an energy I had been attuned to. I felt it move through me. "I did it, I did it!" I said with excitement to myself and emailed Kaia, "Wow! Wow! I did it." From that point, I was able to move the energy myself.

Early in the classes, I was focused on getting the good feeling I would get from the energy. It was like getting high—but clean and healthy, and you felt better after, unlike when using alcohol or drugs. Kaia, however, would caution us over and over, "This is nothing to play with!" and "This can only be used for good." "Be careful," he would warn, especially when he attuned us to Kundalini Reiki. "This is not Kundalini" (referring to the energy that sits at the bottom of the spine, near the root chakra). "This is Kundalini Reiki—there's a difference." He explained the effect that opening Kundalini had on him, taking him about a year to recover. "If it's not opened correctly, you can really mess yourself up."

When I became attuned to Kundalini Reiki is when I began to become more cautious about the energy. After receiving the first level of it, I could not function, and I was glad Tim had started coming to class, so he could drive us home. Although he was also affected by the energy, he was still able to function and drive. "Oh my God! I have to teach. I have got to ground. I can't teach like this," I kept saying. By the next morning, I had grounded.

I had taken a course with Ausar Auset Society on reading the oracles a few years back when I did my work on polygyny, so Tim and I began taking classes with the Ausar Auset community in Atlanta as well. Not long after attuning to Kundalini Reiki, we went to their winter solstice meditation. Before going to the meditation, I used some of the energies to clean myself of negative energy, and it felt like I had a big hole in the top of my head. It felt completely exposed. I said to Tim, as I covered my head with a scarf I was wearing, "This is why in some religions people cover their heads. Particularly those in the priesthood—they're protecting their crowns."

When we left the meditation, the hole felt even larger. I looked up at the trees and skies, and although it was December, I saw a virtual paradise. When we got home, I rushed to the back door to go outside to my backyard. I stood there in the cold winter air and stared up at the trees that encircled the sky for as long as I could.

"This must be what they mean by nirvana," I thought.

Close to thirty years after reading a book I encountered while at Howard about nirvana, I believe I achieved a few minutes of what the author of the book was referring to.

"It must be when one can maintain this state, that they have actually reached nirvana," I concluded.

~~~~~~~~~~

Throughout taking classes we learned a lot about energy work and heal-ing modalities. We learned how to sweep people of negative energy and how to balance their chakras, energy centers through which life force is channeled through the body, to help maximize their own healing energy. We were introduced to and took an interest in crystal healing. "Are you telling me that my love for the earth, which took me down the road to major in geology, was really the road to energy healing?" I asked myself.

I stumbled into something on the Internet about how the Egyptians put the carnelian stone on the heart of the deceased—I had to have one. Tim got a big one. When Kaia asked us to bring a crystal to class so that he could program them for the Kundalini energy, we purchased a Shiva stone, a stone found in one of the holy cities in India that is supposed to increase vitality and enlightenment. I also recalled from African spiritu-ality that stones have memory. I purchased *The Book of Stones* by Robert Simmons and Naisha Ahsian (and later took a course from Kaia on crys-tal healing) and discovered not only the healing and enlightening prop-erties of stones, gems, and crystals, but also that they help facilitate our connection to the ancestors, spirit guides, and guardians.

When Kaia told us that we could also program water, it was right around the time that I discovered Masaru Emoto's *The Hidden Messages in Water*. In this work, Emoto showed pictorially that when water was exposed to words like "love," "thank you," "you're beautiful," and clas-sical music and jazz, beautiful crystals were formed. When it was exposed to words like "you fool," a television, a computer, or a cell phone, or loud music with angry and vulgar lyrics, the crystals were deformed.

Later, we received the axiatonal realignment attunement, which re-connects or realigns us with the planetary and universal grid system through lines along the acupuncture meridians. Axiatonal realignment revitalizes us down to the cellular level not only for optimum physical health but also to be in alignment so that pure intelligence can reveal itself to us. We spent about two to three months attuning to and learning how to attune others to it. We were attuned to this energy before the Christmas holidays.

Because we were also learning about the winter solstice in Ausar Auset Society, particularly the goal of meditation, it became apparent to us how capitalism uses Christianity and the so-called birthday of Jesus to capitalize on the energy around the planet during that time. The winter solstice is the shortest day of the year in the Northern Hemisphere and is the time of the year that people should do inner work such as fasting, meditating, praying, and so forth for preparation for the New Year. It is the beginning of days getting longer or the rebirth of the sun. However, because of consumer capitalism, most people are typically out shopping and preparing for the holidays. And because the majority of us are so out of touch with nature, we do not understand the cycles nor the work that should be done during the specific times of the year, particularly around the winter solstice; this is why most people have such a difficult time following through on their New Year's resolutions.

I decided to do as much as I could before December 21 so that I could spend as much time in meditation as I could until the 25th. For about three days, I washed up, ate, meditated, and slept. When I came out of it, and after the axiatonal reconnection, I felt like the images I see of astronauts when they are floating in outer space. For about a year after that, whenever I would walk, it felt like I was walking on cushions. I still feel like this sometimes when I focus on energy work.

~~~~~~~~~~~

Although we all have psychic abilities, those who are either especially gifted with it at birth or who develop them might become psychics.

In one of Kaia's classes, we spent some time developing our psychic abilities. I was surprised by how on point I was on my first attempt. I encountered a grandmother who tried to use my eyes to see her grandson, one of my classmates I was doing the psychic reading on. "That was scary," I thought before discussing it in class, and even more so after I told him what she looked like and he showed me a picture of her.

I did a second psychic reading on one of my classmates. I started crying as I discussed what I felt with my classmates.

"What happened?" asked Kaia.

"I felt deep sadness," I responded.

The young woman I had done the reading on eyes widened, indicating to me that I had read her correctly. Now I understood why she seemed so strange at times

"Move out of her space," Kaia instructed. He reminded me that we need to cut the strings immediately after doing a reading or healing with someone. "Be careful. You don't want someone's energy to attach to you." Another time he explained, "I see psychics with contorted faces," suggesting that this stemmed from the kinds of energies psychics encounter in their readings.

One of the most significant things that Kaia emphasized was the importance of connecting with one's spirit guide and "light" energies/beings and putting protective energy around ourselves. I think I must have already known this because for as long as I can remember, I have felt a strong presence around me. When I was a teenager, I heard a voice call me out of my sleep one night. When I was a young adult in DC, while I laid in the dark one evening, the presence was so strong, I thought it might show itself to me. "Go away," I told it, "because I am not ready for you." My thinking was "I don't know who you are." Somehow, I knew that there are realms and that if you do not know what you are doing, you could get yourself in a lot of trouble. It went away.

I did not encounter the presence again until I lived in Boston, which was a peak spiritual time in my life, I believe, because I lived near the water (water symbolizes purification, but inspires me and gives me clarity). One night, I went to sleep, and I traveled down a tunnel so fast; faster than anything I know in my conscious mind. When I came out on the other side, there was a very tall dark-skinned man with a white robe and a turban, standing at an elevator. "Go back," he said. "You are not ready."

In one of the first classes with Kaia, he gave us exercises to help us connect with our spirit guide. In my meditation, I saw a man with clothes that looked very similar to the one in the dream, standing at the elevator, but he was faceless. When I came out of meditation, Kaia asked us their names. I started to say "Ausar," but my lips said "Osei." Interestingly, more than a year after that, I found the notes with the information on how to build a shrine I got from the Yoruba priest and it had Osei as my ancestor spirit guide. I did not even remember him telling me that I had an ancestor spirit guide, let alone giving me the name of one. When I searched for the name, Osei Kofi Tutu was the first name that came up. Although my ancestor could be someone else, as there may have been many with that name, a further search on Osei Kofi Tutu indicated that he was crowned the Asantehene, king of the Ashanti Empire in 1701, a position he held until 1717. In light of this, I guess it was not happenstance that my first visit to West Africa would be to Ghana.

~~~~~~~~~~~

Throughout learning under Kaia, we continued to get attuned to different types of energies. It seemed like he was just a reservoir of information—we never stopped learning. Tim and I would leave the class and discuss our experiences and always affirm, "Kaia is baaddd!" That brother is baaddd!" "That's a baaddd man."

As I continued to seek out information on energy healing, I stumbled onto information about ascension. Interestingly, when Kaia started facilitating ascension meditations, I was already ahead. For the very first one he called an initiation meditation, he called the name Isis. Immediately, I connected. It topped even what I had already experienced; I was in a state of bliss for three days. When he said, "You can make the ascension in this lifetime," I was determined that I could do it.

I would later learn that the ultimate goal in various religions is to reach nirvana (the God-realized self, bliss, or heavenly state of consciousness) and to make the ascension (return to God) while in the physical body. According to some ancient teachings, your state of consciousness when you leave the physical body will be the state of your soul at death. Is this why when Jesus appeared to Mary of Magdalene, he said, "Touch me not; for I am not yet ascended to my Father: but go to my brothers, and say to them, I ascend to my Father, and your Father; and to my God, and your God" (John 20:17)? Is it that if she had transferred her energy onto him, it may have prevented him from making the ascension?

I continued to do meditations, particularly after receiving the axiatonal reconnection. I would play Reiki music and meditation tapes produced by Ra Un Nefer Amen of Ausar Auset Society, and I would travel transcendentally. When I would seek my father, he appeared not as the man I remembered, who had grown old and tattered. No, the spirit of the man was young. Other times, I would see what seemed like fairy-looking beings flying over my yard. One of the most extraordinary experiences I had was while meditating one day and asking what I needed to do psychic work, an energy came over me, showering me in blue. Whatever the energy was, it seemed to indicate that I needed to set up a shrine that focused on blue so that I could commune with it.

Before and after taking the energy classes, Tim would talk about things he sees and can do. He says (all the time) that he can communicate with animals and that they can see him and listen to him. He says that he can see his kids no matter where they are, always knows when they are in trouble, and that he travels and catches them on time. He says that he can see entities that most people cannot see. And that it is probably good that they cannot because they do not look like what we would expect them to look like. Some are grotesque-looking, while others are very tall and huge and would scare most people. He talks about being able to travel to other dimensions. He tells me things and either I will have read it already or find it later in the literature.

I had explored shamanism while at Temple but only understood it academically. While we were still doing the energy work, a shaman came to Atlanta to conduct a ceremony. A young woman who enrolled in my relationship course because she read my polygyny book introduced me to the shaman. At that time, I was considering doing a documentary on Black Shamans and Healers and I asked if I could interview him for it, which I did. Soon after that, Tim and I were engaging in one of our conversations and suddenly it occurred to me, "Are you telling me that I have been living with a shaman all these years and didn't know it?"

16
THE ACADEMIC FACTORY

The spiritual awakening dramatically shifted how I would see the world. If I thought I was on the outside looking in; if I was, in fact, in a state of *soul consciousness*, it increased tenfold.

Being a professor, I had fulfilled not only what I thought was my life's purpose, but also a life dream. I, however, struggled with academe throughout my career at GSU. Long before I came to GSU, I was familiar with the "publish or perish" mantra from my experience at Berkeley. I had also heard through the grapevine, "Stay away from a service. You have to publish to survive academe." When I first got to GSU I wanted to publish books. But I was advised by the chair not to do so ("Books take too long") and that I needed to publish articles in peer-reviewed journals so that I would be ready for tenure. I did that and made tenure. After that, I began to pursue writing books, which can take years to complete and publish.

My first book, *We Want for Our Sisters What We Want for Ourselves*, on polygyny, I published under my own company before it was published by Black Classic Press. I also co-authored and self-published *TLC, Talking and Listening with Care* with Khalil. Since my primary concern with the latter work was to help couples communicate, I was not concerned about getting academic credit for it.

After that, I began working on *African American Relationships, Marriages, and Families: An Introduction*. No one had written a book on African American relationships that was comprehensive enough to be used in a course, and I had to pull materials from everywhere, making it challenging. The book took about four summers to complete. I did not know how to make the book appealing to publishers, and when I asked the chair about it, he said to make it a book that can be used in Black family courses. The approach worked.

I mailed a letter and a few chapters to about fifty presses. Someone from Routledge contacted me, indicating that they were interested in the work. Routledge wanted to publish it in an 8½ in. by 11 in. format, which made it more like a textbook. I wanted a smaller book so that it would also have appeal to popular audiences; Routledge decided on the former. As time went on, I realized that although I was fortunate to have the book published by Routledge and get academic credit, I did not have a book for laypeople—it looked too textbook-like, and it was too expensive.

When I came up for my five-year post-tenure review, I proudly came to the dean's office because I had published two books: one by a reputable press, Routledge, and the other by Black Classic Press. When I arrived, I was told that I would get credit for teaching—not research—for the relationships book. Since I had always received excellence in teaching, it was not where I needed the credit. I needed it for research, as I had not published any articles because all my time was spent on books. *African American Relationships, Marriages, and Families* was my second-best work. It was a blow that I never fully recovered from.

Another thing I struggled with was my salary: I recognized early that I was not earning enough to prepare me to retire comfortably and as I was getting older, I started worrying more about it. I was asked by the new chair to head the committee for a new hire. When I first saw that new hire would be coming in at my salary level, I told myself "Just ignore it." But I had been in the department for close to twenty years, was one of its first hires, had published more books than anyone (except for I think one other faculty member), but was earning less income than the other associate professors. "Find another way to make money," I kept telling myself. However, the problem with that is being a professor is a full-time job; trying to do anything else is a drain on your life force. And as you get older, it is much more difficult. Unfortunately, I had already tried that, and it did not pan out.

We had opened a mortgage company. However, because of all the time and energy that went into keeping employees compliant with state and federal regulations and trying to make them understand why we were not doing some of the loans that "big" lenders were allowing them to do, owning and operating a mortgage company was life-draining, to say the least.

Also, being in the mortgage business during the 2007–2009 subprime mortgage crisis was eye-opening. As the mortgage crisis approached, we watched daily as over three hundred lenders (some of the nation's largest ones, many of whom we had been brokering our loans through) go under. This, however, was not surprising considering some of the "exotic" subprime loan programs that they were promoting. For some lending programs, homebuyers needed only to state their income and not show verification of it. The type of loan programs that some of the largest lenders were allowing was unbelievable. Anybody could get a home loan, whether they could pay it back or not.

Since we were brokering mortgages before the crisis, I thought home-buying education might be beneficial and called Ray Carlisle, the president of NAREB's Investment Division (NID). NID was one of the intermediaries who received large grants from HUD (and was probably the only Black one to receive millions of dollars) to provide housing education and counseling. NID trained us and awarded NAARI a grant. Although we started with home-buying classes, our office started filling up with more people facing foreclosure (which was an indication of the coming mortgage crisis). It was shocking to witness the redistribution of wealth as Black people were losing their homes, and investors were buying them up for pennies on the dollar.

While being in both for-profit and non-profit businesses, I would also discover that what I was teaching in my courses about African American marginalization in U.S. society, particularly in the labor force, was real. This became even more evident during the 2007–2009 recession. Black people were showing up at our office in droves, looking for jobs, most of them middle-aged, too old to train for work in the growing global digital economy, and too young to draw social security.

Ironically, although we started the mortgage company to prepare for retirement, I did not pay myself (and Tim paid himself, minimally). I could not take money, while people who were working for us were not earning enough to live. So, working in both GRMI and NAARI, ended up being community work for me.

Despite the challenges we faced in both companies, we helped thousands of people of all races (but mostly African Americans and Latinos) prevent losing their homes to foreclosure. Eventually, for various reasons (including the toll it was taking on us), we had to close the doors to both companies. With regard to our real estate investments, the value of houses that we had purchased for an average of $126,000 dropped to an average of $25,000. Seeing the bottom drop out of the housing market, was the beginning of my awakening from the illusion of it all.

Another factor contributing to my growing disillusionment with academe is how I had begun to see the university. After being introduced to Marxism and at times feeling exploited, I began to see the university as sort of like an "academic factory" and professors as cogs in the wheels of the machine, producing the information that it manufactures to help fuel the capitalistic economy. I also began to see professors as "gatekeepers," determining who we will let through to get the credentials they need to earn a living so that they can support their families to a standard that affords them human dignity.

In addition, I was struggling with the whole scientific enterprise. What we are calling science, ancient peoples had already discovered thousands of years ago; the only difference is that they saw all of existence as the divine in a myriad of manifestations, including the material. Once you have been awakened to this, you begin to see beyond the deception of the veil of materialism gripping Western science, and how it is used to control the world, so that it can be exploited in the name of progress and technological advancement.

As to publishing, ironically, advances in technology are removing the chokehold that big presses had on who gets published and who does not. Notwithstanding that peer-reviewed work ensures that it meets scientific standards, which is necessary, your work is more accepted and given more prestige if it is published by a university press. The question for me was: Why would it not be? Scholars work for the university, and it is the university's agenda they are promoting. And while they do the work, the presses make the money. Your work may also be highly regarded if it is published by a so-called "reputable" press (whatever that means). The question for me was, "What determines a press to be reputable? That it has been around for a long time and may even have a monopoly because it owns the channels of distribution?"

Amazon did for authors what the printing press did for the Bible. The printing press put the Bible in the hands of the people, giving them the power over their salvation (although it imprisoned them in other ways). Amazon gave people the power to publish and sell their work, which means they no longer have to wait for a big publishing company to tell them their work is worthy of publishing, putting their destiny in their own hands (although Amazon is exploitive in other ways). Once you understand how it all works, that you can publish your work, it becomes a matter of who will own and control your intellectual property and your destiny.

Thank God for Black presses like Third World Press and Black Classic Press. Had it not been for Black Classic Press, *We Want for Our Sisters What We Want for Ourselves*, probably my greatest life work, may have never received academic credit because, at first, I published it myself. It was a struggle for the chair to get the university administrators to accept Black Classic Press as an acceptable press. If I were to convince a university or other "reputable" press to publish my work on polygyny, the reality was I would have been asking a "traditional" white press to publish a book that tells Black people to consider a practice that white males had determined to be "barbaric" and something that "savage" (code for "people of color") people did. Also, since many polygynous families have lots of children (which in the United States is associated with poverty and welfare), it would be like giving Black people permission to have a lot of children. The only press that I can think of that may have taken an interest in the work is Brigham Young University because it is a Mormon university and some Mormons still practice polygyny. However, they may not have necessarily been interested in promoting that Black people practice it, nor may they have liked what I had to say about their practice of polygyny.

Near the end of my journey with GSU, evaluators came to evaluate our department, which departments are required to do periodically to assess whether they are carrying out their goals and the strategic goals of the university. When one of the evaluators asked their first question, I had a hard time responding, because I was trying to hold back the tears. I had just had a meeting with the chair, and he indicated that my course load was going to be increased (which he said he had no control over) because I had not published.

I had published *African Male-Female Relationships: A Reader* and published an article in it, but it had also been classified under teaching and I did not get academic credit. Most of the works in the reader were scholarly articles, some of which I edited to make them more current. I was also working on a book of creative essays that mixed social and cultural critique and commentary with academic research (which I was considering publishing myself). To get academic credit, I decided to do something Jeff suggested we do early in our careers: write the chapters, get them published as peer-reviewed articles, and then compile them into a book.

However, because the papers were written in a creative style, they were not getting accepted for publication. A paper based on primary research I had written was also not accepted for publication, probably because my heart was not in it while writing it. At this point in my life, I was not interested in writing papers that almost nobody reads (or understands) other than academics, and it may have reflected in the work. So here I was, straddling the fence, trying to publish peer-reviewed research papers to satisfy the university and trying to publish books that were fulfilling what I thought was my life's purpose—and getting nowhere.

One of the evaluators came over to me to try to comfort me and I told her I was stepping out of the office for a moment so that I could regain my composure. When I came back in, they wanted to know what was going on, assuring me that what I shared with them would be held in confidence. "It's me," I responded. But they insisted that I talk to them.

I told them that I had written two books and that one had been published by Routledge, but that it did not count towards scholarship. Although the brother was rather stoic, the two women were shocked. The one woman who was a chair of an African American Studies Department even gasped.

"But the work is based on scholarship," she said.

"Exactly," I responded.

"With two books, you should have come up for full professorship. Why have you not come up for full professorship?" she asked.

"Because I did not think that I would qualify," I responded.

Being the chair of a department, she started talking about why it was important for professors to come up for full professorship, explaining that they would be able to play a more significant role in decisions at higher levels of the university. When she began to discuss that something seemed wrong about the fact that I was not given research credit, the gentleman reminded her that she could not impose her university standards at this university and began to explain the significance of research for universities to get funding. Although I did not think I would qualify for full professorship, I also did not see where it was worth it.

I recalled that right after I had received tenure, in a departmental meeting with the dean, I inquired about the benefits of becoming a full professor. I asked whether one would receive an increase in their salary, and if so, how much it would be. The response was that one might or might not receive an increase. If they did, it could be $1,000, or it could be $5,000.

My thoughts were "What's the point?" I had seen the résumé of someone who had come up for full professorship, and thought, "Someone has to do all that—and still not know whether they will get an increase. And if they do, it may only range from $1,000 to $5,000? You have got to be kidding me. It's not worth it," I concluded.

Although it was important that I produce work that my peers respected, I could have cared less about the prestige that comes along with being a full professor. I always felt that my work would speak for itself. I was more concerned about my salary. In response to my complaint that I was the lowest-paid associate professor in the department, the other female evaluator began to explain that what I was going through was common for Black women who were professors. We even discussed the conference at MIT, which she indicated that she had attended herself, and I told her that I remember that Angela Davis said that a lot of the women were crying during some of the talks because of what they were going through.

As they continued to talk about academe and African American Studies, I began to drift to that place I go to when I am surprised about what I am seeing or hearing, or when I am trying to figure something out. Looking at where the evaluators seemed to be in the life cycle, and considering where I was in my own life, I looked at them, asking myself, "Are you really into this like that? How can you be this old and still believe in this crap?"

Because of its superiority complex, the university fails to examine itself and the assumptions upon which it is based. When it does, it only does so within the framework it has defined itself in, which is all but cracking at the seams.

Academics, specifically those who are seeking truth, will at some point hit a wall. They will learn that with all they learn and think they know; they are still not able to answer the questions that have plagued humanity since the beginning of time: Who are we? Why do we come here? Where did we come from and where do we go upon death? Since all science has to offer is the big bang theory, one will have to go beyond the academic walls for answers.

The only place to go is to religion. Religion has attempted to answer some of these questions and is probably the closest we are going to get to answers. The problem with religion is that although it may have originated from the truth, it was captured and manipulated to be used as a tool of domination and control.

As time went on, I was becoming increasingly haunted by my book not receiving academic credit and being penalized with an increased course load. The anxiety I had always experienced with teaching was getting worse, making me feel like I was going to have a stroke or heart attack. Because of my teaching style, I was also experiencing a lot of physical pain, some stemming from years of carrying and later pushing and pulling a cart with my teaching materials and student papers. Knowing the reality of how Black people are suffering, many barely making it by the skin of their teeth and wanting to produce work relevant to their lives (and that at least a few might take in interest in reading), I was finding it increasingly difficult to continue to wear the mask and the cracks that had already begun some years ago were deepening. Hearing more clearly now what Du Bois said around the turn of the century in *The Souls of Black Folk*—his double consciousness theory (which is the internal conflict that occurs with attempting to reconcile one's African heritage with European cultural hegemony), I was feeling sort of like a seventh [daughter], born with a veil and gifted, with a second-sight in this

American world—a world which yielded me no true self-consciousness but only let me see myself through the revelation of the other world. It was a peculiar sensation, this double consciousness. I was feeling torn between whether to:

Continue to heed the call of the academic world, or heed the call of my conscious, which nags me incessantly to create work that can potentially reach those whose lives I want to affect.

Take control of my life, my destiny, and publish my work, or give it away to satisfy the academic machine.

Try to be more collegiate, which meant giving more of my life force to the university, or just not doing it.

Dance to the tune of the academy or dance to the tune that stirs my soul—a tune that is seeking truth.

I now knew what Du Bois meant by, "One ever feels [her] twoness (or threeness if you are a woman)—an American, a [Black American]; two souls, two thoughts, two warring ideals in one dark body, whose dogged strength alone keeps it from being torn asunder."[73] And it was taking a toll on both my mental and physical health, and I was getting sicker by the day.

17

A STRANGE ENCOUNTER

One day I was visiting the Little Five Points neighborhood in Atlanta with Tim, and I went into a store that sells African clothing and art, something I do most of the time when I go to that area. As often as I have gone into that store, I never went to the reading section because I did not want to buy any more books. I would tell myself, "Read the books you have." But that day, something pulled me to the book section of the store. I saw one about Shambhala that caught my attention because I had just received a Shambhala attunement (a multidimensional energy of higher vibration that is both a healing modality and is supposed to lead to an expanded level of consciousness) while in class with Kaia.

As I began to browse the pages, an older brother with his front teeth missing came up to me. He started pointing out which books he thought I should purchase and started talking about the earth being out of alignment and the potential crisis we are in: if a meteorite were to strike the earth at one of the nuclear plants, it would be catastrophic. This became more confirmed when I visited the Smithsonian Crystal and Gem Museum. It was a reminder of how often meteorites hit the earth's atmosphere and dissolve and the many that make it through. It also reminded me of dreams, or shall I say visions, I have of something penetrating the sky from the cosmos. The man said the book on Shambhala was a good one, along with others. I discovered that the book was a publication of Malachi York, leader of the Nuwaubians.

I was first introduced to the Nuwaubians while I was living in Boston when people selling books approached me. Some of the information seemed interesting, but since it was my first year of teaching and how demanding it was, I decided I would have to come back to it another time. The last I heard was that the Nuwaubians had built a community in Putnam County, Georgia and that York was being arrested for child molestation charges. I did not know much about the Nuwaubians, but based on my brief introductions to York's teachings, I could see they were radically different from traditional Western religion and empowering for Black people. My thought was he was just another Black leader that the government was finally able to find something to bring him down.

This time, however, the book caught my attention because of the Shambhala attunement I had recently received, and because I was starting to get sick (I was in a lot of pain). I did not know if I had taken in too much energy or if something else was going on. I had stopped doing the energy work until I could get to the bottom of what was going on.

According to the Tibetan Buddhist and Hindu traditions, Shambhala is a mystical spiritual place where highly evolved spiritual beings reside. Since the idea of such a place was introduced to the West, Shambhala has taken on varied stories about where it exists, the many places it can be accessed from, and who and how it is governed. And there have even been expeditions made to find it.

I was taken aback by one of the pictures that looked exactly like an image I saw during some of the ascension meditations I did with Kaia: an old, bearded man with long white hair and a long white robe, standing directly in front of me, looking through my eyes with a microscope. I kept trying to erase the image from my head. Because I thought he was white, my thinking was, "There you go. The image of the old white sage has been so embedded in your conscious, no matter how hard you try to get the image out of your head, it's still there." It is the same with Jesus. One of the reasons I struggle with Christianity is that I cannot get the image out of my head, of the young, bearded white man with blue eyes, sitting on my mother's mantle.

I wanted to buy the book primarily because of the picture but did not want to spend $40 on it. I ran out of the store to bring Tim to meet the man I had just met and for him to see the picture. When I got back, the man was gone. I wondered whether he was sent to lead me to this information. I showed the picture to Tim and asked him if he thought I should purchase the book.

"No," he said. "I have a book at the house."

"What? Are you sure?" I kept asking. "Well, why haven't I seen it?" I asked.

"I am telling you I have the book with all this information at the house."

We went back and forth, and I settled upon waiting until we got home. When we got there, Tim pulled out *The Holy Tablets* (which seemed to contain a lot of the information that was in the book I considering purchasing). I began browsing through it and took it with me when we went out again.

For some reason, while browsing through the book, the energy started rising, and I began to feel that floaty feeling I feel when doing energy work. The contents looked like a mixture of Judaism, Christianity, and Islam, as well as Eastern spirituality. I went immediately to the information on Shambhala. Based on what I was reading about people living underground, I began to think about the caverns I had seen when I was a child and how awestruck I was by the stalagmites and stalactites. How they glistened when the light hit them. What was more amazing was how all that beauty formed in pure darkness.

"You know, based on what I have seen with the underground caverns," I said to Tim, "it is not inconceivable that beings could be living under the earth."

"I know," he responded. "There are other beings who live among us because I see them all the time."

I also discussed what I had read from Malidoma Somé's *The Healing Wisdom of Africa*, about *Kontomblé*—beings who live in caves. In this work, Somé recounts how, when he was a child, while he was chasing a rabbit, he encountered a being that was about the size of a doll but looked like an old man. The being was sitting in a chair in front of a window to what seemed like an entryway into another realm or world. The being talked to him, asking him to be kind to the rabbit. When he told his mother about his encounter, she panicked because she knew he had encountered a *Kontomblé*. Somé indicated that he would have dismissed this experience as a hallucination had he not encountered beings as an educated adult. He also recounts another experience in which a tree came alive: a green being walked out of it while he was going through an initiation. In addition, he indicated that other members of his community have visited *Kontomblé* in caves for help and that he saw and felt the hand of one (which indicated that she was not of this realm) when his family took his sister to get help.

"Everybody is not making this up," I said. And Tim and I had started watching shows like *Ancient Aliens* on PBS History Channel and documentaries about UFOs and people having encounters with extraterrestrial beings. I then finally went to the beginning of the book.

I said to Tim, "This stuff is too out there for me," and I put it down. I began to explain to him why. "First," I said, "it seems to be all over the place—like the ramblings of someone who has mixed up a whole lot of stuff. And it even looks like York might be insane. Second, I mean how did he come up with all the names of these beings from these so-called planets?"

"You really want to know?" Tim asked. "Do you really want to know?"

"Yeah," I responded.

"They come and talk to you." The car went silent.

Upon further investigation, I found that York spent some time in Egypt studying Islam as a child and began his ministry in the 1960s. His ministry made international connections with Islamic imams abroad, but due to clashes with Black Muslims in the United States and being under constant surveillance and investigation, his ministry underwent several transitions throughout his life. The Nuwaubians eventually bought 476 acres of land near Eatonton, Georgia, for close to a million dollars and developed a complex called Tama-Re with an Egyptian theme, which included pyramids. Aerial pictures of this astonishing achievement can be found on the Internet; it looked like Egypt in Georgia. Tim said he had visited the complex and met Maliki York and that he had given him a copy of *The Holy Tablets* personally.

Clashing with Putnam County officials, primarily the sheriff, over building and zoning matters, specifically a night club, and holding festivals on the property, the Nuwaubians were eventually raided by the FBI, and other federal, state, and local forces, and York was eventually convicted of racketeering and child molestation charges, including the transport of minors for sexual use. The property was sold under government forfeiture, the proceeds went to Putnam County, the FBI, and the IRS, and the complex was demolished.

"Why would he establish a community in the South, in Georgia, with pyramids, making him appear larger than the county sheriff? Didn't he understand that this was his territory? Being from the North, maybe he didn't understand how deeply rooted racism is in the South," I said.

"Maybe it was because the land was so cheap in Georgia," Tim responded.

18
THE HEAVEN PEOPLE

"Where are you? I am worried about you," I said to Khalil in an email.

The last time I had seen Khalil was about four years prior when he visited Atlanta from South Africa, where he had moved to. I had reached out to him but did not hear back from him. I went to Facebook, and it looked like he had not been on it for a couple of years. That morning, I was searching my email for something, and another email address that I had forgotten I had for Khalil came up. I emailed him, and ironically, he said that he would be in Atlanta in a week.

When Khalil came to our house for a visit, I was surprised by how different he looked—like he was straight from Africa (as opposed to generations removed, like most African Americans). I thought it was interesting how people start to look like where they live. "It must have to do with the food they eat and the environment," I said to Tim.

While in town, Khalil left Atlanta to visit Ohio (where his family lives) and on his way back he called me. During the conversation, he said, "Pat, I went to visit my brother in prison. Do you believe he's been in prison for thirty years?"

"Wow," I responded, and we talked more about it.

After we got off the phone, my mind went to the place it goes to when thinking about the injustices Black people experience in the United States. "Thirty years...How does a mother lose not one, but two of her sons to prison? One son for twenty years (which Khalil had done) and the other one, a life sentence?"

I began to reflect on the story of Glenn Ford, featured on *60 Minutes*, who was wrongly convicted of murder and spent close to thirty years on death row in Louisiana's infamous Angola prison. When evidence was found exonerating and releasing him from prison, not only was he denied the entitled $330,000 for wrongful imprisonment, but he also died of lung cancer within fifteen months of his release. "How does this happen?" I asked. "How is it that some people come to Earth and live their entire lives in a living hell and then just die? What is that? Is it that they are paying for some past life transgression?" It is hard to believe that Ford did something that terrible in his youth (since he was found not guilty of the crime he was in prison for) that would warrant this kind of life sentence.

During his visit, Khalil announced he was getting married and that he wanted us to come to his wedding in South Africa. He said that he was working with Nelson Mandela's daughters, who launched the House of Mandela wines that are distributed throughout the world.

"Look," as he had said before, "everything will be taken care of when you get there—you will have a place to stay and transportation. Just come."

"We have to see if finances will permit us to," I responded, saying the same thing I said the last time he invited us to South Africa.

Frustrated with me, Khalil said, "Let me talk to Tim."

Although we wanted to go because we thought it was an opportunity that might not come around again, it just was not financially feasible at that time. But within a couple of months, I woke up and found an email from Khalil saying that someone would be sending us a travel itinerary, thinking that if they could send us inexpensive flights, we might be able to go. I emailed him back saying, "Tell them to send the time and date before doing anything." Within a few days, I received an email with the itinerary that looked like the tickets had been paid for.

I emailed him back and asked the cost, to which he replied, "It is already paid for. No worries."

"Are we really going on an all-expense-paid trip to South Africa?" we asked. I think we (or at least, I) did not believe it until we checked with the airlines and the tickets were there.

~~~~~~~~~~

My first impression upon arriving at Johannesburg in the evening was that it looked a lot like Atlanta. It confirmed what I heard from others who had visited the city. My thinking was, "So, I went all the way to South Africa to go to Atlanta." Khalil's best friend and partner, Rasheed, said that living in South Africa was better than living in the United States, but that he did not like it. The next day, I began to understand why.

While riding in the shuttle bus, Rasheed pointed out the walls to us. "Hmm," I thought. At first, my thinking was that the walls are like what we see in business and residential complexes in the United States. But as time went on, we noticed that not only were walls almost everywhere but also many of them had barb wires, with warnings that they were electric.

It seemed that everywhere we went in Johannesburg and surrounding areas there were barb wires. "Why do they have barb wires everywhere?" we asked. It was not to prevent crime, we suspected.

"It was to protect against a potential uprising."

The next day, we were flown to Durban to go to the resort for the wedding. We arrived at King Shaka International Airport. Being in the land of the legendary Shaka Zulu and the people he was the descendant of (the Zulus) was surreal for us. When I investigated Shaka Zulu's legacy, there is a great deal of controversy. It is alleged that under Shaka Zulu's legacy, approximately one million people were killed as he conquered African chieftains to bring them under the Zulu kingdom. How he revolutionized warfare, including under the famous "bull-horn formation," which prepared the people for the wars to come with the English and the Boers is worth noting (although the Zulus were eventually slaughtered by them).

While at the airport, a man that Khalil had invited to the wedding, Sipho, arrived as well. Khalil introduced him to us. I felt an immediate connection with him. I did not know what it was; it was just something familiar about him. Once we arrived at the resort, while I was with Tim on one side of the balcony of the hotel we were staying at, Sipho was talking to others who came on the trip. I could hear that he was talking about the people of the land, so I joined the group.

I said, "I'm interested in the history," and he began explaining that there were the Xhosa people and the Zulus. He was Xhosa, and so was Nelson Mandela. They called themselves "the heaven people" because they believed they had come from heaven. Later at the bar inside the resort hotel, he said he and his wife were the first persons in South Africa to own a McDonald's franchise. He explained that he had owned a coffee shop, and that is how he met Khalil.

Sipho had observed Khalil sitting at the same table three days in a row, and because he had studied psychology, there was something about Khalil that made him decide to introduce himself to him. Referring to him as "a brother from another planet," they became friends. Sipho was aware of the customs around getting married, so when Khalil was ready to marry the woman he had met, he negotiated the bride price with her family for him.

Because Khalil did not own cows (ten cows was the traditional price), Sipho negotiated other personal characteristics and attributes such as his education and résumé, and Khalil had to complete certain tasks. I had researched African family practices and understood that the male was paying for the loss the family would sustain by their daughter marrying.

Although Sipho explained that Khalil was paying for the family losing their "flower" (which confirmed my research), for the first time, I could not get over the funny feeling that it was men negotiating women, like they were property. But in a world dominated and ruled by the force of men, in some ways it made sense that women had men to protect them from other men.

The next morning, Tim got up around 4 a.m. because it was already light, and I got up a little time after him. He went out on the balcony, and while he was recording the sounds of a monkey, the birds, and the ocean, I joined him in silence. As time stood still, I held my hands out like I do when I am doing energy work or in meditation while I gazed upon the heavenly gray ocean that met the matching gray sky. We later came back in. "Can you believe we are in a resort in Africa?" we said in utter disbelief. "We are in Africa. We are in Africa," we kept repeating. "And the best part is we do not have to think about how to pay for it. How blessed are we?"

We ordered breakfast and got dressed for the wedding. At the wedding, I saw more rose petals than I have ever seen in my lifetime as

Khalil's beautiful Zulu bride was escorted to meet him by her brother-in-law and the minister. The reception was no less awe-inspiring. I introduced myself to the bride's mother and father as Khalil's sister. I had no idea that was exactly what he needed. When Khalil got up to make a toast, I was moved to tears, as I watched her mother and father watch him. I had forgotten how gifted Khalil was. I was thinking, "One of our brightest has returned to show the best of what we have produced," and I was so proud.

When Sipho came to speak to us again, he continued the conversation he had started earlier. During the earlier meeting, he said that he had attempted to commit suicide and had written a book about the experience, *There's a Killer in My Head*. I was surprised to see that he had a noose on the front cover. "Why would he put that on the cover of a book?" I asked in silence. "Maybe he does not know the history of lynching in the U.S., and how sensitive this is," I concluded. At the time, I had no idea that lynching was significant in South African history as well.

While he was talking at the wedding reception, I started crying, for many reasons: I was in Africa. I was so glad that Khalil had met and married a woman who was compassionate enough to understand his struggles and patient enough to go through them with him. I was inspired by Khalil's speech and I felt Sipho's pain. But it was more than that. It was the connection between two empaths, a term I had recently discovered, which means for some "those who sense the pain of others." Some feel the pain of the earth, others the pain of the world, others all of it. I sensed the pain of the people through Sipho. He went on to explain that suicide among South African men is high, but it gets little attention. He then went on to say, "My father committed suicide in his seventies. He hanged himself," as he held back the tears. I, however, unable to hold back mine, wondered as I always do "What is it about me that people, even strangers, feel compelled to reveal the most painful events in their lives?"

At one point, I saw Khalil sitting alone at the bride and groom table that he had made sure that Tim and I along with his son, his wife, and two grandchildren sat at. It was the opportunity to tell him that although they married at this stage in their lives to help each other with their destinies, which is something he has always maintained was most important to him, and said it in his vows, that he still had to pay attention to the small things that show a woman that you love and cherish her. I was trying to say, in so many words without saying it, "Don't blow it."

Khalil said to me, "Pat, we are in South Africa; we are at the Indian Ocean." We both felt we were touching those things we had read about.

Later that evening, a woman who at first claimed to be the sister of the bride came up to me and said, "I hear you are Khalil's sister."

"Well, sort of," I said, not wanting to be deceptive.

"Well, how long you have known him?" she asked.

"A long time," I responded.

She went on to explain that she was not the sister of the bride either, as she had originally claimed, but that she was like her sister because she had known her for a long time.

"I was worried," she said, "because we knew nothing about him. Who is he? We kept asking."

Confirming everything I had learned about African family practice, she made it clear that when people marry in Africa, it is two families marrying. So, it is important to know what family you are marrying into. When she said that, at that moment, it became clear why Khalil made sure we made it to South Africa. Saying he was my brother was just the ancestors speaking through me, without my knowing it, telling me to confirm to the family that he was marrying into that he had family— whether it was biological or not—that he had some people in the world—good people—who cared for him like he was family.

When the woman pointed out that she had traveled all over the world and that Africans were the same no matter where you go, she hit that nail right on the head. Since being there, I had observed just that. I had an affinity for the Zulus, and when meeting the bride's sister, I connected with her and felt like I had known her for a thousand years. Just like African Americans, the Zulus had different complexions, wore their hair like ours (straightened, weaved, braided, and natural), and they even partied like we do—doing line dances, getting in the center, and walking down the aisle like they are on *Soul Train*. The reality is *Soul Train* was Africa in America.

In addition to the unforgettable wedding experience in Durban, what was also unforgettable was the pain of the people of South Africa, I was feeling that intensified each day we would go out into the city and see the walls and barb wires, and especially the day we went on tour. As that day continued, the anger I had suppressed from what I had learned about the injustices against Black people the world over began to rise.

When we went to the informal settlements in Soweto, I became infuriated. The tour guide went off her normal route to introduce us to two women who lived there in shanties, makeshift houses made from wood, sheets of metal and plastic, and cardboard boxes. As it always does when I go to impoverished areas with rubble, it occurred to me, "Can't they get together in groups and just pick up the trash?" Are people that ignorant that they cannot figure that out? All they needed to do is establish a central location to dispose of it."

One woman who lived there assists the tour guide when she brings tourists. She was rather happy and enthusiastic about showing us the shanties that the people lived in. We were instructed that we could not give them American dollars. Feeling compelled to do so anyway, we asked, "Why not?" The tour guide responded, "They do not have an ID, which means that they can do nothing with it." The woman took us to the house of a woman who was in her sixties. She lived in a one-room shanty where she did everything including cook for the community on something no bigger than a hot plate, without electricity. The tour guide explained that for the people to get out of the shanties into a house they must win a housing lottery. However, they cannot enter the lottery until they reach the age of forty.

I was done when I heard that. The woman was in her sixties. She had been waiting for over twenty years to get out of that God-forgotten place. I attempted to cover my eyes with my hands so no one could see the tears welling up but to no avail. They were able to see them anyway. Tim was so moved that he gave her all the change that he had in Rands (South African currency). "How can Johannesburg have so much wealth and people live like this?" I asked myself once we got back into the van and throughout my time there.

The woman reminded me of the song "Pearls" where Sade sings about a woman who digs for pearls: "There is a woman in Somalia... She lives in a world she didn't choose. And it hurts like brand-new shoes." After that, every time I would think about South Africa, the song would sing in my head, "There's a woman in [Soweto]... She lives in a world she didn't choose..." I would then pray: "God, please get that woman out of there. God, please help the people of South Africa."

The assistant then took us to her house, which she was proud of. She bragged about all the things she had done, including digging out more space in the hole she was literally living in, and putting down tile. Others had bigger spaces because they assumed the space next to them that was available each time one of the shanties are demolished, which is done when someone wins the housing lottery. She had mustered up enough to have a flat-screen television that she would only be able to use if she were able to siphon electricity from somewhere. "Some people attach electricity, but the authorities come and cut it because it is potentially dangerous," she said. The shanties were worse than the worse living conditions I had ever seen in the United States. Since her shanty was more developed than others, I imagined she may have thought she was a class above the rest. "It goes to show, it is all relative," I thought.

"They just need to take a bulldozer and just bulldoze those shanties," I said to Tim. "Are you telling me some multimillionaire or billionaire can't work out a deal with the government and just come in and develop this area?" I thought about calling Ray and telling him, "There is a real estate development opportunity in South Africa." After I gave it more thought, "There is nothing in it. That's why nobody sees this as an investment opportunity. Most of the people do not work, so they will not be able to pay rent. I mean the people could build it themselves. All they need are the materials, and it would give them something to do," I said.

"Yeah, but they would have to do major work to bring in electricity, water, and sewage. That would be extremely costly," Tim explained.

When we visited the Mandela Mall with the giant statue of Nelson Mandela outside of it. "This looks like Lennox Mall in Atlanta. Is this what Mandela did?" I asked. "Opened up South Africa so that corporate conglomerates can come in and exploit peoples' labor, paying them low wages?" When I went into the mall and saw Black people in low-paying service jobs, "It's just like in the United States thirty or forty years ago. It's just that apartheid ended thirty years after it ended in America," I said.

As I thought more about it, I began to wonder what South Africa produced and offered to the world market in contemporary times. I reflected on the closed diamond mines we also saw on the tour: although Black South African people were literally worked to death and the country, or at least the majority of native people accrued little or no benefits.

South Africa used to supply 95 percent of the world's diamonds. Later, the gold mines were discovered. "I guess the corporation conglomerates do provide jobs," I said. "Other than that, what would the people do to earn a living so that they can feed their families?"

Before visiting the shanties, we visited Nelson Mandela's Family Museum in Orlando, Soweto. It is also called the Mandela House, the house he lived in before going to prison, which is in the complex where people who live in the shanties must win the lottery to get in. The house contained many of the accolades he received for his struggle for South African people's liberation from white rule. We were informed that Winnie Mandela's house was nearby and that she still lived there, as did Desmond Tutu (which "he rarely occupies because he travels a lot," said the tour guide).

The tour guide explained that when the apartheid laws were passed, 92 percent of the land had been designated for the Afrikaners and the rest of the land had been designated for Black Africans, coloreds, Indians, and other people of color. Because they were all subjected to laws under apartheid, this is why coloreds and Indians participated in the struggle against apartheid. "How do you come into somebody else's land," we asked, "and take 92 percent of it and leave them 8 percent?" Soweto, a township outside of Johannesburg, was one of many throughout South Africa that Black Africans were relegated to live on under apartheid legislation. Tim and I asked over and over, "What is wrong with these people?"

We visited the Hector Pieterson Memorial Museum, with the photo of Mbuyisa Makhubo holding this thirteen-year-old youth, with his sister Antoinette Sithole running beside him. Peterson was one of the first students to get shot in the 1976 student protest (although the tour guide said that he was not even participating in the movement). An estimate of ten to twenty thousand students organized a peaceful protest in response to being required to be taught in and learn the Afrikaans language on a 50:50 basis, with the other language being English, which they preferred. Although they organized a peaceful protest, police opens fire on them killing 176 to 700 (although South Africa reported only 23). The legislation only added insult to injury with the Bantu Education Act of 1953, which said that Black Africans must be taught at an early age that they are not equal with whites.

Since there was strict censorship disallowing journalists from reporting, filming, or videotaping, the photo of Makhubo carrying Hector Peterson was one of few. After being questioned by the authorities, Makhubo fled the country. His mother said that in 1978 she received a letter from him, but after, that his family never heard from him again. Pieterson's sister Antionette Sithole gives tours at the Hector Pieterson Memorial Museum.

We visited the Regina Mundi Catholic Church in Rockville, Soweto, in the Moroko neighborhood, where some of the protesters fled to. It is also the place that people met for meetings, like how freedom fighters met in churches during the Civil Rights Movement. The police, however, opened fire on students while they were inside the church. Some students were injured, and furniture, decorations, symbols, and other items in the church were damaged. The walls still show damage by the bullets. Right in the center, behind the pulpit, was a big statue on the wall of the crucifixion of Jesus.

"There goes that white Jesus," Tim said.

"White supremacy at the highest level," I responded. "White supremacy is so deeply ingrained in people, no matter how much they try, they can't get that white Jesus out of their minds."

The Apartheid Museum showed just how brutal the white Afrikaners were to the Black people of South Africa. There was a section with ropes with nooses hanging from the ceiling. "Oh, my God. I am not going to be able to handle this," I thought because it evoked images of Black people being lynched in the United States. When you see the photographs of the lynchings, some images will get etched in your memory forever.

For example, *Without Sanctuary*, a photographic exhibit about lynching in the United States came to Atlanta in 2002. Although there were numerous gruesome photographs (some of them group hangings), the one that got etched in my conscious is that of an elderly Black man, who was dead, but was sitting up in a chair, with white guys standing on both sides of him, smiling as one of them held a mop on his head. "These people have absolutely nothing inside them that is remotely human," I thought when I saw that. Another image I stumbled onto was that of the lynching of a Black woman whose hair was filled with dirt from the ground. All I could think of is what the events before the hanging must have been like. "Was she dragged?" I asked. "And what other gruesome things happened before she was strung up on a tree by those monsters?"

I would learn that the Afrikaners were outright murdering Black people, and not only without recourse, but it was also state promulgated. The nooses represented how Black people were killed or threatened to be killed and how it be would be reported that they committed suicide.

As we continued going through the museum and digesting the awfulness of apartheid, I began to wonder how Khalil's grandchildren, who were 11 and 14 were processing the information; whether they were too young to see such awful things, and how it might affect them. The picture and video I will never forget, and neither will Khalil's grandson, who seemed sad when he bought up the images of the cops pulling a young man over barbed wire. The footage of the brutalities bought me back to the footage of the dogs and water hoses in the apartheid in the South in America during the Civil Rights Movement. And it made me sick to my stomach. What was more mortifying to think about was that we did not see in those gruesome pictures and video footage.

When we left the museum, it started raining hard and even started hailing. I wondered whether the water was getting into the shanties and whether the people were not only getting wet but drenched. Although I know that people have lived like this since the beginning of time, I still could not help but think about how miserable it must be to live exposed to the elements—all the time.

For Black South Africans, encounters with Europeans have resulted in a lot of suffering and a lot of life lost. Nelson Mandela (whose original first name was Rolihlahla, which means "troublemaker") as well as an untold number of men, women, and children who suffered terribly, lost their lives, or became political prisoners.

While serving the 27-year prison term, he continued the struggle from his prison cell. In 1985 when violence swept the country and economic sanctions were being imposed, and international governments and agencies, put pressure on South Africa to end apartheid and release Mandela, Pieter Willem Botha, then the president, negotiated with him offering to release him under the condition that the African National Congress (ANC) would end the armed struggle, and he refused. When Botha made the offer again in 1988, he refused again.

When Mandela was released from prison by F.W. de Klerk, who was now the head of the National Party (NP) and who would become the president, Mandela ran for president under the (ANC) party. He was voted in by the majority Black vote and became the first president of the new democratic South Africa. During his presidency, Mandela traveled widely, meeting heads of state and wealthy elites all over the world. He won numerous medals and honors from countries throughout the world including a joint Nobel Peace Prize with de Klerk.

Concerned, however, that the white elite would pull out of South Africa, taking their money with them, and wanting to attract foreign investment into South Africa, he moved away from ANC's goals to nationalize the banks, land, and gold mines, putting them under state control, and adopted liberal economic policies.

Through these policies, Blacks gained back the land that was taken from them through the 1913 Native Land Act, helping to relieve some of the suffering stemming from poverty. To bring peace to South Africa, Mandela also sought to reconcile differences between NP and ANC and Afrikaners and Black Africans. However, he was accused of being more concerned with appeasing Afrikaners to the detriment of Black Africans and was ultimately seen as a sell-out by some Black Africans, including his ex-wife, Winnie Mandela. It has been reported that the policies and programs under his administration have helped millions of Black Africans rise out of abject poverty.

Notwithstanding the progress that has been made since the dismantling of apartheid, from what I could see, it seemed that far too many Black South Africans were still languishing under the crushing effects of poverty. And it is not the kind of poverty that we know in the United States. It is the kind without safe, affordable, and decent housing, without safe running water, without inside plumbing, and without electricity. In light of the tremendous amount of wealth that I could see in Johannesburg, there is something terribly wrong with the living conditions I saw people living under in Soweto, especially in the informal settlements, and Soweto is only one township in over forty throughout South Africa.

It was not just what I saw in Johannesburg and Soweto. It was not just the barb wires that were revolting. There was something so thick in the air, you could cut it with a knife—that made me feel sick. While on the tour, the tour guide made it clear that many Black South Africans hate Afrikaners. "Maybe the air is thick with hate." I thought, "Just like I can smell racism, I can feel hate."

When we saw the barb wires on the expressway as we were leaving for the airport to return to Atlanta, it confirmed for us that they were there to keep the people out. "What kind of crime are they trying to prevent on the expressway?" Tim and I both asked. No matter how much I tried to see South Africa through the eyes of Khalil (who thought South Africa was great and liked living there), the barb wires were a constant reminder of the brutalities and injustices that Black South Africans have experienced and the abject poverty and suffering gripping many of them.

"I don't care what Khalil says about how great South Africa is. I hate this place," I said, as I struggled to hold back the tears.

19
YEARNINGS FOR ETERNITY

It is interesting that I would visit Egypt for the third time and the African American Museum within two months of each other. Returning to Egypt with Tim was a bucket list item for me.

About two-and-a-half years after the South Africa trip, when my brother, Bruce, left his old life behind (including his marriage, six-figure executive position with a non-profit organization, house, and luxury cars) to go on a spiritual journey around the world, called me, and said he was in Egypt, I decided I might have to let go of my goal to do an Afrocentric tour and go then. Bruce had come to visit us over the Christmas holidays, and with the hope of helping him to find his African roots, I took him to a seminar that was being held about Kemetic spirituality. I thanked God that he had come during that time. When we talked, he said that even though he had already visited Egypt, he would go back if I were to come over there.

So, I booked a trip and chose a flight that connected in Rome because I wanted Tim to visit Rome. The trip, to Rome, however, was less eventful than I had remembered when I visited in the 1990s. This could be because, just like before, we were rushed and did not have a chance to do an educated tour. We just did it ourselves. Because we visited on Easter Monday, the Sistine Chapel was closed, so I missed it again. When I had visited in the 1990s, I was astounded by the detail in the architecture of St. Peter's Basilica and the statues inside of it. This time I was less awed; maybe because I had already seen it. However, when I saw the statues lining the top of buildings (which I did not remember), now having had a spiritual awakening, "Oh, my God. They represent the guardians," I said to Tim. I would later find that the statues on the front of the building are Jesus, the apostles, and St. John, and on the colonnades are statutes of 140 saints that consist of martyrs, popes, bishops, virgins, etc.

As we approached the obelisk, Tim asked excitedly, "Do you see that? Do you see that?"

"See what?" I asked.

"That light?" He pointed up to the sky.

I looked to where he was pointing, squinting my eyes. "No," I responded.

He proceeded to take out his phone to take a picture. When he showed the picture to me, there was a light beam in it that you could not see with the eye, or at least, I could not see it.

"It is a curve to another dimension," he said, something he talks about from time to time, where he sees things in spaces that most of us do not see. "There is a lot of power coming from that obelisk; it is going far in the sky, but you cannot see that far because the sun is too bright. It is here because they wanted to tap into its power."

With the obelisk taken right out of Egypt and what the architecture and statutes symbolize, although I speculated it before, this time I was sure that I was visiting Egypt in Rome. The Romans were so inspired by what they saw in Egypt, they wanted to duplicate it. After touring St. Peter's Basilica, we caught the hop-on-hop-off bus to take a tour of other churches and the Coliseum and then got back on the train to the airport to head to Egypt.

When we arrived in Egypt, it was late evening. Bruce had arranged for someone to pick us up from the airport. He had also contacted a tour guide and had already been to the Egyptian Museum in Cairo, so the next day we went to it on our own. It occurred to me, as it had in the past, when I saw mummies on some of the shelves, "You think you are resting in peace, and somebody has dug up your body and put it on a shelf." This was my third trip to Egypt, but I was just as astounded as I was before by the sheer number of artifacts in the museum, how massive some of them are, the spiritual concepts they represent, and the feelings they evoke when seeing them. And particularly what they represent for me: Black people created the greatest civilization known in the ancient world. After we left the museum, all three of us went to the Nile and stood gazing at it in utter amazement that we had the opportunity in this life to be standing at the Nile—together.

The following day, Bruce called the tour guide to take us on a tour of the Great Pyramid complex at Giza and the Step Pyramid at Saqqara. When a short-statured, mild-mannered, warm, enthusiastic, Arab fellow showed up, I knew he was the right person; at the very beginning of the conversation, he said that the pyramid was symbolic of the *Merkaba*, which means "the eternal house of the soul." Kaia would refer to the Merkaba as if it were a vehicle of travel when he would lead us in meditation. When I searched for the meaning of it on the Internet, it seemed to be associated with mystic Judaism, but I knew there was more to it. *Ka* and *ba* meant "soul" and "spirit" in the ancient Egyptian language, so I speculated that Merkaba had Egyptian origins. However, I did not know what *mer* meant, and based on how the tour guide explained it, I am assuming it means "eternal house." So, when questions that I have been seeking answers to are answered without my even asking, I know I am at the right place.

Since I had already been to the pyramid complex in Giza and had been to the light show (which opened my understanding a bit of why it was so significant), I think the excitement I got from it this time was the fact that I was there with Tim and Bruce. Tim and I had frequently discussed the Great Pyramid. Tim believed that it was a portal for otherworldly visitors. And the first energy attunement I got that shifted my whole paradigm was called Sekhem, which Patrick Zeigler, an international teacher, said he received when he slept overnight in the Great Pyramid.

The tour guide was enthusiastic and shared a lot of information about not only ancient Egypt but also contemporary Egypt. He said he was excited about taking us on the tour because of our sincere interest. I am sure our interest in his journey also helped. We would learn about his sick wife, and how he struggled to take care of her while he had to also provide for his family. He explained to us how contemporary Egyptians, particularly Egyptologists (who earn a living as tour guides), were struggling financially because of the effect the 2011 revolution had on the tourist industry, which subsequently led to a downturn in the Egyptian economy.

Every time I visit Egypt, I learn more. The tour guide explained the mummification process, and why ancient Egyptians painted the person's face on the coffin or sarcophagus. When a person died, first the brain was removed through the nostrils and thrown away. The rest of the organs (except for the heart) were removed through a cut on the left side of the body, mummified, and put in a canopic jar. The heart was left in the body so that it could be weighed in the halls of justice in the afterlife. After that, the body would be covered with salt to dissolve the fat and absorb the moisture, and then wrapped with linen. The body was then put in a coffin (for some, several coffins for added protection), which would then be put into a sarcophagus. The face of the person was painted on the sarcophagus so that the soul could find its way to the body.

This would be the first time I would visit the Step Pyramid, the oldest one built during King Djoser's reign during the third dynasty of the old kingdom (circa 2670 BC), by Imhotep (Djoser's chancellor, high priest, and the architect of the Step Pyramid). We had used the Step Pyramid as a symbol in our relationship book *Soul Partners*, and now here I was standing right in front of the oldest pyramid known.

I did not know before arriving there that there was an Imhotep museum. I had discussed the numerous contributions that it is believed that Imhotep made to the world (in medicine, architecture, mathematics, astronomy, science, and other subjects) in my courses, and now here I was at the Imhotep museum. Although the museum was filled with artifacts (as to be expected), what stood out to me is that the jewelry, pottery, sculptures, and other pieces of art that we create today look the same as those created by Black people thousands of years ago. But what stood out, even more, is that the paint was still vibrant. So, not only were Black people the creators of paint, but their paint could also last for millennia!

Outside of the Egyptian Museum, on the right side of it, is the Auguste Mariette Memorial, who was its first director. A statue of him sits on top of a sarcophagus, surrounded by twenty-four busts of Arab and white men, called "fathers" of Egyptology, because of the role they played in shaping and developing Egyptology. "hmm," I thought. "They are following in the footsteps of the Egyptians, leaving busts of themselves so that they attain immortality." It is the same thing I thought when I encountered the works of E.A. Wallis Budge, who translated the

Egyptian texts because entry into ancient Egypt at least in the English language would mean entry through his works. A gallery dedicated to the French Egyptologist, Jean-Philippe Lauer, who spent seventy-five years of his life restoring the monuments means that he will be remembered right along with Imhotep. Those who attach themselves to ancient Egypt, I believe, once they understand what the Egyptians were doing themselves, are attempting to achieve immortality—at least in the earthly realm—by the contributions they were making in keeping their monuments alive.

After the tour, we caught a taxi into town for dinner. It never ceases to amaze me how poorly people in other parts of the world live, and how much we take for granted in the United States. Cairo was incredibly dirty; the air quality is horrifying, I am assuming because of the sand, and there seem to be no air quality regulations for automobile emissions. In some places, particularly downtown, the buildings had no windows; it made you wonder what those windowless places looked like on the inside. When I saw the meat that was being grilled and served in the outside restaurant we went to, it made me wonder if it came from the sheep, which we saw eating trash.

The next day, we went to the train station to purchase tickets for the overnight train to take us to the port where the cruise down the Nile would begin. The train station looked like something out of a Humphrey Bogart movie; it felt like you were in the 1940s and people were smoking cigarettes on the inside of the train station. When we tried to sit on benches on the console outside as we waited for the second train with the overnight quarters, we were told that the few available seats were reserved for Egyptian citizens (which we speculated is an indication of how Arabs treat the Nubians. We believe some thought we were Nubians). We had to get up.

Tim got into two scuffles before we got to the overnight train. In one, an official took him in the back office and tried to shake him down, writing on a piece of paper "370 American dollars." Tim said he told the guy he didn't understand, and just got up and left. While on the train, some Egyptian guys started harassing Tim over his seat. I had moved to the front to get away from the vent that was over me in the icebox train and had fallen asleep. Bruce was sitting in another seat. Tim said the guys just kept hovering over him, talking, until he stood up over them (they were all short) and said, "I've had enough." One of the men said, "Oh you're mean," while another one went to get the attendant. After the ordeal was over, he discovered that the ticket clerk had put the wrong date on the ticket, giving us tickets for the same seats for the next day. When the attendant came, he never said anything about it and told the guys to just sit somewhere else.

When we got to the overnight train, we were as excited as little children because we had bunk beds and our rooms were right next to each other. However, the train was so cold, and the dirty air coming out of the vent blew directly on me, which made the ride a miserable experience.

Things got much better when we boarded the nice cruise ship, where we were treated well. Tim and I were so excited about doing a tour on the Nile that we bought cartouche rings (an oval or oblong with a line at one end indicating that the text inside is a royal name; it also means protection) with our Egyptian names (Ra Heter and Mu Skher Aakhu, given to us by a *shekhem*, a priest in Ausar Auset Society) printed on each other's ring in hieroglyphics.[74]

No matter how much I had read or heard about Egypt, there was nothing, I mean *absolutely nothing*, that could have prepared me for what I would see in cities and towns along the Nile. It was not just the sheer magnitude of some of the ancient temples, statues, columns, and other structures, it was the detail in which their spiritual concepts are etched on them, the feelings they evoke, and their astounding majesty—almost all constructed by Black people millennia before Europe or Christianity as we know it today was born. It is no wonder that peoples from all corners of the earth that visited them, including the Greeks, Romans, and later other Europeans (even Napoleon Bonaparte, who was supposed to have started Egyptology) were so moved by them. They adopted their concepts as their own, laying the foundation of their philosophies and religion (including Christianity), and attempted to emulate them in their statues and architectural structures.

While visiting the Valley of the Kings, I would learn that when a king was crowned, the digging of his burial chamber began and continued until his death. That means that the longer he was king, the deeper in the earth was his burial chamber. The grandeur of the Mortuary Temple of Hatshepsut is beyond words. One could tell when the Greeks dominated because Isis (the Greek name for Auset) began to look more

Greek on some of the temple walls. Also, we found that some of the temple's walls and other structures had been defaced during the Roman Empire when they were attempting to stamp out any spiritual-religious practices that were not in alignment with Christianity.

While on the ship, I got as sick as I did when I visited Israel. It started from the dirty air blowing on me in the sleeper train. I asked the same question that I asked while in Israel: "Am I going to die here?" It made me think about Asa Hilliard, a world-renown Kemetic scholar, and professor at GSU, who dedicated his life to researching and bringing to us knowledge from Egypt. I had always believed he was an Egyptian ancestor who returned to tell us who we are. So, I found it ironic that he would die in Egypt.

After we got off the ship to return to Cairo, I found that the hotel we stayed at in the interim had a doctor on site. When he came to the room with an assistant and an IV, I was shocked that he was rolling in an IV, but was glad because based on the poverty I was seeing in Egypt, I absolutely did not want to have to go to an Egyptian hospital. Recognizing that a "bug" in Egypt might be much too much for me to handle, I told him, "Give me an antibiotic—whatever it will take to knock this thing out." He gave me a prescription. When we got back to the hotel in Cairo, we got it filled, and after a few days, I started to feel better.

Since we had time left over, we spent the last few days just hanging out in Cairo. We contemplated traveling to Alexandria and Greece. We were already in the land, and it would be a lot cheaper than traveling back from the United States. I also did not get to visit the city of Abydos, where Osiris (the Greek name for Ausar) is supposed to be buried, or Abu Simbel, where the Temple of Ramses II, one of the greatest kings in Egypt, because he kicked out the invaders, is located. Since I had gotten sick, I was still feeling weak and did not have the strength to do more travel. Not seeing these areas would give me a reason to return to Egypt.

Because I spent more time in Egypt on this visit, I could really see the women this time. Although most of them dressed in the traditional Muslim black abaya (based on the Islamic principle of modesty in dress, hiding their curves) and the iihab (head covering; other spellings are hajab and hijab) you could still see how overweight and out of shape a lot of them were. This is probably because of their poor diets and the seeming high content of sugar in some of the food. "It's unfortunate that Muslim women have to cover their beauty in that dull black," I thought.

Many not only looked really poor but also depressed. My eyes met the eyes of a few women and men when I noticed that they were looking at me, which I assumed was because they thought I was an Arab (because of my complexion), but it may have been because I had on bright colorful clothes! I did cover my head (with scarves) and body (with long sleeve shirts and pants) most of the time I was there, not only to repel the hot sun (which I am sure is also a reason they cover) but also to repel the sand. It makes you feel dirty, and I did not want it to blow in my hair.

One night, we met some young female Egyptologists, who Bruce had met when he visited Egypt the first time. In our conversation, one of the women, of Turkish origin, kept talking about how she was glad to be an Egyptian and suggested that the ancient Egyptians were her ancestors.

The more she repeated that the more upset I became. Trying to be kind (and not wanting to mess up the night with really nice and sincere young women), I refrained from saying what I was thinking: "You are not the descendants of the Egyptians. The ancient Egyptians were African people (although I did say that). Everyone else are the descendants of transplants and conquerors." I left the gathering pretty upset but continued to process so that I could reconcile the feeling of anger that raises its head when I think of the wholesale theft of not only African peoples and their resources but also their legacies with trying to be healthy and evolve spiritually.

Within a day or two, it came to me very clearly: The Egyptians are the ancestors to all of us. It is not so much who the people were (although African Americans need to know the greatness of their ancestors), it is what messages they were attempting to leave humanity. The messages they would leave were so important, that they were not only etched in stone but they would also be put on monuments so majestic that they cannot be ignored.

And some souls who encounter them, are so stirred they cannot rest until they heed their call to seek out the mysteries behind them.

Those who do so will find their way to their wisdom, themselves, and ultimately the way to eternal life.

~~~~~~~~~

Besides the election of the first African American president, the establishment of the National Museum of African American History and Culture (NMAAHC) must be one of the most, if not the most, significant achievements for African Americans in the twenty-first century thus far. But it is significant not just for Americans, it has international implications. When I had seen on *60 Minutes* that the museum was being built, I was overwhelmed with disbelief. It was one hundred years after Leonidas C. Dyer (a Republican from Missouri, who served in the House of Representatives from 1911 to 1933) introduced a bill for an African American monument (the first legislation was introduced in 1915 for a memorial for Black soldiers who fought in the Civil War and other wars). I also found it ironic that fifteen years after I took the European tour, there was an African American museum. Just imagine now when people from all over the world visit the nation's capital to see all the achievements of white Americans, they will also be able to see the achievements of Black Americans as well.

As I strolled through the museum, I began connecting what I had just experienced in Egypt with what I was seeing there. I recognized that the African Americans who were fortunate enough to have their achievements and contributions exhibited in the NMAAHC are not only there for visitors all over the world to see, but also that they would be immortalized.

Although the NMAAHC is an extraordinary accomplishment, what I noticed (and always do) is that the sports and entertainment exhibits seemed to stand out more. I think it bothered me because African American achievements in sports and entertainment seem to be more valued than achievements in other areas. Although I know that it is a function of a superficial and materialistic culture that focuses on wealth (and all the things it can buy) and the way media exploits it (because of all the money sports and entertainment rake in), it still bothers me nevertheless. It is as if those who act or throw or maneuver a ball in extraordinary ways, (although there is something to say for such talent) are more valued than the thousands of people who commit their lives to other worthy causes. I also attributed it to the fact that it was because many of their descendants were still alive, and they had the items to donate or could make substantial financial contributions.

In addition, some African Americans in the sports and entertainment industry who are still alive could make generous contributions, earning them a statute of themselves, like Michael Jordan (he donated $5 million) or earning a space in the museum named after them, like the Oprah Winfrey Theater (she donated at least $13 million). Although I am sure their generous contributions were needed, it speaks to the fact that if you have the wealth, you can buy your way into immortality—something wealthy people have been doing for a long time. Even among the ancient Egyptians, it is not hard to see the vast inequalities that must have existed as only kings, queens, priests (who were supposed to represent the gods), and others with wealth and status had access to the substantial amount of resources it took to create statutes of themselves, and for their burial chambers. One can see why monarchies the world over were overthrown. However, at least among the ancient Egyptians (especially for kings and queens), the measuring stick was morality. In morally bankrupt societies like the United States, it does not matter what one does or who one harms to achieve the kind of wealth that allows them to buy immortality—at least in the earthly realm.

According to the ancient Egyptians, those who make it through the Hall of Judgment achieve eternal life and can visit their body at will. The face was painted on the sarcophagus to help the soul find his or her body. Since the soul may live around the body, visiting the grave and making offerings helps to keep the person alive. This explains the practice of libations, where African people set a plate of food and pour libations to their ancestors. One is considered alive as long as one is remembered. It also explains ancestor shrines; honoring the ancestors helps to keep them alive. The genius of the ancient Egyptians is that they left monuments so awe-inspiring that people all over the world want to visit their tombs, keeping them and the messages they wanted to share with the world alive, and potentially forever because they are etched in stone.

But I think it is even more to it than that. It speaks to the yearnings of all of us to feel relevant; to feel special, not only when we are alive, but also special enough to be remembered, even after death—for eternity.

PART III
UNVEILING CHRISTIANITY

20
CHRISTIAN QUESTIONS

Although I had been to Egypt three times and had been awakened (on some level) through the energy work and from what I was learning through the literature, I still was not clear. I had bits and pieces of information, but I was still not clear as to how it was all connected. And I still struggled with Christianity. Specifically, I could not understand why Black people found it so appealing. And considering how horrible white Americans had been to Black people, I could not understand why Black people would worship a white image of Jesus.

One reason that I struggled with Christianity is that I could not get that white, blue-eyed, blond hair image of Jesus that used to sit on my mother's mantle when I was a child out of my head. One day while in class, I asked the students, "When you think of God, what does he (or she) look like?" I left the question open, and we never discussed it. I wanted them to go home, think about the question, and work it out for themselves. To me, if you are a person of African descent and your image of God is white, then you have internalized white supremacy at its highest level.

From what I had learned while at Temple, I speculated that Black people were drawn to Christianity because Judaism (upon which it is founded) is based on African theology and because the Hebrews were African people. Or perhaps it was the promise of the coming of a savior, who will save us from oppression. Perhaps it is the extraordinary wisdom in the theology and the promise of eternal life, which I also suspected came from Black people. Maybe it is how powerfully the soul-stirring sermons are delivered by gifted Black ministers.

Or is it because the church offers the only place where Black people can be independent, where we can commune with each other, where we can be free, without having to wear the mask; a place where we can lay our burdens down? Where else we can cry, scream, shout, and fall apart without being judged? Sometimes when I visit Black churches, I feel like I am walking into a pit of pain. Once, a young woman standing next to me began sobbing so, I was shaken to the core. I wanted to reach out to her and hold her and tell her everything is going to be alright, but I froze as I fought to hold back the tears. I guess I feared that my pain might start flooding out, and I would fall apart too. Sometimes, I let the tears flow, but only so much, as I go to that place deep within, pleading with God, "Please help our people. Please help humanity."

Whatever the case may be, I struggled with Christianity. I knew the truth was there because of the way it resonated with my soul. When I first moved to Atlanta, I must have visited every church in my community and some outside of it: famous mega-churches, small, medium, and large; non-denominational; Baptist; Methodists; and even the Shrine of the Black Madonna, which is founded on Black Liberation theology (defined by James Cone its primary creator, "as a theology that sees God as concerned with the poor and weak in society"). I eventually settled on Beulah Missionary Baptist Church, primarily because of how genuine the minister seemed (and because it is close to my house), but only visited from time to time when I got spiritually low or was seeking an answer to something. But something just would not let me join the church.

I could not get past what I had already learned about the history of Christianity, specifically its crimes against humanity. Also, something just did not sit well with me about the story of Jesus and who he was supposed to be. The idea that he is the only way to God also did not make sense to me. In addition, I had difficulty with what seems like fear-based theology and all the violence, especially in the Old Testament. This made it difficult to get through it, especially after attending energy classes that focused on love and light.

I thought about just abandoning Christianity altogether. But since it is supposed to have the largest following in the world (over two billion people), I thought it would be foolish to abandon it without further investigation. So, I did what I always do when I really need to understand something, I searched the literature.

Upon investigation this time, I would find that there is the conventional story told in religious textbooks (at least the ones written for college, general laypeople, and Christians) and the scriptures themselves. And there is alternative information that challenges the story surrounding the birth, life, death, and resurrection of Jesus, who he was, and to my surprise, whether he even existed at all! This section is a brief overview of Christian origins and its history (some of which is considered speculative by scholars and writers) and how African Americans became Christian. In Part IV, "Unveiling the Christ," I expand more on what some scholars speculate about the story of Jesus.

21
JUDEO-CHRISTIAN BEGINNINGS

I felt it necessary to begin my research on Christianity with the history of the peoples the religion is supposedly founded by the Hebrew people. Reading the Old Testament and the Tanakh, one cannot help but be moved by the fact that the Hebrew people were God-centered people. It seems they did nothing without being conversant with God. But this is not surprising. Peoples all over the world were God-centered, and they had relationships with and prayed to gods that, according to their theologies, the creator God put in place over both the cosmic and earthly realms. Almost nothing was done outside being conversant with the gods, especially for African people. The idea that Judaism is the first monotheistic religion and others were polytheistic is a misunderstanding and/or misrepresentation of peoples' spiritual practices by Western scholars, especially the spiritual practices of African people.

Although most people believed in a God who was the creator of the universe, some peoples' rationale for focusing on lesser gods or deities was that the creator God had too much to do attending to the universe, so he created a hierarchy of beings or powers to attend to affairs in both the cosmic and early realms. Even Hebrews consorted with "otherworldly" beings such as cherubim, angels, and archangels to guide them. African peoples had oral traditions (the Egyptians had both oral and written traditions and writings in caves and on stone are still being discovered all over the world). So, it is harder to ascertain the religious-spiritual practices of many African and other peoples throughout the world without being conversant with the keepers of their oral traditions. The Hebrews also had an oral tradition until it was put into writing.[75]

Generally, the history of the Hebrew people is intertwined with war and conflict. This history, although may not be intended to do so, reveals who the people were, and potentially the societies that influenced their culture, including their religious ideas. It has been speculated that the unpredictability of the violent storms and periods of flooding, alternating with droughts around the Tigris and Euphrates Rivers or Mesopotamia (the Greek name for "land between two rivers"), created competition for arable land, where the Hebrew people are supposed to have originated. This led to continuous conflict and warfare among the peoples who lived in these regions. Outlined in *Table 1* is a timeline showing their history in Mesopotamia, Egypt, and Palestine.

The Hebrew story as people all over the world begins with creation. And like most other people, creation began where they are. It then details how they left the city of Ur, settled into Egypt, their exodus out of Egypt under the leadership of Moses, who established their laws, the rise of the Kingdom of Israel (under Saul), and the subsequent kingdoms under David and Solomon and their conflicts, including their conquests and defeats. Since they lived among the Sumerians and the Amorites, spent four hundred years in Egypt, and settled among the Canaanites, Hebrew theology was likely influenced by all of these civilizations. In terms of Egyptian influence, Moses was raised among the Egyptian elite and was therefore likely to have been initiated into its priesthood. The Hebrews had been subjugated by the Assyrians (after the Kingdom of Israel was destroyed), the Babylonians, the Persians, the Greeks (until the Maccabean revolt in 166 BCE, where they were allowed independence), and then by the Romans (who were brutal especially against insurrections) as they struggled to maintain their cultural identity and political independence, until the revolt in 66 CE when they were crushed by the Romans in 70 CE.

Table 1

Hebrew Timeline

Mesopotamia	Palestine	Hebrews
5200-3500 Ubaid People 4000 Sumerian Civilization 4500 Uruk 2750 Dynasty of Ur 2334-2218 Akkadians 2000 Amorites	3500-2000 Nomads settle in the region	
1728-1686 Hammurabi Code-first code of law		2000 Reside in Ur, 2000 -1700 Settle into Palestine among the Amorites 1700 Go into Egypt
1595-1100 Staggering periods of Hittite dominance 1520-1170 Periods of Kassite Dominance	1550-1200 Palestine absorbed under Egypt	1400 Lead out of Egypt into the Sanai desert by Moses
1200-612 Assyrian Period	1276 Philistines arrive 1100 Philistines conquered Palestine, make Gaza their capital and gain control over the Hebrews	1200 Settle into Palestine and wage war against the Canaanites

	1080 Kingdom of Israel Founded 1000 David captures Jerusalem 931 Kingdom of Israel Hebrews divided into 2 states-Israel (10 tribes the wealthiest) & Judah (2 tribes)	970-931 King Solomon; First Temple Built
	722 Assyrians invade Palestine	Israel dispersed (lost tribes of Israel, State of Judah continues)
612 Fall of Assyrians 586/598 Chaldeans (New Babylon)	598 Babylon invade Palestine	The Kingdom of Judah destroyed, Jews transported to Babylon as slaves
539 Persians King Cyrus conquers Babylon	539 Palestine claimed by the Persian Empire	Jews return to Palestine, Second Temple Period
312 Seleucus (assumed bulk of territory Alexander conquered	334 Alexander the Great claims Palestine (bought 70 territories under Greece)	166 Maccabean revolt Jews regain independence
	63 Palestine taken over by Rome	Jews lose independence
	70 CE Romans squash Jewish Revolt	Jews defeated; the second Temple destroyed

*All periods refer to BCE unless CE is specified.

22
THE COMING OF A MESSIAH

The coming of a messiah (the word originating from the Egyptian word *messu*, which means "anointed one," "king," or "savior"), had been prophesized throughout Hebrew scriptures. Like most peoples throughout the ancient world, Jews were governed by divine or sacred kingship. The king was believed to represent God on Earth; he was a high priest and the intermediary between God, who expressed his will on Earth, and man. He was also a "political" messiah, who was supported and often controlled by a council of priests. Thus, the sacred and secular were indistinguishable, and the king was a religious, political, and military leader. Also, in many cultures throughout the world, there was the expectation that an "angelic" messiah (whether he was a king or not), someone who had attained the highest level of spiritual evolvement, would come every so often (six hundred to two thousand years) to help humanity.

By 63 BC Palestine was occupied by Rome, and the Judaic monarchy had all but been extinguished under Roman domination. There was the anticipation of the coming of a "messiah," a "king" who would deliver the Jews from the oppression of the Romans and reestablish a unified Hebrew state, like the one that existed in the time of David and Solomon. Such an individual would establish a righteous kingdom— the "Kingdom of God" or the "Kingdom of Heaven"—that among things, would fight against their captivity, oppression, and persecution, protect them from foreign invasions, enforce the laws of God that were given to Moses, and gather the Israelite people from around the world back to their land.

It is against this historical backdrop and within in this political milieu that Jesus (whose name was "Yeshua," in Hebrew, Jesus comes from the Greek word "Iesous," and is the transliteration of the Hebrew "Jeshua," "Joshua," or "Jehoshu.") was supposed have appeared around 30 CE, in Roman-occupied Palestine. Since it had been prophesized that such a person would be coming, and Jesus's followers may have thought that he might be that person, and Jesus himself (according to scripture) thought he was that person, then it is not a surprise that numerous scholars and writers have speculated that Jesus was a political messiah. Also, considering that the sacred and secular were not separate, one might speculate that being a political messiah also encompassed being a high priest, making him a religious-political king.

During its rule, Rome appointed promulgators or governors in the areas that it dominated, including Palestine. Within this political structure, the Jews consisted of four primary sects: Sadducees, Pharisees, Zealots, and Essenes.

Sadducees were the upper-class who served as administrators in the Roman state and as high priests in the Second Temple period. They believed in a strict interpretation of the written law, but did not believe in the oral law, and monopolized Temple activities and appointments. They also were socially more liberal and assimilated into Greco-Roman culture. The Sadducees did not survive after the destruction of the Temple in 66 CE.

Pharisees, who were the majority, emerged as a distinct group after the Maccabean revolt because of their different perspective regarding the law. They believed in both the written and the oral law—the teachings of the prophets—and followed the spirit of the law but preferred to interpret it in ways that reflected the times. They also did not assimilate into Greco-Roman culture and were at odds with the Sadducees because they were perceived to be collaborators with or "sell-outs" to the Roman government.

Zealots (named so because they were "zealous" for the law) were nationalists, who believed in war against Roman oppression and rule and were responsible for waging insurrections and continuous guerilla attacks against the Romans, for which they often suffered brutal executions.

Essenes (a term derived from the Aramaic term *aschai*, which means "a bather") separated themselves into ascetic communities and are believed to be the authors of the Dead Sea Scrolls or *The Book of the Disciplines*, discovered in 1947 in Qumran Caves in the Judean Desert of the West Bank. The Essenes were called "morning Baptist" or "morning bathers" because they bathed every morning to purify themselves from impurities. The Essenes followed Jewish laws but practiced more strict dietary laws (they were vegetarians) and did not believe in or participate in animal sacrifices. Some sources indicate they believed in equality of the sexes and practiced celibacy (although marriage was permitted by some).

In light of these sects and his ministry, there is speculation about Jesus's background. It has been speculated that he was a Pharisee because of his position on the law (he was literate in Jewish law). Others speculate that he was an Essene because his ministry seemed in line with their lifestyle: he mingled with both sexes and all classes, and he taught everywhere, not just in the synagogues, and Jesus was possibly an "angelic" messiah since they were expecting one. It was also speculated that he was a Nazarene; it was said that he was from Nazareth, but the city did not exist at the time (although a village may have, leading to the belief that it was a mistranslation).

There is speculation that Jesus may have been initiated into Egyptian and other mystery schools (during that time, Egypt was the go-to place for the highest level of learning and initiation into the mysteries), and that he was a *Therapeutae* (the Egyptian word for doctor or healer), which seem to be evident because of his miraculous healings. In addition, some speculate that Jesus may have acquired some of his knowledge from Buddhist philosophies because some of his teachings seem to echo Buddhism. Buddhist monks had been proselytizing in Alexandria during Jesus's time

Jesus supposedly appeared as an associate of John the Baptist (which seems to indicate that he was an Essene), who called for repentance and ritual washing, or baptism for "initiation" into Judaism. John the Baptist was speculated to have been associated with the Zealots, as indicated by the fact that he dressed in animal skins and ate nothing but locusts and wild honey. Jesus continued the ministry that John started after he was executed by the Roman procurator because his movement which preached "the Kingdom of God was at hand," was seen as potential for a rebellion, and thus was seen as a political threat to Roman rule.

According to the Gospels, Jesus was turned in by Jewish priests to be crucified by the Roman procurator Pontius Pilate. Since many Jewish sects existed, and it was common (and accepted) that many claimed to be the Messiah (all the Jews needed to do was let events play out to see if the claimant was really who he said he was), it is believed that the story that the Jews had Jesus executed was added later to promote the idea that he was just an "angelic" versus a "political" messiah, who would present a threat to the king of Rome.

After his execution, according to the Gospels, Jesus was resurrected and was supposedly seen by Mary Magdalene (which means "of the town of Magdala") and other disciples and followers, leading them to believe that he had physically risen from the dead. Forty days after his first appearance in the garden, the resurrected Jesus supposedly appeared to the disciples and ascended to heaven. After his ascension, the disciples were supposedly shaken by a force during the Pentecost (in Jewish tradition, forty days after the first harvest), which they believed to be the Holy Spirit. Because it was believed by some of his followers that he had resurrected from the dead, it was also was believed that Jesus would return and establish the Kingdom of God on Earth.

After the death of Jesus, the movement; referred to as the "Nazarene movement," the "Jesus movement," as well as the "Jerusalem Church," (although there was no definite church, just a way to describe a movement headed by James and Peter as there was only one Temple and synagogue) separated into two broad divisions.[76] In the first century, it was divided primarily between the apostles; James and Peter, who now headed the movement, and Paul who became an apostle after Jesus's death. In the second and third centuries, the division would become more marked by the Orthodox Church and the movement within the Church known as Christian Gnosticism (the Greek word for knowledge). Orthodox Church fathers would deem the Gnostic Church fathers as *heretics* and fight their doctrines which they considered *heresy*. In the Fourth Century at the Council of Nicaea, held in 325 CE, the Orthodox Church would adopt Paul's brand of Christianity, adopt many ideas from the Gnostics (and other mystery religions) and metamorphose them into Christian dogmas and rituals and then seek to destroy all Gnostic and other records.

23

JAMES AND PETER VERSUS PAUL

The first division in Christianity was between the apostles and Paul. After Jesus's death, the movement would be headed by James (it is believed that James led the movement because he was the successor to Jesus via his bloodline, which is characteristic of divine kingships, but only until Jesus returned), and Peter, who was a charismatic spokesperson and leader.[77] It is thought that the first converts to the Jesus movement were the Nazarenes, the Ebionites, and the Greek proselytes who had already accepted Judaism, its teachings, and many of its practices, without undertaking the whole of its law (specifically circumcision). The Nazarenes and Ebionites could have been sects within the Essenes and just called by different names. It is also thought that they were almost indistinguishable from the Pharisees because they adhered to Jewish law.

Although the apostles were gaining Jewish converts, it was primarily through Paul (formerly Saul) that the movement would spread to Gentiles (non-Jews). According to the Gospels, before Saul changed his name to Paul, he persecuted Christians by throwing them into prison and even played a role in Stephen (one of Jesus's seventy-two apostles) being murdered. However, Saul was converted when one day, while traveling to Damascus, he unexpectedly fell to the ground and experienced a vision of Jesus, who asked him, "Why do you persecute me?" after which he was blind for three days.

However, there are some speculations that Paul may not be who he said he was. According to the scriptures, Paul was a Hebrew of the Tribe of Benjamin and a Pharisee. Although Paul himself said that he was a Pharisee, and that that he had been trained under Gamaliel (a highly respected figure in the rabbinical writings and was given the title "Rabban," as the leading sage of his day), there is speculation that he may have fabricated his story: and that he was a Greek who had converted to Judaism (according to accounts from the Ebionites, who considered him a false prophet).[78] There is also speculation that his name changed from Saul to Paul after he had been initiated into a mystery system, and it was the mysteries that influenced his theology.

The apostles and Paul began to clash around beliefs about who Jesus was and how converts would be accepted into the fold. The apostles held that converts should adhere to Jewish law and did not see the faith as a new religion. Neither did Jesus, and it speculated that because he was a devout Jew, he would have been shocked at such a notion. As time went on, controversy emerged regarding whether Gentiles should be required to convert to Judaism, that is, become "full" Jews, being required to adhere to Jewish law (including their dietary laws and circumcision). Around 50 CE, it would be determined in a council of the apostles that Gentiles, like other "God Fearers," could be accepted into Judaism if they adhered to four of the seven primary laws: abstain from idol worship, fornication (adultery, incest, sodomy, and bestiality—premarital sex was not regarded as a grave offense), eating animals that have not been

drained of blood, and murder. The other three primary laws were robbery, eating limbs cut off from live animals (assumed to be implied by
the other laws), and an injunction to set up courts of law to administer
justice (which applied to nations that convert to Judaism). These laws
were Noahide laws, those of the sons of Noah, which the Gentiles or
"God Fearers" had to follow to become attached to Jews without becoming full Jews.[79]

With regard to who Jesus was, fundamentally, the Nazarenes and
Ebionites believed that Jesus was a human being, born to Mary and Joseph; that he was a wise man; that he had died and been miraculously
resurrected; and that he went to paradise and would return to establish
the Kingdom of God on Earth. However, although he never met him,
Paul started preaching a different message about who Jesus was, essentially a "new" religion, and was promoting that people could come into
the faith, without adhering to Jewish law in general and circumcision in
particular. When Paul's message; essentially that Jesus was an "otherworldly," or "divine" being vs. a "this-worldly," "human" being, who
came to Earth to be "sacrificed," to atone for our sins, was found to be
unacceptable by the apostles (and the Pharisees) he re-envisioned himself as an apostle to the Gentiles and turned to recruit non-Jews by offering them minimal adherence to Jewish law; particularly circumcision
(understanding that it would be deterrent) which was later accepted in
the council of the apostles (around 50 CE).

Jewish resistance to Paul's message under his "new religion" is revealed primarily in Acts of the Gospels, where his life was threatened
several times and some Jews even conspired to kill him. He also underwent a trial in Rome, and it is where it is believed he was eventually murdered somewhere between 64 and 67 CE during Nero's Persecution of
Christians.

Under Paul's "new" religion, all one had to do is believe in the Gospels about Jesus, join him through faith, accept him as one's lord and
savior, pray in his name, accept baptism (initiatory rebirth), and one had
access to all the privileges that were available to the Jews. This meant
that not only Jews, but non-Jews could have a personal relationship with
God; access to the Kingdom of God, and the potential to gain everlasting life.

As the new religion began to stabilize, these themes found their way into the Epistles (Letters of Paul written 20-30 years after the crucifixion) and they along with the Gospels of Mark (65-70 CE), Matthew (70-80 CE), Luke (80 CE), John (date uncertain), and Acts (believed to be written by apostle Luke, 85-90 CE) and other Epistles of the apostles. Although these dates are given as to when the Gospels and the New Testament were written, there is no evidence that any of the writings existed within 120 years after the crucifixion, and further no evidence that they were written by eyewitnesses of the facts.[80] Paul's version of Christianity, however, would later become of the "New Covenant" as distinguished from the "Old Covenant between God and Abraham" or the "New Testament."

24
ORTHODOX VERSUS GNOSTIC CHRISTIANITY

The second division in Christianity that occurred in the second and third centuries had to do with differences between Orthodox and Gnostic Christians. Gnostic Christianity (the Greek word for knowledge) was based on knowledge and the initiate's mystical journey into self-knowledge as the pathway to the Divine; mystery religions that existed thousands of years before the advent of Orthodox Christianity. Orthodox Christianity was based primarily on Paul's theology (which was based on the mystery religions—interpreted as literal vs. allegorical). The *Nag Hammadi Library,* a collection of 52 second-century Gnostic texts that were found in 1945, at an archeological site-Jabal-al-Tarif, in Nag Hammadi, a city in Upper Egypt, provides some insight into Gnostic Christianity. Their discovery is an interesting story.

According to Elaine Pagels, in *The Gnostic Gospels,* Muhammad Ali al-Samman, and his brothers (shortly before they had murdered to avenge their father's death) who were digging for *sabakh,* a soft soil used to fertilize crops, found the collection in a red earthenware jar. When they first stumbled onto the jar, they hesitated to open it for fear of releasing a jinn (a spirit). However, realizing the jar might contain gold they smashed it and discovered thirteen papyrus books, bound in leather. Muhammad Ali took the papyrus home and piled them on straw near an oven. Not knowing their value, his mother burned much of the papyrus in the oven along with the straw she used to kindle the fire.[81]

Later, fearing that the police investigating the murder would discover the books, Muhammad Ali asked a priest to keep one or more for him. The priest sent one of them to a historian to evaluate their worth. After that, some of the manuscripts changed several hands. They would be sold on the black market through antiquities dealers in Cairo, confiscated by Egyptian government officials, deposited in the Coptic Museum in Cairo (ten-and-half of the thirteen books called codices), smuggled out of Egypt (a large part of the thirteenth codex) and offered for sale in the United States. They would eventually find their way to a professor in the Netherlands and bought by the Jung Foundation in Zurich. Some of the texts also got caught up in a lawsuit and were held hostage by scholars who wanted "firstmanship" (to be the first to publish it) because it would give them international fame. The texts were eventually released, and after sixteen hundred years of being buried (it is believed that they may have been buried by a monk from a nearby Monastery of St. Pachomius in Upper Egypt) and over thirty years after their discovery, the texts would be translated by a collaborative effort from scholars from all over the world and published by Harper and Row in 1977.[82]

Because the Gnostic texts vary ranging in type (from poems to letters to the gospels by some of the disciples themselves—those excluded from biblical canon), and in content (descriptions of God, the origins of the universe, the origins of man, instructions, secret knowledge, etc.), it is difficult to make a definitive statement about them. What they do reveal is that some of the ideas were contrary to Orthodox Christian doctrine (which was based on Paul's "mystery" theology) and perhaps, secret knowledge that Orthodox Church fathers wanted to keep from the laity. Some of the Gospels that were excluded from the biblical canon include the *Gospel of Mary*, the *Gospel of Thomas*, the *Gospel of Phillip*, the *Gospel of Truth*, and the *Gospel to the Egyptians*. Some of the books attributed to the disciples are the *Apocryphon* (secret book) *of John*, the *Apocryphon of James, the Book of Thomas the Contender*, etc.

Some Orthodox Church fathers devoted their lives to refuting and denouncing so-called *heresies*. In fact, most of what we knew about the Gnostics, could only be found in these refutations before the discovery of the *Nag Hammadi Library*. Some of the most renowned fathers include Justin Martyr, Hippolytus in *Refutations of All Heresies*, Tertullian, in *Prescriptions Against the Heresies*, and Bishop of Lyons, Irenaeus in *The*

Destruction and Overthrow of Falsely So-called Knowledge which was written in five volumes. Among those whose doctrines were bitterly attacked and refuted were Basilides, Marcion, Valentinus, Gnostics, and numerous other sects. Interesting to note is that Tertullian, an African Bishop, condemned the pursuit of knowledge as heresy, and said that one should not even enter into a discussion about it; as it leads to confusion, and the "rule of faith," should be one's only guide (even if it does not make sense). Although the conflict may have begun with theological differences such a conflict would eventually lead to the Orthodox Church using its version of Christianity (Paul's version) to establish political authority and using such power to condemn any doctrines not in line with its own as *heresy*, and those who promote it as *heretics*.

Although the Orthodox and Gnostic Church fathers and may have varied in their perspectives below are some general differences between the two:

• Orthodox: There is only one God who created everything. God, Jesus his Son, and the Holy Spirit are one substance. God incarnated in the flesh as Jesus Christ to save us from our sins. Jesus died and was resurrected in the flesh and later ascended to heaven. All one needs to do is accept Jesus as one's lord and savior, ask for forgiveness of one's sins, get baptized, and participate in the Holy Communion. It is about faith.

• Gnostic: The God that Christians naively worship as the God of the Universe, or the Supreme Being is the "Creator," a "second God." The God of the Universe; God of the "preexistence" "the depths," the Supreme Being (who created the "second" God would not need to be "jealous," nor would he have to establish that "I am God and there is no other.") The "Creator God" "second God" is the God that the Jews worship.

The way to God is through self-knowledge which is a lengthy process that one matures into before one is initiated into the mysteries. When man matures into gnosis (knowledge) he will learn that it is through self-knowledge that he comes to know the true God. Once he comes into true knowledge, gnosis, he is liberated from the control of the "Creator God." Jesus was a man in a physical body, who received the Christos when he was baptized, and it left him when he was crucified—thereby he died a man and was resurrected in spirit. Jesus as redeemer received the Christos, to show us the way to redemption, which is to redeem man from ignorance that blinds him.

25

ESTABLISHMENT OF ORTHODOX CHRISTIANITY

For the Orthodox Church to establish its authority, according to Pagels, it first had to establish the successorship of the bishop through Peter. Since it was unlikely that Jesus gave Peter authority while he was alive, since Jesus had predicted during the last supper that Peter would deny him three times before the rooster crowed, it had to be established that Jesus gave Peter authority after his death, even though his brother James became the head of the Jerusalem Church as his bloodline, heir to the "throne."

To do this, the Orthodox Church had to establish that Jesus had a "physical" resurrection, not only to give Peter authority but also to make the resurrection a historic event.[83] Also, as Pagels notes, we know that Peter claimed that the resurrection happened, and we know that he took charge of the group as its leader and spokesman. However, the Orthodox Church took it further; by stating that Peter was the first to see Jesus after the resurrection, it legitimized his authority as the successor to him, although, according to the Gospels of Mark and John, Mary Magdalene—not Peter—was the first to witness the resurrection. In the *Gospel of Mary* (which was excluded from the Bible), she says she saw Jesus in a vision.[84] In addition, establishing that only the apostles had the power to ordain future leaders as successors, in effect put the power to determine who would be the authority to a select few.

Important to note is how the three-tier hierarchy in the development of Christianity helped the Orthodox Church become established. At first, followers of the new faith met in private meetings in homes and catacombs (underground tombs and passageways that people used for religious practice). As Christian beliefs, rites, and church organizations began to stabilize, it would lead to the development of early Catholicism (Catholic means "universal"). Church structures begin to form with *episcopos* ("overseer" or "bishop") assisted by a council of *presbyteroi* ("elders" or "priests") and deacons ("severs"), whose special duties were to care for the needy. The church, becoming the center of life for many, served as a mutual aid society and a place for religious fellowship. As Orthodox Christianity continued to evolve, the bishops governed the church in geographical areas called dioceses, and the parish priests led the communities in which the church got a foothold. Those who governed major cities became known as archbishops.

Interesting to note is that because the Essenes were widespread, residing in both Judea and Egypt, had apostolic founders, divinely inspired scriptures, and the same allegorical mode of interpreting them, the same order of performing public worship as Christians, had parishes, churches, bishops, priests, deacons, and festivals that were identically the same as Christians, and had communities established in Rome, Corinth, Galatia, Ephesus, Philippi, Colossae, and Thessalonica (whom Paul addressed his letters to, as well as the doctrines of the Nazarenes), it is believed that they are the foundation upon which Christianity is founded.[85] However, because the Essenes all but disappeared by the second century, it is thought they may have been absorbed into the new Christianity because they were the original Christians before the term Christianity was being used, and those whose brand of Christianity did not fall in line with Orthodox Christianity would eventually be deemed heretics.

One way in which the Orthodox Church attempted to gain authority was to require every church to follow its hierarchal structure; this would put each under the authority of a bishop.[86] However, such a structure differed radically from that of the Gnostics. The Gnostics refused to rank their members into superior and inferior orders within a hierarchy and followed the principle of strict equality. Their meetings were held based on the drawing of lots, where all—men and women alike—could serve as a priest, bishop, or prophet. Because each meeting was held in such a manner, the role that participants played could never become permanent ranks.[87] Since the Gnostics believed that the God that the Orthodox Church worshiped was an "imitation" God, who had humanity under His spell, they were under no obligation to worship him; lest they be under the authority of those under the authority of this God. Some Gnostic fathers did follow the rules of the Orthodox Church; however, they also held private meetings, while others conducted their meetings according to their own rules.

As indicated earlier, for one to come into the "secret" knowledge of the Gnostics, they had to spend years in study that would lead to awakening before they would be initiated into the mysteries. This means that the Gnostics would only appeal to a small number of people which was acceptable for them. Also, being that they had purported to know secret knowledge made Christian Gnostics seem elitist, which Orthodox Church fathers viciously attacked.

Pagels notes that these major differences in how people would come into faith and the organizational structure may have been some of the reasons why the Orthodox Christian Church was eventually so success-ful. It was the ease at which members could join the faith and the ease at which new churches could establish their structure. However, it would be when the Orthodox Church gained military support from Rome and the penalty for heresy escalated that it would eventually gain power.

Although in its early stages Christianity was not officially recognized in Rome, its general policy was to tolerate all groups that did not present a clear threat to Roman rule. However, some Roman emperors did scapegoat Christians (primarily Christian Jews, who were the majority) and authorized their persecution when there was a threat to Roman sta-bility. For example, Nero (r. 54–68 CE) instigated their persecution to deflect blame from himself for a disastrous fire in Rome. It is believed that Paul was martyred during these persecutions. Persecutions were or-dered under Aurelius (r. 161–180 CE); Christians were fed to wild beasts. They were also persecuted under Decius (r. 249–251 CE), Valerian (r. 253–260 CE), and Diocletian (r. 284–305 CE), under whom the greatest and most widespread atrocities occurred during Rome's rapidly disinte-grating state.

In 300 CE, Armenia became the first nation to adopt Christianity as the religion of the state. In 313 CE, Constantine, along with Licinius, who ruled the Eastern part of the Roman Empire, became co-emperors and issued the Edict of Milan (312 CE), which was a decree of religious toleration and the decriminalization of Christian worship. Before that, Constantine was one of Diocletian's commanders and became emperor of the Western region of the Roman Empire after his death. Before go-ing to battle (of the Milvian Bridge) with the Roman emperor Maxentius, Constantine saw a cross of light over the sun and Greek words that trans-lates to "In this sign, you will conquer," which for him meant that he had protection under the Christian God. Others have said he saw "IHS," the Greek beginning of the name of Jesus.

In 325 CE, Constantine (after becoming the emperor alone; it is speculated that he had Licinius murdered in 323 CE) sponsored a council of bishops at Nicaea, which established that Jesus was one substance with God and was not created, because he saw it to be expedient to his imperialistic aims (discussed later). In 380 CE, Theodosius I outlawed the worship of "pagan" gods and made Nicene Christianity the official religion of the Roman Empire. By 389 CE, the council of bishops at Carthage rendered the final codification of the scriptures that were established as the New Testament.

Over time, several other councils were held where invited bishops squabbled over who Jesus was and the Trinity, and to condemn heresy or false teachings. However, the split now would be the differences between the Eastern Orthodox Church and the Western Church, both of which were vying for power. The Council of Chalcedon (451 CE) made the bishops of the most important cities, Constantinople (capital of the Byzantine Empire), Ephesus, Alexandria, and Jerusalem, patriarchs. The patriarch of the Eastern Orthodox Church (of the Byzantine Empire) was called the ecumenical or universal patriarch while the patriarch of Rome came to be called the Pope or the Supreme Pontiff because he was considered to be the successor to Peter, who was considered the successor to Jesus.

26
CHRISTIAN CRIMES

The Middle Ages marks the period when the Roman Empire fell to invading Germanic tribes (476 CE) Goths, Visigoths, Vandals, Saxons, Vikings, Franks, etc. With warfare within and between the various Germanic tribes and no single powerful secular government, the Catholic Church, with its central ecclesiastical form of governance, rose to become the dominant power in the West. In other words, the Catholic Church and its clergy became the central political authority throughout Europe, which meant the Pope became the senior civilian official in secular affairs in Rome, and bishops increasingly became the authority in civil affairs in other cities. Throughout the Middle Ages, papacy power depended upon the Pope's relationship with rulers of the various regions, some of whom attempted to carry out their political agendas (some even placing their administrators in the church hierarchy). Some

Popes (depending on how power-hungry and corrupt he was) used decrees or prohibitions, and indulgences (payment for the remission of sins), and threatened excommunication, to control rulers and force them to comply with the Catholic political-religious agenda.

The Catholic Church eventually lost much of its political power as the wealthy supporters (Barons) of kingdoms came to recognize the dangers of the church using its power to seize their land and property, using the crime of heresy or whatever other crime it could come up with. It was eventually reduced to an independent state in Vatican City; although because of its previous imperialism (starting in 313 CE), the Catholic Church (which includes independently owned and operated churches, institutions, and organizations) is now one of the largest nongovernmental landowners in the world with holdings estimated at 177 million acres of land; over 277,000 square miles.[88] It has more than 26,000 properties in the United States alone, including hospitals, long-term care facilities, schools, colleges, universities, housing developments, parking lots, etc.

Interestingly, during the Middles Ages (considered the Dark Ages in Europe, and one can see why), the papacy, Supreme Pontiffs—the so-called successors to Peter and Jesus, individuals who are supposed to represent God on Earth—were responsible for some of the most heinous crimes committed against humanity. Two practices that were authorized by the Church were the Crusades and the Inquisitions. The Crusades were religious so-called "holy wars" that were carried out by religious-military orders (recruited from criminal and mercenary classes) like the Knights Hospitallers, Knights Templars, and Teutonic Knights to stamp out heretics (the Gnostic Christians whose beliefs were different from Orthodox Christianity) and to wage war against the Turks, Muslims, and others who had invaded lands previously held under the Roman Empire.

The First Crusade (1096 CE) was against the Turks, who had invaded the Byzantine Empire, and Muslims, who had seized Jerusalem, conquered some lands in the Byzantine Empire and expanded to India, Central Asia, North Africa, the Middle East, Southern Italy, and the Pyrenees. However, when something with evil aims begins and is haphazardly done so, it is difficult to determine the direction it will go or what the outcome will be. Although some sources indicate that the Church initially did not see Judaism as a threat to Christianity and probably because it claims to be founded on it, under the First Crusade, called "the People's Crusade," thousands of Jews were massacred in what is called the Rhineland Massacres. For nearly two hundred years (1096–1291 CE) several Crusades were carried out. Many men were willing to join because of hopes of receiving absolution (remission of their sins and entry into heaven) and increasing the quality of their lives. As was promised by the papacy, some became extremely wealthy as they seized the properties of those they massacred. Ultimately, it is estimated that close to two million people were murdered in these brutal campaigns—so-called "holy wars" or Crusades for God.

Inquisition was another practice that was established to wipe out any spiritual-religious practice, not in line with Catholicism including Greek philosophy, Gnosticism, magic, divination, which were referred to as heresy, and apostasy (desertion from Christianity). In fact, the Greeks, Romans, and the Church fathers extracted the mystical aspects and "magic" of the Black Egyptians, where Greek philosophy, Gnosticism, and the mystical aspects of Judaism were derived from (to be discussed later). They used these powers to conquer and control the world and then to make sure that no one else could use such powers, made these non-Catholic spiritual-religious practices a crime.

Under the Inquisitions, an inquisitor would inquire into a belief or practice, determine whether the accused person was guilty of heresy, and attempt to teach them the correct doctrine or practice. If that did not work, they would turn them over to local authorities, who would establish a tribunal, prosecute them, and carry out punishments, which included but was not limited to wearing a big colorful X on the outside of their clothing, public scourge, confiscation of property, imprisonment, and execution. The original aim of the Papal Inquisition (established by Pope Gregory IX c. 1232) according to some sources, was to avert mobs and local authorities from outright murdering so-called heretics without going through the process. However, such a practice was used to confiscate property, enriching the inquisitors, local authorities, the clergy, and ultimately, the Catholic Church.

During European world expansion, the Spanish (1492 CE) and Portuguese (1536 CE) Inquisitions were operated completely under royal Christian authority throughout their colonies and territories throughout the world with the specific aims of forcing Jews and Muslims to convert to Christianity. In addition, an estimated five-hundred thousand people were burned at the stake for witchcraft throughout Europe between the fifteenth and seventeenth centuries. But worse than meeting such a fate, was the inhumane torture that so-called witches were subjected to, to make them confess and accuse others, who would also be tortured (to confess) and burned at the stake. All one needs to do is an Internet search to see the instruments of torture. It will make one ask as I did when I first discovered a book (which I do not recall the name) while at Temple; what kind of mind would come up with such instruments? What kind of human being (if that is what you want to call them) would want to bring that kind of harm to another human being?

Added to the Catholic Church's list of crimes against humanity is the 1494 Tordesillas Treaty in which it divided the world outside of Europe (370 degrees west of Cape Verde, off the coast of Africa) between Portugal (who got the world East of the line) and Spain (who got the world west of the line), without any regard for the millions of people who already lived in these lands. The need for labor in these newly so-called "discovered" Americas would eventually culminate into the Transatlantic slave trade, where European nations and Christian missionaries, who were claiming to "civilize" the so-called "savage," "infidel," and "heathen" people they would encounter. They were given permission to covet the land and natural resources and enslave, maim, and murder millions upon millions of people of color throughout Africa and the Americas. After that was done their political, family, kinship, and spiritual-religious structures were destroyed under colonialization—all in the name of Jesus. With all the crimes committed against humanity (which I just cannot seem to forget), if that does not turn one off from Christianity, I do not know what else would.

27

HOW BLACK AMERICA BECAME CHRISTIAN

Protestantism was essentially the outcome of a protest to some of the doctrines, practices, and abuses occurring under the Catholic Church. One abuse was how indulgences were being used. Indulgences were certificates that one could receive for engaging in acts of penitence or devotion to be remitted of their sins. They were issued by the Pope to decrease the amount of time a person would have to spend in purgatory—

an intermediate state that sinners supposedly go to (referred to as the fourth dimension in other spiritual-religious systems, where ancestors may reside, but not necessarily a hellish place) to be purified before entering into heaven. The problem was that indulgences were being issued without much consideration and essentially as a fund-raising mechanism for the church. The extensive rites and sacraments that Christians had to engage in under Catholicism were troublesome as well.

Martin Luther, who was troubled by the abuses and who saw the faith as more of an inner experience, spearheaded the protest by posting ninety-five theses or points of debate on the door of the All Saints Church in Wittenberg, Germany in 1517. Such an act would lead to the beginning of the Protestant Reformation, "reform" of the Church, and would eventually usher in a new style of Christianity, with one of the most significant tenets being that all people are equal before God. Over the next centuries, different sects within Protestantism developed, including but not limited to the Puritans, Baptists, Quakers, Methodists, Pentecostals, Seventh Day Adventists, etc., who were distinguished by variations in their theology, rites, and practices. Some of them were bought to America with the first English settlers.

According to Albert J. Raboteau, in *Slave Religion*, early on in American history, there was a great deal of controversy around converting enslaved Africans to Christianity. Although European nations used missionary work as a disguise for colonizing and robbing the world and urged the Christianizing of enslaved Africans and Native Americans, it would create potential problems on plantations. Planters were against it for several reasons.

One reason was that it would take up the day (Sunday) that was allotted for enslaved Africans to work the land that was given to some to feed and clothe themselves (so that slaveholders would not have to). Some also worked for the slaveholders on Sunday, which mean that they would lose profits from their labor. Another reason is that slaveholders would have to spend time instructing them, which would also detract from profit-making. Because of the language and cultural barrier, they reasoned that Africans could not be instructed because they were too 'brutish.'[89] Clergy even reported that some slaveholders could not be persuaded that Africans and Indians were other than beasts.

In an attempt to convince slaveholders to teach Africans about Christianity, they had to convince them that they were "not merely Slaves and upon the same level as Labouring Beasts, but as *Men*-Slaves and *Women*- Slaves," had "bodies" with "limbs and members," and "voices and continence" like themselves; they were capable of reason and understanding, and they had souls that were capable of being "eternally happy."[90] Essentially, they had to be convinced of their basic humanity and that the African was "thy brother."[91]

The greatest reason for the resistance was that it was thought that African Americans would begin to see themselves as equal brothers in Christianity and that they would have some claim to fellowship. Such a claim would have threatened the master-slave order. Thus, the idea of "spiritual equality;" the idea of treating them like men, caused many to reject the idea of Christianizing them.

Resistance to converting enslaved African Americans to Christianity, however, would gradually change with the revival movement, called the "Great Awakening" beginning in 1740. Blacks and whites would attend revival camps of the evangelizing Presbyterians, Methodists, and Baptists. An increase in the conversion of Blacks was due to several factors. One is that "in the heat of religious fervor, slaveholders became more indifferent about their own involvement and potentially the involvement of their slaves."[92] Another was the emphasis on the conversion experience versus religious instruction, making Christianity more accessible to illiterate enslaved Blacks and slaveholders. Religious leaders focused more on conversion and less on the process of religious instruction, minimizing complex explanations of doctrines, which made it easy to understand. There was also more focus on heavy emotion.

Another factor is that the "Baptists and Methodists did not insist on a well-educated clergy... All one need have is a converted heart and gifted tongue" to preach.[93] Enslaved African Americans who showed a talent for exhorting, exhorted to both Black and white audiences and there are accounts of a few enslaved African Americans, because of their talent for exhorting, being set free. Although they preached in both Black and white congregations, enslaved Black preachers became the predominant preachers under the authority of the slaveholders on plantations. Black preachers also became the predominant preachers for free Blacks when they became too numerous and separate services were held for them and when a separate church was formed when whites withdrew because Blacks were present.

Particularly interesting is that until some states passed legislation restricting Blacks from preaching, the Baptists gave more leeway to their Black members to preach. Baptist churches licensed and ordained those who felt they had the call to preach and demonstrated that they had the gift; Methodists licensed them as exhorters. The Methodist founders, John Wesley, Francis Asbury, and Thomas Coke were opposed to slavery, and it was the only denomination that attempted to institutionalize its opposition. Because of this stance, slaveholders attempted to keep enslaved African Americans away from the Methodists. At a Baltimore conference in 1780, the Methodists asked traveling preachers who held enslaved African Americans to promise to set them free, and in a later conference, even threatened to exclude ministers who failed to comply.

However, this would change when Coke was threatened by a mob, served with indictments in two counties in Virginia, and a woman offered fifty pounds to a crowd to give him one hundred lashes. Seeing Southern resistance to freeing enslaved African Americans, the Presbyterians, Baptists, and Methodists, who initially condemned slavery, shifted their stance to defending the conversion of African Americans to make them "better" slaves. Both Black and white preachers began teaching slaves to obey their "masters."

Although such messages of docility may have been taught by some Black preachers, there is evidence that others taught a different message: some African Americans began to equate spiritual equality and freedom with earthly equality and freedom. Some attempted to gain their freedom by escaping, while others being influenced by Christian ideology, used secret and religious meetings to recruit members and plan revolts such as the Gabriel Prosser plot of 1800, the Denmark Vesey revolt in 1822, and the Nat Turner rebellion in 1831, where sixty-five people were killed, with fifty-five of them being white.

Because of Baptist and Methodist openness, it is not surprising that by the end of the century with the Second Great Awakening in 1790, free and enslaved African Americans were among those swelling the ranks of the Baptists and Methodists and is likely the reason why both are the predominate denominations of African Americans today. The first known separate Black Baptist churches that were formed were the African Baptist or Blue Stone Church in 1758 in Mecklenburg, Virginia, and the Silver Bluff Church between 1773 and 1775 in Silver Bluff, South Carolina. The first Methodist church dates to 1787 when Richard Allen,

Absalom Jones, and other Blacks mistakenly worshiped in a gallery of St. George's Methodist Episcopal Church in Philadelphia; they did not know it was closed to Blacks and were pulled from their knees during worship. Subsequently, they withdrew from the church. The Free African Society, which assumed both secular and religious functions was founded in 1787, and from it came the first Bethel African Methodist Episcopal Church in 1794, with Richard Allen as the pastor. Because African Americans encountered racism and desired autonomy, a meeting was called by Allen to meet in Philadelphia to establish a new Wesleyan denomination, the African Methodist Episcopal Church (AME).[94]

Because the Black Church has been the primary American institution in which African Americans found independence, self-worth, dignity, and respect, continues to provide mutual aid and has been the foundation for social and civil rights activism (including the Civil Rights Movement), it is understandable why African Americans embrace Christianity to the level that they do. Some of the achievements African Americans made under the Black Church are astounding, including the founding of Black colleges and universities. The AME founded Wilberforce University in 1856, the first institution of higher learning founded by African Americans in the United States. It also founded Morris Brown in Atlanta, Georgia, in 1881 and the *AME Review*, the first Black journal. Some institutions of higher learning established by Black Baptists include Morehouse and Spelman Colleges in Atlanta, Shaw University in Raleigh, North Carolina, and other junior and four-year historically black colleges and universities (HBCUs). It also has several conventions including the National Baptist Convention, U.S.A, Inc., National Baptist Convention of America, Progressive National Baptist Convention, Inc., and other regional and state conventions.[95]

The answer to my question of why Christianity is the most followed religion in the world is because, with all the crimes of coercion, including outright torture and murder, people did not have a choice. By the time Church-sanctioned crimes would come to a halt, the job had already been done. Also was the ease with which people could come into the faith and establish an organizational structure. In nations where Christianity is the religion of the state, it is the only religion that most people are familiar with and it is the most accessible, especially in the United States. In some American cities, especially in urban centers where the majority of African Americans live, Christian churches are the most prevalent and can be found on almost every other corner.

But I would later find that there may be even more to it. There may be an even greater reason why African Americans find Christianity so appealing.

PART IV
JOURNEY TO CONSCIOUSNESS

28
A SEARCH FOR TRUTH

We are all on a journey.

But for many of us, we only become aware of this as we go through our journey, and as we awaken to the reality that we are one. Since most of us know our origins, at least in this lifetime, we just go on with the business of living. However, for some of us, whether we know our origins or not, there is a yearning. Our soul burns with the question of "Who am I?" As we search for an answer, this question becomes the larger question of "Who are we?"

I would first find the answers to these questions through Black Studies. Black Studies would lead me to Africa. Learning about the history and culture of African peoples, including their spirituality, would reveal to me who we were before we became "Made in America," "Negroes," African Americans, or Black people. Being conscious of the tremendous gifts African peoples had given the world and becoming conscious of African cultural practices, especially their spirituality, gave me a profound sense of connection, and explained a lot about African American cultural practices.

However, after years of being on my journey in African American Studies, my mother died. The shock of her death was so destabilizing, that I had no choice but to search deeper if I were going to survive her death. Overcome with grief, questions that kept whirling around in my mind for months on end were "Why do we come here to go through all that we go through, and then just die, disappear, as if we had never been here?" and "Where do we go after death, if anywhere?"

In African spirituality, there is a great deal of emphasis placed on our ancestors. I believed I had connected with my father on a few occasions after he died. When we found out that my nephew (who was more like a little brother) had contracted HIV, during a fit of grief over his pending death, I felt my father's presence and him telling me everything was going to be alright (other family members said they had a similar experience) and it had a calming effect on me. I saw him in a dream before one of my younger sisters died (which I was not aware that he was warning me about until after her death when I visited his gravesite). In a few other dreams, he lived up the street from our house on Ten Broeck Street (which said to me that he was close by). And in meditations, I would see the spirit of a younger man.

But I was not making any connections with my mother, especially through that pitiful shrine I had set up, and every time I would see her in my dreams, she was mute. I, however, did feel her presence at my sister's house a couple of times. Because I was not connecting with her, at least in a way that was satisfactory for me, I began to doubt whether this ancestors thing was real; whether it was just a figment of our imagination, because of how difficult it is to deal with the death of those we love.

One day, I called my sister Gina, who was more grief-stricken than I was, and said, "I know where Mommy is. She is in the freaking ground, that's where she is." Because I was struggling so much, I thought it might be time to try to find my biological mother again because it might help with the anguish I was experiencing and the deep disconnect I was feeling again. I had attempted to find her several times throughout my life but became extremely discouraged because adoption laws made it difficult and just gave up.

When I first attempted to find my biological mother, I contacted a private investigator, who was charging $5,000 at the time, which in my twenties was not possible to come by at all. I had somehow gotten a copy of my original birth certificate when I was in high school but lost it. I, however, had looked at it so many times, I remembered the information on it. When I tried to get another copy of it (with my birth name), I received a letter stating that I (or at least the person with that name) did not exist. Disgusted, and frustrated to tears, "Oh, so I don't exist," I kept repeating over and over.

Another time, I called the woman (who I believe was trying to help me) who at first called me to ask some questions before she sent me the birth certificate of the woman she thought might be my biological mother. I called her back to ask some questions and she said that she did not know what I was talking about. I later found out the name and location of the maternity home that I was born in and wrote them to request my records. I received a letter stating that they could confirm that I was born there, but that was all the information they could provide me. I called my mother's attorney who handled the adoption to ask if he would assist me, and he said, as far as he was concerned, an adoption never took place. I finally called another attorney, and she indicated that under New York State's adoption laws, my birth records had been sealed.

This time, with the Internet making it easier to find people, the cost to find someone had gone down. I sought out a private investigator (PI) who only charged $950, and a few weeks later, she called me to tell me that she had found my mother. Ironically, ten years earlier, a PI referred to me by a colleague had already found her and had given me a list of possibilities, with her being the first on the list. Because her married name sounded Chinese, I was skeptical, and therefore did not follow through on it. After the PI gave me her contact information this time, saying she was 150 percent sure it was my mother, I called her. We met and began to cultivate a relationship

Although finding my biological mother helped me stabilize because it filled a gaping hole that it seemed nothing could fill, it still did not satisfy my soul. The awakening with the energy work had stimulated something much deeper. However, still not quite sure of what I was seeking, I continued to search the literature. As I searched, a few questions came to me: "What did the earliest humans, at least those that we know of, have to say about our origins?" Might not they have an answer to this question as well as other age-old questions of why we come here, why there is so much suffering, and what happens after death?" I would find that a lot of what the ancients said was shrouded in mystery, available only to the devout seeker. Only through years of study and practice would one be privy to the highest level of knowledge—although whatever that knowledge was, much of it had been purposely destroyed (discussed later). Fortunately, some of what was left or dug up are now accessible on the Internet.

However, in any course of any study, one needs a guide to point one in the right direction. Otherwise, you may find yourself stumbling around in the dark (as was the case with me). Although I did receive some information, in the energy classes, I felt like I needed more to be clear. I needed to know how it was all connected, and somehow, I knew finding out the origins of Christianity might provide the link. While searching, I came across an ancient Egyptian saying: "When the student is ready, the teacher (or master) will appear." I found this to be true. When you are seeking the knowledge of the ages, it will find its way to you. And in most cases, it will not come to you until you have awakened enough to receive it. If it comes before that time, you will find yourself reading what you find over and over, which is what I was finding myself doing.

Each time I would encounter a different religion or spiritual system, I would find that it has its own body of knowledge and/or scriptures. Trying to read the scriptures, let alone grasp the deeper and hidden meanings behind them, is almost impossible to do for a single religious or spiritual system, let alone more than one in one lifetime (or at least the life I have left), especially without a guide. As I continued to search, specific knowledge of different religions came to me based on the questions I was asking. I, therefore, did not come by what I found in any systematic way, and what I did find, I would review it enough just to get a general understanding of it.

Some of what I share in the pages that follow came to me directly from the universe as I interrogated it, and then I would find literature to affirm it. Other insights came through someone I may have met, but mostly through the works of others. The underlying question for me at this juncture became "What is the truth?"

According to the wisdom of the ages, there are two paths to truth. One way is through knowledge, and the other way is through practice. Practice includes the cultivation of virtues, meditation, contemplation, purification, piety, etc. If one comes to the truth by either path, there might be such a thing as self-initiation. Although there is much more knowledge from the ages, I am sharing that which I found to be most significant, based on the questions I needed answers to in my journey. If you have found this work, my hope is that helps you with yours.

29

GODS ON EARTH OR ANCIENT ASTRONAUTS?

One day, before doing the more extensive search on religion and Christianity, Tim and I went to a YouTube channel that we watch on television occasionally and stumbled onto a video that would leave us stunned, sitting looking into space. The narrator suggested that heaven was not just out in the cosmos, as we had always imagined it to be, but a specific place or planet in the cosmos. I was also taken aback by another video that we stumbled upon about the Anunnaki, whom the creators essentially suggested were ancient astronauts from somewhere in the cosmos who had at one time come to Earth and enslaved humanity. There was something about the story that resonated with me, and during that time, there was a nagging feeling that I should go back and look at *The Holy Tablets* by Malachi York again.

As I began to read the first chapter, this time something said, "There is truth here; keep reading." I would have another paradigm shift and would spend days in contemplation. Before the advent of religion, most people's mythos contained stories of gods visiting Earth from the cosmos. Based on what I was reading *in The Holy Tablets*, two major questions occurred to me:

'Suppose who we are calling gods are beings from somewhere else in the universe, another planet? And suppose, just suppose that beings from somewhere else in the universe were involved in the creation of humanity?"

As I continued to read *The Holy Tablets*, I realized that the work contained mounds of knowledge, but as I had asked before, I asked, "Where is he getting this information?" I went to the introduction. York indicated that the work was inspired by numerous other works that contained the knowledge of the ages. I had found on the Internet that York had studied in Egypt and that he had connections with imams abroad. I wondered whether he had been initiated and was privy to information that the uninitiated are not privy to. But as I continued to read, I would find that much of the information seemed to be derived from the Abrahamic (Judaism, Christianity, and Islam) and Eastern religions. The book also contains a lot of information that is based on science. What was interesting, however, is the extensive amount of information in the stories about the creation of the universe, our solar system, Earth, and the Anunnaqi (his spelling).

According to *The Holy Tablets*, The All (the creator of the universe) appointed Anu, an Anunnaqi who is known by different "tones" (i.e., names) as El Eloh, Yahweh, Allah, and God to head the Anunnaqi. Anu appointed other Anunnaqi known in tones as Eloheem, Neteru, etc. to be caretakers of our solar system. Much of the extensive information and stories regarding the events and affairs of the Anunnaqi, including their decision to create human beings, I would later discover, were derived from the Sumerian tablets. Revealed in *The Holy Tablets* also is the creation of good (from the agreeable Anunnaqi) and evil (from the disagreeable Anunnaqi) and the events and affairs of the Anunnaqi (Anu, his sons Enki and Enlil, and the other great gods). Included were also stories about the agreeables and disagreeables (from whom Satanists, Luciferians, Reptilians, etc., who are from different galaxies and planets, evolved). In addition, contained in *The Holy Tablets* are some of the biblical stories, including but not limited to the story of Cain and Abel, and Jesus's story (which includes information not found in the Bible and with an interesting spin—particularly, that Simon had been crucified, not Jesus).[96]

What I found most interesting is not only how extensive the information about the affairs and events of the Anunnaqi (gods) is, and the extensive amount of time it took for these events to occur, but also that most of the events predate the Genesis story of the flood! Even more astounding is that throughout *The Holy Tablets* is the beautiful art that depicts the Anunnaqi and most of the prebiblical and biblical characters as Black people with wooly hair! How empowering is this for Black people? No wonder the powers locked York up and threw away the key. York was sentenced to 130 years in prison.

An Internet search on the Anunnaqi would lead me to ancient alien/astronaut theorists, some of whom I was already familiar with. For example, I already knew about Giorgio Tsoukalos and David Hatcher Childress from watching *Ancient Aliens* on the History Channel, a series that documents ancient ruins throughout the world. Because of how advanced some ancient societies were, some ancient astronaut theorists speculate that the advancements of ancient peoples came from astronauts who traveled to Earth from somewhere in the cosmos, or at least they had learned from them. Searching specifically for information on the Sumerians would lead me to Zecharia Sitchin.

I would find that Sitchin was the most prolific of the writers who wrote about the ancient astronauts and had numerous works. I decided to read *the 12th Planet* since I believed his first work would lay out the premise for his following works. Although this work seems to be written for a popular audience (as opposed to an academic audience) it is supported by scientific evidence. Sitchin provides extensive information from transliterations primarily from Babylonian tablets (which he, as well as other scholars claim, are forgeries of the Sumerian tablets) and numerous other works to support his theory of ancient astronauts. Based on biblical history, scientific evidence (or lack of it), and speculation, Sitchin then comes to his own conclusions. The stories are quite like those in *The Holy Tablets*. However, I think the difference between the two is that York's renderings of the Anunnaqi are ethereal (light) beings (which we cannot see) while Sitchin's are anthropomorphic, physical beings.

According to Sitchin's transliterations, the Anunnaki (also referred to as Nefilim, "gods of heaven") came to Earth on Nibiru, which is a planet (and home of the gods), which serves also as a spaceship, that orbits the solar system every thirty-six hundred earth-years and carries with it smaller spacecraft by which these ancient astronauts traveled to Earth. Once getting to Earth, Anu returns to his heavenly abode but leaves his two sons, Enlil (god of the sky and later god of the earth) and Enki (god of the earth, who later becomes Ea, the god of the deep waters) and an Assembly of Seven (other Anunnaki great gods), who Enki makes commanders of cities on Earth. A total of nine hundred Anunnaki were involved in this undertaking that began approximately 450,000 years ago, with three hundred being Igigi, who navigated the space flights (and stayed on the spacecraft) and six hundred who came in groups of fifty at a time to Earth.

The original place of landing when Enki first came to Earth was the ocean. Subsequent landings were in Tigris-Euphrates, "the land of two rivers" area in Mesopotamia, which was the place of choice for landing and a spaceport for travel back and forth, according to Sitchin, because it was the most suitable of the other two potential places (the Nile and Indus Valley) because it is long and flat. Also, because of the need for petroleum (fuel for space travel), the Tigris-Euphrates area was the most suitable because it contains some of the world's richest oil fields, and its "bitumens, tars, pitches and asphalts, flowed up to the surface naturally."[97] Although the Nile has oil, the area must be drilled to bring up the crude oil, and Indus Valley has no oil.

The primary reason the Anunnaki came to Earth was to mine for gold, "the metal of the gods." Under the rulership of Anu, Enki, Enlil, and the rest of the Assembly of Seven, the other Anunnaki provided labor, mining for gold (a much-needed resource for Nibiru) in the "lower world," the South African mines. Because the Anunnaki felt exploited and overworked, they staged a mutiny where they burned their tools and surrounded Enlil's house, who is now at the helm of the gods' rulership on Earth. Enlil calls a meeting with the Assembly of Seven, summoning his father, Anu, to leave his heavenly abode and join them, and they meet to address how to deal with the mutiny. Anu, who had already heard their cries in heaven, has compassion for the laboring Anunnaki. and decide that the workload is too heavy. Enki comes up with an idea: create a primitive worker to "bear the yoke," to carry the toil of the gods. The Assembly of Seven voted and accept this proposition.

The Assembly then summoned Ninti (who was called by various names such as "midwife of the gods," "mother of the gods,' "birth goddess," "lady who gives life," and "lady whose hands opens") to create a *Lulu*, a man or a primitive worker. At first, the Anunnaki attempted to create a worker by mixing apewomen with animals. This resulted in creatures that look like humans with wings, lions with human heads, and so forth, similar to what you see in pictures in ancient Greek stories. This led to the conclusion that the only mixture that would work would be one with apewoman and the Nefilim themselves. Then at a *shimiti* ("house where the wind of life is breathed in"), Enki prepared "a purifying bath" and Ninti mixed the blood of a slain Anunnaki, with clay (Adamu-which means dark red-dirt soil) and Adapta, (biblical Adam), or *Homo sapien*, who would be the "model man" was created.[98]

Sitchin indicates that the work of Ninti and Enki was, in reality, genetic manipulation, where the sperm of a male god was inserted into the egg of an apewoman, *Homo erectus*. After the model man was created, fourteen more birth goddesses were assembled, and "seven bought forth males, and seven bought forth males."[99]

After a time, humankind became so wicked, even engaging in abominations that lead to the defilement of the purity of the younger gods,

Enlil sought to destroy them. He first tries pestilence and sickness, but that does not work. He then tries famine. This leads to such extreme starvation and deprivation that Earthlings began to practice cannibalism; that did not work either as they continued to multiply. Sitchin suggests that this is because Enki, who was not in agreement with his brother Enlil and the great gods, went around their decision, finding ways to feed humanity.

Since neither of these tactics worked, another council of the Assembly of the Gods was called, and it was decided that the way to destroy humanity was to not tell them about a coming flood. Although he took an oath (that he did not want to take) with the other gods to keep the coming flood a secret, Enki, who loves mankind and does not want to see his creation destroyed, instructed Utnaptashim to build a ship for his family and to make room for two of every kind of animal. Utnaptashim does so and allows those who helped him build the ship to board it as well.

When the flood was about to occur, the Anunnaki, "trembling" with fear, cram into space crafts, leave Earth, and orbit it as they watch it become engulfed by water. However, as they watch humanity turn to clay, they feel deep sorrow. Not realizing how close they had become to the Earthlings, they become grief-filled, and deeply regretted their decision to not tell humanity about the flood. Enlil, on the other hand, was upset when he finds that the seed of humanity survived the great flood and suspected that Enki revealed the secret to Utnaptashim. When Enlil inquired as to whether Enki had done so, he responded that Utnaptashim was able to get the information himself as he was "an exceedingly wise man.

Feeling bad about what happened, the Anunnaki decree to work with humanity and to teach them information that only the gods were privy to, such as the art of agriculture, domestication of animals, etc. Divine kingship was then passed from heaven to Earth, where the kings were chosen by the gods and served as intermediaries between the gods and humanity. This, according to Sitchin, is how divine kingships, practiced throughout the ancient world, particularly in Mesopotamia, Egypt, and the Indus Valley originated. Interestingly, like the Sumerians, the Egyptians claimed that the gods lived among them and were their first kings.

Sitchin proposes that a primary reason why there may be truth to the stories found in the Sumerian tablets, particularly those about the creation of humanity, is the gap of time between when man's ancestor, apes, first appear on the scene (some 25,000,000 million years ago) and the length time it takes them to evolve to ape-like men some two million years ago, and then the sudden appearance of the *Homo sapiens* some 200,000 to 300,000 years ago. The question, according to Sitchin, is what happened in the middle? Perhaps it could be that humanity was created through genetic manipulation by ancient astronauts. If humanity first evolved from apewoman and then was genetically manipulated by alien astronauts, the theory of evolution does not conflict with creation; they go hand-in-hand.

Another reason that Sumerian stories may be true, according to Sitchin, is that within the twenty-five thousand tablets that were found, the stories of the creation of the universe, solar system, and the Earth, and the events of Anunnaki are written as if they were a matter of fact, just like the other records of their day-to-day living. Additionally, some of the stories are consistent with the biblical stories in terms of the unfolding of events and the time in which they occurred. In addition, the sudden rise of Sumerian civilization, a period when there were extensive advancements in building, writing, music, art, etc., their complex legal system and extensive educational system which dates as far back as 3800 BC (although *Homo sapiens* can be found to exist some 200,000 years ago) may indicate ancient astronaut influence. This is especially since some claim to have no idea of who the Sumerians were, where they came from, or how and why their civilization appeared (although there is now evidence that the early Sumerians were Ubaidian people of non-Semitic origin–code words for African people, who settled in southern Mesopotamia).

~~~~~~~~~~~

Written before Sitchin's work about ancient astronauts is Erich Von Daniken's *Chariot of the Gods*. In this work, Daniken makes the case for his theory that whom the ancestors call gods could very well have been astronauts from another planet, who had the technology to navigate the cosmos in the same way that if we were to land on another planet with technology we currently have. If we found people who were technologically speaking 5,000 years behind us, they might think of us as gods. Given the estimated number of species that live on Earth (8.7 million), how persistent life is (bacteria can exist in extreme temperatures, deadly chemicals, and in lethal water surrounding nuclear reactors), the age of the universe (thousands of millions of years old) and how vast the universe is, it is highly likely that there are other planets with favorable conditions that can support other or similar intelligences.

Daniken supports his case with technology that is found all over the ancient world such as precise maps that could only have been derived from an aerial view (e.g., the Turkish navy admiral Piri Reis' map); gigantic parallel lines found in Nazca, Peru (which seem to indicate an air field); enormous drawings on the mountain sides in many parts of Peru (one, which is 820 feet high, carved on the high red walls of the cliffs in the Bay of Pisco, and can be seen from a distance of at least twelve miles); precise calendars (the Mayan calendar, with calculation to last for sixty-four million years); the great Idol of Tiahuanaco (over twenty-four feet long, twenty tons and records the state of the heavens 27,000 years ago); huge structures or stones (e.g. a stone block in Sacsahuamán, near the Inca fortress in Cuzco, some estimate to range from 120 to 300 tons); and other megalithic and architectural structures (the Great Pyramid of Giza, 570,000 square feet at the base and 2.3 million stone blocks at 5.9 million tons of mass). In addition, people themselves from all over the ancient world, such as the Pre-Inca people, Sumerians, Assyrians, and Egyptians, have similar stories, saying that the stars are inhabited and that gods traveled through the heavens in fireships and sky boats, came, and left, some promising to return.

Cave drawings of figures wearing bulky space or diving suits, helmets, and antennae (or horns), and flying vehicles with wings and wheels (metal birds) are also found all over the world. The "Mahabharata (Indian scripture), the Bible, the *Epic of Gilgamesh* (Sumerian), the texts of the Eskimos, the American Indians, the Scandinavians, the Tibetans, etc. tell the same story of flying gods, strange heavenly vehicles and frightful and catastrophes connected with them."[100] In addition, the Mahabharata (Drona-Parva and Karna Parva) and the Bible (in the Story of Lot and Sodom and Gomorrah) chronicle airships that sprout fire, quicksilver, and other weapons mass of destruction that has effects similar to hydrogen and atomic bombs.

David Hatcher Childress in *Technology of the Gods* provides extensive information on the advanced technology of ancient societies throughout the world. It includes everything from electricity to heavy machinery to atomic weapons. He, however, argues that ancient man was as intelligent as we are today, and were the originators and creators of ancient architecture and technology. To name a few some include elaborate and advanced sanitization sewage and plumbing systems; bathrooms with toilets; ceramic and colorful basins and bathtubs; massive irrigation, dams, and hydraulic systems found in Egypt, Ethiopia, and Arabia; wet chemistry and lead-based technology to make cosmetics; soap (comes from Egyptian word *swab*); fleets of ships in Egypt; earthquake-resistant houses; seismographic technology; mechanical clocks; gunpowder, tear gas, typewriters, etc. found in China; and other technology found all over the world. *Ancient Aliens: The Official Companion Book* contains essays from astronaut theorists Eric Von Daniken, Giorgio Tsoukalos, David Hatcher Childress, and other producers of *Ancient Alien* on the History Channel; some of whom have authored their own works as well. In addition, are others with different slants such as Graham Hancock's works, *Fingerprints of the Gods,* and *Magicians of the Gods*, who claim that some catastrophic event wiped out earlier civilizations.

Unfortunately, a lot of information about ancient societies was lost because ancient texts were destroyed due to attempts to suppress knowledge. An ancient book in South America (which was supposed to contain all the wisdom of antiquity) was destroyed by the sixty-third Inca ruler Pachacuti IV. Thousands of texts were burned in South America by zealous and fanatical Christian monks and missionaries. Five-hundred thousand volumes (which were supposed to have all the traditions of mankind, and housed the book entitled *The True History of Mankind over the Last 100,000 Years*), were partly destroyed by the Romans with the burning of the Library of Alexander; and the rest were burned on the order of Caliph Omar centuries later, and by Moslems to heat baths. An unknown number of texts were burned by the converted Paul (of the Bible) at Ephesus. Two hundred thousand works (astrological, historical, and philosophical) were ordered to be destroyed by the Chinese emperor Chi-Huang (builder of the Great wall) in 212 BC, for political reasons.[101]

A few that survived, speak of advanced civilizations and the cataclysms that destroyed them. Similarly, they talk about wise people who lived in harmony with the earth and knew the working of things. However, at some point, because man fell out of harmony with nature, catastrophe struck the whole Earth. Unfortunately, we find ourselves re-peating the patterns of our ancestors.

Although I do not think the ancient astronaut theory is far-fetched, there are some problems with the way the term "civilization" (which means an advanced stage of social and cultural development and organ-ization) has been used. In Western scholarship, civilization has histori-cally been undergirded with notions of earlier man (who made fewer ma-terial advancements) as uncivilized, unintelligent, "savages." Such no-tions led to the enslavement, colonization, and genocide of peoples all over the world by Western nations. However, to suggest that because some societies were more "civilized" than others, simply because they made more material advancements, would be like saying that because the United States has made more material advancements than other peoples throughout the world, it is more "civilized." Although earlier societies may have not made as many material advancements, does not mean that they were less intelligent than modern man. It may be a matter of what they focused on. In fact, because many societies were spiritually focused and lived in harmony with nature, they may have not wanted to use more than they needed.

As we know, Western nations are far more developed than other parts of the world primarily because of centuries of slave labor and from the pilfering of the natural resources of nations of color. In addition, societies do not always develop at the same pace over the same period of time.

Another problem with ancient astronaut theory has to do with Su-merian societies being the oldest civilizations (although Gobekli Tepe in Southeast Asia is now believed to be the oldest –9000 BCE; Egyptians said their civilizations went as far back as 17,000 years and older). A lot was found in Mesopotamia thereby leading to the discovery of the Su-merian tablets because using the Bible as a historical reference, there was a lot of exploration in Mesopotamia where biblical stories were supposed to have originated. The reality is, what we find depends on where we dig. We certainly are not going to find ancient life or "civilizations" where we do not dig. And just because we do not find something does not mean that it did not exist.

There is also the enigma of the theory of evolution that proposes that modern man evolved from apes, or that man and *Homo erectus* share a common ancestor. However, the link between the two has not been found. Nor has a common ancestor been found. Is it possible that the reason a link between the two has not been found is simply that it does not exist? Is it possible that although humanity shares a lot in common with apes, they did not evolve from them nor share a common ancestor? And regarding the Sumerian stories of the creation, and by extension the Judeo-Christian story, one will find that this story is just one of many. There are probably as many creation stories as there are peoples in the world, and in many of these stories, their origins began where they are. But despite some of the problems with all of this, there seems to be some merit to some of the theories and ideas, particularly both evolution and creation, and this is what makes ancient astronaut theory worth considering.

When I was at Temple in the 1990s, I was invited to the home of one of my colleagues, who had invited others as well. Some of them started discussing reports of ancient astronauts having built the pyramids. Being suspicious of white supremacy, and being a new scholar, I challenged them saying, "This is just white people saying that Black people did not have the intelligence or ingenuity to build such massive structures. Don't believe it," I said. I completely dismissed such a notion, until now. I did not turn on the television much in those days, nor paid attention to popular trends (and still don't) because working two part-time jobs while pursuing a doctoral degree was overwhelming and I simply did not have time to do so, which is why I did not know much about ancient astronaut theory until I started watching the *Ancient Aliens* series recently. I did not know anything about Sitchin's work or the work of others either. Like most things, I stumbled into it while doing an Internet search.

When the scholarly community examines peoples' cosmologies, they are examined within the framework of myth or mythology. Mythology is defined as myths dealing with the gods, demigods, and legendary heroes of a particular people. Based on this understanding, in my courses, I taught that myths should not be taken literally, and that mythology was created by societies to provide explanations for the origins of the universe and how we got here, but specifically were used as guidelines for moral behavior and the organization of societies.

The problem with the definition of myth is the part of it that defines it as unfounded, false, imaginary, and unverifiable. Because stories of creation are classified as myths, this means that they are undergirded by the notion that they are unscientific (not verifiable by observation or experiment; not real). However, if science is based on observation or experiment, the question is, how can stories of humanity being created by God or gods be considered unscientific if such stories are universal to the human experience?

What the Ancient Astronaut theorists are suggesting is that perhaps creation stories are not myths. Perhaps the stories we are calling myths did happen. Perhaps the beings we are calling gods are astronauts who visited the earth and even created humanity. To think that human beings would be the only intelligent beings in the universe with advanced technology would be foolish. And there are too many reports of people being abducted by beings that do not look like us for this not to be taken seriously. The problem is how such information is presented, particularly in popular media. It is the sensationalism that goes along with it and the fear that surrounds it. The phrases "extraterrestrial" or "alien" just means "not of Earth." If the creator of the universe created Earth, God would be considered extraterrestrial because it would be impossible for God to create Earth or the universe while standing on Earth.

Regardless of the questions that remain unanswered, it is highly likely that in the vastness of the universe, there exists life that is similar to life as we know it, as well as different from how we know it. It is also highly likely that there are places in the universe where technology far surpasses what humanity has created. I used to believe that because Earth and life on it are so insignificant in the grand scheme of things, no one or nothing would even care enough to bother to make voyages to Earth. At times, humanity seems so desolate that if there were gods who at one time had an interest in us, it seems they have all but abandoned us. And, in some of the stories, this is exactly what the people said. Nevertheless, I think that it is highly likely that beings from out there somewhere make visits to Earth, and that they are even living among us now.

Even though I have become more of a believer now (not necessarily that ancient astronauts built the massive stone structures found throughout the world, although being in communion with the gods may have inspired them, but for reasons which I will discuss later), I still have a difficult time shaking the feeling that Western arrogance and white supremacy underlies some of the ancient astronaut theory (although people the world over said the gods came from the sky). When I look at all the advancements that humanity has made in architecture—the extremely tall and massive structures we see all over the planet, advances in communications, Internet, and artificial intelligence, astronomical observatories, space stations, satellites, bio-medical advances, and the list goes on and on, and the advancements and technology that is growing by the day, the question for me is how can anyone say that ancient peoples could not have been as intelligent as we are today? It is an utterly ridiculous notion to me.

It would be like after we blow up the world and destroy everything in the coming catastrophe, a few thousand years from now when humanity evolves again and begin to search for the past, and find some of the massive structures and tall buildings in Dubai (the city with the tallest building) China, Chicago, New York and other places throughout world, or when they discover the space stations and satellites, and the Large Hadron Collider (a particle accelerator—in which the goal is to move small particles (smaller than quarks) at high speeds to uncover their mass), the largest machine in the world, referred to as the "Big Bang Machine" in which the goal ultimately is to find out the origins of the universe; that is what was behind the so-called big bang, they might say, "Gods or astronauts must have come from out of space and did all this, because surely people who are foolish enough to destroy themselves, could have not possibly been intelligent enough to create this kind of advanced technology." Or when they find the biblical scriptures indicating that God would destroy the world with fire and brimstone, future peoples conclude, that God destroyed the world—not man himself.

It is suggested that ancient astronauts helped to build the massive structures found throughout the world because surely if ancient man did not have the equipment to do it, then, perhaps the aliens may have done so, or at the least, giants did so. And old and recent digs have discovered giant bones. But my response to this is that giants live among us now. We see them every day, using their talents in spectator sports, performing some of the most incredible feats. This may be why we are so captivated by sports, and the sports industry capitalizes on it, making billions of dollars. But giants come in different forms; we find them in industry, arts, politics, martial arts, and in the spiritual arena. We need only to open our eyes.

Regarding whether our ancient ancestors were intelligent enough to develop the technology that has been found and is still being discovered all over the world, I surmise that some of the disbelief has to do with them being people of color. It is like saying that people before "Western civilization" (essentially code words for white people) could not have had the intelligence to develop the technology or create the massive structures that they did.

When in the Abrahamic traditions it is said that God (or the gods) did not want humanity to eat from the Tree of Knowledge, the question for me has been "Why not?" Why would God not want humanity to have access to knowledge? When I read in the *Book of Enoch* that the Watchers were teaching humanity things that they should have not been teaching them, again the question for me was "Why not?"

In the face of imminent mass destruction, I think I can finally see why. When I read in one of the Sumerian translations that Enlil was upset that the gods were teaching "wretched" humanity information that only the gods should be privy to, I think I got it; "wretched" is the operative word. What would we do with such information? Would we use it for the good of humanity or would we make a mess of things? I think the answer is quite clear.

Knowledge in the wrong hands can lead to catastrophe. Unless man (with knowledge) has cultivated a certain level of moral aptitude, it can lead to destruction. The fact that we have created weapons of mass destruction makes it inevitable that this is where we are headed. As the saying goes, "You keep playing with fire, you will eventually get burned."

30

CAUSES FOR THE FALL OF EMPIRES

Some of us who engage in scholarship collect books like people collect other things they love. Some books we may only read a few paragraphs of. Other books, we may read enough to ascertain whether we need to read them ever, and if so, whether we will do so now or in the future. And, some others, we determine that they are not worth the read, and still with others, with our limited time on Earth, we realize that we may never have the chance to read.

When C. F. Volney's *The Ruins of Empires* (which I had forgotten I had) fell off a shelf one day when I was looking for another book, it was as if the gods were saying to me, "It is time to read this more intently now." I had purchased the book over twenty years ago while at Temple, read through it quickly, but knew I would have to come back to it one day. To my surprise, over three hundred years ago, Volney articulated what I have thought and felt (but did not have enough information to articulate) about how we govern ourselves, the causes for human suffering, and outlines how religion developed, came to be monopolized, and used as a tool of manipulation and control.

I found Volney's background interesting. He was born of modest means in Craon (a commune in France). He received a small inheritance, which he decided to spend on studying in Syria and Egypt. Although his studies would lead him to accumulate wealth and climb the ranks of the French government, he would spend a great deal of his life in search of truth and contemplating the state of man. Traveling through and studying cities in ruin and ancient monuments of the Ottoman dominions and the ancient provinces of Syria and Egypt, and those who once inhabited them, he would find, robbery, devastation, tyranny, and wretchedness. Such discovery would leave his heart heavy with sorrow and indignation (as is mine, and I am quite sure many others).

One day, while in solitude and reflecting on, and conversant with the ruins, "the ashes of their inhabitants, and the memory of their former greatness" according to Volney, his eyes filled with tears, and he "sank into a gloomy mediation on human affairs, and a profound melancholy soon befell him."[102] Then a genii, an apparition, which he refers to as "Genius of tombs and ruins," appeared. Among many questions, the genii ask: How long will man shut his eyes to the truth, light, and reason? How long will he blame fate as the author of his calamities? If just for a moment, man can suspend the delusions that fascinate his senses, if just for a moment his heart can reason, then he ought to interrogate the ruins and read the lessons that they present to him.[103]

The genii continues by asking other questions. If nothing has changed with regard to creation; that is the laws of the heavens have not changed;[104] the sun has not stopped emitting its rays, the seas do not withhold their vapors, the rain and dew are not suspended in air, the mountains do not withhold their springs, and the plants do not withhold their seeds and fruit, essentially the heavens do not deny, Earth, and Earth does not deny its inhabitants the blessings it formerly dispensed, then why is the present not what former generations were? If these now desolate, but once powerful places lay in ruin, he asks, is it "the arm of God which carried the sword (now guns) into your cities, and fires (now bombs, missiles, and biological weapons) into your fields, which has slaughtered the people, burned the harvests, rooted up trees and ravaged pasture or is it the hand of man?"[105] Further, after man (kings and governments) in their pride have committed rapacious, murderous wars and heinous crimes against the earth and humanity, and pestilence and famine follow are not these catastrophes the wrath of God, or are they of man's own making? It is man's own folly that leads to his misfortune.

Volney then responds to the genii with the question I have also asked: if man is blind, shall his misfortune be also his crime? In other words, just why is there so much suffering? Why do so many people, especially those who have nothing to do with the crimes of a few, come to Earth only to suffer? Volney states what I have witnessed and the deep sadness I have felt myself:

I have wandered over the earth, I have visited cities and countries and seeing everywhere misery and desolation, a sense of the evils which afflict my fellow men hath deeply oppressed my soul. I have said with a sigh: is man then born but for sorrow and anguish? And I have meditated on human misery that I might discover a remedy...I will interrogate ancient monuments on the wisdom of past ages; I will evoke from the tombs the spirit which once in Asia [and Africa] gave splendor to states and glory of nations: I will ask the ashes of legislators: *By what secret causes do empires rise and fall; from what sources spring prosperity and misfortunes of nations; on what principles can the peace of society and the happiness of man be established?* [106]

To these questions, the genii responds saying that since Volney seeks truth, with sincerity, his prayers shall not be in vain, and that he would reveal to him the sciences of the ages and the wisdom of the tombs. He then proceeds to take him in flight, where he now sees Earth from regions above (like Enoch in the *Book of Enoch*). Interestingly, while showing him the ruins of the Nile—Ethiopia and Egypt—the genii points out that "A race of men now rejected from society for their *sable skin and frizzed hair,* founded on the study of the laws of nature, those civil and religious systems which still govern the universe."[107]

The genii then explains the condition of man in the universe, how man evolved from a "primitive" state to societies, the principles upon which societies are founded, the twin sources of evil, the origin of government and laws, the general causes of the prosperity of ancient states, and their ruin, among other things. I shall outline a few as Volney did.

- On the Condition of Man in the Universe: Man, like everything in the universe, is governed by natural law. These laws are present to man; they warn his understanding, act upon his senses, and give every action its reward and punishment. If he knows the laws, those elements that surround him, and his own nature, he will know when his behavior is contrary to these laws and how to correct them. If he follows the laws, he will be protected.[108]

- The Primitive State of Man: An orphan, abandoned by the unknown power that had produced him, self-love, aversion to pain, and the desire for happiness would lead man to produce comforts.[109]

- Principles of Society: "Wandering in the woods and on the banks of rivers in pursuit of game and fish, the first men, beset with dangers, assailed by enemies, tormented by hunger, by reptiles, by ravenous beasts, felt their weakness; and urged by a common need of safety, and a reciprocal sentiment of like evils," they would find that if they "united their strengths and resources, they could augment their powers and protect their enjoyments, thus *self-love* would become the principle of society. Self-love then is the moving principle of every individual and is the foundation of every association. The observance of that law of our nature has determined the fate of nations. However, man would fall into a labyrinth of errors, which would lead to calamities.[110]

- Sources of the Evils of Society: Some men, "not content with the abundance that the Earth offers or that is produced by industry, wished to accumulate enjoyments and coveted those possessed by fellow men." The strong one rose against the weak one to take the fruit of his labor; the weak one invoked another weak one to repel the violence. Then the two strong ones said: "Why fatigue ourselves to produce enjoyments which we may find in the hands of the weak? Let us join and despoil them; they shall labor for us, and we will enjoy without labor." And the strong, seeking to oppress, and the weak resisting, "men mutually afflicted each other; and a general and fatal discord spread all over the earth," generating a continued chain of misfortunes.[111]

The same self-love, which was the principle of happiness and perfection, became blind, disordered, and "transformed into a corrupting poison; and cupidity (greed), offspring and companion of ignorance, became the cause of all evils that have desolated the earth." Biased by the twin sources of ignorance and cupidity, into false ideals, man has mistaken or broken the laws of nature, thus, they are the sources of all the torments of man. It is ignorance and cupidity "that has armed man against man, family against family, tribe against tribe, [leaving] the earth a theater of blood, of discord, and rapine." The twin evils of ignorance and cupidity, then are the evils that have caused the ruins of empires.[112]

- Origin of Government and Law: Becoming fatigued with their evils, the pain they were inflicting, and the misfortunes they caused each other, man established judges to arbitrate their rights and settle their differences; eventually this would become the convention.[113]

What I found most interesting in this treatise is that the genii, according to Volney, lays out the evolution of religion, which he characterizes as having eight systems.[114]

1. First System—Origin of the Idea of God: When man first found himself on Earth, he was at the mercy of the forces of nature—the elements. Being at their mercy, he discovered two realities:

1. Power: They (the forces of nature, the elements) have power over him and excited in him sensations of pleasure and pain; good and evil.
2. Love: He developed love or aversion towards them; he desired-or dreaded their presence—fear gave rise to religion.

Applying the same practices that he did with his fellow man—appease those who are stronger or those who would cause him harm—he reasoned that by praying to the intelligence of the forces, he could supplicate them. Out of this the idea of God and religion sprung every being; every force of nature was a power, a genius. Thus, the first men conceived of a universe filled with innumerable gods. From here, the forces of nature, the gods, and genii were divided into beneficent and malignant; good, and evil. These two forces would become universal in all religious systems.

2. Second System—Worship of the Stars, or Sabeism: As men began to unite in society, agriculture emerged. Since vegetation depended on celestial influence, it became necessary to know the cycles of the sun, moon, stars, and planets. Astrology emerged and became the first religion.

3. Third System—Worship of Symbols or Idolatry: As agriculture evolved among the people along the Nile, and they began to observe more intently the effect of certain star systems on terrestrial productions, they found it necessary to individualize and group them. Groups of stars were named according to the animals that were most present and/or their manners or natures, and from this emerged the zodiac (wheel of animals). Once the calendar was developed, people no longer needed to observe the heavens and lost sight of their original meanings. Such a loss would result in confusion about the use of animals, which would lead to the propagation of animal worship. This practice would spread from the Nile to throughout the whole ancient world, through commerce, war, and conquest.

Contributing to the confusion was the difficulty that came with the development of language. The difficulty of turning sounds to signs, ideas into written language—hieroglyphics (developed by the Egyptians)—gave rise to illusions, ambiguities, and errors. There was also the development of a priestly class. Because agriculture required continuous observation of the stars, there emerged a need for a few people to study the cosmos. Those who did were exempt from labor, and society provided for their maintenance. With such provisions, they would spend their time in study and observation, leading them to become acquainted with nature and the secrets of her many operations. Such knowledge was then transmitted to their families and friends, leading it to become the exclusive privilege of a few families. Because they were able to predict future celestial events, heal disease, and perform other feats, people thought them to be in alliance with celestial powers and took them to be interpreters and mediators between the celestial and terrestrial worlds. From this would emerge a class who, under the name of religion, would monopolize an "empire of mystery," which would eventually become the ruin of every nation.

Because of misguided and erroneous ideas about how animals became associated with the stars, the animals and their attributes, as well as other natural phenomena, such as rivers, mountains, and objects were passed over to the gods and became symbols of nations (i.e., the development of totemism).

4. Fourth System—Worship of two Principles, or Dualism: Two principles of nature were observed—producing and destroying—which evolved around the equinoxes: six months of procreating and multiplying (spring/summer) and six months of breaking down and nearly dying (fall and winter). These two powers of nature would become genii/angels of light, fecundity, and creation; and genii/angels of darkness, destruction, and death. The two opposing forces represented the good god (who receives the worship of love and joy, with festivals, dances, offerings of flowers, etc.) and the evil god (who receives the worship of fear, pain, tears, mourning, blood offerings, and cruel sacrifices), symbolized in animal form. Examples include the serpent in Christianity, who represents Satan or parts of animals, and the devil with horns, which is found in religions throughout the world.

5. Fifth System—Moral and Mystical Worship or System of a Future State: Metaphorical language to describe celestial cycles of birth, death, and rebirth was derived from the equinoxes and solstices, which were called "the gates of heaven" among the Egyptians. This gave birth to the idea of a future state, or afterlife, where man would undergo divine judgment. Divine justice would be metered out by the God of the Universe, and each person would be rewarded and punished according to his or her earthly deeds. Such ideas served as a grand equalizer for injustice and were transmitted from Egypt to Judaism, Christianity, Islam, and other religions.

6. Sixth System—The Animate World, or Worship of the Universe under Diverse Emblems: Theologians began to see the world as unlimited and eternal. All phenomena were multiple expressions of God being

the cause and effect, the moving principle with variable laws that moves everything. Also, was the idea that "nothing can be annihilated in the world; that the elements are indestructible; that they change their combinations but not their nature; that life and death of beings are but different modifications of the same atoms; that the world is eternal..." This idea was also transmitted from Egypt to the Indians, Druids, Japanese, Tibetans, Chinese, and is found in Judaism, Christianity, and other religions.

7. Seventh System—Worship of the Soul of the World: The moving principle is distinguished from things moved. God is seen as the igneous principle, the fluid called ether; the subtle principle that animates the soul; spirit. All beings are thought to be portions of God himself. Since God is eternal and since there is a piece of God in man, our souls are immortal.

8. Eighth System—The World-Machine: Worship. . . of the Demi-Ourgos, or Grand Artificer: Losing the chain of ideas or ignorant of the facts on which they were founded, theologians would derive that the world was a machine and God as Demi-Ourgos or Grand Artificer (taking the world out of the realm of eternity). Since the Demi-Ourgos had to have intelligence, they (the Greeks) derived the concept of *logos* (reason or word). Because there was the acceptance of a soul of the world or the solar principle (from Egypt), the theologians found themselves obliged to compose three grades of divine beings: The Demi-Ourgos or working god; the *logos* (word or reason); and the spirit or soul (of the world) and this would become the basis of the Christian Trinity (God as Father, Son, and Holy Ghost). Because early concepts got confused and religion strayed from their original intent, it would eventually become nothing more than a corrupt "political engine to conduct the credulous vulgar," and even credible men would be duped by their own delusions.[115]

In summary, religion began when man began experiencing pain and pleasure from the powers of nature. Wishing to avoid pain, excited in man the first law of his nature—self-love. Through self-love, men learned to unite their strengths and resources for the safety and well-being of all. Learning from relationships with his fellow man, that he could win their favors, or disfavor by his actions, men began applying these same principles to appease the forces of nature that affected their lives by worshiping and praying to them. Man, also personified these forces in nature, giving them names.

As societies became agricultural, particularly with the inundation of the Nile, peoples along the Nile Valley began to understand the necessity of observing and studying the cycles of the celestial bodies—sun, moon, star systems, and so forth—and their impact on agricultural production. From these observations, two opposing forces emerged: light versus dark, and good versus evil; the ideas of rebirth and the afterlife began with the observation of the celestial cycles—the equinoxes and solstices. Errors and misinterpretations of the Egyptian spiritual system led to confusion in worship and practices. Corruption by the kingly and priestly classes led to the monopoly of the mysteries, and because of ignorance and cupidity, men would violate the natural laws—specifically the law of self-love. Ignorance and cupidity resulted in wars, slavery, and other atrocities, and subsequently the fall of empires.

31

THE HIGHEST PLEASURE

Aside from Volney's *The Ruins of Empires*, I think ancient Eastern spirituality did more than any other spiritual system to answer my question of why there is so much suffering. While I was doing the energy work, I began searching the Internet to gain more insight into what I was practicing. This search would take me to New Age spirituality.

I researched New Age spirituality and it seemed to be founded on the works of the Theosophical Society, founded by Helena Petrovna Blavatsky and Henry Steel Olcott in 1875. It has also been suggested that New Age spirituality originated in Europe's Age of Enlightenment, and even before. Whenever it began, New Age spirituality seems to be an amalgamation of the spiritual traditions and wisdom of Kemetians (Black Egyptians), Traditional Chinese Medicine, Reiki (Japanese), mystical Judaism and Christianity, and other Western esoteric traditions such as Hermeticism, Rosicrucianism, Freemasonry, and most of all, Indian spirituality, (including the Tantric tradition of the Black Dravidians). Many of these traditions are Egyptian in origin.

Although New Age spirituality is a mix of numerous religions and spiritual practices, Helena P. Blavatsky and others (Annie Besant, Charles Webster Leadbeater, and Alfred Percy Sinnet) of the Theosophical Society focused primarily on India's religion and probably did more than any others during that time to translate it and bring it to the West. I got a copy of both *Isis Unveiled* and *the Secret Doctrine*, by Helana P. Blavatsky, and some of the works of others that helped me understand the science of spirituality include, including the *Etheric Double* and the *Astral Body* by A.E. Powell and *Ancient Wisdom*, by Annie Besant. The Theosophical Society also has a substantial amount of information at https://blavatsky.net/Wisdomworld/index.php.

I was particularly drawn to India's spirituality because of the profundity of its philosophy, the purity of its sacred scriptures, the magic in some of its practices, but particularly the science behind it. But I was turned off by the way dark-skinned or Black Indians have been oppressed under India's caste system; the very people from whom India more than likely obtained its great philosophy, scriptures, and spiritual practices. "Hinduism" was at first a Persian geographical term used to refer to people who lived beyond the River Indus and was not a religion. However, by the end of the eighteenth century, it came to mean "followers of Indian religions."

Although some scholars suggest that Hinduism is Indo-European in origin, it is doubtful that the warring and conquering Aryans—who went to war for no real cause other than to fight and steal—had little or no religion of their own. The Aryans simply took the oral philosophy and spiritual practices of the Indus Valley Black people and translated them to Sanskrit (the language of the Indo-European people—whatever that means), producing a written spiritual tradition that they called the Vedas and Vedic literature, and passed it off as if they were the originators of it. According to the Greek historian Diodorus, Egyptians claimed that Osiris had traveled to India, bringing the Black Egyptian philosophy and spirituality. And it is commonly known that the Black Dravidians are the originators of the Tantric practices (the magical aspects) of India's spirituality.

Regardless of the origins of Indian spirituality, the meager amount of material that I managed to explore of India's tremendous scriptures, the Bhagavad-Gita, which means" song of the Lord," and some of the

Upanishads (which means to "sit down near an illumined teacher") led to a transformation of consciousness for me and gave me some probable causes as to the condition of man—or at least why there is so much suffering.

The primary principles that underlie Indian philosophy and life, in general, are *dharma* (the order of the universe, laws of nature), social order (i.e., rights, duties, laws, conduct, virtues, and right way of living), and the practices necessary to sustain them; *Samsara* (wandering into the cycle of birth, disease, death, and rebirth); *moksha* (liberation from wandering into the cycle of birth, disease, death, and rebirth), and *karma*, the law of cause and effect (i.e., what you sow, you will reap as you repeat the cycle of birth and death).

According to Indian spirituality, there are four primary aims (*purusartha*) of life: *kama*, pleasure, and emotional fulfillment; *artha*, economic gain, and prosperity; *dharma*, righteousness; and *moksha;* liberation. These four aims correspond with the four *ashrama*s, or stages of life: student, householder, hermit, and renunciant. The first three aims; pleasure, gain, and dharma, are dealt with in the householder stage. Once one retires, they enter the hermit stage, where they begin the quest for liberation, which leads to the renunciant stage—renouncing the world for spiritual life.

The Bhagavad-Gita was revealed to Arjuna, a warrior, by his childhood playmate and cousin, Krsna, who reveals to him that he is the Supreme Godhead when Arjuna desires to withdraw from a war between two families for domination of their kingdom. The Bhagavad-Gita evolves around five primary concepts. These are *Isvara* (the Supreme Godhead), *jivas* (living entities), *praktri* (material nature), *kala* (eternal time), and *karma* (activity). The Supreme Godhead, living entities, material nature, and time are eternal. Karma, or activity, is not eternal and can change according to the perfection of our knowledge and our practices.

The Supreme Personality of the Supreme Godhead, Krsna (who is also known as Vishnu—maintainer and Shiva-destroyer, and other names depending on the tradition) is the—maintainer of the universe and created the first living being (Brahma) and other gods who preside over the material world. According to A.C. Bhaktivedanta Swami Prabhupada's interpretation of the Bhagavad-Gita, there is a material sky and an eternal spiritual sky; there are material planets and spiritual planets. In the spiritual sky, there are innumerable spiritual planets. The eternal spiritual sky has its nature, just as the material sky. What we see in the material world is a mere shadow of the spiritual world. It is like when one sees a tree in a reservoir of water; the branches go downward and the roots upward. No planet in the material universe is free from the principles of material existence.

The abode of the Supreme Godhead is the eternal sky. "It is not illumed by the sun or moon, nor by fire or electricity, because the spiritual sky is already illuminated."[116] The Supreme Godhead is the eternal, the transcendental, unborn, the greatest; he is the creator and enjoyer.

All living beings have the same qualities as the Supreme Godhead but in minute quantity. Since the Supreme Godhead is eternal, and we have the same qualities, we are, therefore eternal. When Arjuna looks upon the field and sees that he is about to go to war with respected people—grandfathers, uncles, and great souls, teachers who are worthy of his honor and respect—he becomes grief-stricken and tells Krsna he will not fight. In response to this, Krsna explains the non-permanence of happiness and distress, comparing their appearance and disappearance to the coming and going of the winter and summer. Krsna goes on to say, "You are mourning for what is not worthy of grief. Those who are wise lament neither for the living nor the dead" (2:11). He then goes on to explain the eternal nature of the soul.

o No one is able to destroy that imperishable soul (2:17).

o For the soul, there is neither birth nor death at any time. He has not come into being, does not come into being, and will not come into being. He is unborn, eternal, ever-existing, and primeval (2:20).

o As a person puts on new garments, giving up old ones, the soul similarly accepts new material bodies, giving up the old and useless ones (2:22).

o The soul can never be cut to pieces by any weapon, nor burned by fire, nor moistened by water, nor withered by the wind (2:23).

o It is unbreakable and insoluble and can neither be burned nor dried... It is everlasting, present everywhere, unchangeable, immovable, and eternally the same (2:24).

o It is invisible, inconceivable, and immutable (2:25).

Krsna asks, "How can a person who knows that the soul is inde-structible, eternal, unborn and immutable kill anyone or cause anyone to kill?" (2:22), As "He who dwells in the body can never be slain. There-fore, you need not grieve for any [body] or living being" (2:30). Krsna then explains to Arjuna that since Arjuna reincarnated as a warrior, he must fight and that in the unavoidable discharge of his duty, he should not lament.

Generally, according to Prabhupada's interpretation of the Bhaga-vad-Gita, a fundamental problem with humanity is that we think we are in control. However, since the Supreme Godhead is the controller, we are not in control. The Supreme Lord is the creator and enjoyer; we are just cooperators. Through cooperation, we enjoy, but we are only coop-erators in the enjoyment of God's creation. We come to know the mate-rial world through our five senses or nine gates: two eyes, two ears, two nostrils, a mouth, genitals, and an anus. Because we are living in a body and come to know the world through our senses, this means we are ma-terially conditioned, which also means that our consciousness is materi-ally conditioned. Such conditioning leads to false consciousness and false ego.

Material nature is not independent but is acting by the direction of the Supreme Godhead. It has three qualities or "modes:" goodness, pas-sion, and ignorance. When we come in contact with nature, we become conditioned by these three modes. Because the living entity has become conditioned by the material world, he acts under the spell of these three modes of nature. Also, because we have different kinds of bodies that correspond to one of these three modes of nature, we are inclined to act according to the nature of that body.[117]

The mode of goodness is conditioned by a sense of happiness and knowledge. Although this mode is purer than the two others and can lead to pure goodness—a state in which one can understand the science of God—one may be still bound by the mode of goodness of a material nature. Such persons repeatedly become philosophers, scientists, etc., and repeatedly become entangled in the cycle of birth, disease, old age, and death.[118]

The Mode of Passion is born of unlimited desires and longings. So, the embodied living entity is bound to material fruitive actions (those in which there are expectations of material profit or reward). One born of the mode of passion may get satisfaction from industry, owning as much as he can, and giving to charity. Actions done in the mode of passion because they are of the material world and fruitive, result in unlimited desires and longings, and ultimately, misery.[119]

The mode of ignorance can lead to darkness and delusion, which can further lead to madness and foolishness because the person has no understanding.[120] In summary, according to the Gita:

> From the mode of goodness, real knowledge develops; from the mode of passion, greed develops; and from the mode of ignorance develop foolishness, madness, and illusion...Those situated in the mode of goodness gradually go upward to the higher planets; those in the mode of passion live on the earthly planets; and those in the abominable mode of ignorance go down to the hellish worlds.[121]

Above the three material modes is eternal time and under eternal time are activities, karma. All living entities are engaged in activities and entangled in the actions and reactions to their own karma. These activities are being carried out from time immemorial and we are suffering or enjoying the fruits of our labor. In every aspect of life, we either enjoy the results of our work or suffer the results. Since we are engaged in activity from time immemorial, we are caught in a continuous cycle of birth, old age, disease, and death. That is, after giving up one body, we enter another one the same way that we put on and take off clothes. Even for those living entities, traveling from one planet to another in the material world, they will still find the inconveniences of birth, old age, disease, and death. No planet in the material universe is free from principles of material existence.

How do we become liberated from this cycle of birth, old age, disease, and death? First, let go of our bodily conception of life; we must understand that we are not our bodies. Liberation means freedom from material consciousness and becoming situated in pure consciousness.

When we are attached to the material world, through our senses, we will stay bound to it. Although activity in the material world brings us pleasure, it also brings misery. There is nothing in the material world that brings pleasure that does not also bring misery. It is only when we let go of attachment to our material nature, to the material world, will we find true happiness, the highest pleasure: Krsna, the Lord, the Supreme

Godhead, the storehouse of all pleasure. We experience the highest pleasure by being in service, a devotee to the Supreme Lord. To live in the world is to be in service, which means that no one is exempt from providing service to other living beings. Because of this truism, *"the rendering of service is the eternal religion of living beings* [italics my own]."[122]

It is only by letting go of attachment to our material reality and becoming a devotee to the Supreme Lord that one can experience Krsna (God) consciousness, and subsequently the highest pleasure. Becoming a devotee means rendering service without attachment to fruitive results. Ultimately, giving up attachment to temporary activities in the material world and taking up activities prescribed by the Supreme Lord will lead to Krsna consciousness, the pure life, and the highest pleasure. When one reaches the state of Krsna consciousness, one can end the cycle of birth, disease, old age, and death in the material sky, and return to the eternal spiritual sky, the abode of the Supreme Godhead—the Lord.

32

BREAKING THE KARMIC CHAINS

Since breaking the chains of karma is crucial to becoming liberated from the cycle of birth and death, understanding how it works is worthy of expanding on, which Annie Besant (a theosophist) does in her work, *Ancient Wisdom*. As stated already, karma is the law of causation; cause and effect and means action. According to the laws of karma, all actions are effects of previous causes, and each effect becomes a cause of future effects. One's karma is the aggregate of one's many lives. Although many of us think of events that occur as chances, accidents, or miracles, according to Eastern spirituality, these do not exist. It is being ignorant of the law that makes us think in this way. Nothing can strike a man that he does not deserve; because he does not remember it does not mean the law will fail to work.

The three types of energy that one sends forth that can affect one's karma are one's thoughts, desires, and physical actions. When energy is sent forth, it has an effect on who generates it and on those who come within one's field of influence. Thought is the most potent in the creation of karma. It creates mind stuff and mental images, and these shape the mental body. Thoughtforms leave the generator and live a quasi-independent life; they also keep a magnetic tie with the person and affect others, establishing karmic links between the thought creator and these others (e.g., relatives, friends, and enemies), and help determine his future human associates.

Every thought modifies the mental body, and the mental faculties in each successive life are made by the thinking in previous lives. Even death (of the physical body) does not stop this process.

The present body facilitates the process by working up mental images into an organ referred to as a faculty that returns in the next birth on the physical plane; part of the brain in the new body is molded to serve as the organ of this faculty. It then forms the mental body for opening life on Earth. The brain and nervous system are shaped to give the mental body expression on the physical plane. Knowing this law, a person can make the mental character one desires to possess.

The second type of energy, desire, affects the astral body (the vehicle of our desires) our fate after death, and the nature of the astral body in the next birth. Our desires attach to objects, and therefore toward an environment in which they may be gratified. For example, sending out hatred and revenge could link one to someone who then commits murder. Desires for earthly things draw the person toward where the objects are most readily attainable. Because a person is born according to desires, it can determine the place of rebirth and surroundings, and bring persons, objects, and influences.

The third type of energy; physical actions, also generates much karma, but is primarily the effect of past thinking and desires. Depending upon whether one spreads happiness or unhappiness on a physical level will determine one's physical surroundings in future lives, and whether they are good or bad. For example, if someone bought suffering and misery through their actions to others in past lives, they will live in misery and suffering in future lives.

Other factors in the workings of karma are that every force works on its own plane, it can be discharged, and it determines three bodies in the future. The higher the plane, the more potent and persistent the force. Because motive is on a higher plane, it is more important than the action. The knower of the laws of karma works diligently to choose the best path, paying careful attention to motive, moving beyond selfish motives, and purifying his heart. The general principle of force belonging to the plane it was generated on has far-reaching importance on the path of liberation. The motive of obtaining physical objects works on the physical plane and will attach a person to the physical plane; one who has no motive other than divine service cannot attach to anything because he has no motive.

The lords of karma, who work in various capacities—recorders of karma, agents on Earth, knowers of the record of every man, and so forth—are the great spiritual intelligences who keep the karmic records and complicated workings of karmic law. Some karma can be exhausted or worked out in a single life or body. Other karma, however, because it is so incongruous with a single life has attached its liabilities with other souls that are not incarnated at the same time. This karma requires different types of bodies and different types of environments and will take several lifetimes to discharge. Using their omniscient wisdom, the lords of karma combine portions of that record to form a plan for the single life. They decide on the nation, place, family, and parents depending on the combination of hereditary diseases and hereditary fitness of their nervous system, and the garment of the reincarnating soul (i.e., the physical body) suitable for the exhaustion of the aggregate of causes which can be worked out together. Further:

> This aggregate of causes fixes the length of that particular life; gives to the body its characteristics, its powers, and its limitations; brings into contact with the man the souls incarnated within the life-period to who he has contracted obligations, surrounding him with relatives, friends, and enemies; marks out the social conditions into which he is born, with their accompanying advantages and disadvantages; selects the mental energies he can show forth by molding the organization of the brain and nervous system with which he has to work; puts together the causes that result in troubles and joys in his outer career that can be brought into a single life.[123]

A soul must return to Earth until he has discharged all his liabilities and exhausted all his karma. But since by being born again he creates fresh karma, the question that arises is how to put an end to all of this; how can the soul attain liberation? The keys are to understand the role of desire and how to discharge karma.

Regarding the role of desire, if the soul attaches itself to any object, he will be drawn to the place where the object is for gratification. Most of what we do via action is motivated by a desire for some material object or result. Action has no power to hold the soul. "But the ever-renewed desire for fruit constantly spurs the soul into fresh activities and thus new chains are continually being forged."[124] Desire then is the binding element in karma, for when the soul no longer desires any object on Earth or in heaven, his tie to the wheel of reincarnation that turns the three worlds is broken.

Liberation then begins with the practice of voluntary gradual renunciation of the fruits of action, by denying oneself the objects and doing so habitually, until one is content to do without it. As he does this, he must be careful not to neglect his duty because of his indifference to the fruits it brings. It is further explained:

> When he attains perfection in this, and neither desires nor dislikes any object, he ceases to generate karma; ceasing to ask anything from the earth or from *Devachan* (Heaven) he is not drawn to either; he wants nothing that either can give him, and all links between himself and them are broken off.[125]

This ceases the generation of new karma. To get rid of old karma, chains must be allowed to wear out gradually or be broken deliberately. To exhaust or burn up karma from previous lives or put an end to karma generated in the present life, one can neutralize or counteract forces that would bring them into manifestation by sending equal and opposite forces against them (for example, sending strong thoughts of love and goodwill). One can also use this knowledge to find a wronged person whether in this world or another and pay his karmic debt by seeking an opportunity to serve them. In addition, the karmic debt of a soul can be paid by neutralizing every force of hatred by radiating love and compassion in every direction. Whether one is knowledgeable of the laws of karma, living by these principles, one may unconsciously discharge their karmic liabilities.

33

THE FOUR NOBLE TRUTHS & EIGHT FOLD PATH

I had already encountered the story of Siddhartha Gautama's life on a television program before my encounter with Indian spirituality. I think I connected to his story because I, as he did, grieve the suffering of humanity. The question for me for as long as I can remember has been "Why so much suffering?" Why is it that some people are born into good fortune while others are born into so much pain and suffering? And I have also spent my life, when not bogged down with the responsibilities of living it, searching for the truth. Because Siddhartha Gautama (more commonly known as the Buddha, "the enlightened one") left his wealthy family, choosing a life of a homeless monk, in search of answers to both questions, I thought I might also find answers in his teachings.

In brief, according to legend, Siddhartha was born in a forest in Lumbini (modern-day Nepal), where his mother had him while on her way back home to Dewadaha to her parents, Suddhodana (whose name means "pure rice") a king in Kapilavastu, and Maya. Five days after Siddhartha's birth, a naming ceremony was held, where eight of 108 Brahmins (priests) were requested to predict Siddhartha's future. They indicated that he was "distinguished by thirty-two principal characteristic marks of a Divine Being and eighty minor ones by virtue of the infinite amount of merit accumulated by the practice of duty and charity" over many lifetimes.[126] They also highlighted physical characteristics, particularly his feet, which indicated that Siddhartha was a grand being. It was predicted that Siddhartha would either become a world emperor or that he would attain the Buddhahood (Perfect Enlightenment).

However, one of the Brahmins, the youngest one, predicted that Siddhartha would enter the holy orders and that he would become an omniscient Buddha of the world. When his father inquired what visions would induce him to pursue the religious life, the young Brahmin indicated that Siddhartha would see four visions that would determine his destiny—an old man, a sick man, a dead man, and a man of the holy orders.

Since Siddhartha's father desired for him to be an emperor of the world, he lavished upon him all the luxuries that wealth can attain and befitting a prince and attempted to shelter him from seeing these four individuals. However, one day, Siddhartha requested for his chariot to be made ready so that he could visit his garden (in the *Gospel of Buddha*, it was the city). During this outing, he saw a very old man, toothless, bald, with a wrinkled face, and shriveled skin hanging loosely on his bones, who was bent over, trembling, and barely holding himself up with a crutch. This deeply saddened him. Later (one account says that day, others say on other days), he saw the second person: a sick man rolling in agony on the ground weeping and groaning unceasingly; his foul body oozed pus from his sores. Siddhartha then saw the third man: a foul-smelling corpse, which caused him to feel even more anguish and deep sorrow. He later saw a man of the holy order.

After reflecting on the misery and suffering in the world, desiring to find answers to end such suffering, and wishing to sever the ties that bound him to the world, Siddhartha determined that he would pursue the Buddhahood. He gazed one last time at his beautiful wife and son (while they were asleep), feeling grieved at the pain of leaving them, and he gave up worldly pleasures, his kingdom, and went into the homeless life.

Siddhartha would first sit at the feet of two of the most learned Brahmins, but he would find no satisfaction in their teachings, particularly the concept of self or ego migrating from body to body, and some of the practices, specifically the killing of animals for sacrifices (something that I have also found disturbing). He would then spend six years pursuing the ascetic life with five bhikkhus (monks), eventually living off one grain of hemp seed (some say rice) a day. He nearly starved to death. One day, after someone gave him food to bring him back to life, and after seeing the limitations of such a pursuit, he decided to sit under a Bodhi tree until he achieved nirvana. After attaining Perfect Enlightenment, his ministry would begin. It is founded on the illusion of self as the primary root of suffering, the Four Noble Truths, the Middle Path, and the Eightfold Path.

A primary premise of Buddhism (as with Indian spirituality in general) is that one must detach from the world and this can be done by letting go of desire. The question for me was: Why would God give us desire if we are not supposed to desire? Especially since it is the driver of action. However, as I continued to explore, I would not only find answers to why there is suffering but truth, light, and a very clear pathway to enlightenment and an end to suffering.

The Buddha concept of the self can be summed up as: "There is truth and self. Where self is, truth is not. Where truth is, self is not... Self as egoism, and individual separateness, begets envy and hatred, vice and evil. Self is the yearning for pleasure and the lust after vanity...[and] truth is the correct comprehension of things...The attainment of truth is possible only when the self is recognized as an illusion."[127]

The four noble truths are the noble truths of: suffering, the origins of suffering, the extinction of suffering, and the path that leads to the extinction of suffering.

• The Noble Truth of Suffering—is decay, death, sorrow, lamentation, pain, grief, and despair. These forms of suffering come from the five groups of existence: corporeality, feelings, perception, formations, and consciousness, which are mere combinations of things that are transient and keep changing into different combinations of things. For example, a house, a being, an individual, or a person does not really exist. They are a combination of materials of one or more of the five existences. All formations are transient and that which is transient is subject to suffering.

• The Noble Truth of the Origins of Suffering—is craving that gives rise to fresh rebirth. Everything is in perpetual change, continual dissolution, and renewal. Everything is dependent on everything. e.g. clinging on craving, craving on the karmic process of becoming, becoming on rebirth, and rebirth on decay, death, sorrow, lamentation, pain, grief, and despair. Since craving is the basis upon which everything else is dependent, then it is craving that keeps one in the perpetual cycle of birth and death, and ultimately is what causes suffering.

• The Noble Truth of the Extinction of Suffering—is done by the extinguishing of craving. The extinction of craving leads to the extinction of clinging, which leads to the extinction of the karmic process of becoming. This leads to the extinction of rebirth, decay, death, sorrow, lamentation, grief, and despair, and thus the extinction of suffering.

• The Noble Path that Leads to the Extinction of Suffering—is the Middle Path and the Eightfold Path. Understanding the Middle Path means seeing and knowing that neither of the two extremes—indulgence in sensual pleasure (and its vulgarities), nor living the ascetic life (and self-mortification and pain)—are profitable. It is the Middle Path that leads to peace, enlightenment, and nirvana.

The eight-fold path is the right understanding of the four noble truths, and right-mindedness, speech, action, living, effort, attentiveness, and concentration.

1. Right Understanding of the Four Noble Truths is knowing what is karmically unwholesome (greed, hatred, and delusion), and what is karmically wholesome (unselfishness, benevolence, and wisdom). It is also knowing the two kinds of Right Understanding and the two kinds of the Eightfold Path: the "mundane," practiced by the "worlding," and the Ultra-mundane, practiced by disciples or the "noble ones."

2. Right Mindedness is thoughts free from lust, ill-will, and cruelty.

3. Right Speech is abstinence from lying, tale-bearing, harsh language, and vain talk.

4. Right Action is abstaining from the killing of living beings, stealing, and unlawful sexual intercourse.

5. Right Living is avoiding the wrong way of living and a livelihood that is the right way of living.

Right Mindedness, Right Speech, Right Action, Right Living, yields worldly fruit and brings good results. These are called *mundane* right-mindedness, speech, action, and living. However, abhorrence of the practices of wrong-mindedness, speech, action and living, and being turned away from the world, and conjoined with the path; with the holy path being pursued, is *Ultra-mundane*, Right Mindedness, Right Speech, Right Action, and Right Living.

6. Right Effort is the effort to control the senses; it is the effort to avoid, to overcome, to develop, and to maintain. It means one teaches their mind to *avoid* the <u>arising</u> of evil, and demeritorious things that have not yet arisen; to *overcome* evil and demeritorious things that have <u>already arisen</u>; to *develop* the will to arouse, meritorious conditions that have <u>not yet arisen</u>, and to *maintain* the meritorious conditions that have <u>already arisen</u>, and not let them disappear, but to bring them into growth, to maturity and to the full perfection of development. For all these efforts one puts forth energy.

7. Right Attentiveness is the four fundamentals of attentiveness: contemplation of the body, contemplation of feelings, contemplation of mind, and contemplation of mind-objects—phenomena. It is contemplating their rising and passing away; whether they are one's own or someone else's; understanding that they are here, and they are there and living independently of and unattached to anything in the world.

8. Right Concentration is dwelling in the four fundamentals of Right Attentiveness and the four fundamentals of Right Effort.

Developing concentration to understand things as they *really* are; that is the arising and passing away of the five groups of existences; corporeality, feelings, perceptions, mental formations, and phenomena; abandoning delusion and craving; and developing tranquility and insight is the Middle Path that leads to peace, enlightenment, nirvana, the end of the cycle of birth, old age, disease and death, and the end of suffering.

The Four Noble Truths referred to as the "liberating insight," is liberating in and of itself and the Eightfold Path provides a clear pathway to liberation. For one who is interested in pursuing the Eightfold Path, "Buddha the Word, The Eightfold Path (500 BC)," provides a detailed step-by-step guide.[128]

34
THE COMPANY OF THE GODS

As I continued to search for truth, almost all the information, if not all (that I would find), would lead me to Egypt. Because numerous works indicate that all three Abrahamic religions, the Eastern religions, and Greek philosophy are founded on Egyptian religion, my thoughts were (and always is), if you really want to know the truth about something, seek from where it originated. Numerous texts indicate that Central Africa along the Nile Valley is where everything, including religion, originated, and Egypt is where the origins of symbols, language, mythology, and religion were preserved and given expression.

These texts include *The Gods of the Egyptians, Vols. I & II*, a translation and interpretation of various Egyptian texts by E. A. Wallis Budge; *The Natural Genesis* and *Ancient Egypt the Light of the World*, both extensive and extraordinary works of research on the origins of symbols, language, mythology, and religion, by Gerald Massey; and *The Origins and Evolution of*

Religion and *The Signs and Symbols of Primordial Man* by Albert Churchward, and numerous other works. The people of the Nile Valley, (referred to as the Nilotic people) were those who inhabited the Congo, Ethiopia, Kenya, South Sudan, Tanzania, Uganda, Egypt, and other countries and who spoke Nilotic languages. In fact, Massey goes as far as to assert that Africa is the birthplace of all things human, stating:

> I have not been shown nor do I perceive any reason for doubt in the truth of my generalization that Africa and not Asia [where the biblical story begins] was the birthplace of articulate man and therefore the primordial home of all things human; and that the race which first ranged out over the world, including the islands of the north [Britain] and the lands of the southern seas [Australia]...was directly Kamite;...Egypt itself is old enough to be the mouthpiece of the first articulate language, the oldest intelligible witness to the natural genesis of ideas, the sole adequate interpreter of the primary types of thought.[129]

Churchward also states:

> Except one knows and understands the Primordial and *Ritual* of Ancient Egypt, it is impossible to trace back the history of this world—the history of all religions, and the history of all mankind...Research has led us to bring forward such evidence, as furnished by the records and monuments of the country or nations of the world, where we find the same signs and symbols, the same myths and legends, the same sacred ceremonies and identical religious beliefs, which when correctly interpreted proves that only one conclusion can be definitely arrived at...that the first or Paleolithic man was the pygmy who evolved in Central Africa at the sources of the Nile or Nile Valley, and that from here all originated and were carried throughout the world...Egypt alone preserved the primitive gnosis and gave expression to the language of signs and symbols, and it was here that the first elemental powers were divinized—here that Totemism, Stellar, Lunar and Solar Mythology originated.[130]

Particularly tracing the genesis of humanity through language, Massey found that:

> The result is to show that the most ancient names and words are Kamite, not Aryan nor Semite. That is, they are words still extant in Africa, which can be brought out of that land together with the Black race, but cannot be got into it backward from Europe, or Asia, America, or Australia.[131]

Furthermore, it was found that certain root words are common to all languages, and thus point back to a unity of origin, with Kemet being the origin of that unity. Churchward further points out that Kemet is the origin of all language and mythology in the British Isles, Akkad (a city in ancient Mesopotamia), India, and New Zealand, in Hebrew and Christian theology, and of zodiacal and extra-zodiacal celestial signs. Thus, any gaps in knowledge that exist about the genesis of language, mythology, theosophy, and religion exist because the Kemetic element has been omitted.

Also noteworthy is what Massey had to say about mythology. The Greek words "myth," "mythos," and "mythology" are derived from the word *muthos*, which means "a saying." He notes, "the *muthoi* or myths did not begin in Greece or originate in any other Aryan language; nor with the sayings which are fading metaphors of mythology and the utterances of its second childhood" (in other places outside of Egypt). Nor is Myth a mere word in Greek."[132] The Greek word *muthoi* ("sayings") represents the Egyptian *mutu*, *mutun*, *mote*, and *mut*, which have similarly different meanings, but in essence means "mystical sayings." In these mystical sayings were the mysteries, like the *smiriti* of India, uttered only by word-of-mouth to the ear alone. Because these mysteries, the hidden oral wisdom, and the *dark sayings of old*, were only to be said not written, *Muthos*, therefore, denotes anything delivered by word-of-mouth.

Suffice it to say, since what was written (and even what was written that has been misunderstood, misconstrued, and falsified) did not contain that which is uttered by word-of-mouth, one can only surmise that a lot of the mystical aspects of the mysteries have been lost, even from Egypt. Massey asserts this as well, explaining how the Greeks misunderstood Egyptian "mythos" word-of-mouth wisdom, and although they named their divinities after Egyptian divinities, they did so without knowing their origins and meaning. He states that nothing could be more fatal than to try to understand the meanings of Egyptian mythology than to try and do so through the eyes or interpretations of Greece and Rome. Further, "the utterly misleading way in which Egyptian physics were converted by Plato and his followers into Greek metaphysics makes Platonism only another name for imposture."[133]

~~~~~~~~~~

Egypt's political history helps to contextualize just how broad its reach was and how significant its influence was on the world, particularly as it pertains to its theology and its mystery religion. Egypt's history is divided into an Early Dynastic Period and Kingdoms (old, middle, and new), when Egyptian kings ruled; Intermediate, and Late periods, when nomarchs, provincial governors, or outsiders ruled and/or when there was instability.

Since no records can be found in the Early Dynastic Period and Old Kingdom (3100–2345 BCE, over one thousand years) detailing their wars like other ancient societies had, it is speculated that early Egyptians were not so much interested in conquest as they were in the preservation of their own society. Most of their conflicts were internal and had to do with civil unrest, and/or competition over who would rule. Conflicts beyond their borders did not begin until the Middle Kingdom (ca: 2040-2025 BCE to 1786–1640 BCE) with expeditions into Nubia and Palestine and reached an apex in the Third Kingdom, after defeating and kicking the Hyksos out, who invaded around 1650 BCE and ruled for about one hundred years. After that, more focus would be put on imperialistic aims, at least by some kings, especially early in the New Kingdom (ca. 1550–1070/1069 BCE). One might speculate that Egyptians had learned well from invaders and incorporated a military approach of going to the enemy before they come to them.[134]

Cheikh Anta Diop in *Civilization or Barbarism* describes not only the wide reach of ancient Egypt's vast empire (and the first known in the world) in the sixteenth century BC, during the XVIII dynasty, but also how powerful it was. According to Diop, under Thutmose III, Egypt had conquered the whole Eastern Mediterranean (Crete, Cyprus, the Cyclades, etc.) and Western Asia including Syria, the country of Akkad, and Babylonia. "In total according to Thutmose III's *Hymn of Triumph*, engraved on the 'poetic stela' at Karnak, 110 foreign states were conquered and integrated to different degrees into the Egyptian empire."[135]

Diop notes that "fourteen hundred years before the Roman Empire, Egypt created the first centralized empire in the world."[136] And it was not one held together by the threat of war; it was a force much stronger than that. The idea that the king's power came from the god Amon-Ra, creator of the universe, to maintain peace, justice, and the law, was the unifying force. Because the king "in the righteousness of his heart," exercised the divine will of the God Amon-Ra—not just Egypt's national God, but the God of the Universe—all people were compelled to respect and obey him."[137]

Within Egypt's vast empire, some states that came under Egypt's domain were divided into administrative districts and placed under Egyptian governors. In some towns, princes were replaced by Egyptian generals, and in others, a chief was replaced by another vassal by anointing him with oil. Garrisons were stationed at strategic points in important towns and parts. Each vassal state that came under Egypt paid annual tributes (and whenever they asked for favors), making Egypt extremely wealthy. Year after year, these came in the forms of war service, money, gold (7, 770 pounds of electrum, white gold, was paid in one year), silver, copper (3,648 tons from the Island of Cypress in one year), lead, ivory, chariots (some filled with wood, others plated with electrum, and others decorated with silver and gold), slaves, horses, bulls, cows, asses, small livestock, tusks, gems, lapis lazuli, vases, and jars of incense, honey, and fine oil.[138]

With such a wide reach, it is not surprising that Egyptian theology would be found in the lands that came under its domain, and that Amon-Ra, the sun god, would become integrated with the God of peoples in the regions in both the East and West.

~~~~~~~~~~

Egypt is where we find the first concepts of monotheism, heaven, the Trinity, the virgin birth, resurrection, the afterlife, eternal life, and other major theological constructs found in Abrahamic religions. In fact, ancient Egyptians claimed that gods once inhabited the earth and mingled with men; that Egypt was once a land of gods and men. Interesting to note is that one of Egypt's ancient cities and spiritual centers was called Anu (also spelled Annu) before the Greeks called it Heliopolis, "city of the sun." One might speculate a link to the Sumerian god Anu and considering that Egyptians indicated that gods lived among them, there may be some truth to the ancient astronaut theory (or they may be referring to those who were so evolved they were thought to be virtual gods on Earth, discussed later).

As indicated earlier, Anu is the Sumerian god, whose abode was heaven, and whose sons were Enlil and Enki. Interestingly, the Egyptian Annuian theological system, namely the Ennead nine gods also called the Company of the Gods emerged to be the primary of three Company of Gods; Company of Great Gods (of Anu of heaven), Company of Little gods (of Earth) and third, name unknown (of the underworld). An was also the name of God among the Dravidians (Nile Valley people who inhabited Indus Valley), who had built great civilizations before the Aryan invasion. Henry Heras, in "Anu in India and in Egypt," indicates that:

Anu, undoubtedly being an Aryan tribe, bear that name which 'appears to be of non-Aryan origin'... It is well known that very soon the Aryan tribes accepted a number of dogmas of their Dravidian predecessors, into their own religion, first little by little and hesitatingly, but later openly and without fear, until finally the whole religion of the Dravidians was amalgamated with their own religion.[139]

The Aryans also accepted the dogma of monotheism and later accepted the very name of their god, Anu, whose name means "the Lord." In addition, "their contact with one of the Dravidian tribes that were inhabiting the neighborhood of the Indus Valley, called the tribe of the Sivas, was the final reason for accepting the old Dravidian god," who was worshiped as both Siva (one of India's major gods) and An, after whom Anu had been named.[140]

Sifting through the mounds of information to decipher major theological concepts of Egyptian religion can at first be daunting because of the various names of the Supreme God and the pantheon of demigods, or "little gods." Budge, however, explained the role of predynastic Nile Valley civilizations in dynastic Egypt. Knowing how African people (and others all over the globe) practiced spirituality before the rise of world religions also helped to understand Egyptian spirituality. Like how spirituality was practiced among people throughout the world, specifically among Africans including people along the Nile, all of existence was seen as imbued with divine force or spirit. It was generally held that the God of the Universe gave birth to forces that were referred to as gods, deities, demigods, and other names (depending upon the culture), who were responsible for carrying out various functions and maintaining different aspects of the universe. As with other societies throughout Africa and the world, some peoples accumulated a litany of names for these various forces. Among the Egyptians, the generic terms for God and the forces were *Ntw* ("Neter") *Neteru*, respectively, which is probably where the term "nature" originated.

Each city had names for the Supreme God and numerous other names for the Neteru. According to Budge, one of the oldest goddesses was Het-Her. Noteworthy is that Massey confirms that before the evolution from polytheism to monotheism, where the one primordial Father-God emerged to be the Supreme God, there was the Mother-God. He states:

> There is no fatherhood in the first Pleroma of the gods who are a family of seven, born of the genitrix of gods and men...individualized fatherhood was comparatively late as a human institution, and that the father could not be recognized in heaven before he had been discovered on Earth. The mother is everywhere first and foremost, as she was in nature as the bringer-forth was observed and typified long before the human mind could inter into the cause, or the fatherhood had been established.[141]

According to Budge, in predynastic Egypt, every village and town had its own God and/or group of gods whose power increased or declined depending on the prosperity of that community. When Egypt was broken up into nomes (which were originally city-states but became more like provinces with governors after unification) a certain God and/or group of gods became representatives of that nome and obtained pre-eminence over all the other gods. Budge notes that "the whole country of Egypt from the Mediterranean Sea to Elephantine was divided among the gods, and it became customary in each nome to regard the god of that nome as the 'Great God' or 'God' and to endow him with all the attributes possible."[142] The goddess of Dendra was Het-her (Hathor in Greek); the Goddess of Sais was Neit (Net, Nit); the God of Memphis was Ptah; the God of Edfu was Heru (Horus in Greek); the God of Hermopolis was Tehuti (That, Tat, Dehuti, Thoth in Greek); the God of Thebes was Amen (Amun, Amon); the God of Busiris (and Abydos) was Ausar (Aus, Osiris in Greek); and God of Annu (Heliopolis, On) was Tem (Atum, Tum, Ra). Sometimes a God would be the representative of more than one nome.

In every nome, there was a temple located in the capital city of that nome with a body of priests connected to it to carry out various duties in service of the gods and other functions such as maintenance of the buildings, religious education, etc. Generally, people of one nome were hospitable to the gods of another one, and to those who settled among them. The priests of the gods, who were a power of their own, having no authority over them (and may have even held more power than the king) were also hospitable to the God/Company of Gods of others. And when they were given power over another nome (due to war), they never attempted to suppress them but integrated them into their own pantheon. Thus, when the priests of the Great God Ra of Annu rose to supremacy, they integrated Ra with their god Atum and Company of Gods (of Annu). Care was made to include as far as possible every god and goddess who had been worshiped in past generations. Thus, in Annu, Atum (or Tem) became Atum-Ra (Ra-Atum, Tem-Ra, Ra-Tem), and in Thebes, Amen became Amen-Ra and the Company of the Gods of Annu rose to supremacy.

When the Theban prince of the god of Amen rose to supremacy after the conquests of the Hyksos and as King of the North and South, Thebes rose in supremacy, and the God, Amen-Ra became the greatest of the Great Gods with the accompanying Annuian Company of Gods.

Something that has always been curious to me was why Egyptians represented their gods with the heads of animals and as animals. What was also curious is the practice of totemism, and why animals were significant, even in the practices of shamanism throughout the world. The works of Volney, Massey, and Churchward helped to affirm conclusions that I was beginning to draw on my own. They explain that early man did not make the gods in his image but saw superpowers in nature because he was too helpless in the presence of these powerful forces to see himself in them. Because of this, gods and goddesses were first represented by these powerful forces in the form of zootypes; such representations would precede anthropomorphic representations. These zoo types of the divine would later be expressed in sign language—hieroglyphics.

Massey notes that zootypes "can be traced to their original habitat and home in Africa and nowhere else upon the surface of the earth."[143] Egypt is where they were perfected and later dispersed throughout the world. However, because the Greeks were ignorant of the Egyptian hieroglyphics, and even more so, did not understand that they were giving reverence to the superpower or divine attribute possessed by the animal they thought that Egyptians were worshiping animals. This misunderstanding was also repeated by the Romans.

Preceding the expression of divinities in sign language (symbols as zootypes) is totemism, which was found to be practiced throughout the world, and also thought to have originated in Africa. Totemism is beliefs in mystical relationships with an animal, animal part, rocks, plants, etc. With this relationship, totems became the basis of group identity, which further came to be used to distinguish one group from the other. In terms of how a mystical relationship developed, it is conceivable that some of our first teachers, guardians, and guides were animals. It was through observing what food and water they did or did not eat and drink, their general natures, their behaviors, and how they affected the lives of the people they came into contact with that determined whether they would be perceived by that group as a friend or foe of man.

If one applies one of the Egyptian Principles of Correspondence "As above so below; as below so above," (to be discussed later), it means everything on Earth, has a correspondence in the cosmos' a form before the physical manifestation originated (what Plato was referring to his forms, which he derived from Egypt). With this understanding then, it is conceivable that the powerful attributes of animals, like the all-seeing eye of the hawk and the swiftness at which it takes flight, or the ear of the dog that hears, guards, guides and protects, plants, and gems, crystals and stones, etc. were seen as having correspondences "above" or in other interdimensional realms. In other words, a force, deity, demi-god, or Neter may have been responsible for their creation and maintenance. With this understanding, it makes sense that animals would assume mystical significance.

Connecting with the superpower of the animal, connected the people with the deity, energy, force that was responsible for it. The animal (and the intelligent force) would then be seen either as a protector, guide, and good force, or an evil force (if such an animal bought harm). If the priest, magi, diviner, or medium could access the deity of the animal, then he could access its power and/or how to work with it for the benefit of the society (or at least, appease and control it), particularly if it had the potential to bring harm. Such might also explain why animals and their parts hold special significance for shamans, especially when they go into trance, see animal guides in their passage to other realms, and why the animals and their parts would be used to facilitate rituals where humans sought to connect with the divine.

Interestingly, the Greek historians Diodorus Siculus and Plutarch in *Biblica Historica* and *Moraila*, respectively, also inquired into why animals were so highly serviced, honored, and prohibited from being killed (they thought Egyptians were worshiping animals). They found several reasons expressed by the Egyptians themselves. For example, the sacred bulls, Apis and Mnevis, were honored because they helped man discover the fruits of the earth and the labor they provided in farming. Sheep give birth to lambs twice a year and they provide wool for protection and decorous covering. They also provided milk and cheese. The dog was useful for hunting and man's protection. Cats protected against asps (venomous snakes). The crocodile, being in the Nile, provided security against robbers who infested Arabia and Libya and dared not swim the Nile because of fear of them. The ichneumon prevented the Nile from being impassable because of too many crocodiles. These animals were said to crush the eggs of the crocodiles, and when the crocodiles went to sleep with their mouth open, the ichneumon would go into the center of the crocodile's body and rapidly gnaw through their bowels, killing them, and getting out unscathed. The crocodile was also revered because, like God, it can see without being seen (it has a thin transparent membrane extending down for its forehead to cover its eyes). The ibis will not approach or drink unwholesome or tainted water, which helped the people know what water not to drink, and was a protector against snakes, locusts, and caterpillars, and the hawk protected against scorpions, horned serpents, and small animals with noxious bites.

Siculus explained in some detail the extraordinary amount of resources that went into the care of some of the animals including the superior foods they were fed, the pedigree of those whose care they were under, the penalty of death if one were killed, and the extensive rituals (mummification, for example) and mourning that occurred if one died. The type and amount of care bestowed on some animals among Egyptians, it seems was like that bestowed on animals in contemporary America by pet owners, veterinarians, zoos, endangered species conservatory organizations, etc. Such care for animals may have been unheard of in other parts of the world during the times of Plutarch and Diodorus when many people all over the globe were (and still are) struggling with basic survival.

Although Massey, Churchward, and other scholars surmised that the Greeks, Romans, and later anthropologists misunderstood totemism, and thought that African people were worshiping animals, it is not inconceivable that some peoples did, and that Egyptians may have as well. Just as many people today misunderstand religious ideas, where and how they originated, the meaning behind and the significance of certain practices, and often take what is meant to be allegorical as literal, then it is probable that early peoples may have done the same thing. Thus, rather than revering the divinity or attribute of the animal, people started worshiping the animals themselves.

~~~~~~~~~~

Monotheism, or at least the idea of a Universal God, originated with African peoples and was articulated in hieroglyphics by the Egyptians—not with Moses of Judaism, as it is generally thought. Although this is the case, I have wondered why monotheism is held to be superior to polytheism in Western thought. Although Marimba Ani in *Yurugu: An African-Centered Critique of European Cultural Thought and Behavior*, as the title suggests, is an extensive work on how through *Asili* (the logos of a culture within which its various aspects cohere) *Utamawazo* (culturally structured thought), and *Utamaroho* (the vital force of a culture set in motion by the *Asili*), Europe came to world domination.

In her chapter, "Religion and Ideology," she offers interesting insights into the role of monotheism in Christianity. First, important to note, as Ani does is that the spiritual essence of Christianity originates chronologically with "older cultures" and traditions. Second is the importance of distinguishing between religion and spirituality. "Spirituality rests on the conception of a sacred cosmos that transcends physical reality in terms of significance and meaning...Religion refers to the formalization of ritual, dogma, and belief...that may or may not issue from a spiritual conception of the universe. Most often it functions to sacralize a nationalistic ideology."[144]

Third, is that although monotheism is found in earlier religions, and existed right beside polytheism, monotheism was valorized and used by the Hebrews and later Europe under Christianity. If one goes by the biblical account, Moses was raised in Egypt among the elite (Pharaoh's daughter found him in the bushes on a riverbank), and he became an Egyptian priest. This means that he went through Egyptian mystery schools and was trained in Egyptian theology. Therefore, it is highly likely that his theology and his monotheism were shaped by Egyptian theology. In fact, Churchward indicates that Moses received his priestly education in Heliopolis and was learned in all the Osirian and Amen-Ra doctrines. It was found recorded on papyri that the Egyptians used to believe and say they were the *chosen people of the Lord.*

Ani explains the role of Plato's influence, the Judaic heritage, and Judaic cultural chauvinism in the development of the monotheistic idea in Christianity, and how it was used as a political tool in the imperialistic and expansionist aims of Europe. As it regards the platonic influence, in brief, Plato, building on the ideas of Thales (who studied in Egypt and Babylonia), Anaximander, Pythagoras (Aximander's student, who had spent twenty-two years studying in Egypt), and other Greek philosophers such as Parmenides and Heraclitus, set forth that there are laws that govern the universe, and the world could be understood in terms of physical phenomena. It was a radical break from supernatural explanations—the workings of the gods—and a purely rational and materialistic explanation of the physical world. Plato's works, *Euthyphro, Apology, and Crito* are not only interesting but also insightful in terms of the *elenchus* or Socratic method, whereby Socrates (whom a Delphi oracle said was the wisest man in Greece, which he did not believe and sought to test it through questioning other wise men), would question so-called "wise" men, challenging them to question their assumptions (many of which were based on wants and desires of the gods) and to think critically. This rational approach to understanding the world would lay the foundation of modern Western science.

Egyptian-influenced Greek philosophy derived the universe as boundless and God as the *logos* or the first cause or first principle. This was undergirded by the idea that everything else, even the gods, came after (so why be subjected to their whims?). The first cause underlies the idea of monotheism. Monotheism is thousands of years old among ancient Egyptians, Africans, and other peoples; however, it would be identified with Plato's absolutism (absolute truths, which Plato confused as the same thing), and codified and formalized in Judeo-Christian religion. Absolute and so-called "pure" monotheism expressed as an ideal or value in Christian cultural chauvinism served as the basis for the devaluation of other cultures, clumping them all together under "paganism,'" although other cultures' religious ideas are the foundation upon which Christianity is based.

As far as the role of Jewish heritage, it is the 'codification' of their religion, or rather their nationalistic political and cultural ideology in the form of the written word, that holds dominant value in Western culture. Written codification potentially does several things according to Ani. First, it gives the impression of cumulative activity, that the culture is more cumulative. Second, it is seen as evolutionarily superior to cultures that codify their tradition through other media. Third, it imparts the illusion of historicity, and therefore so-called "universal truth."[145]

Ani notes that although Kemet kept written records, the religion was more cosmic, mythic, and symbolic in its intent: Kemet presented a conception of the universe as spirit, written text was buried with the dead, and much of its knowledge could only be transmitted orally by priests in their mystery schools. However, it is not so much that their records were written, it is rather the *value* that was placed on them in the West. The oral tradition held just as much value if not more value among the Kemetians (as it did among Africans in general and peoples all over the globe). This was especially the case for secret knowledge. The recording of Judaic religious laws gave birth to the idea of scriptures, and "within the European context 'culture' and 'law' are reified and, therefore through writing, are deified, religion has greater force and is 'truer,' because it is codified in writing."[146]

The Judaic cultural chauvinistic monotheistic ideal would also be transported into Christianity. Ani notes that for "Europeans the one-god idea, like written codification represents a socio-technological 'advance' along the evolutionary spectrum."[147] God had chosen the Hebrews, setting them apart as one nation among nations to be the recipient of laws, and by observing them, they would be an example among peoples of the world. Those who worshiped many gods or images were irreligious, and this justified violent hostility toward them. The scriptures below show this.

> If your brother, your mother's son or your son or daughter of the wife of your bosom, or your closest friend entices you in secret say, "Come let us worship other gods"—whom neither you nor your fathers have experienced—from among the gods of the peoples around you.....show him no pity or compassion and do not shield him, but take his life. Let your hand be the first to put him to death and the hand of the rest of the people thereafter. Stone him to death... If you hear it said, of one of the towns that the LORD your God is giving you to dwell in, that some scoundrels from among you have gone and subverted the inhabitants of their town, saying, "Come let us worship other gods" put the inhabitants of that town to the sword, and put its cattle to the sword. Doom it and all that is in it to destruction: gather all its spoil into the open square and burn the town and all its spoil as a holocaust to the LORD your God. (Tanakh, Deuteronomy 13:7-13:17)

Such ideas would serve as the precursor to the formulation of monotheism in Christianity, which is thought to be evolutionarily superior. Christianity was to "save" all the people and provided Europe with a tool to serve its imperialistic aims. This, however, would begin with a schism between Judaism and Christianity. Ani notes that "While their God was projected as the one 'true' god for humankind, the emphasis and essential feature of Judaism was not the possibility of worldwide application, but rather the specialness of the Jewish people...Important to note is that Jews as other people claim their specialness. They, however, were 'chosen' to fulfill God's prophecy, by presenting a normative example to other peoples, but not through conquest" (although as shown in the scriptures above, they promulgated violence against other peoples).[148]

Jewish nationalist formulation was based on cultural solidarity, self-determination, and social cohesion, which served as self-defensive mechanisms for their extreme minority circumstances and encouraged group identification for efficient sociopolitical organization and consolidation. A critical difference between Judaic and European Christian theology is Jewish refusal to recognize Jesus as the son of their God. Even earlier in Christian history, Paul sought to bring Gentiles into the fold; this was rejected by Jewish nationalists. Ani further notes that the Judaic vision was elitist isolationist; the European vision was expansion under the cloak of universalism, control, and exploitation of other groups.

Early in the development of Christianity, Constantine decreed a policy of tolerance for Christianity (although it is also noted that he may have genuinely embraced it) as well as Christianity's monotheistic one-God idea as expedient to his imperialistic aims in Roman territories and those that he wanted to come under the Roman Empire. He may have envisioned a one-God, one-world empire, and a one-world emperor—himself—which would eventually culminate into the Holy Roman Empire. As European states and Christianity continued to develop, in the way that Jews were to be an example in the world, Europeans would now become the so-called "chosen" people whose mission was to save souls.

Under the banner of saving souls, Christianity with its "universal," monotheistic, one-God formulation would serve as a tool along with other ideas such as white supremacy, which would come later in European imperialism and expansionism, and be used in the enslavement and slaughtering of millions of so-called "heathen," "pagan," "uncivilized," and "savage" people during their expansion into the New World, the Transatlantic slave trade, and the extraction and exploitation of their labor, land, and materials under colonialism.

~~~~~~~~~~

In the *Legends of the Gods*, by E. A. Wallis Budge one finds the origins of monotheism and the Trinity found in Abrahamic religions and others throughout the world. In the Annuian (On; Heliopolis) story of creation, the Supreme God referred to as Neb-er-tcher (Lord of the uttermost limits) first emerges out of the watery abyss Nu (speculated to be the origins of the term Anu), and out of a desire from his own heart, created himself out of himself, saying, "I am he who came into being...out of Nu [a watery mass] ... I found no place whereon I could stand. I worked a charm upon my own heart.... I laid the foundation ... and I made everything which had form."[149]

Neb-er-tcher, through "utterance" or word, gave form to a god named Khepra, the creator God or creative principle (origins of the second God in Gnosticism). He is also known as Ra at noonday and Tem/Atum in the evening. [150] Neb-er-tcher laid down the foundation through Maat (truth, justice, law, and order) and Tehuti (wisdom). Neb-er-tcher then created other gods, Shu (air) and Tefnut (moisture), declaring "from being the ONE, god (or, the only god) I became three gods" (one of several trinities in Egypt).[151] Shu and Tefnut give birth to Nut (heaven/sky) and Geb (Earth), who give birth to five gods (two couples); Ausar (Osiris) and Auset (Isis); Set and Nephthys; and Heru-Ur (the elder). In some renderings of the story, the gods then create humanity. In others, humanity was issued directly from God, Neb-er-tcher himself.

One also finds miraculous and immaculate (i.e., virgin) birth, resurrection, and eternal life in the events in the lives of the gods. In brief, in a quest for the throne, Osiris is deceived by his brother Set and seventy-two conspirators to see if he could fit into a chest that was designed to fit his body size (others also tried to fit into it). When Osiris gets into the chest, it is closed shut. The conspirators take the chest and throw it into the Nile. Distraught at the death of her brother-husband, his grief-stricken wife, Isis, searches all over Egypt until she finds the chest. She attempts to restore Osiris back to life. While doing this, Isis fans his body with her feathers (after she uses her godly magical powers to transform into a bird) and produces air, causing his inert members to move. After that, she draws from his essence and conceives the child, Horus (miraculously and immaculately).

With the help of her sister, Nephthys (who is essentially abandoned by Set), Isis continues to try to nurse Osiris back to life. However, while hunting, Set discovers the chest containing Osiris's body, dismembers it, and disburses it throughout the land of Egypt. Isis searches Egypt over again until she finds each part of Osiris's body, except for his phallus. Unable to restore him, she, Horus the Elder, Anpu, Nephthys, and Tehuti, mummifies his body and sends him to the underworld, where he becomes the first resurrected God (in the afterlife), establishes eternal life, and becomes the king of eternity.

Before his death according to legend, Isis and Osiris brought a lot of good to the people of Egypt and vast corners of the earth. Isis discovered both wheat and barley, which grew wild over the land, along with the other plants; Osiris showed the people how to cultivate these plants. Isis, calling on the powers of the god Maat, established laws for a just and peaceful society. Osiris founded the city with a hundred gates, built temples in honor of his mother and father, built golden chapels for the ancestors and gods, and taught the people how to honor them. Osiris discovered the vine and taught the people how to cultivate it, how to harvest the grape, the uses of wine, and how to store it. He also taught them how to use barley to make beer. To Osiris's discovery also are the olive tree, ivy, and myrrh. Isis taught women the medicinal use of herbs; the magical powers of perfume; how to comb, curl, and braid their hair; and how to birth children. Isis was also possessed with the power of the use of words that could heal the living and revive the dead.[152]

Because of her many benefactions, Isis has been referred to as "The Lady with a Thousand Titles," some of which include: "Queen of Earth," "Lady of Heaven," "Lady of Light," "Great Lady," "Divine Mother," "Mother of the Gods," "Mother of God," "Chamber of the Birth of a God," "Lady of Abundance," "Queen Bee," "the Beautiful Goddess," and "She who weeps." Egyptians believed that the Nile began with the tears of Isis splashing from the heavens as she mourned the death of Osiris.[153]

Osiris, having bestowed much upon humanity in life and having been the first to establish a place where humanity can go after death, a place where they could achieve everlasting life, is hailed as the greatest of the gods. To his honor, he has also been called by many names. Some among them include: "The firstborn son of unformed matter," "the god of gods," "king of kings," "Lord of lords," "prince of princes," "the prince of gods and men," "king of eternity," "lord of everlastingness," "the soul that liveth again," "one who giveth birth unto men and women a second time," and "he who engenders life in both the dead and living."[154]

Although Siculus tells of the history of Egypt as it is told by the Egyptians, Plutarch (and later scholars) suggests that the stories are probably "myth" and should not be taken as literal but as allegorical of celestial bodies. For example, according to Plutarch, the stars, the sun, and the moon were thought to represent forces and their impact on terrestrial phenomena such as the rising and generative effects of the Nile and vegetation and the forces of darkness versus the forces of light (e.g., Set versus Osiris and Horus), and so forth. Churchward reasons that the first mythos probably evolved around the stars (the Great Bear with a primary focus on the pole star and those of the big dipper—since they are the brightest stars in the sky) and is also the reason that the number seven is significant: seven glorious gods of the Egyptian; the seven days of the week; the seven celestial bodies; the sun, moon, and five planets (those most visible in the sky and also closest to the Earth); the zodiac, etc. Later, as humanity began to recognize the sun as the generative power of all of life, the sun rose to supremacy and gave birth to the solar mythos, which gave rise to solar gods found throughout the world.

Although Plutarch believed the story of Isis and Osiris to be allegorical of the celestial mythos, because a tomb of Osiris is supposed to exist in Abydos, with those of early kings, and because one can find tombs for Osiris (according to legend, Isis is supposed to have had a tomb placed at each of the places that she finds his body parts) throughout Egypt it is speculated that there may be some truth to the story and that "myth" may have been interwoven with fact and they were elevated to gods; if Isis and Osiris were not gods on Earth as the Egyptians said they were. Regardless of what historians and scholars speculate as to what is historical and what is allegorical or myth, Budge notes that although Plutarch collected many facts about the legend of Isis and Osiris, "there is no evidence that he had the slightest knowledge of the details of the original African legend of these gods as it was known to the Egyptians say under the VI Dynasty...[and] he never realized that the characteristics and attributes of both Isis and Osiris changed during the long history of Egypt and that a thousand years before he lived the Egyptians themselves had forgotten what the original form of the legend was."[155]

He also notes that "as the importance of Osiris declined that of Isis grew and men came to regard her as the great Mother-goddess of the world."[156] Because of the role that she played as a loving and devoted wife and mother, Isis was regarded as the eternal mother of life, love (bringing men and women together and giving them children), virtue, goodness, happiness, peace, immortality, and of all living things. The message of the priest of her cult was carried from:

Egypt to the Islands of Greece and to the mainland, to Italy, Germany, France, Spain, and Portugal, and then crossing the western end of the Mediterranean it entered North Africa, and with Carthage as a center spread east and west along the coast.[157]

Isis is also identified with numerous Greek, Roman, and Eastern goddesses. In Rome, she was worshiped as the Black Madonna. A college of the servants of Isis was founded in Rome. Several temples were built to her honor in Rome, Greece, and the East, and festivals were recognized in public calendars in these regions of the world.[158]

35

EMERGING FORTH INTO THE LIGHT

As indicated previously, what makes Egypt captivating to visitors, I assume (because of the effect it had on me) is the sheer magnitude, size, and majesty of the temples, monuments, and tombs in honor of the gods and kings who were considered to represent God on Earth, and Egypt's concepts of resurrection, afterlife, and eternal life. I had been to Egypt three times, and I still did not fully awaken to the extent to which the monuments had to do with the afterlife. More importantly, the role of the desire for eternal life in shaping morality; that is, how man conducts his life on Earth determines what happens to his soul in the afterlife is probably the most significant contribution Egyptians made to the world in general and the world's religions in particular.

Egyptian cosmology held that there existed Earth, the underworld or the Tuat, and heaven or Aaru (field of reeds or rushes—eternal life). Before the soul could gain entrance into Aaru, it had to get through the Tuat, which presented many dangers. Budge, in *The Egyptian Book of the Dead*, notes that the underworld is the origins of Hades in Greek mythology and hellfire in Abrahamic religions. However, although the Egyptians had a concept of the underworld, it was not in the center of the earth, and it was not hellfire. It was beyond the sky and consisted of twelve hours or divisions, which the soul had to pass through in the boat of a million years with Ra, who makes the journey every evening before he "comes forth by day" at which time he is renewed. In other words, as the sun rises in the east and settles in the west, the soul was a rising and setting sun.[159]

When Ra and his Company of Gods make their daily journey through the twelve divisions of the Tuat, at each gate or hour are serpent guardians and other gods to help him ward off attacks of fiends and monsters, and specifically the most notable Apep, the monstrous serpent, who endeavors to obstruct the passage of the boat. Before the soul can enter the boat with Ra and other Company of Gods, the soul must have been funeralized properly and must know the "words of power" to first enter the boat; the names of the gods at each hour or division of the Tuat, and have served them while on Earth. In the Annuian system, if the soul makes it through successfully, it rises again. During this journey, the soul must make forty-two declarations to pass through forty-two assessors before he enters the Judgment Hall, where his heart is weighed against the Maatian feather of justice. Tehuti records the outcome, and if successful, the soul can pass through the gate where Osiris, the king of eternity sits. From here, the soul achieves eternal life and can enter into the boat of Ra, where he "comes forth by day" and is free to roam (make visits back to Earth, I am assuming, where his body lies), or he enters into the field of reeds, where all his needs are met. If the soul is not successful in making it through the Tuat, it is devoured forever. Budge notes, that because the soul is annihilated in the Egyptian theological system, there, therefore, is no concept of hell or eternal damnation.

What assisted the person in navigating through the Tuat successfully were spells referred to as *Coming Forth by Day* or *Emerging Forth into the Light*, commonly known as *The Book of the Dead*. Such spells first appear at the end of the fifth dynasty in Egypt's age of pyramids, referred to as the *Pyramid Texts* (written on tomb walls). They were eventually adapted for private use and carved into coffins, referred to as the *Coffin Texts*, for those who could afford a sarcophagus. *Coming Forth by Day* texts were later developed from the *Coffin Texts* and put on coffins, shrouds, wrappings, and bandages. They contained information about the landscape of the Tuat; the names of the gods; what needed to be said to gain entry through their gates; and transformation spells that allowed the soul to change into different forms (e.g., a falcon, snake, or lotus flower, etc.); and spells to drive away snakes, crocodiles, and insects. Since the body also needed to be protected so that the spirit or *ba* could return to it, it was mummified and protected with the spells, images of the gods, magical objects, small amulets, or charms, placed around and wrapped in the

bandages, on the mummy and on the coffin itself. The Papyrus of Nes-
tanebetisheru, a high priestess and the daughter of the high priest of
Amun, Panedjem II, is one of the largest surviving complete rolls, 123
feet long (before it was cut into ninety-eight separate sheets). The Papyrus of Ani (originally seventy-eight feet long), also one of the most complete papyri that were found, provides insight into the actual journey
through the Tuat.

The gods of the Ennead play significant roles in helping the soul get
through. What is particularly interesting is the passion with which the
gods and Ani ask to be accepted into God's domain. In the first stanza
below, Ani asks that his heart not stand in opposition against him, and
in the second, Tehuti supports him:

> Ani: O my heart which I had from my mother! O my heart which
> I had from my mother! ... Do not stand up as a witness against
> me, do not be opposed to me in the tribunal, do not be hostile
> to me in the presence of the Keeper of Balance... Do not tell lies
> about me in the presence of the gods.

> Tehuti: Hear this word of very truth. I have judged the heart of
> the deceased, and his soul stands as a witness for him. His deeds
> are righteous in the great balance, and no sin has been found in
> him...[160]

Interesting is that in the first stanza the soul accuses itself, which it
seems would have serious implications for how what one does while on
Earth in the physical body affects one as one goes through the Tuat.

36
UNVEILING THE CHRIST

The extensive work, *Bible Myths and the Parallels in Other Religions*, by T.W.
Doane, *Christianity Before Christ*, by J.G. Jackson, and *The Christ Conspiracy*
by Acharya S., and numerous other works claim that Christianity is
founded on so-called "pagan" religions. Because much of the story of
the life and death of Jesus appears to be constructed on the mythos of
earlier peoples, some scholars go as far as to assert that there is no

historical personage of Jesus; although this is counter to what is generally accepted by most mainstream scholars.

They inform us that numerous "Pagan Christs" lived or were supposed to have lived hundreds, even thousands of years before Jesus. The most known of them were Osiris and Horus of Egypt, Krsna and Buddha of India, Mithra of Persia, Quetzalcoatl of Mexico, Adonis of Babylonia, Bacchus of Greece, and Attis of Phrygia. When one examines their traditions, myths, and legends, one finds that as a rule (although variably): they are said to have been born on or near December 25 (near the winter solstice and the Christmas holidays). They are typically born of a virgin mother and/or are of royal descent. Their births are announced by a star, their coming is prophesized, and they are visited by prominent men (wise men, shepherds, priests, magis, etc.). They are said to have been born in a cave or stable. They are tempted (while fasting and/or in meditation). They are slain (by crucifixion or hanging). They descend into hell. They are resurrected somewhere about March 25 close to the vernal equinox, spring, the Easter holiday, and they ascend to heaven.

Scholars also explored the origins and meanings of some of the life and death events of these saviors and suggest that they are derived from the stellar and solar mythos. Acharya S. points out the significance of the savior as symbolic of the sun in her chapter the "Son of God, is the Sun of God." First citing from the Book of Ecclesiastes 1:9 "there is nothing new under the sun," she notes that that the Christian Gospels are mere astrotheological and non-historical recordings of the mythos found in virtually every culture all over the globe. She further notes:

> In many places and eras, the sun was considered the visible proxy of the divine and the most potent bestower of *Spirit* [italics my emphasis]. It was regarded as the...progenitor of all life and matter...it represented the Archetypal Man as human beings were perceived as solar entities...The sun was also considered as the 'Savior of the world,' as it rose and brought light and life to the planet. It was revered for causing seeds to burst and thus giving its life for plants to grow; hence it was seen to sacrifice itself in order to provide fertility and vegetation. It was the 'tutelary genius of universal vegetation' as well as the god of cultivation and the benefactor of

humankind. When the sun 'dies' in the winter so does the vegetation, to be 'resurrected,' in the spring...[161]

Thus, "Because of the importance of the sun, for millennia, people around the world people have built solar temples, monuments and entire religions with priestesses and priests of the Sun, along with complex rituals and accouterments."[162]

Throughout the world, the sun had been represented as a solar deity because it is the generative force and giver of life. The "son" of the sun is the regenerative life force that is reborn daily, annually, and processionally. Manly P. Hall in *The Secret Teachings of All Ages* notes that the Egyptians divided the life of the sun into four parts or seasons and that the "Solar Man" goes through these four seasons. He is born during the winter solstice (represented by the Egyptian Horus with one lock of hair, which symbolizes survival through the darkness of winter); at the vernal equinox (spring), he is a beautiful youth; at the summer solstice (when nature is the strongest and most fecund), he is in the prime of his maturity; at the autumnal equinox, he is an aged man, moving to winter darkness (death).[163] The other elements found in mythos throughout the world that seem to originate with solar mythos and/or that predate the Christian savior are as follows:[164]

- Slaughter of the Innocents: A standard element in the sacred king tradition found in mythos whereby the reigning monarch tries to prevent a prophecy from being fulfilled, a king will be born who will overthrow him. Found in the Isis, Osiris, and Horus story, as well as numerous other stories (Sargon, Nimrod, Krsna, Oedipus, etc.), is the flight of the virgin mother with her infant to prevent attempts made to destroy him. He eventually grows into manhood and carries out this purpose.
- Virgin Birth: During certain ages, the constellation Virgo (which represents the virgin) rose with the sun.
- Three Wise Men and Announcement of His Star in the East: "Represents the three stars in Orion's belt 'whose rising announced the coming of Sothis, the Star of Horus/Osiris: that is Sirius, the brightest star in the sky, whose coming heralded the annual flood of the Nile...The gifts bought by the magi, gold, frankincense, and myrrh were what was always offered by the Arabian magi to the sun.'"[165]

- Born in a Manger/Cave: "Represents winter and the setting of the sun when it appears to go underground or in the underworld, which is the womb of both the heavens and Earth. It 'was originally identified with the womb of Mother Earth, the logical symbolic birth and regeneration.'" Also, the birthplace in Bethlehem, now considered the birthplace of Jesus long before the Christian era, was the birthplace of Adonis/Tammuz.[166]

- The Temptation: Many saviors (Horus, Buddha, Manu, Quetzalcoatl, Zoroaster, etc.) were tempted in the wilderness. It represents the struggle between day and night, winter, and summer, dark and light.

- Descent into Hell and the Resurrection: The sun makes an annual descent southward until after midnight on December 21st (the winter solstice), it appears to stop for three days, and then starts to move northward again. During these three days, "God's sun" had "died" and was "born again" after midnight on December 24th. December 25th (Christmas) is celebrated as the birth of saviors all over the world.

- The Crucifixion: The "crucifixion" is the "crossification" of the sun through the equinoxes. It is a scapegoat ritual in which the son of God, the sacred king (in some cases, his son, or a criminal, or animals), was sacrificed or put to death atone for our sins. The sins of the community were put on the head of a person or animal, who was sacrificed to rid the community of its sins. In some instances, the victim was slain by having his heart pierced by a sacred lance. It was practiced throughout the ancient world and has happened thousands of times around the globe.

- Ascent to Heaven: Several gods and goddesses around the world ascend to heaven in one way or other; the Mount of Olives in Egypt was the mountain of Amenta termed the "Mount Bakhu," which was the mount of the olive tree but was represented by Judea as the local mount of olives.[167]

- Jesus as the Lamb of God and Fish: The crucifixion occurs during the vernal equinox in the sign of Aries the lamb; fish represent the age of Pisces.

- The Twelve Disciples: Represents the twelve signs of the zodiac. As the sun goes through the twelve months, it also circles the signs of the zodiac, which means "wheel of animals." It is speculated and generally agreed that their names originated among the Egyptians (and earlier Nile people) with the presence or dominance of animals and/or their attributes and other symbols or events when the sun is in each of the constellations. The following is how the signs correspond with an animal or other natural phenomenon.

○ Aires (ram or lamb): the season of sheep raising, plowing, and goat breeding.

○ Taurus (bull or ox): the season of plowing.

○ Gemini (twins): goat breeding season; two kids or goats are frequently born two at a time.

○ Cancer (crab): the sun reaches its most northern point in the constellations, and then returns toward the south moving backward like a crab.

○ Leo (lion): time of year when the heat is most powerful, and the lion the most ferocious (like the sun) of animals, driven from the desert, appears on the Nile.

○ Virgo (virgin): the harvest season; when young girls were sent out to glean the field.

○ Libra (the scale of balance): the sun moves in this constellation when the day and night are of equal length.

○ Scorpio (scorpion): season of unhealthy weather and plagues, which were imagined to strike like a scorpion.

○ Sagittarius (the archer): hunter season when hunters shot game with the bow and arrow.

○ Pisces (fish): when fishing season was at its height.

○ Capricorn (goat): the sun reaches its lowest point and then begins to climb toward the north again as the wild goat climbs toward the summit on the hill.

○ Aquarius (the water carrier): time of winter rains.[168]

~~~~~~~~~~

Something else that I was curious about as a child and adult was communion or the Eucharist. During the last supper, according to Matthew 26, "Jesus took bread, and blessed it, and broke it, and gave it to the disciples and said, 'Take, eat; this is my body.' And he took the cup and gave thanks, and gave it to them, saying 'Drink ye of it; for this is my blood of the new testament, which is for many for the remission of sins'" (26–28). The question for me has always been: "Why would I want to eat somebody's body or drink their blood?" I searched for an answer to this question and would find that human sacrifice might be the source of this ritual. At least, this is what some scholars speculate. Churchward indicates, without any uncertainty, that the mother was the first in the line of human sacrifices and explains its connection to the totem. The totem was first used by Nilotic Africans to distinguish blood relationships within tribes with the blood mother being used to trace the line of descent. The totem first represented two phases: it was first given to the girl when she attained womanhood as the badge by which she, as the mother of her children, would be known; secondly, it included food districts that were represented by the totem of the family or tribe. "*The Totem was first eaten by members of the group* [italics his emphasis] as their own special food. Later, this was altered, and the totemic food was only eaten very sparingly by the tribe with that totem; it became *tabu* or sacred to them. The tribe was appointed the totem's preserver and cultivator and was named after it."[169]

In terms of human sacrifice, he explains: "The Totem then represented the Maternal Ancestor, the Mother who gave herself up for food to the tribe and was eaten absolutely alive after she had ceased to bear children, because she should never die, but always be alive."[170] Churchward asserts, "*This was the primitive Eucharist and was the foundation of all such rites. The 'body and blood,' were veritably eaten whilst alive, and no morsel, however, small, was allowed to remain uneaten*" [italics, his emphasis].[171] He also points out that it was a sacred feast in which each member of the tribe was expected to participate. Although the practice has died out in most if not all parts of the world "her *Totemic Zootype is eaten sacramentally* once a year in place of the human mother."[172] In addition, he notes that this is the origin of one of the principal doctrines of Christianity.

Doane explains that the Eucharist was practiced among the Egyptians to celebrate the resurrected Osiris, who ate a sacred cake or wafer, which was mystically symbolic of "flesh of his flesh." Bread and wine were bought to the temples by worshippers as offerings. It was also practiced among the Therapeutae, Essenes, Pythagoreans, Greeks, Melchizedek (high priests of the Israelites), the Persian magi, and in Mithraism, from where the Eucharist is believed to have been transported into Christianity.

The death and resurrection are speculated to have originated with vegetation cults, which are thought to predate stellar and solar cults with the death and resurrection of crops and plant life. Jackson notes that many ancient peoples made annual human sacrifices to vegetation gods. First, the king, who was thought to represent God in human form, was killed because the prosperity of the society depended upon his well-being; a weak and feeble king meant the society would suffer; therefore, they were replaced by their sons. When they got tired of being killed, their sons were sacrificed. After a time, condemned criminals and animals were sacrificed. The fact that such victims were slain while bound to a sacred tree, with their arms outstretched, might explain crucifixion on a cross.

In addition, the resurrection of the victim was believed to occur after a time, with three days being the most common, their resurrection representing the return of vegetation.[173] Acharya S. notes that both the Eucharist and the Passion stem from the scapegoating fertility ritual, where the vegetation god-king is conducted in precession and put to death as a sin offering to atone for our sins. His blood and flesh were eaten (a cannibalistic rite, which is now allegorical) or spread upon field crops so the crops would produce abundance. It is analogous to spring and renewal of vegetation and has been practiced thousands of times all around the globe.

It has been suggested that using the crucifixion as Jesus being the "sacrificial lamb" helped to get rid of the practice of human sacrifice throughout the world. Unfortunately, millions of people were "sacrificed"—outright murdered—during the various periods of Christian expansion, throughout the Roman Empire, during the so-called Dark Ages, the slave trade, and during colonialism.

A point of interest is that Madame Blavatsky in *Isis Unveiled*, was adamant that Jesus Christ was India's Krsna. When I read Paul Carus's *The Gospel of Buddha*, who predated Jesus by about five hundred years, it was like reading straight out of the Christian Bible. Doane makes comparisons between Krsna, Buddha, and Jesus, finding numerous parallels. All three of them were born to virgins; they were from a royal bloodline (although they were born of a virgin); their conceptions were celebrated (by devatas or angels); their births were announced by a star; the heavens rejoiced at their birth; they were visited by wise men who bought them highly valued gifts; they were born while their fathers were away paying taxes (Krsna and Jesus); they spoke to their mothers while they were yet infants; their lives were threatened by kings who thought they might overthrow them; their fathers were warned by a heavenly voice (Krsna) and in a dream (Jesus) to take the child and flee to another city, and they were possessed with knowledge beyond their years as child students.

For both Jesus and Krsna, one of the first miracles they performed when mature was the curing of a leper, they descended to hell, both were pierced, crucified, and resurrected, and bodily ascended to heaven. And all three saviors are to be judges of the dead on the last day. There are also numerous other parallels. Doane notes that the mythos of Krsna may have been borrowed from early Indian saviors (who also probably got it from Egypt) and that Buddhism may have borrowed from the Egyptians, as well as the Krsna mythos. However, they both predate Christianity, and it is clearly obvious that the Christ Jesus (as distinguished from Jesus, the historical man), borrowed from the Buddha, if not Krsna as well.[174]

Although scholars show the Bible myths and their parallels in religions throughout the world, and strong parallels can be found between India's Krsna and Buddha, Massey and Churchward indicate that the Christian mythos, like all others, is founded on Egyptian mythos since it all originated with Nilotic peoples. Particularly, the mythos of Jesus the Savior is founded on Horus the Savior, which is based on the stellar and solar mythos that goes back at least ten thousand years. Because much of the story around the gospel of Jesus appears to be constructed on the mythos of earlier saviors, some go as far as to assert that there is even no historical Jesus.

Using substantial evidence from numerous sources, Acharya S. argues that the whole Jesus story was manufactured in the Catholic Church's "holy forgery mill." First, there is little recorded history by the primary historians (Titus Flavius Josephus and Tacitus) during the time that Jesus purportedly lived. The seemingly insignificant amount of information that is found is believed to have been interpolated. Second, the four Gospels (the so-called inspired works of the apostles), were written (or rather forged) in the middle of the second century, around 150 CE, about 120 years after the supposed crucifixion. No New Testament texts can be found in writings before the second century of the Common Era, and despite claims that the Gospels were authored by apostles, there were no translations of manuscripts written in Hebrew or Aramaic by Jewish apostles, because they were originally written in Greek.

Because of all the writings that were supposed to be authored by the apostles, it took years to distinguish which writings were "inspired" and which were "spurious." Numerous were written by unknown authors (and some, Christian fanatics), and it took a thousand years for the New Testament to be finalized or canonized. In addition, in the Epistles of Paul (which are argued to be also fictitious), there is no mention of the historical background of Jesus or any of his sayings. The letters deal with spiritual constructs found in various religions, cults, sects, and mystery schools that existed for hundreds, even thousands of years.

The Christ or Christos concept existed before the invention of Roman Christianity, and Christian sects existed before the advent of Jesus Christ as Nazarenes, Essenes, Ebionites, Therapeutae's, etc., although they were not yet called Christians. Since there were numerous, cults, sects, mystery schools, secret societies, and brotherhoods, with varying ideas, vying for supremacy, the Council of Nicaea was held to unify them under one "universal" Catholic Church. According to Acharya S.

> The name, 'Jesus Christ,' or 'Christ Jesus' was put together for the first time at the Council of Nicaea, uniting Jesus who represented Jesus of the Druids, Yeshua/Joshua/Jesus of the Israelites, Horus/Iusa of the Egyptians, IES/Iesios of the Dionysians/Samothracians, and Christ representing the Krishna/Christos of India, the anointed of the Jews and the KRST of Egypt, among others. Further, evidence that the phrase 'Jesus Christ,' did not exist prior to the Nicaea Council is that it does not exist in Greek or Latin prior to that time.[175]

Because people have always waited for messengers, avatars, messiahs, mahdis to incarnate (in some cases, every six hundred years), the Church exploited this. Jesus was carnalized and historicized not only to rebut the Gnostic intelligentsia who saw some Church fathers as ignorant fanatics but also to distinguish him from other "mythological" personas the world over who had not appeared in the flesh. In the earliest New Testament, written by Marcions, Jesus was neither Jewish, historical, or incarnate. Bringing Jews into the fold and historicizing and making Jesus (who was prophesized to come) was done to legitimize that the

Church had received its authority from the Jewish "Messiah," although Judaism and Christianity are essentially two different religions. In addition, the story was manufactured to reflect that the Jews, rather than Rome, had crucified Jesus, thereby exonerating Rome and to further justify Rome's destruction of the Jews. After manufacturing the Jesus story, every effort was made to destroy all traces of the first two centuries of the Christian Era. Acharya S. notes:

> In the third to sixth centuries, whole libraries were burned, schools and universities destroyed, and citizens' books confiscated throughout the Roman world on the pretext of defending the church against paganism. Under the early Christian emperors, people were framed by ecclesiastical investigators who planted 'magical writings' in their houses then legally confiscated all possessions.[176]

Further, after the Council of Nicaea in 325 CE, per the orders of Constantine, censorship was heightened, leading to the centuries-long obliteration of millions of texts, including those in the Library of Alexandria. Even the death penalty was enacted for reading unapproved books. Pope after pope continued the assault on books and learning, some actively engaging in book burnings. In the eleventh century, the Library of Palatine Apollo was burned, and the Council of Trent (1545–1563) reconfirmed the policy against "heathen" learning. In addition, "Christians demolished and desecrated the temples, statues and sacred site of the predecessors" and the erection of Christian churches on the ruins of "pagan" temples and sacred sites was common and served to obliterate evidence of the previous deities and worship. Additionally, millions were tortured and murdered for centuries.[177]

Although attempts were made to purge the history of Christianity's beginnings, some important texts did survive, providing evidence of its development. According to Acharya S., the Syrian Gnostics were attempting to create a synchronistic religion that would encompass the wide variety of cultures around the world and began writing the various sayings and deeds of the personas of the celestial mythos and savior cults that had been transmitted orally within the brotherhood for millennia. Meanwhile, in Palestine were various Jewish sects such as the

Jewish/Samaritan priesthood of the Masons, some astrologers, the Za-
dokites/Sadducees, and others, who dispersed after the destruction of
Palestine into various other brotherhoods and branches, including those
at Antioch and Alexandria. She continues:

> The new influx reignited the centuries-old internecine struggle for
> supremacy over each other and the Gentiles. Thus, began the con-
> spiracy to set the ubiquitous solar hero sayings and narratives in
> Judea. In the middle of the 2nd century, the original Gnostics
> schools began to dissent from the Judaizing and historicizing ac-
> tivity, objecting that their original work was not meant to be taken
> literally. At the end of the 2nd century, the historicizing push in-
> creased with the success of the Roman play for domination, and
> the canonical Gospels were completed somewhat, although they
> were continuously reworded to agree at least superficially with
> other newly forged manuscripts. This...went on for centuries until
> relative uniformity was achieved with dozens of councils as well.[178]

Baigent et al. in *The Messianic Legacy* note some interesting details
about Constantine and how Roman gods were reconciled with Christianity. When Constantine decreed tolerance for Christianity, Sol Invictus
("Unconquered Sun") and Mithra ("Genius the Celestial Light") were
the dominant Roman gods. Constantine had been initiated into the Sol
Invictus cult and was its chief priest. The Sol Invictus god (which originated in Syria) had been introduced to Rome a century before Constantine, was monotheistic, and held to be the sum of all the attributes of
other gods, but subsumed other gods without the need to eradicate them
(like the priests did with Amon-Ra among the Egyptians).

Mithraism is speculated to have originated in the Hindu-Kush mountain area. The god found in India (Varuna the "Light God") and the chief
god of Zoroastrianism in Persia, Mithra ("the Genius of Celestial Light"
and "Defender of Truth and All Things Good"), were also popular in
Rome. It was by an edict promulgated in 321 under Constantine that
Christianity adopted Sunday ("the sun's day," as other days are named
after planets) as the Sabbath day, dissociating it from its Judaic origins.
Also, until the fourth century, Jesus's birthday was celebrated on the 6th
of January. However, for the cult of Sol Invictus, the most important day
(based on the winter solstice as with other mystery religions), for rebirth

was December 25th. Michael Baigent et al. sums up how the god from Sol Invictus and Mithraism aligned perfectly with Christianity:

> So close was Mithraism to the cult of Sol Invictus that the two are often confused. Both emphasized the status of the sun. Both held Sunday as sacred. Both celebrated a major birth festival on 25 December. In consequence, Christianity could also find lines of convergence with Mithraism—the more so as Mithraism stressed the immortality of the soul, a future judgment, and the resurrection of the dead. The Christianity that coalesced and took shape in Constantine's time was in fact a hybrid, containing significant skeins of thought derived from Mithraism and from the sun cult. Christianity as we know it is in many respects closer to those pagan systems of belief than to its own Judaic origins.[179]

After the Council of Nicaea in 325 CE, where it was established that the Father, the Son, and Holy Spirit were of one substance, in an attempt to suppress the opinions contrary to the church, Constantine issued a decree that the property of the Gnostics whom he addressed in a public notice as heretics "be confiscated and handed over incontestably and without delay to the Catholic Church, and other sites become public property; so that hereafter no opportunity be left for [them] to meet [so that their] unlawful groups may not dare to assemble in any place either public or private."[180]

~~~~~~~~~~

As indicated previously, I was curious about how Black people in America (and in Africa and the diaspora for that fact), could worship a white image of Jesus. This would lead to the question of how Jesus even became a bearded man of European descent. It is speculated that this image was derived from Serapis, a combination of Egypt's Osiris and Apis (an ox) represented as Osiris's attributes once he passes to the underworld, Osorapis. The story is that Ptolemy I Soter, the first Greek pharaoh of Egypt after Alexander, wanted to produce a supreme deity that would be acceptable to both the local Egyptian population and the Greek immigrants and visitors. According to Plutarch, Ptolemy I saw a statue in his dreams. When he inquired about it, a well-traveled man, Sosibius, informed him that what he saw was a statute of Pluto (Greek god of the underworld) in Sinope. With great difficulty (in one account, it took three years for the King of Scydrothemis to agree; in another account, it was stolen) Ptolemy I had the statue moved to Alexandria.

Manetho, the Egyptian historian, and Timotheus, an expositor of the sacred law, convinced Ptolemy I that the statue was not Pluto or any other god; that it was none other than Osiris (or Serapis, his other title). Ptolemy I, placed the Greek looking statute with the attributes of one of the oldest Egyptian gods, Osiris combined with those of various Greek gods, (Egyptian priests were accustomed to combining the attributes of various gods, although many of the Greek gods had already acquired some of the attributes of Osiris) in Alexandria, and had the Serapeum Temple complex built, that centered around his worship.

The original elaborate temple complex, located on the west bank of the Nile near Ṣaqqārah, was a monument (cemetery) to the deceased Apis bulls, the sacred animals of the god Ptah (of Memphis). As early as 1400 BC, the area was used as a cemetery for the bulls. Ramses II (1279–1213 BC) designed a main gallery and subsidiary chambers that were repeatedly enlarged by succeeding kings, to serve as a catacomb for the deceased Apis bulls who, in death, became assimilated to the god Osiris as Osiris-Apis. The Greeks living near Ṣaqqārah worshiped this god as Osorapis, which under the Ptolemaic dynasty became Serapis, and the temple was thereafter called the Serapeum. Through the syncretistic Gnostic sects, who sprung up around Alexandria in the second century, Serapis would also acquire the attributes of the healer, the judge of the living and the dead, and the Supreme Being whose manifestation on Earth was the Christ. A letter of Hadrian (Roman emperor from 117 to 138) written to Servianus (his brother-in-law) is revealing:

> Those who worship Serapis are also Christians; even those who style themselves the bishops of Christ are devoted to Serapis. The very patriarch himself, when he comes to Egypt, is forced by some to adore Serapis, by others to adore Christ. There is but one God for them all; him do the Christians, him do the Jews, him do all the Gentiles also worship. There can be no doubt that the head of Serapis... supplied the first idea for the conventional portraits of the Savior.[181]

The statue would be destroyed during the destruction of the Serapeum Temple complex at Alexandria, and the great library by Theophilus, the patriarch of Alexandria, and his followers in 391 CE, with the encouragement of Emperor Theodosius's edict that was addressed to the magistrate and military government of Egypt, prohibiting the worship of "pagan" gods. Although this would signal the final triumph of Roman Christianity not only in Egypt but also throughout the Roman Empire, the image would be transported to Rome, and later during the Medieval and Renaissance periods in Europe, a white, bearded Jesus would be proliferated in their art and imposed upon people throughout the world during European world conquest and domination beginning in 1492 CE.

Finally, Doane summed up what some of the Gnostics and other sects during the time that Christianity was being invented, what other scholars and writers have expressed, and something that I and I am sure people all over the world have felt and thought in some way or other: "The Great God of the immense universe looks too small upon the cross of Calvary, and the human family is too large, has too numerous virtues and vices to be perfectly represented by and depended on one Rabbi of Galilee."[182] Furthermore, I, as Doane and I am sure numerous others, just find it too hard to believe that:

> God himself...was manifested in the flesh; that that Being who pervades the universe had been confined in the womb of Mary [or the womb of any other woman as implied in other saviors]; that his eternal duration had been marked by the days and months, and years of human existence; that the Almighty God had been scourged and crucified [and would ask himself why he had forsaken himself]; that his impassible essence had felt pain and anguish; that his omniscience was not exempt from ignorance; and that the source of life and immortality expired on Mount Calvary [italics his emphasis].[183]

37

PIERCING THE VEIL OF ISIS

"I pierced the veil of Isis," said my twenty-something-year-old cousin, Julius, after I sat down at a table at a hotel to have a chat with him. "I pierced the veil of Isis," he said again, and he repeated several more times during our brief conversation.

I was visiting Berlin, Maryland, where my biological mother lives, who I had met a few years before this strange encounter with my cousin. I found it particularly interesting that she lives in the really small town of Ocean Pines, about seven minutes away from my non-biological cousin, Rosalind and her husband Freddie (who had helped me participate in the Hal Jackson's Talented Teen Pageant in New York City when I was fifteen) had moved to. I had met Julius about two years before this meeting at his sister's wedding near Boston. My mother told me some years before this encounter that they were concerned about him. I speculated that he might be engaging in Reiki, or energy work since she said he was talking about crystals. I told her I would talk to him to see where his head is.

When I came into the room where some of my blood relatives had gathered in a hotel in Ocean City, he was there, but not present. I found it interesting that although I was sitting in a room with my blood relatives, the connection felt nothing like I feel with my family I was raised with (who had come to Maryland as well, and whom I could not wait to get back to). I felt some connection because I knew consciously that they were my blood relatives, I had spent some time around them at the wedding, and because my mother talks about them. When I got ready to leave with my mother and father (her husband, but not my biological father), Julius came out like a humble servant to escort us out. Once we got to the lobby, my mother and father seemed like they were not ready to leave and began watching some of the activities. Julius began talking, so I suggested that we sit down for a moment so I could hear what he was saying.

I do not recall what I asked, but I do recall that he kept repeating that he pierced the veil of Isis. Although I used the story of Isis and Osiris in my relationship books, it was the first time that I had been awakened to the "veil of Isis," as something to even seek to pierce. "They will only reveal information to you if you are worthy of it," he said, "and they will only give it to you if you use it to serve." He also said, "They will trick you. They will give you what you ask for, and then take it all back." I don't recall what he said about the daemons (which are different and spelled differently and here to distinguish them from demons—evil spirits), but I remember that he said something about them; I had been searching the Internet for information on them.

In this brief conversation (that probably lasted no more than twenty minutes), this young man in his twenties revealed things I had been searching for information about, without my even asking. It was as if the gods were speaking directly to me through him. When I got home, I searched the Internet for information on the veil of Isis and the daemons.

The veil has fascinated me since I can remember. It started with my first memory of seeing a black veil on the faces of Jacquelyn Kennedy at John F. Kennedy's funeral and Coretta Scott King at Dr. Marin Luther King Jr.'s funeral on television when I was a child. It became thematic in my work on polygyny once I discovered that in ancient Mesopotamia the veil was used to separate classes of women. It privileged some women over others based on their status with men (generally their marriage status, leaving women who were not married and did not wear the veil unprotected). And the veiling of women seemed to have carried over into Islam. I think it was the words "Isis" and "Unveiled" that drew me to Madam Blavatsky's work, *Isis Unveiled*, and subsequently to her other work *The Secret Doctrine,* and the numerous other works by members of the Theosophical Society that reveal the mysteries in India's religion.

In ancient Egypt, the veil meant something different. Plutarch wrote that on a statue of a goddess in Sais, Egypt, there was an inscription that read, "I am all that has been and is and shall be, and no mortal has ever lifted my garment." It is speculated that this statue is Isis (it is also speculated to be Neith) and that it refers to "things hidden in plain sight;" the forces that are governing the world right before our very eyes that we cannot see.

38
THE "DEMONS" OF SOLOMON

In my search to understand who the daemons (their Latin name and *daimons*, their Greek name) were (or are), I found that it is how the Greeks referred to the elementals (which is the name of the forces that reside in and/or govern the elements of earth, water, fire, and air, or nature spirits that are discussed later). Although daemons are benevolent and serve good purposes, the Christian fathers (some of whom said they were conversant with them), clumped them all together as "demons" or evil spirits. I also found the work, *Iamblichus on the Mysteries of the Egyptians, Chaldeans and Assyrians*, which is a detailed response to a letter written to an Egyptian named Anebo (although the responder is said to be Iamblichus himself) requesting that he explain in every manner possible the difference between gods, archangels, angels, daemons, genii, archons, heroes, and other deities, which he does. The response is insightful however, it goes way beyond the scope of this work. I have mentioned it here for those interested in seeking it out.

The search also led me to *The Three Magical Books of Solomon*, a volume by Crowley, Mathers, and Conybear. Although it is revealing with regard to Solomon's practice of magic (and I am assuming is derived from Hebrew or Jewish mysticism), what I found particularly interesting is what it reveals in the chapter, "The Testament of Solomon," about how he used the "demons" those of an evil nature to build the Great Temple of God.

The testament begins with Solomon describing how a boy of his chief deviser of the Temple, whom he loved, was growing thinner by the day. He questioned the boy, asking him how it is that he was giving him double wages and a double supply of food, but day by day and hour by hour he was growing thinner. The boy responded that after he is released from work on the temple, one of the evil demons comes and takes away half his pay and half his food and that at night, he sucks his right thumb. Disturbed by this, Solomon enters the temple and prays with all his heart and soul, night, and day, that the demon is delivered into his hands so that he could gain authority over it. In response to this, a ring consisting of an engraved stone was given to him by Archangel Michael from the Lord Sabaoth, and he was instructed to use it to lock up all the demons of the earth and use them to build up Jerusalem.

Solomon gives the ring to the boy and instructs him that, when the demon shows up, to throw the ring at his chest, and then run to him. The boy follows his instructions, and upon meeting him, Solomon asks who he is, under what zodiacal sign he was subjected to, and what angel frustrates him. After receiving the information, he needs to bind him, Solomon seals him up and puts him to work on the Temple. Now having him at his mercy, Solomon asks this demon who the prince of the demons is, gives him the ring, and instructs him to use it in the same manner as the boy, to bring to him the prince of all the demons. After meeting the prince of the demons, Solomon asks him his purpose, to which he responds, "I destroy kings... I excite them into desires for wicked sins, and evil heresies, and lawless deeds; and they obey me, and I bear them on to destruction... I inspire men with envy, and [and desire] for murder, and for wars... and other evil things. And I will destroy the world."[184]

Solomon binds him also, and this opens the way for Solomon to summon them all; some singularly, others in groups. In the same line of questioning, Solomon asks who they are (their names), and their purpose or pursuit. The responses from a group of seven were as follows:

- "I am Deception," I deceive and weave snares... I excite heresies."
- "I am Strife... strife of strife."
- "I am battle...and cause the well-behaved to scatter and fall foul one of the other..."
- "I am Jealousy... I cause men to forget their sobriety and moderation... [I split the husband from his wife] and children from parents and brothers from sisters."
- "I am Power...By power, I raise up tyrants and tear down kings. To all rebels I furnish power."
- "I am Error...I lead the errant souls away from all piety."
- "I am the worse of all... I make [one]worse off than [they were] ...If one were wise, he would not turn his steps towards me..."[185]

Solomon summons numerous other demons whose purpose is to lead men astray. He also asked them as he did others their name, their purpose, under what star they lie or pass, what archangel or angel frustrates them, and using this information, he binds them and puts them to work on the Temple.

While in this pursuit, Solomon was warned by one of the demons that his glory would be but for a season and short would be his tyranny over them; the demons would one day have free range over mankind who would revere them as if they were gods. Another demon warned Solomon that the temple would be destroyed, the jars they were bound in would be broken by the hands of men, and they would go "forth in great power hither and thither and be disseminated all over the world."[186] The spirit of God departed Solomon, according to his testament, after being lured by a woman of "idol" gods to worship them and build temples to them, after which he became the "sport" of idol gods and the demons.

The testament was supposedly written by Solomon before his death to warn the Children of Israel to not underestimate the power of the demons. I guess what happened to Solomon is what my cousin meant when he said they will give you what you ask for and then take it back. Interestingly, given the corrupt state of affairs in the United States and the world over, and based on what the demons say they do, if they are not running rampant now, I don't know what else is.

39

THE ELEMENTALS

When I was doing energy work (before doing more extensive research on religion), I decided to ask flowers in my yard to tell me their stories. I wanted to attune to their energy so that I could bring it to women to help them get more in touch with their femininity. One morning, while attempting to attune to flowers, something spoke to me as clearly as if it were standing right in front of me telling me that the flower had been bought here a long, long time ago. It also revealed to me that all plants, flowers, trees, things of nature have beings, some of whom are their creators, others who bought them here from other places, and/or others who are their guardians or custodians. Therefore, I was taken aback when I found information that affirmed this experience in *The Secret Teachings of the Ages* by Manly P. Hall.

Hall obtained information about the elementals from Franz Hartmann's work on Paracelsus (*The Life and Doctrines of Philippus Theophrastus Bombastus of Hohenheim, Known as Paracelsus*). Hartmann indicates that Paracelsus learned the rudiments of alchemy, surgery, and medicine under his father, studied under monks as a child, and later acquired his knowledge of the occult arts under two celebrated adepts of magic, alchemy, and astrology in Germany. He also speculates that Paracelsus later learned under Eastern adepts in India, where he was taken as a prisoner by the Tartars. This is especially believed because much of Paracelsus's information is similar to Indian spirituality that was unknown in the West during that time. He also traveled to Egypt, Arabia, Israel, and Constantinople.[187] Since a lot of what is described about the elementals is similar if not the same as African spirituality, one might speculate that this is where his information is derived from.

According to Paracelsus, the elements (air, fire, water, and earth) are twofold—they consist of gross corporeal substance (the visible) and a subtle vaporous principle (the invisible). In essence, there is a physical fire, air, water, and earth, and *spiritual* fire, air, water, and earth. The general term "elements" has been applied to the lower or physical aspects of these four primary principles, and the name "elemental" to their corresponding invisible, *spiritual* principles. The substance constituting the body of the elementals is the visible corporal flesh (which we inherited from Adam), and flesh (not inherited from Adam) that is not subject to the limitations of the corporeal flesh. However, the elementals have flesh, blood, and bones; live and propagate offspring; and eat, talk, sleep and act, and therefore, cannot properly be called spirits.[188] Because they occupy a space between men and spirit, they might be called "spiritual matter" or ether. Hall further explains, according to Paracelsus:

> Whereas man is composed of several natures (spirit, soul, mind, and body) combined in one unit, the elemental has but one principle, the ether out of which it is composed and in which it lives. [They] are completely isolated in their own ether and have no intercourse with those of other ethers, but as man has within his nature centers of consciousness sensitive to the impulses of all the four ethers, it is possible for any of the elemental kingdoms to communicate with him under proper conditions... Nature spirits cannot be destroyed by grosser elements such as material fire, earth, air, or water, for they function at a rate of vibration higher than that of earthly substances. Being composed of only one element or principle (the ether in which they function), they have no immortal spirit and at death merely disintegrate back into the element from which they were originally individualized. No individual consciousness is preserved after death.[189]

The nature spirits or elementals live in the four elements: the undines (water), sylphs (air), gnomes (earth), and the salamanders (fire). These descriptions of the elementals were substituted for Eastern terms by Paracelsus according to Hartmann because they were more in harmony with

German mythological conceptions. "The species of the elementals move only in the element to which it belongs and neither of them can go out of its appropriate element, which is to them as the air is to us, or the water to fishes; and none of them can live in the element belonging to another class. To each elemental being, the element in which it lives is transparent, invisible, and respirable, as the atmosphere is to ourselves."[190] These four elementals are further described below. I, however, have removed the European names and just described them according to the element to which they belong.

- **Earth elementals** are spirits that dwell in earth ether. They live, and in some cases "work in so close a vibratory rate to the material earth that they have immense power over its rocks and flora, and also over the mineral elements in the animal and human kingdoms...The [earth elementals] work with the stones, gems, and metals, and are supposed to be the guardians of hidden treasures."[191]

"The tree and forest spirits include the sylvestres, satyrs, pans, dryads, dyrdalis, hamadryads, elves, brownies, and little old men of the woods...Every shrub and flower is said to have its own nature spirit, which often uses the physical body of the plant as its habitation," some dying when the plant or tree they are a part of dies. Trees also have their nature spirits, but they are much larger. The earth elementals are of various sizes—most of them much smaller than human beings, though because of the extreme mobility of the element in which they function, some have the power of changing their stature at will. Philosophers, initiates, and mystics of the ancient world have said that they are generally friendly, easy to govern, loyal, and faithful, and will serve man; however, they can be tricky, malicious, difficult to manage, and treacherous, particularly if their trust is betrayed or if one seeks their aid for selfish purposes or to gain power. The earth elementals marry and have families. "Some wear clothing woven of the element in which they live...in some instances their garments are like a part of themselves and grow with them, like the fur of animals." It was thought that some "would only be visible at certain times and only to those *en rapport* with their ethereal vibration," while it was also believed "that many nature spirits have constitutions capable of functioning in the physical world."[192]

- **Water elementals** "function in the spiritual essence called humid (or liquid) ether." Because their "vibratory rate is close to the element of water, [water spirits] are thought to control, to a great degree, the course and function of this fluid in nature. The water spirits are known by names such as oreades, nereids, limoniades, naiades... sea maids, mermaids and potamides... water nymphs [deriving] "their names from the streams, lakes or seas in which they dwelt." The ancients said that they resembled human beings in appearance and size, while others inhabiting smaller streams and fountains were smaller. "It was believed that some were occasionally capable of assuming the appearance of normal human beings and actually associating with men and women." They were said to be "emotional beings, friendly to human life and fond of serving mankind... that the songs of the undines were heard in the West Wind and that their lives were consecrated to the beautifying of the material earth."[193]

- **Fire elementals** are the spirits of fire who live in spiritual ether, which is the invisible part of the fire element. Without them, material fire cannot exist. Because of the fiery element in which they live, man is unable to communicate successfully with them; everything that comes in their presence turns to ashes. In ancient times (as today), incense was used as a medium for the expression of these fire spirits. There are many families of them, differing in appearance and size; some are visible as small balls of light, others are lizard-like in shape and about a foot or more in length, and others are huge flaming giants in flowing robes.

- **Air elementals** are spirits of the air that live in "the invisible, intangible, ethereal substance, similar to our atmosphere but far more subtle." They are believed "to have temples and sacred places in which the gods really dwell, and they hear their voices and receive their answers and are conscious of them and hold converse with them, and see the sun, moon, and stars as they really are...[The air elementals] were believed to live among the clouds and in the surrounding air, their true home was upon the tops of mountains." However, it is also said that they "have no fixed domicile, but wander from place to place—elemental nomads, invisible but ever-present powers in the activities of the universe."
"The [air elementals] sometimes assume human form for short periods of time. Their sizes vary, but in most cases, they are no larger than

human beings, and often considerably smaller." They are said to have "accepted human beings into their communities and have permitted them to live there for considerable periods of time." They are also said to "gather round the mind of the dreamer, the poet, and the artist, and inspire him with their intimate knowledge of the beauties and workings of nature," and that the qualities common to men of genius are said to come from their cooperation with them. The [air elementals] labor at snowflakes and the gathering of clouds; the winds are their vehicles, and they are thought to be the highest of all the elementals because air has the highest vibratory rate.[194]

All the elementals were given as their throne one of the four corners of creation: earth (north), fire (south), water (west), and air (east). They have rulers like the queen of bees or the leader of animal herds. In addition to the various elements they work through, they labor with or through the tissues of animal and human bodies that correspond to their nature. Bones (of the mineral kingdom) belong to the earth elementals, vital essences and liquids belong to the water elementals, the liver and bloodstream belong to the fire elementals, and gases and the nervous system belong to the air elementals.

Based on this information about the elementals, one might surmise that some adepts and others who seem to possess great magical powers, as well as some of those who control and amass great wealth from metals, stones, gems, plants, etc. may have learned how to communicate and work with the elementals.

40
THE "MAGIC" KEY

Many of the works discussed thus far would profoundly shift my consciousness. However, I think it is works founded on Hermeticism, or ancient Egyptian secret knowledge, that bought it all together for me.

One such work is *The Kybalion*. Authored by The Three Initiates (William Walker Atkinson, either alone or with others, is speculated to be the author). *The Kybalion* outlines seven principles of truth that were abstracted from Hermetic philosophy or Egyptian secret knowledge and were passed down from student to teacher, from mouth to ear throughout the ages. These principles are briefly outlined here as an introduction and a lens through which to understand the ancient Egyptian mysteries that follow. For a more in-depth understanding, one might seek out the work for oneself.

The Kybalion starts with the fundamental truth that under and behind all outward appearances or manifestations, there is a substantial reality known by many names but called "The All." The All is unknowable, undefinable, infinite, living mind—spirit—the name given to this highest conception. Without attempting to remove the veil of the Unknowable, according to *The Kybalion*:

>   1. The All must be all there is—nothing that exists outside of The All, else The All would not be The All.
>   2. The All must be infinite in time or eternal; it must have continuously existed forever, as something can never evolve from nothing.
>   3. The All must be immutable or not subject to change in its real nature.

The All, being infinite, absolute, eternal, and unchangeable, it must follow that anything finite, changeable, fleeting, and conditioned cannot be The All. And while The All is The All, it is also *In All* [italics my emphasis].[195] The seven principles are as follows:

1. The First Principle, the Principle of Mentalism, embodies the truth that "All is Mind." Although The All is Spirit, which in itself is unknowable and undefinable, it may be considered and thought of as a universal, infinite living mind.[196] "The phenomenal world or universe is simply a Mental Creation of The All, subject to the Laws of Created Things; the universe as a whole and parts or units, has its existence in the Mind of The All, in which we 'live and move and have our being.'"[197] The nature of energy, power, and matter, are all subordinate to the mastery of the mind.

We can endeavor to know the workings of the higher planes by examining those on our own plane. This might begin with the question: "How does man create?" The answer is: he creates by making material outside of himself and he procreates by self-multiplying, transferring a portion of his substance to his offspring. However, The All has no material outside of The All, and cannot transfer or subtract a portion of Himself or reproduce or multiply Himself (since The All contains the All). Again, the question is: "How does man create?" The answer is: he creates mentally. It follows then that The All mentally creates the Universe. Therefore "The Universe and All it contains, is a Mental Creation of The All. This translates to the truth that All is Mind!"[198] Possession of the understanding that All is Mind gives one the "Master Key," which unlocks the mental temple of knowledge into which one can enter.

2. The Second Principle, the Principle of Correspondence, holds that "As above, so below, as below, so above." It embodies the truth that there is harmony, agreement, and correspondence between the Three Great Planes, which consists of seven sub-planes, which also consist of seven sub-planes. They are the following:

I. *The Great Physical Plane*, which as shown below includes three planes of matter A, B, and C; The Plane of Ethereal Substance; and three Planes of Energy A, B, and C. The three planes of matter consist of different forms of matter, solids, liquids, and gases (A); radiant matter (B); and more subtle forms of matter (C). The Plane of Ethereal substance is that which pervades all universal space and act as a medium for the transmission of waves of energy, such as light, heat, and electricity, and is the connecting link between matter and energy (although ancient and now science recognize that it is all energy, vibrating at different frequencies). Energy Planes A, B, and C comprise ordinary forms of energy known to science: Energy Plane A with seven sub-planes of heat, light, magnetism, electricity, and attraction (including gravitation, cohesion, etc.); while Energy Planes B and C consist of finer forms of energy that were not yet discovered by science by the time of the writing. [199]

i. The Plane of Matter (A)—solids, liquids, gases, etc.
ii. The Plane of Matter (B)—more subtle form of matter; radiant matter
iii. The Plane of Matter (C)—the most subtle and tenuous matter
iv. Plane of Ethereal Substance—pervades all universal space; is the connecting link between matter and energy
v. Plane of Energy (A)—heat, light, magnetism, electricity, etc.

vi. Plane of Energy (B)—not yet discovered

vii. Plane of Energy (C)—not yet discovered

II. *The Great Mental Plane* as shown below includes the Plane of Mineral Mind and Elemental Mind A; Plane of Plant Mind and Elemental Mind B; Plane of Animal Mind and Elemental Mind C and the Plane of Human Mind. Minerals and plants have material bodies and forms just as man's body is a material form and is not himself. Minerals and plants may be called "souls" in a sense and are living beings of a lower degree of development, life, and mind—just a little more than the units of "living energy," which comprise the higher subdivisions of the highest physical plane. The Animal plane is familiar to us and just below that of man. The Elementals Mind A, B, and C are between the plane of the mind of mineral and plant (A); plant and animal (B); and animal and man (C), respectively. Elemental Mind A, B, and C are invisible to the average man but recognized by occultists.

i. The Plane of Mineral Mind

ii. The Plane of Elemental Mind (A)

iii. The Plane of Plant Mind

iv. The Plane of Elemental Mind (B)

v. The Plane of Animal Mind

vi. The Plane of Elemental Mind (C)

vii. The Plane of Human Mind

III. *The Great Spiritual Plane* consists of beings we refer to as angels, archangels, and demigods. On the lower planes dwell the great souls we call adepts or masters (and one might imagine that even on lower planes are ancestors who are not adepts?). Above them are the angelic hosts, and above them are the divine beings or gods. Divine beings and angelic hosts (army of angels) take the greatest interest in the universe and play an important role in its affairs."[200] They also occasionally intervene in and assist in human affairs; superimpose their knowledge and power upon the world and this has led to "legends, beliefs, religions, and traditions of the race, past and present."[201]

3. The Third Principle, the Principle of Vibration, holds that "Nothing rests; everything moves; everything vibrates...Differences between various manifestations of the universal power are due entirely to the varying rate and mode of vibration...All between the poles of spirit and extremely gross forms of matter are millions upon millions of different rates and modes of vibration..."[202] Even "every thought, emotional or mental state has a corresponding rate and mode of vibration."[203] The Principle of Vibration underlies the power used by masters and adepts, who can use one law against another and change the vibrations of material objects or forms of energy and perform what is commonly called "miracles."[204]

4. The Fourth Principle, the Principle of Polarity, "embodies the truth that all manifested things have 'two sides;' two aspects;' 'two poles;' a 'pair of opposites;' with manifold degrees between the two extremes..." expressed in the saying, "All truths are but half-truths." "Spirit and matter are but two poles of the same thing, intermediate planes being merely degrees of vibration." Likewise, light and darkness; good and evil; heat and cold, east, and west, etc. as well as phenomena on the mental plane; love and hate; courage and fear are the same things at two ends of the same pole with different degrees of vibration between them.[205]

5. The Fifth Principle, the Principle of Rhythm, "embodies the truth that in everything there a to-and-from movement; a flow and inflow; a swing forward and backward; a pendulum-like movement; a tide-like ebb and flow; a high-tide and a low-tide; between the two poles" that manifests on the physical, mental and spiritual planes.[206] There is also an action and reaction; an advance and a retreat; a rising and a sinking; manifest in all phenomena of the universe... With all things of shape and form; they swing from action to reaction; from birth to death; from activity to inactivity—and then back again."[207] With all worlds, nations, governments, philosophies, great movements, creeds, there is birth, growth, maturity, death, and then new birth. The Principle of Rhythm applies to "the universe, suns, worlds, men, mind, energy, and matter...It is manifest in the creation and destruction of worlds; in the rise and fall of nations; in the life of all things: and finally, in the mental states of man."[208] Even with The All there is "ever the Outpouring and the Indrawing; the

Outbreathing and Inbreathing…" In all phenomena, "the swing of the pendulum is ever in evidence."[209]

6. The Sixth Principle, the Principle of Cause and Effect, holds that "Every cause has its effect; every effect has its cause; everything happens according to law; chance is but a name for law not recognized."[210] "Although nothing happens without a cause or a chain of causes; no 'thing' ever causes or 'creates;' another 'thing.' Cause and effect deal merely with 'events.' An 'event' is 'that which comes, arrives or happens, as a result, or consequent of some preceding event'… No event 'creates' another event but is merely a preceding link in the great orderly chain of events flowing from the creative energy of The All."[211]

7. The Seventh Principle, the Principle of Gender, embodies the truth that the masculine and feminine principle is manifested in all phenomena. On all levels, the masculine principle seems to be that of directing certain inherent energy toward the feminine principle and starting into activity the creative process [while] the feminine principle is always doing the active creative work. Each principle is incapable of operative energy without the assistance of the other; the masculine is always present in the feminine form, and the feminine is always present in the masculine form.[212]

In summary, according to *The Kybalion* "he who knows these [seven principles of truth] … possesses the Magic Key before whose touch all the Doors of the Temple Fly open."[213]

41

UNVEILING THE MYSTERIES

In *Stolen Legacy*, George James explains in great detail how Greek philosophy that supposedly came from some of its most noted philosophers, Pythagoras, Socrates, Aristotle, Plato, and others, was derived from Egyptian theology. He provides insight into its mystery schools, their objective, and how expansive their reach was. He also explains how Egyptian Memphite theology is the source of the modern science of the atom; how the Atum (the sun god) is the atom (with similar attributes, and underlies much of Greek philosophy), and how the Ennead nine

(Egyptian nine gods) is the source of the Nebular hypothesis (which is the theory that everything has been created from nebular clouds; gas and dust from stars forming and dissolving and planets that coalesce from them. Our solar system was created from gas and dust coalescing into planets while orbiting the sun). According to James:

1. The earliest theology of salvation is Egyptian. However, salvation means freedom from the prison of the body (this is the origin of Christian salvation and India's liberation from the cycle of birth and death). The most important objective of the mystery system was for man to become god-like (some say to be a god), and for the soul of man to be liberated from the prison of the body. If he were to be liberated while in the body, he would see the gods (the equivalent to India's nirvana, or the bliss state); and join the Company of the Gods in the afterlife.

2. The Egyptian mystery system, like the modern university system, was the center of life, with three levels of students: (1) Mortals, probationary students who were being instructed, but not yet experienced the inner vision; (2) The Intelligences, those who had attained the inner vision, mind, or nous (intellectual apprehensive); and (3) Creators and Sons of Light, those who had "become identified with or united with the Light" (true spiritual consciousness). They have also been referred to as initiation, illumination, and perfection.

3. Their learning consisted not only of the cultivation of ten virtues but also the seven liberal arts (where we get our university liberal arts from), which were intended to liberate the soul. They included
    :
    i.   Grammar, Rhetoric, and Logic: the disciplines of the moral nature
    ii. Geometry and Arithmetic: the science of transcendental space and numeration
    iii. Astronomy: the knowledge of latent forces in man and the destiny of individuals
    iv. Music (or harmony): living the practice of philosophy and "living in harmony with God until the personal soul became

identified with God" opening the way "for it to participate in the music of the spheres."

4. Egyptian temples were built to be a microcosm of the macrocosm; they resembled the constellations and heavens surrounded by pillars, recording the number of constellations and the cycle of the planets. The temples contained several levels: large courts where the congregation assembled, the hall of priests, and the innermost chamber called the Adytum, the Holy of Holy of Holies; the place of the shrine, and the abode of the Gods, which was entered only by the high priest.[214]

He further explains that Egypt's Temples of Luxor and Karnak sat one and a half mile apart; between them, a double row of sphinxes lining an avenue sixty feet in width presented the most extraordinary entrance the ancient world had ever seen (even today). "She surpassed in her astonished architecture, all other nations that have existed upon the earth." James continues:

The majesty of Egypt...with the splendor of its architecture, the hieroglyphs of the temples, the obelisks, and the sphinxes before the shrines, the linen vestments and the shaven heads and faces of the priests, the endless and obscure ritual. ...The staunch faith of the Egyptians, together with their mysterious forms of worship, led to the universal conviction that Egypt was not only the Holy Land but the Holiest of lands or countries and that indeed the Gods dwelt there.[215]

James further notes that Egypt became the world center for pilgrimages, and the Temple of Luxor was the only "grand lodge" (governing body) of the ancient world. It had minor branches or "lodges" throughout the ancient world in Europe, Asia, Africa, North America, South America, and probably in Australia. Some of the places include Palestine at Mt. Carmel, Syria at Mt. Herman in Lebanon, Babylon, Median, India on the banks of the Ganges, Burma, Athens, Rome, Croton, Rhodes, Delphi, Miletus, Cypris, Corinth, Crete, Central and South America (especially in Peru, among the American Indians, the Mayas, Aztecs, and Incas of Mexico).[216]

Egyptian mystery knowledge was also disseminated throughout the world during Greek, Persian, and Roman invasions. The Persian invasion opened Egypt to Greek immigration, and in 525 BC, Thales was the first to be initiated in its mystery schools. Because it was regarded as the educational center of the ancient world, like the United States is today, students flocked to its schools. Later, Alexander the Great (r. 323 BC) and Aristotle (his mentor and friend), who came and set up a research center in Egypt's Library in Alexandria, claimed authorship of many of its books. Because of the invasions, numbers of Egyptians fled not only to the desert and mountain regions but also adjacent lands in Africa, Arabia, and Asia Minor, where they lived secretly and developed the teaching which belonged to their mystery system.[217]

Finally, James makes it clear that the Temple of Luxor "was the seat of government, having organized the ancient world into a universal or 'catholic' brotherhood with jurisdiction over all minor lodges and schools wherever they were. And whether we call it the mysteries, or Greek philosophy or Free Masonry, the system was one and all the branches came out of that one and were subordinate to it."[218]

~~~~~~~~~~~

In *The Kybalion*, the Three Initiates also note the significant role that Egyptian secret knowledge has played in religions and philosophies throughout the world.

> From old Egypt have come the fundamental esoteric and occult teachings which have so strongly influenced the philosophies of all races, nations, and peoples for several thousand years. Egypt, the home of the Pyramids and the Sphinx, was the birthplace of the Hidden Wisdom and Mystic Teachings. From her Secret Doctrine, all nations have borrowed. India, Persia, Chaldea, Medea, China, Japan, Assyria, ancient Greece and Rome, and other ancient countries partook liberally at the feast of knowledge which the Hierophants and Masters of the Land of Isis so freely provided for those who came prepared to partake of the great store of Mystic and Occult Lore which the masterminds of the ancient land had gathered together.[219]

They then go on to explain that in ancient Egypt dwelt the great adepts and masters who have never been surpassed, and who seldom have been equaled. Because they wished to learn from them, aspirants from all over the world would enter into the doors of the Temples of Egypt, and afterward, travel the four corners of the earth, "carrying with them the precious knowledge which they were ready, anxious, and willing to pass on to those who were ready to receive the same."[220]

Among these great masters dwelt one whom masters themselves hailed as "the Master of Masters." Believed to have incarnated in the oldest dynasties of Egypt, Tehuti (Teh, Tehu, Tehut, Dheuty, Dheuti, Tut, Thoth), considered the inventor of writing, arts, and science is referred to as "the great, great," "twice-great," "thrice-great" "Lord of Books," "Revealer of the Hidden," "Mighty in Speech," and "Scribe of the Gods," among other titles.[221] In *The Progress of Religious Ideas: Through Successive Ages*, Child notes:

> The Sacred Books of Hermes [Tehuti]...containing the laws, science, and theology of Egypt, were declared by the priests to have been composed during the reign of the Gods, preceding that of their first king, Menes. Allusions on very ancient monuments prove their great antiquity. There were four of them, and the subdivisions of the whole make forty-two volumes... They were deposited in the inmost holy recesses of the temples, and none but the higher order of priests were allowed to read them. They were carried reverently in all great religious processions.[222]

She further notes how these sacred books were disposed of:

> These books were very famous, and later were much sought after for alchemical purposes, especially for that of making gold. The Roman Emperor Severus collected all writings on the mysteries [and I am sure, extracted the information] and buried them in the tomb of Alexander the Great; and Diocletian destroyed all their books on alchemy lest Egypt should become too rich to remain tributary to Rome.[223]

What remains of ancient Egyptian's secret knowledge can be found in the Hermetica literature, upon which the Greeks transposed the name of their god, Hermes, calling him Hermes-Trismegistus, which means "three times great," or Thrice-Great Hermes. The Hermetica is a collection of Greek transliterated Egyptian texts from the second and third centuries that were translated into Latin and compiled into a *Corpus Hermeticum* by Italian scholars during the Italian Renaissance. The most notable scholar was, Marsilio Ficino, whose translations went through eight editions before 1500 CE and twenty-two editions between 1500 CE and 1641 CE. English translations include *The Divine Pymander*, translated (or first published) by John Everard in 1650, *Virgin of the World*, translated by Edward Maitland and Anna Kingsford in 1885, and *Thrice Greatest Hermes*, translated by G.R.S. Mead in 1906.

One of the most significant fragments of ancient Egypt's secret knowledge is the Poemander, which means "Knowledge of Re," the Egyptian god Ra.[224] It is believed to lay the foundation for the rest of the dialogues in which Tehuti is teaching or "initiating" Greek-named Egyptian disciples or initiates Asclepius, Tat, and King Ammon into secret knowledge.[225] Included in the knowledge also is the *Virgin to the World*, where Isis (Auset) is initiating her son Horus (Heru) into secret knowledge.

In the Poemander, while in meditation, a persona's mind (whom in one translation it is Tehuti; in others, it is Tehuti speaking to an initiate) has an encounter that is described as follows:

Me thought a Being more vast in size beyond all bounds called out my name and saith: What wouldst thou hear and see, and what has thou in mind to learn and know?

And I do say: Who art thou?

He saith: I am Man Shepherd; Mind of all Masterhood; I know what thou desirest and I'm with thee everywhere.

[And] I reply: I long to learn the things that are and comprehend their nature and know God.

He answered back to me: Hold in thy mind all thou wouldst know, and I will teach thee.

And in a twinkling of an eye, all things were opened to him, and he saw a limitedness vision and all things turned to light. The "Man Shepherd," "Mind of all Masterhood," "understanding of Re" (or his own mind after having been illumed with the "light"), then reveals to him "secret" knowledge. This secret knowledge expanded on in dialogues where Tehuti is teaching disciples or initiates includes but is not limited to the origins of the universe, the creation of humanity, the regions from Earth to the heavens, the types of beings occupying these regions, their makeup, and the roles they play in the universal order, the cause of and how humanity can avoid evil and suffering, what happens upon death, how souls are rebirthed, and other knowledge. These works are dense with knowledge, and one would have to seek them out themself to reap fully the benefits of the knowledge that they contain. I have outlined briefly below some of what was most significant in my search for truth.

The Origins of the Universe and Humanity

In the Hermetic literature, there are two versions of the origins of the universe and humanity. In *The Divine Pymander*, the *Mind* of the Universe—God through word, brings forth another *Mind* or *Workman*, who fashion the sensible (material world). This Workman sets about whirling circles bringing into existence formations with boundless beginnings and indeterminable ends. The elements of nature descend downward forming air-winged things, water things that swim, and four-footed things.

The *All Mind* also brings forth a human being, who first descends to the sphere of the workman, there attaining attributes of seven powers. He then breaks through the circumference of the circles and becomes intertwined with nature, who forms a frame (body) for him, bringing forth seven androgynous beings who are eventually split into male and female and are instructed to multiply.

In *the Virgin to the World*, God first brings forth nature and fills the heavens with ether and air. He then creates a myriad of souls who inhabit sixty regions in a hierarchy with sixty degrees of purity (with the first region being the purest) and instructs them of the laws that they should follow. He mingles together the rest of the elements, earth and water, and with certain powerful and mystic words, and breathing breath into the liquid protoplasm, formed beings of human shape. What was left of the protoplasm, he gave to the loftiest souls inhabiting the region of the gods about the stars and instructed them to make beings in their image. They did just that, creating birds (with the lightest part of the proto-plasm); the quadruped (with the thickest part), fish (which needed a moist vehicle), and reptiles (of the cold and heavy part). But some of the souls sought to find out what the protoplasm was made of thereby trans-gressing the laws. Because they transgressed divine laws, they were incar-cerated into a fleshly body, with the opportunity through right living, to return to the heavenly abodes.

The Structure of the Universe and its Inhabitants

With regard to the structure of the universe and its inhabitants, ac-cording to this knowledge, there are four provinces governed by fixed and immutable laws—heaven, ether, air, earth—and sixty regions that become more subtle as they expand outwards. In heaven dwell the gods, stars, and powers of providence, who are ruled by the Maker of the Uni-verse. In the ether, the planets are ruled by the sun. Between the moon and the earth reside the souls of the genii, who are governed by the moon. On the earth, man and animals are governed by kings (or in to-day's terms, it would be whatever governmental system is established). In the region between the moon and Earth, souls abide there in a hier-archy according to their nature and virtue. They are not hindered by air, and they can ascend and descend without obstacle. They can flow across it without mingling in it, or confounding themselves with it, just as water flows over oil.

All things in the universe are differentiated by quality and quantity, are moved by act and operation (their nature), and increase and decrease by augmentation and diminution. Therefore, there is no death or destruc-tion. All beings that the world contains constitute a type, some of which are imbued with the act and operation of generation and reproduction of themselves. The various types include gods, genii, humanity, animals, plants, and minerals. All types have souls—even beings that sustain themselves by roots fixed in the earth; however, they are without sensa-tion.

Divinity forms a type, and all individualizations are immortal. Indi-viduality is part of a type. For example, man is part of humanity. Eternity belongs only to types; the individual perishes. All types are imperishable; individualities are not imperishable. For example, man is a mortal, humanity is immortal. Bodies can only be formed by the divine will; individualities cannot be characterized without the aid of the genii like the education and training of animals cannot be conducted without humanity. Individuals of all types mix with all types. The nature of the gods is to do good, the duty of men is to be pious (and obtain knowledge of God), and the function of the genii is to chastise and have control over mundane things including our bodies, which serve them as instruments.

Although the regions and the souls occupying them are based on a hierarchy, where those farthest from the earth are higher, they are all one substance. "Intelligible Essence rules heaven; heaven directs the gods, under these are classed the genii, who guide mankind."[226] In all the orders of gods, there is an intelligible part. They range from those whose principle is pure spirit to those who are both spirit and sensible, which means that humanity can perceive them. The genii reside in regions of the sky (and I am assuming according to their nature and virtue). Some genii who become joined to the individuality of the divine type become neighbors and associates of the gods; others who preserve the character of their type and are properly called genii love that which relates to mankind. Those genii that reside with the gods watch over human affairs and fulfill the wills of the gods using the "storms, tempest, transitions of fire and earthquakes, famines and wars (for punishment and impiety). Operation is the essence of the genii; in some, there is both good and evil operation."[227] The genii:

> Preside over mundane affairs, they shake and overthrow the constitution of states and individuals; imprint their likeness on our souls, are present in our nerves, our marrow, our veins, our arteries, and our very brain substance, and in the recesses of our viscera. At the moment when each of us receives life and being, he is taken in charge by the genii who preside over births, and who are classed beneath the astral powers.[228]

Although "the genii permeate the body and impress its own energy on the soul, the reasonable part of the soul is not subject to the genii, it is designed for the reception of God... therefore those who are illumined neither the genii nor the gods have any power in the presence of God. Men who are not so illumined; both body and soul are directed by genii, to whom they cleave, and whose operation they affect."[229]

Humanity is comprised of two parts: divine likeness and a body, which is the envelope for the soul. With this double origin, he is both mortal and immortal, "which differs in mode and duration." The mortal part is comprised of the elements (earth, air, fire, and water) and remains upon the earth. Upon death, the mortal part is restored to the earth, and the immortal part (mind, soul, conscious, and reason) mounts to heaven. The nature of the soul has to do with the union and mixture of the four elements, producing varieties among souls and bodies.[230]

Although a lot of questions were asked throughout these various dialogues, and some of the responses are outlined above, I have highlighted a few of the questions that were most curious to me and the response below.

Why Man Lives in the World and Not with God

When The All Mind created the second God, because he was so enamored with this being whom he had drawn from himself, who was so perfect, he created humanity. The All Mind gave humanity a body and spirit and two natures—eternal and mortal—so that through his double origin, he could contemplate this being, admire it, adore what is celestial and eternal, and cultivate and govern that which upon the earth.[231] Those "who have an affinity with the Gods through the intelligence he shares with them and through piety is the neighbor of God...[those] who have an affinity with genii; approximate himself to them, and [those] who are satisfied with human mediocrity; remain a part of the human type."[232]

How Different Souls are Born

The gods themselves decide who will be kings befitting humanity (at least when monarchies ruled; one might imagine that currently, it would be those who are born or propelled into wealth and privilege; giving them the freedom and power of kings). The king is "the last of the gods and the first of men... When he sojourns upon Earth, his divinity is concealed, but he possesses something which distinguishes him from other men and approximates him to God."[233] The soul in him comes from regions higher than the soul of common men. Souls destined to reign on Earth descend for two reasons: There are those who in former lives lived blamelessly, and their position was in preparation for the divine state. And there are holy men who, for some slight infringement of divine law, receive a penance where the suffering and shame of being incarnated into a physical body are mitigated. "The condition of these individuals in taking a body resembles not that of others; they are as blessed as when they were free."[234]

As to their various characteristics, "the variety is not in the soul, [as] all are royal; but it is due to the nature of the angels or genii who assist them. Those souls destined to such offices are not without ministers and escorts. If the genii or angel is war-like, the soul in their charge takes that character; if they are gentle, the soul follows a path of peace; if they are friends to judgment, the soul loves to judge, if they are musicians, the soul sings, if they love truth, the soul is that of a philosopher."[235] Generally, the soul follows the teachings of its guardians.

As to gender, for souls, there is no distinction between male and female. The distinction only exists between bodies—not between incorporeal beings. However, some are more energetic while others are gentler, and this belongs to the air in which all things are formed. The female and male are distinguished by the combination of elements. Among females, the combination is more cold and moist; among males, it is more hot and dry, which gives them greater vivacity and energy.[236]

What distinguishes those who are wise is the organ of vision, which is enveloped in tunics; a coat or layer enveloping a part or organ. When they are thick and dense, the sight is dull, and the soul cannot see far and discerns only as through cloudy weather, that which lies immediately before his steps. When they are subtle, clear, and transparent, the sight is clear.[237]

What Happens When a Man's Life Ends?

Because the multitude is ignorant of the reason of things, they are troubled by the approach of death and fear it. "Death occurs by the dissolution of the body wearied with its toil. When the number which maintains unity is complete; for the binding power of the body is a number, the body dies. And this happens when it can no longer support the burdens of life."[238] The dissolution of the body occurs when the union of the soul to the body separates. When the soul is separated from the body, it is judged according to its merits. If found pious and just, it is allowed to dwell in the divine abodes, but if it is found to be defiled with vice, it "is precipitated from the heights to depth, and delivered over to the tempest and adverse hurricanes of the air, fire, and water. Ceaselessly tossed about between heaven and Earth by the billows of the universe, [it] is driven from side to side in eternal penance; [and its] immortal nature gives endless duration to the judgment pronounced against [it]."[239]

There are "two ministers of universal providence [who controls what happens at death]; one is the guardian of souls; the other is their conductor who sends them forth and ordains for them bodies. The first minister guards them, the second releases or binds them, according to the will of God."[240] "The law is supplemented by two energies; memory and experience; memory directs in nature the preservation and maintenance of all the original types; experience provides every soul descending into generation...with an appropriate body; passionate souls assume vigorous bodies; slothful souls sluggard bodies; active souls active bodies; gentle souls gentle bodies; powerful souls powerful bodies...every soul should have a body befitting it."[241]

Souls do not "return confusedly, not by chance, into one and the same place, but each is dispatched into the condition which belongs to him and this is determined by that which the soul experiences while yet he is in the tenement of the body, loaded with a burden contrary to [its] nature. An example of this is as follows. Suppose there should be shut up in the same prison, men, eagles, doves, swans, hawks, swallows, sparrows, flies, serpents, lions, leopards, dogs, hares, oxen, sheep, and certain amphibious animals such as seals... and at the same moment all the creatures were [set free]."[242] The men would seek cities and public places; the eagles the sky; the doves the lower air; the hawks, the higher expanse; the swallows to places frequented by men; sparrows to orchards; swans to districts where they can sing; flies to the proximity of the grounds (around humans); lions and leopards to the mountains; the wolves to the solitudes; dogs the tracks of men, and so on. In this same way, the soul goes to the abode befitting it.

The Torments of Humanity and How to End Suffering

The twelve torments of humanity include ignorance, sorrow, intemperance, concupiscence, injustice, covetousness, deceit, envy, fraud or guilt, wrath, rashness, and maliciousness. These can be purged and lead to regeneration by the ten powers of God or virtues, which include:

knowledge of truth (for ignorance), knowledge of joy (for sorrow), temperance (for intemperance), continence (for concupiscence and injustice), communion (for covetousness), truth, accompanied with good, life, light and unity (expels, deceit, envy, fraud, wrath, rashness, and maliciousness).[243]

In every order, some individuals transgress the laws of their being. For example, some people act against reason. Some animals act against their nature. Evil arises from a lack of prudence and knowledge of things of the universe. When ignorance asserts itself, vice develops. *The worst evil is not knowing God.* Knowledge and understanding of divine law/religion—the basis of all things—leads to the contempt of all vices in the world. Men suffer when their desire and attachment to their mortal part hinder them from their divine part. "They are deceived when they are drawn after the image of things without seeking for the true reason of them."[244] They also suffer because they are lovers of bodies. Terrestrial things, possessions which the body desires, are foreign to divine thought. "Such things are called possessions because they are not born with us; they are acquired later. They are then foreign to us...even the body itself is foreign to us."[245] Perfection is attained when man renounces his senses; when his virtue preserves him from the desire of things that are foreign to himself.

42

THE INITIATE'S PATH

Unveiling some of the mysteries of the universe is enlightening in and of itself. However, one might venture to say that it does not pale by comparison to the experience of illumination that can come about through initiation.

Charles Vail's *The Ancient Mysteries and Modern Masonry* provides great insight into the purpose of initiation and how it was practiced among various peoples throughout the ancient world, especially those who had been influenced by the Egyptian mystery system. Because the events surrounding the birth, life, death, and resurrection of Jesus the Christ parallel events in the lives of earlier saviors such as Horus, Krsna, and others, the controversy around whether he was a historical versus a mythical figure might also be explained by the initiate's path. Vail notes that although the narratives are the same, what is being described is not the physical life of these saviors but the "inner mystic life." Their biographies might vary, but their paths as initiates were the same.[246]

According to Vail, "antiquity held that there was a science of the soul, a knowledge of things unseen, a gnosis..."[247] "Gnosis of God [was] the science of sciences."[248] It was a sacred science of a higher instruction that taught man how he could transcend his limitations and how he could be liberated from finite consciousness and become one and identified with the infinite. The gnosis taught that "a soul purified from all stain," could see, hold communion, and unite with the Gods in this life.[249] It could transcend, while still in the body into "the higher vehicle; a body that can never die."[250] This "higher instruction was not only given by perfected initiates who could function on the higher planes, but the assistance of angelic hierarchies was also invoked and those exalted Beings came to teach and elevate by their presence...and impart their light..."[251] Ultimately, the goal of initiation was "to make [man] a God, either by union with a Divine Being without or by the realization of the Divine Self within..."[252]

To be recognized as a candidate for initiation, the person had to be "pure and holy and possess a well-developed and well-trained mind."[253] After having attained the "good life," he could enter into preparation for initiation. Certain conditions had to be fulfilled and attributes acquired for the aspirant to be "worthy and well qualified, duly and truly prepared.[254] During this period, the candidate was said to be treading the "Probationary Path," which leads up to the 'Strait Gate,' beyond which is the 'Narrow Way.'... "[255] Some of the attributes that had to be acquired include:

1. Being able to discriminate; that is being "able to distinguish between the eternal and the temporal, the real and unreal so that the unreal world becomes real to him. He must set his [attention] on things above, loosen the ties on world objects and fix his aspiration on things pertaining to the unseen." In other words, the candidate had to make an "allegiance to the Higher Self."[256]

2. Being devoted to what is right without regard to his own gain or loss; he had to become indifferent to personal reward as the fruit of good actions; and cease craving for earthly reward, especially once he realizes their impermanent character.[257]

3. Meeting six qualification which includes control of his thoughts; control of his actions; detachment from any doctrinal belief; letting go of resentments; steadfastness in being turned aside from his purpose; and "faith and confidence in the power of his master to teach the truth, and in himself to grasp it... "[258]

Vail points out that the "Path Proper" was divided into five stages. In the first four stages, the neophyte had to cast off the ten fetters (discussed in the previous section) that bind him to the cycle of rebirth and keep him from realizing the highest state of consciousness. "When these fetters are cast off, [he]is ready for the fifth state—full adeptship; to become an "Adept-a Christ Triumphant."[259]

In the first step or "at the first great initiation, the "Divine Child" was born in man." This first step was purification, which was done by water or fire. The candidate was purified from the corruptions of the world which he was about to leave. "Purification of the body was symbolic of purification of the heart."[260]

In Egyptian mysteries and those upon which many mystery religions were founded, purification by water symbolized the "primeval waters" whereby the initiate was "begotten again," born the Divine Child, and called "Moses a word signifying in Egypt, from the water, or by the water, which was symbolic of purity and designated the birth of the pure initiate" (Moses of the Hebrews probably got his name through initiation).[261] Once the "Christ Principle" is born in the soul and the spiritual consciousness is awakened, the soul continues an evolutionary process, whereby at each stage "it becomes again as if were a little child, born into that higher life of the initiated."[262]

Vail explains that the "Mystic Christ who is in every one of us, is born and lives, is crucified, [and] rises from the dead... "[263] He then explains how the events in the birth, life, death, and resurrection in the story Jesus is the story of the mystic life of the initiate.

Every such child is beset by perils that do not befall others. The dark powers seek his undoing, but the Christ child once born cannot be destroyed. He grows in wisdom and spiritual stature until the time comes for the second great initiation, symbolized by the baptism 'by water and spirit,' which confers on him the powers necessary for the Teacher. He then goes forth into the world to labor, and is led by the Spirit into the wilderness, and is there exposed to severe temptations. The evil powers strive to lure him from his set purpose, bidding him to use his unfolding powers to secure worldly ends. But triumphant over those temptations, he uses the powers which he would not employ for his own needs, to save the world. This devotion of service leads him to the third great initiation symbolized by the Transfiguration. He ascends... the sacred mountain of initiation... where he is to meet the baptism of the Holy Ghost and of Fire the final and last state of the 'Way of the Cross.' He is now ready for the fourth initiation symbolized by the passion. He has become victorious over the lower nature and is willing to nail it to the cross. [However, because] of the darkness and horrors of the final trial, it seems that even the Father has forsaken him. His inner vision is blinded, and he thinks himself alone...but he is still steadfast, and with an unconquering trust he yields up the lower life, and descends into hell, that no region in the universe may remain untrodden. But liberated from the material body he sees the light once more... and is ready for the fifth Initiation, symbolized by the resurrection and ascension.[264]

Vail further explains the final stage in the initiation process:

The candidate was received by the initiating Hierophant at the proper time and place, usually in a secluded chamber in a temple or pyramid, and laid on the stone floor with arms outstretched; sometimes on a wooden cross, which was hollowed out to support the human figure...He then passed into a deep trance. The body was placed in a sarcophagus of stone, a vault or tomb beneath the floor of the Hall of Initiation and carefully guarded. [In the] meantime, while the body was dead and buried, he himself was fully alive in the invisible world...and undergoing what was called the tests of earth, water, fire, and air. He then put on his perfected Bliss Body, which was now fully organized as a vehicle of consciousness. After the third day the cross, bearing the body, was lifted up and carried out into the air... ready to greet the rising sun. At the moment the rays touched the face, the perfected Initiate, the Horus or Christ rose from the dead, resuscitated the body, and glorified it by his resurrected body, no longer a natural man, but a spiritual man, having overcome death and hell.[265]

These initiation rites, which symbolize the stages through which the initiate passed, were called the "Initiation of the Cross" by the Gnostics and the "death rite" in Egypt. This story, according to Vail, was the path of every initiate, including Jesus of the Gospels.

Knowing the initiate's path provides yet another (but the same) pathway, to the highest state of consciousness, the bliss state, heaven on Earth, and realization of the Divine Self. Initiations are still done all over the world, especially among indigenous peoples and in African and African American communities in the United States. However, their methods and aims may be different from those of the ancient world and may vary widely.

43
SETTING FACE-TO-FACE

Egyptian and Eastern knowledge did more than anything else to expand my consciousness. As to what happens upon death, there was nothing more eye-opening, than the *Tibetan Book of the Dead*, also referred to as the *Bardo Thodol*, which means "Liberation in the Intermediate state through hearing, or on the After-Death Plane." The *Tibetan Book of the Dead* is so similar to *The Egyptian Book of the Dead*, that it is speculated that they have common origins (although, the former was more than likely derived from the latter since Egypt's theology, was spread throughout the world). In essence, the *Bardo Thodol* is an instruction guide for how to navigate in the intermediate period following death (*antarabhava*). More specifically, it is a book of instructions to guide the dying and the dead, during the forty-nine days they are in the immediate state between death and rebirth, the Bordo.

The Bardo is undergirded by the idea that there are two states of consciousness: birth consciousness and death consciousness. However, just as the body is under constant change, so is one's state of consciousness. While one is dying and after death, there are successive states or chains of consciousness in the intermediate stage or Bardo state.

In this immediate stage, there are three states that one can attain: The first is *Dharma-Kaya*: the void, the uncreated, unshaped, unmodified, boundless light, the source of life eternal, Perfect Enlightenment. The second state is *Sambhoga-Kaya*: offspring of the unmodified and manifestation of all perfect attributes. The third state is *Nrmana-Kaya*: divine incarnation among sentient beings, those immersed in the illusion of *samsara* (wandering between the cycle of birth and death) in phenomena in worldly existence.[266] In the third state are the six *lokas* (worlds or realms of rebirth) of the samsara. The six lokas include *Sura* (god or the deva world), *Asura* (titan, demi-god or the *asura*-world) *Nara* (man or the human-world), *Trisan* (the brute world), *Preta*, (the unhappy ghost or the *preta*-world), and *Hung* (from *hunu*, meaning "fallen" or hell or the hell-world).[267] There are also six poisons or enemies. They are pride, jealousy, ignorance, anger, greed, and lust.[268]

Operation in the immediate stage through hearing means that when one is dying or after death, there is a guide to help one navigate through the immediate state or the Bardo. The goal of the guide (who is typically the guru of the individual, a brother in the faith, or a close friend) is to summon the spirit of the deceased. This is referred to as "setting face-to-face" to direct him to remember the Clear Light of the Void of Realty so that he might be liberated from the cycle of birth and rebirth at the moment of death. If he is not able to attain liberation at that point, the individual will guide him through each stage of Bardo consciousness so that he might attain liberation, and if he fails, guide him to a womb of rebirth.[269]

The first stage is the *Chikhai* Bardo, which occurs immediately after death. In the three to four days before actual death, while the individual is dying, he is directed by the guide to recognize the Clear Light of the Void or Pure Reality and at the moment of death to liberate himself. If he does, he will not experience the intermediate or Bardo state and will attain liberation—the *Dharma-Kaya*. This state may be as short as a snap of a finger or may last for several days.[270]

If he is not able to liberate himself, he will enter the second stage of the *Chikhai* Bardo, the Secondary Clear Light. In this stage, the Clear Light is dimmer, and the consciousness principle is outside of the body. It enters a state that is like a dream. Not sure if he is dead, he asks himself, "Am I dead, or am I not dead?" In this dream state or illusory body, he sees relatives as he had been used to seeing them and may even hear wailings. Although he sees and hears, his karmic illusions will have not come yet, and the Clear Light dispels the power of karma. If the Clear Light of the second Bardo is recognized, liberation will be attained. If not, he enters the third stage.[271]

The third stage of the Bardo, the *Chonyid* Bardo, is the stage that the karmic illusion rise. At this stage, the deceased can hear all the weeping and wailing of his family and friends, and although he can see and hear them, they cannot see and hear him. His consciousness also experiences sounds, lights, and rays, which frighten and terrify him. However, he is instructed to take heed to the fact that what he is experiencing is unable to harm him because he has lost the body and is incapable of dying. The apparitions are his own thought-forms. In this stage, the deceased will encounter peaceful and wrathful deities.[272]

After the swoon (which lasts three-and-a-half days) the deceased will ask, "What happened?" On each of the first five days, the radiance of different orders of peaceful deities or wisdoms (with different names on each successive day that he does not make it successfully through the preceding day) will appear in bright, glorious, dazzling lights of different colors (according to the element and that of the deity) with an accompanying duller light (of the same or different color) and strike at him. In the setting face-to-face, the deceased is instructed to not fear and flee from the brighter lights, and to not turn to the duller light (which is his karma), and to pray special prayers.

If he is successful in recognizing or merging with the wisdom of that Bhagavan (deity) and the order that came with it, he will attain Perfect Enlightenment in the *Sambhoga-Kaya* in whichever realm (Central, North, South, East, or West of that particular order) that came to receive him. In other words, if he does not fear the first bright, glorious, and dazzling light (which is his pure self), he will obtain the Perfect Light in *Sambhoga-Kaya*. If he is overcome by illusion or flees from the bright light, the deity of the second day, as well as his evil deeds meriting hell, will come to receive him. This continues until all the peaceful deities are met unless he is successful in one of the days and attains Perfect Enlightenment.

Continuing to wander in the samsara because of having failed to recognize the wisdoms or the deities of the first five days of the Bardo, on the sixth day, the deceased will encounter the lights of the Five Orders, called the Lights of the Union of Four Wisdoms, and their attendant deities. This is a total of forty-two deities (seems like the forty-two assessors in *The Egyptian Book of the Dead*), who are perfectly endowed from the four directions of his heart, who will strike at it. However, in the setting face-to-face, he is instructed that they are the radiances of his heart and have not come from any other place than his intellectual faculties. Appearing also will be illusory lights of the six lokas, who will come along with the six radiances of wisdom. He is also instructed to abide in non-thought; if he is attracted to them, he will assume a body in any of the six lokas and suffer samsara miseries. He is also instructed to concentrate on the radiances of Wisdom of Five Orders of Buddhas and to pray a special prayer.[273]

On the seventh day, the Knowledge-Holding Deities come to receive him along with the pathway to the brute world, produced by the obscuring passion and stupidity stemming from intensified propensities. He is also instructed to pray a special prayer, and if he is attracted to them, he will fall into the brute world, which will lead to limitless miseries of slavery, dumbness, and stupidity.[274] On the eighth to the fourteenth days, blood-drinking, multiple-headed, humungous (the smallest being eighteen people in size, the largest being as large as heaven), orders of wrathful deities come to receive him. They are the same as peaceful deities but in different forms. The deceased is instructed that rather than being awed, fearful, and fleeing, to recognize that they are not real, are apparitions of his own mind bought on by his karma, upon which he is instructed to pray special prayers. If the consciousness principle is still unable to achieve liberation, he enters the *Sidpa* Bardo.[275]

In the *Sidpa* Bardo, the deceased has now taken on a desire body (a thought-form hallucination with the same propensities of the human body) and will see forms and hear. Other sense organs will be keen, which is all an indication that he has wandered further into the Bardo. Since he has lost the gross body, he has the power to traverse continents and go through physical objects like hills, boulders, and houses without being impeded. When he sees his relatives and tries to speak to them and they do not reply, he now knows he is dead, feeling great misery. He may even try to find his body so that he can enter back into it.

In the *Sidpa* Bardo, the deceased will be tossed around by the ever-moving winds of karma—and happiness and misery will depend on his karma. If he has bad karma, all sorts of frightful things will strike at him and threaten to devour him. During the judgment (which occurs in the

Sidpa Bardo) the Lords of Death will consult a mirror, and upon finding bad karma, will torture him, cut off his head, extract his heart, pull out his intestines, drink his blood, eat his flesh, gnaw at his bones, and hack him in pieces—and the deceased will revive again and again. Such hacking will cause intense pain and suffering. However, he is instructed that he has only his mental body (which is void), that he cannot die, and the Lords of Death are merely his own hallucinations.[276]

Having now wandered further down the *Sidpa* Bardo, the lights of the six lokas will appear; one of the places he is to be born through the power of his karma will shine most prominently. Despite that he has wandered further down the Bardo, he is still capable of attaining Perfect Enlightenment, and is still instructed on steps on how to do so by the guide. Some steps include letting go of attachment to worldly objects as they are of no use to him now; abstaining from impure thoughts that bring about anger, and concentration and meditation on the compassionate one, tutelary deities, prayer, etc. If the individual, through great weakness in devotion and lack of familiarity (because he was not taught as to these matters), is not able to understand, illusions may overcome him, and he will wander to the door of wombs. The guide then instructs him on five methods to close the womb door (one of the most interesting ones is avoiding visions of males and females in sexual union). If he is still unable to attain liberation, he will be instructed on how to choose the womb door that he will be reborn in, which begins with what continent he will be born on.[277]

The entire *Bardo Thodol* document found in the *Tibetan Book of the Dead* has much more detail than space allows here, as with much of the information that has been summarized throughout this work. The intent was to introduce the various concepts so that one might seek out the entire works themselves. It is noted that the object of secret initiations, as a rule, was the culmination of a figurative death. "The instruction given in the *Bardo Thodol* serves to recall to the dead man the experiences of his initiation and the teachings of his *guru*, for the instruction, at bottom is nothing less than an initiation of the dead into the Bardo life, just as the initiation of the living was a preparation for the beyond."[278]

Whether one is initiated or not, the genius of the *Bardo* treatise is that not only does it provide a guide for the science of death, but a guide for the science of life. If it is true that one's state of consciousness upon death (and one's memory) is the state one will find oneself in when one enters into the Bardo or intermediate state of consciousness, it might behoove one to use the *Bardo Thodol* as a guide for right living while in the gross body so that one is prepared for death, especially if one is seeking liberation from samsara, wandering between the cycle of birth and rebirth. That is one might use the guidelines in the previous chapters, to purify one's thoughts, desires, and actions (the various ways in which we create karma) from the six poisons or enemies of pride, jealousy, ignorance, anger, greed, and lust (and others outlined in previous chapters). It might also be wise to not only read the *Bardo Thodol*, but do so thoroughly, meditate on it and commit it to memory. Most importantly, if one seeks the light in all situations and circumstances and in their daily life then it seems they will naturally turn to the light in death.

Although the *Thodol Bardo* is a guide for the person who is setting face-to-face with the dying and dead, to instruct them through the Bardo state, as they go through different states of consciousness after death, they are in fact, sitting face-to-face with themselves!

CONCLUDING REVELATIONS

Being raised in an adoptive family during the height of the Civil Rights and Black Power movements and struggling with Christianity and why it was so appealing to Black America, would raise questions of who I am, who we are, and eventually, other age-old questions of how we got here, why there is so much suffering and what happens after death. The search for answers to these questions would lead me to Black Studies, and Black Studies would lead me to Africa. Africa would lead me to African spirituality. It is in Egypt (and spiritual systems influenced by it) that I would not only find answers to these questions, but truth, or at least as close to it as one can get.

What did the search reveal to me? First, aside from reasons already explained throughout this work, I would find that Christianity may be so appealing to Black people because they (or at least their ancestors) are the originators of it. The theology of the son of God, the Christ, immaculate conception, virgin (or miraculous) birth, salvation, reincarnation, afterlife, eternal life, and other theological concepts found in Christianity originated with Nile Valley people and were given expression and articulated in writing (some in stone) in Black Egypt. These ideas would spread throughout the ancient world through Egyptian imperialism, trade, invaders, conquerors, and by those (including Greek philosophers) who came from all over the ancient world to study in Egyptian mystery schools.

Before the "invention" of religion, Egyptians, as most people all over the world, saw everything as sacred. They recognized that all matter is a manifestation of the divine, that matter is the grossest form of spirit, and that it adheres to laws set in motion by Divine intelligence. Since the sun is the light, the generator, giving vital force to all of life on Earth, the sun rose to supremacy, becoming "God" and "king" on Earth in ancient Egypt and those who came into contact with its spiritual science. Since they saw the microcosm as a mere reflection of the macrocosm, the physical reflection of the spiritual, the king became the reflection of the spiritual sun or light on Earth. Even Reiki (universal life force) is derived from Ra (also spelled Re), the Egyptian god of the sun, or the light.

In Egyptian theology, there was one infinite and eternal source from which all things were generated. That source generated another source that gave form to the world, giving rise to duality. Thus, just as the physical sun gives life and light to the physical world, the spiritual sun gives life and light to the spiritual world. Humanity is also dual in nature; physical and spiritual, mortal, and immortal. As the physical sun gives life to the body, the spiritual sun gives light to the soul. With the attainment of knowledge, cultivation of virtues, purification, and piety, we have within us the ability to attain Perfect Light; reunite with the infinite and eternal source; be released from our duality, and end the cycle of birth and death. This theology, created by African people, laid the foundation of Western science, Greek philosophy, secret societies, fraternal orders, and the world's Eastern and Western religions, including Christianity.

The mythos around the birth, life, death, and resurrection of Jesus can be found among various mystical personas in religions all over the world that predate Christianity, with the oldest being found in Egypt (at least articulated in writing, as Central Africa, Kush, and Nile Valley peoples predate Egypt). Thus, if Jesus of the Gospels did walk the earth and was crucified in the Roman style of execution, it is more than likely that he had already gone through the initiation process that every other initiate went through and was resurrected, reaching the highest level of illumination or the Christ-state, before his final physical death.

In *The Initiatory Process in Ancient Egypt*, Max Guilmot gives an account of how initiates were initiated in the final days of their journey in Abydos, where lies Osiris, the first resurrected god of eternal life and judge of the dead that we know of.

The initiate would be led (ritually) by Anubis (the conductor), where he would go through a series of doors (guarded by guardians) in the temple or underground (in deep recesses of the earth, the place of humanity's physical birth) where the tomb of Osiris lies, until he comes to the Hall of Judgment. If he is found to be pure, he is initiated into the mysteries. Guilmot notes that to reach the tomb of Osiris, the initiate had to step down into the holy water (the source of Christian baptism). After entering the holy water, he comes out reborn; like a new sun, he goes down into the abyss, and then emerges from it as a "sun," reborn.[279] Initiates would undergo three days in the final stages of the initiation whereupon they would die a physical death; they would die to the material world and be resurrected into the Perfect Light. Interestingly, with long periods of fasting (some as long as forty or more days), initiates may have undergone a near-death experience (if not died). This might explain why the authors of the Egyptian and Tibetan Books of the Dead were able to describe what happens at death.

Death and resurrection through initiation into the mysteries had therefore been practiced thousands of years before Jesus of the Gospels. These experiences of the initiate were incorporated into the mythos surrounding Jesus of the Gospels. Attempts were then made to destroy the knowledge of the mysteries and the story (which perpetuated a physical death and resurrection) was then forced upon the world during the Roman Empire and later during European world conquest and domination in the fifteenth century.

But the worst of the crimes against humanity do not lie here. It is telling people that Jesus is the only pathway to salvation, and then through torture and murder, forcing this on people all over the world. It is also the suggestion that one can violate the laws; specifically, the law of cause and effect, and that all one needs to do is ask for forgiveness, even if their violations cause irreparable harm to others (that may last for generations) or to the planet. It is the notion that Jesus, who supposedly died over two thousand years ago, died for our sins (which suggests that we can continue to transgress laws without repercussions). Most importantly, it is not telling people that the way to God, the way to salvation, is through themselves.

I would find that no matter their orientation, people all over the world have recognized that there are other realms with inhabitants with whom we can communicate. Among the Yoruba, it is the Orishas. In the *Book of Enoch*, it is the Watchers. Among the Jews, Christians, and Muslims, it is the angels and archangels. Among the Greeks, it was the daemons and the genii. Among the Hindus, it is the devas. For the Theosophy or New Age spirituality, it is the ascended masters. Among the ancient Egyptians, it was the Neteru. Just as there are different states of matter, that cannot be seen with the naked eye, there are different dimensions or realms that humans may or may not be able to access because of the limitations of our physical sense faculties. Those who are vibrating at higher frequencies may be able to access these realms. Such is the case with those who are born with a natural ability or higher capacity to see, hear, and know—clairvoyants, clairaudients, clairsentients—and those who develop these abilities.

As I continued to awaken, I came to understand what it means that everything is an illusion. Everything that has form is a different combination of the same thing and exists only for a while before it changes its form. Therefore, being attached to anything is not wise because eventually it will change, and even you will change, losing your own physical body. I understand why, when some people "see" the light they give up everything, even their wealth, and go into the "forest" schools (where nature teaches you) to live the ascetic life. As every breath you breathe, every morsel of food you eat, every step you take, every word you speak, something is changing—perhaps, dying—so that you may live. And while you live, you are creating new karma (even with your thoughts) that may keep you wandering in the samsara.

Other things would also be revealed to me: Hidden in plain sight are all the forces at work, right before our very eyes that we cannot see. The *Book of Enoch* opened my eyes to the fact that behind the stars, the sun, the moon, the winds, the rains, etc. there are intelligent forces, constantly at work, keeping all these things in order. And although the universe is abundant, there are storehouses of winds and rains, and if we do not pay attention to what we are doing, we will mess up the balance of things, and there will be devastating consequences.

I would find that:

○ For everything seen, there is the unseen.

○ The master, the adept (whatever his or her tools), has mastered the art of the unseen.

○ In every order, there are those who transgress the laws of their being; man, who acts against reason; animals who act against their nature; etc. And this might explain Fallen Ones, Fallen Angels, Lucifer, Satan, Beelzebub, the devil, and demons found in Abrahamic religions, and why there is evil in the world.

○ Consciousness at a minimum means awareness of our connectedness with everything in the universe. The more diligent one is in the pursuit of unity, the more unified one will become, and the more the mind of the universe will reveal itself until at last one achieves it.

I would also find that:

○ The greatest mystery is that of the self.

○ The more pure one becomes the more one will be able to communicate with pure consciousness.

○ When we learn the science of nature, about the elements, about the elementals—the science of our ancestors—we learn the science of ourselves. This indeed is the path and where the truth lies.

I would find some of the mysteries of the universe, the science of spirituality, a clear understanding of the principles of truth, particularly the law of cause and effect; you reap what you sow, the middle way, a clear pathway to the light, to heaven on Earth, and *ultimately*, the science of death. That is, how to "die" while staying alive if one is to be successful in their pursuit of eternal life.

I would also find out why that although I am a scholar, I struggled with it so. Scholarship is necessary because it helps us to establish a standard for whether the information is to be taken seriously. However, scholarship in Western science is entrenched in materialism, which means that only that which can be observed by five physical sense organs is taken as "real" and therefore taken seriously at least in the scientific world, and anything that falls short of this is considered pseudo-science. Because this approach to knowledge does not take serious matters of the spirit, of the unseen, then it is disjointed, disunified with the whole of the universe, and can only take us so far. In addition, scholarship that does not take seriously the oral tradition, the mythos, or sayings; that which is only passed from mouth to ear, misses a big part of what we are calling knowledge. And this fundamentally may be why religion and religious leaders (although the allegory in the scriptures and how they often interpreted leaves people in ignorance) are so much more powerful and effective, and why the intelligentsia is powerless and ineffective in reaching a great majority of the people whose souls hunger for the truth and the light.

Finally, as to answers to the question of our origins, I am sure if one were to search the mythos of people all over the world, they would find that although the stories vary, what they share most in common is that the original abode of humanity is the heavens. They would also find that in every religious and spiritual system (at least in the ones I encountered) the fundamental teachings are the same. This may be because they all come from the same source. As to answers to the questions of why we come to Earth, why there is so much suffering, and what happens after death, I was eventually led to the answers that the earliest inhabitants that we know of on Earth left behind. Those who peopled the Nile; those who thought that the answers to these questions were significant enough to be etched in stone; those from whose theology peoples all over the globe have borrowed from, including India and Tibet.

It is Africa, the birthplace of humanity, and ancient Egypt, whose answers to these questions, outlined throughout this work, that I found to be satisfying to my soul. I believe I now understand clearly what the most ancient of our ancestors meant by "Know Thyself."

~~~~~~~~~~

One day, I was in class, and a student began discussing how she was conscious, but that her sister was not. I asked her to tell me what she meant by "conscious." I do not recall what her answer was, but I do remember my response, "You know, there is a difference between Black consciousness and consciousness." She looked at me perplexed. "Black consciousness," I explained, "is awareness of the African global experience. Consciousness is awareness of our connectedness to everything in the universe." But I would discover that it is even more to it than that.

In the speech that would celebrate the end of my journey with GSU, I was surprised that Dr. Molefi Asante, under whom I began my journey in Black Studies, who was invited to speak on my behalf, not only seemed to be at a similar level of consciousness concerning the state of humanity but also expanded upon and articulated my own idea of it. Thus, in addition to awareness of our connectedness, it is an awareness of the reality that humanity has come to a place where we have the capacity at any moment to erase ourselves out of the universe. And this is why humanity must be taught the laws, especially the law of cause and effect, "you reap what you sow," and the consequences of not paying attention to it.

One day, I was searching for information on the Internet and stumbled onto the term "democide." Because it piqued my interest, I researched it further, and would find the work by R.J. Rummel, *Death by Government*. In this work, Rummel, finding "genocide" and "mass murder" lacking as comprehensive nomenclatures to describe the various ways governments kill people, defines democide as: The murder of any person or people by a government, including genocide, politicide, and mass murder. More specifically, *democide* is any action by a government that is designed to kill or cause the death of people by deadly prison, concentration camp, forced labor, prisoner of war or recruit camp conditions. It includes:

(a) killing medical or scientific experiments on humans;

(b) torture or beatings; encouraged or condoned murder, or rape, looting, and pillage during which people are killed;

(c) a famine or epidemic during which government authorities withhold aid, or knowingly act in a way to make it more deadly;

(d) Imposing measures intended to prevent births within the group;

(e) forced deportations and expulsions causing deaths.[280]

According to Rummel's extensive statistics, 169,202,000[281] people were murdered by governments in the twentieth century and over 133,147,000[282] were murdered by pre-twentieth-century governments. These numbers do not include those who are casualties of war (when it was not intentional) but do include murders that are considered war crimes or crimes against humanity (for example, the mass murder of prisoners of war).

Although it seems impossible that anyone could realistically attain an accurate count of the number of people who are murdered, since in many places in the world, especially "Third World" countries in the early pre-twentieth century, some nations did not keep records of their populations, let alone records of how many people were killed, particularly when entire populations were extinguished. However, murder by governments that remotely approach anywhere close to these figures is horrendous, to say the least. In another study, it was found that from 1,400 to 2,000, there have been 3,708 conflicts, reaching a death toll of close to 150 million people.[283] If this is the death toll from 1,400 to 2,000, it is highly feasible that the death toll from war before that time was high as well. Man's inhumanity against humanity is beyond words, to say the least. One can imagine if there is an Almighty God watching humanity, he/she must terribly be disappointed. If we are the creation or descendants of gods or ancient astronauts, if they were to return, as ancient civilizations have said, they would be equally disappointed.

Humanity has now entered an era where we have the capacity for space war. But not the kind of war where we fight an invading enemy from somewhere in outer space, as depicted in science-fiction (although that is a possibility as well), but against ourselves. It may also not be the kind of war that is fought in space, where spacecraft are attacking each other with laser beams (although considering where we are going with technology, this might also occur at some time in the future), but right here on the ground, with "virtual" children (that is how young some of them are), guiding missiles and bombs to satellites and people with no real connection to them as human beings or no moral comprehension of what it is they are engaging in, as if they are in computer games. Interestingly, because they are already desensitized to violence in gaming, they are already prepared to become agents of death and mass murder.

The very person who was responsible for the invention of dynamite, Alfred Noble, tried to make amends for it by creating the Noble Peace Prize so that he could leave a legacy for a more noble act rather than as an "agent of death," as he was described in an article in which it was mistakenly thought that he, rather than his brother, had died. Einstein makes note of this in a speech in 1948 when speaking to the guilt that physicists must feel for creating weapons of mass destruction.

Although humanity has achieved unbelievable super-technologies, we have not even begun to scratch the surface by comparison to supernatural technology. Unfortunately, the discovery of super-technology has led to the creation of weapons of mass destruction, and man's arrogance has bought him to the brink of destruction. As of 2017, nine countries were in possession of 9,220 (this number varies depending upon the source) nuclear weapons worldwide, with Russian and the United States possessing most of them. Other countries with nuclear weapons include France, China, the United Kingdom, Pakistan, Israel, India, and North Korea. What is tragic is that the name of some of the ancient world's highest principles, represented by gods or goddesses, have been appropriated to weapons of mass destruction. This is observed in India's nuclear bomb tests called "Smiling Buddha" and "Shakti" (which actually does mean destroyer), or militaristic groups like The Islamic State of Iraq and the Levant (ISIL), also known as the Islamic State of Iraq, (ISIS) in Syria. When I was looking for images of Isis (the Egyptian goddess) online one day, nothing but images of war and destruction came up. What a travesty. One must click on Egypt at the top to find images of the goddess Isis. Before ISIS, that was not necessary.

It is not only weapons of mass destruction (including biological and chemical) that puts humanity in danger of extinction, but it is also our lack of regard for the effects of our activities on the planet, including depletion of the ozone layer; emission of greenhouse gases; water, air, soil, and land pollution; deforestation; mining; electromagnetic pollution; satellites, and more. When things get unbalanced, nature is going to do what it does: it is going to regenerate and balance things out, even if it means that it is catastrophic for humanity. In *the Virgin to the World*, Tehuti prophesized:

Egypt, once the holy land beloved of the gods and full of devotion for their worship, will become the instrument of perversion, the school of impiety, the type of all violence. Then, filled with disgust for everything, man will no longer feel either admiration or love for the world...darkness will be preferred to light, and death will be deemed better than life, nor will any man lift his eyes to heaven. In those days, the religious man will be thought mad; the impious man will be hailed as a sage; savage men will be deemed valiant; the evil-hearted will be applauded as the best of men. The Soul, and all that belongs thereto—whether born mortal or able to attain eternal life—all those things which I have herein expounded to thee, will be but matters for ridicule, and will be esteemed foolishness. There will even be peril of death, believe me, for those who remain faithful to religion and intelligence. New rights will be instituted, new laws, nor will there be left one holy word, one sacred belief, religious and worthy of heaven and of celestial things. O lamentable separation between the Gods and men! Then there will remain only evil demons who will mingle themselves with the miserable human race, their hand will be upon it impelling to all kinds of wicked enterprise; to war, to rapine, to falsehood, to everything contrary to the nature of the soul. The earth will no longer be in equilibrium, the sea will no longer be navigable, in the heavens, the regular course of the stars will be troubled. Every holy voice will be condemned to silence; the fruits of the earth will become corrupt, and she will be no more fertile; the very air will sink into lugubrious torpor. Such will be the old age of the world; irreligion and disorder, lawlessness, and the confusion of good men.[284]

Not only does it seem the gods left Egypt, but it seems they have left the earth. And most of what was prophesized is occurring now. At the time of completing this work, we are witnessing, for the first time in human history (at least that we know of), a global shut down because of a pandemic stemming from a coronavirus virus called COVID-19 that emerged in Wuhan, China. Since the whole wide world, at least those parts that national and international news have enough information or deem significant enough to report on (one barely sees what is going on in many "Second" or "Third" World countries), it seems like this is the planet's way of shutting humanity down so that it can regenerate since we don't seem to know how to do it ourselves and to get us to pay attention to what we are doing. If we can get through this, it should serve as a warning for what is to come, if we continue the path that we are on.

In the oldest religions that we know, Egyptian, Sumerian, and even in Hinduism, Buddhism, Abrahamic traditions as well as other religions throughout the world, it was thought that humanity had become so corrupt that it needed a savior, like Isis, Osiris, Horus, Krsna, Gautama the Buddha, Jesus the Christ, and others, whether they are divinity in flesh or have evolved over many lifetimes and incarnate to help humanity. And in light of the reality that there are other realms, and these realms are inhabited by beings that might even take an interest in humanity, the mythos or sayings that the heavens rejoice and celebrate upon the birth of these saviors on Earth may not be far-fetched. I mean we must believe that someone or thing, perhaps interstellar, will intervene to help humanity keep from destroying ourselves.

~~~~~~~~~~~

While I was walking to my car at the gas station one day and looking up at the gray sky, I noticed the trees that lined the sidewalk across the street. Although they were relatively young, I saw the ancientness in their form and that their ancestors have been changing colors for a very long time. I thought to myself, "I can't believe I am still here." Some people say life is short, but not for me. With all the roads I traveled, even in this life, it seems I have been here for a very long time. When I go to these places, where it seems time stands still, I know for sure my soul has been on this journey much longer than I have. I don't know why it took me so long to find the reason for my soul's journey to Earth this time. But I think I found it. I don't know why it took me so long to find the pathway back. But I think I did this time. The real work now begins.

The ancients say that God is unknowable. But when I stand still—I mean really stand still; when I go into the bliss state a will—and see the splendor of the flower, the tree in her majesty, the bird in flight, the oceans that have touched the shores for a million years, the winds dancing their majestic dances, the earth giving abundantly, the heavenly skies, the celestial bodies that grace us with their light, but most of importantly, when I look—I mean really look—into the face of my fellow man (and woman), I swear, at times, it seems like I am looking right into the face of God.

And it is in these moments, that I know for sure, that I have seen glimpses of eternity.

END NOTES

[1] *Journey to Enlightenment | THE RABBIT HOLE with Deepak Chopra*, 2013, https://www.youtube.com/watch?v=NYi4hqjFfuc.

[2] John C. Greene, *The Death of Adam: Evolution and Its Impact on Western Thought* (New York: The New American Library of World Literature, Inc., 1961), 183.

[3] Greene, 179.

[4] Greene, 187.

[5] Greene, 193–94.

[6] Greene, 193–94.

[7] Greene, 224.

[8] Greene, 235.

[9] Greene, 326.

[10] Greene, 326.

[11] Molefi Kete Asante, *Afrocentricity: Theory of Social Change*, Revised, Subsequent edition (Trenton, N.J: Africa World Press, 1988), 1.

[12] Molefi Kete Asante, *Kemet, Afrocentricity and Knowledge* (Trenton, N.J: Africa World Press, 1990), 28.

[13] C. Tsehloane Keto, *Introduction to the Africa Centered Perspective of History* (London: Research Associates School Times Publications, 1999), 14.

[14] Keto, 15.

[15] Keto, 8. (The Greenwich Meantime, an observatory in Greenwich, London, was used as the international civil time standard. It has been superseded by Universal Coordinated Time (UTC), which is now the primary standard used to regulate clocks and time).

[16] Keto, 9.

[17] Keto, 9.

[18] Keto, 9.

[19] Keto, 19.

[20] Keto, 19.

[21] Keto, 19.

[22] Keto, 19–20.

[23] Asante, *Kemet, Afrocentricity and Knowledge*, ix.

[24] Martin Bernal, *Black Athena: The Afroasiatic Roots of Classical Civilization*, 1st edition (New Brunswick, N.J: Rutland Local History & Record Society, 1987), 108.

[25] Bernal, 108.

[26] Asante, *Kemet, Afrocentricity and Knowledge*, 64–65.

[27] Cheikh Anta Diop, *The African Origin of Civilization Myth or Reality* (New York: Lawrence Hill Books, 1974), 3.

[28] Diop, 4.

[29] Diop, 7.

[30] Asante, *Kemet, Afrocentricity and Knowledge*, 64.

[31] Diop, *The African Origin of Civilization Myth or Reality*, 2.

[32] Asante, *Kemet, Afrocentricity and Knowledge*, 61.

[33] Diop, *The African Origin of Civilization Myth or Reality*, 28.

[34] Dixon, *African American Relationships, Marriages, and Families: An Introduction*, 2nd Edition (New York: Routledge, 2017), 13.

[35] Dixon, 14.

[36] Dixon, 14.

[37] Chancellor Williams, *Destruction of Black Civilization: Great Issues of a Race from 4500 B.C. to 2000 A.D.*, 3rd Revised Edition (Chicago: Third World Press, 1992), 255–56.

[38] Arna Bontemps, *Great Slave Narratives*, 2nd Printing Edition (Boston: Beacon Press, 1970), 27–31.

[39] Bontemps, 31.

[40] Bontemps, 32.

[41] John W. Blassingame, *The Slave Community: Plantation Life in the Antebellum South*, Revised Edition (New York: Oxford University Press, 1979), 262–63.

[42] BlackFacts.com, "(1909) Ida B. Wells, 'Lynching Our National Crime,'" Blackfacts.com, accessed October 23, 2020, https://www.blackfacts.com/fact/1909-ida-b-wells-lynching-our-national-crime; "The Daily Star - Google News Archive Search," accessed October 23, 2020, https://news.google.com/newspapers?nid=1297&dat=19090602&id=4PRNAAAAIBAJ&sjid=sI-oDAAAAIBAJ&pg=3567,2905466.

[43] Maulana Karenga, *Introduction to Black Studies*, 2nd Edition (the University of Sankore Press, 1993), 129.

[44] Karenga, 134.

[45] Karenga, 130.

[46] Karenga, 132–33.

[47] "Ida B. Wells-Barnett (1862-1931) and Her Passion for Justice, Black Women, African American Women, Suffrage, Women's Movement, Civil Rights Leaders," accessed October 23, 2020, http://people.duke.edu/~ldbaker/classes/aaih/caaih/ibwells/ibwbkgrd.html.

[48] "Mob Violence and Anti-Lynching Campaign - A Voice for Justice - The University of Chicago Library," accessed October 23, 2020,

https://www.lib.uchicago.edu/collex/exhibits/voice-for-justice-life-and-legacy-ida-b-wells/mob-violence-and-anti-lynching-campaign/.
[49] John Hope Franklin and August Meier, eds., *Black Leaders of the Twentieth Century* (Chicago, IL: University of Illinois press, 1982), 159.
[50] *FLH Testimony Before the Credentials Committee*, accessed October 23, 2020, https://www.youtube.com/watch?v=IRCUUzpfV7k&t=24s.
[51] C. Eric Lincoln, "The Black Church Since Frazier," in *The Negro Church in America/The Black Church Since Frazier*, ed. E. Franklin Frazier and C. Eric Lincoln (New York: Schocken, 1974), 166.
[52] Nafeesa Muhammad, "The Nation of Islam's Economic Program, 1934-1975," April 2, 2020, https://www.blackpast.org/african-american-history/the-nation-of-islams-economic-program-1934-1975/.
[53] Dona Richards, "African American Spirituality," in *African Culture: The Rhythms of Unity*, ed. Asante Molefi Kete and Kariamu Asante Welsh (Trenton, NJ: Africa World Press, 1989), 12.
[54] Jacob Carruthers H., "Science and Oppression" (Chicago, IL: Kemetic Institute, 1991).
[55] Robert Williams L., "The Death of White Research in the Black Community," *Journal of Non-White Concerns* 2, no. 3 (April 1974): 116–32.
[56] Clinton M. Jean, *Behind the Eurocentric Veils: The Search for African Realities* (Amherst: University of Massachusetts Press, 1992).
Philip Slater, *The Pursuit of Loneliness: America's Discontent and the Search for a New Democratic Ideal*, 3rd edition (Beacon Press, 2016), Introduction, https://www.amazon.com/Pursuit-Loneliness-Americas-Discontent-Democratic-ebook-dp-B01AEPR4DQ/dp/B01AEPR4DQ/ref=mt_other?_encoding=UTF8&me=&qid=1596491404.
[58] Paula J. Giddings, *When and Where I Enter: The Impact of Black Women on Race and Sex in America* (New York: W. Morrow, 1984), 86.
[59] Donna Franklin, *Ensuring Inequality*, Revised edition (New York, NY: Oxford University Press, 2015), 27–28.
[60] Malcolm Jarvis, Interview with Malcolm "Shorty" Jarvis, 1994.
[61] Jarvis.
[62] "Lynching Statistics," Lynchings by State and Race, accessed May 25, 2020, http://law2.umkc.edu/faculty/projects/ftrials/shipp/lynchingsstate.html.
[63] Aminah McCloud Beverly, *African American Islam*, 1 edition (London: Routledge, 2014), 85.

[64] "H. Rap Brown 'Violence Is as American As Cherry Pie'" n. For fear that he would radicalize other prisoners, Amin was transferred to United States Penitentiary Administrative Maximum Facility (USP Florence ADMAX), a Supermax prison in Colorado. He was later transferred to United States Penitentiary in Tucson, Arizona, where he is fighting cancer at the time of this writing., accessed May 26, 2020, https://www.youtube.com/watch?v=8WFFDm-Wyvw.

[65] I have found various numbers; estimating that the number of people Dubois interviewed himself ranging from 2500 to 5000.

[66] W. E. B. Du Bois, *The Philadelphia Negro: A Social Study* (New York: Schocken Books, 1967), 388.

[67] Du Bois, 394.

[68] Randall Robinson, *The Debt: What America Owes to Blacks*, Reprint edition (New York: Plume, 2001), 2.

[69] Robinson, 1–6.

[70] Robinson, 8–9.

[71] "A Short History of Colonialism in Congo, 1885-1997," libcom.org, accessed May 26, 2020, http://libcom.org/history/short-history-colonialism-congo-1885-1997.

[72] Gerda Lerner, ed., *Black Women in White America* (New York: Vintage Books, n.d.).

[73] Du Bois, *The Philadelphia Negro: A Social Study*, 215.

[74] A cartouche is an oval with a line at one end at right angles to the oval, indicating that the text enclosed is a royal name. The ancient Egyptian word for cartouche was *shenu*, and the cartouche was essentially an expanded shen ring, which means "protection."

[75] Hebrew law (the Torah), the first five books of Moses, was first put into writing somewhere between 1200 BC to 100 BC (the Torah is used interchangeably with the Tanakh, which includes the law, the prophets, and the writings; called the Old Testament by non-Jews). The Talmud, the oral part of the law (which consists of how the written law was to be executed and followed) that was supposedly transmitted orally by Moses to the council of elders and others who were invited to listen, was put into writing somewhere between 190 and 200 CE (called Mishna) by Rabbi Judah the Prince (Yehudah HaNasi, who was very wealthy). The part which is the summary of discussions, interpretations, and elucidation of the oral Torah (called Germara) was put into writing somewhere between 450 and 500 CE. Two versions of the Talmud are

the Jerusalem one (300-350 CE) and the Babylonian one (450-500 CE), which is considered the more authoritative version.

[76] Hyam Maccoby, *The Mythmaker: Paul and the Invention of Christianity*, Seventh Printing. edition (New York: Barnes & Noble Books, 1998), 119.

[77] Maccoby, 123.

[78] Maccoby, 60.

[79] Maccoby, 140–43.

[59] J. A. Giles, *Hebrew and Christian Records: An Historical Enquiry Concerning the Age and Authorship of the Old and New Testaments;* (London: Thubner & Col, Ludgate Hill, 1877), 9.

[81] Elaine Pagels, *The Gnostic Gospels*, Reissue edition (New York: Vintage, 1989), xiii–xiv.

[82] Pagels, xiii–xxxvi.

[83] Pagels, 6.

[84] Pagels, 11.

[85] T. W. Doane, *Bible Myths and Their Parallels in Other Religions* (Forgotten Books, 2012), 422.

[86] Pagels, *The Gnostic Gospels*, 39–40.

[87] Pagels, 41–42.

[88] Timothy Schuler, "Mapping One of the World's Largest Landowners," *Curbed*, October 18, 2017, https://www.curbed.com/2017/10/18/16483194/catholic-church-gis-goodlands-esri-molly-burhans.

[89] Albert Roboteau J., *Slave Religion: The "Invisible Institution" in the Antebellum South*, New edition (Oxford: Oxford University Press, 1980), 100.

[90] Roboteau, 101.

[91] Roboteau, 101.

[92] Roboteau, 132.

[93] Roboteau, 133.

[94] A. M. E. Church, "African Methodist Episcopal Church: Our History," AME Church, accessed May 21, 2020, https://www.ame-church.com/our-church/our-history/.

[95] C. Eric Lincoln and Lawrence H. Mamiya, *The Black Church in the African American Experience* (Duke University Press Books, 1990).

[96] Malachi York, *The Holy Tablets*, 1st Edition (Holy Tabernacle Ministries, 1996), 1456–60.

[97] Zecharia Sitchin, *Twelfth Planet: Book I of the Earth Chronicles*, Reprint edition (New York, New York: Harper, 2007), 285.

[98] Sitchin, 348, 350–51.

324 Glimpses of Eternity

[99] Sitchin, 358.

[100] Erich von Däniken, *Chariots of the Gods*, trans. Michael Heron (New York: Berkley Books, 1999), 60.

[101] David Hatcher Childress, *Technology of the Gods: The Incredible Sciences of the Ancients*, 1st Edition (Kempton, IL: Adventures Unlimited Press, 2000), 13–14; Däniken, *Chariots of the Gods*, 69.

[102] C.F. Volney, *The Ruins of Empires* (Baltimore, MD: Black Classic Press, 1991), 8.

[103] Volney, 9.

[104] Volney, 10.

[105] Volney, 10.

[106] Volney, 13.

[107] Volney, 17.

[108] Volney, 20–21.

[109] Volney, 22.

[110] Volney, 23–24.

[111] Volney, 25.

[112] Volney, 25–26.

[113] Volney, 26–28.

[114] Volney, 110–49.

[115] Volney, 145–49.

[116] A. C. Bhaktivedanta Swami Prabhupada, *Bhagavad-Gita As It Is* (Los Angeles, California: The Bhaktivedanta Book Trust, 2001), 21.

[117] Prabhupada, 686.

[118] Prabhupada, 686–87.

[119] Prabhupada, 688–90.

[120] Prabhupada, 693.

[121] Prabhupada, 14–17, 698 ; 14–18, 699.

[122] Prabhupada, 19.

[123] Annie Besant, *The Ancient Wisdom: An Outline of Theosophical Teachings* (Wheaton, Illinois: The Theosophical Publishing House, 1977), 286–87.

[124] Besant, 297.

[125] Besant, 298.

[126] Henry Alabaster, *Wheel of the Law*, Reprint edition (Kila, MT: Kessinger Publishing, LLC, 1942), 111.

[127] Paul Carus, *The Gospel of Buddha* (Seattle, WA: Pacific Publishing Studio, 2011), 18.

[128] "Buddha, The Word, The Eightfold Path (500BC)," accessed September 12, 2020, http://www.columbia.edu/itc/ealac/moerman/fall2000/edit/pdfs/wk4/thewor.pdf.

[129] Gerald Massey, *The Natural Genesis*, vol. 1 (Baltimore, MD: Black Classic Press, 1998), viii–ix.

[130] Albert Churchward, *Signs & Symbols of Primordial Man* (Brooklyn, NY: A&B Publishers Group, 1994), 2–3.

[131] Massey, *The Natural Genesis*, 1:10.

[132] Massey, 1:135.

[133] Massey, 1:8.

[134] "Egyptian Chronology," Digital Egypt for Universities, accessed May 27, 2020, https://www.ucl.ac.uk/museums-static/digitalegypt/chronology/index.html; "List of Rulers of Ancient Egypt and Nubia | Lists of Rulers | Heilbrunn Timeline of Art History | The Metropolitan Museum of Art," accessed May 27, 2020, https://www.metmuseum.org/toah/hd/phar/hd_phar.htm.

[135] Cheikh Anta Diop, *Civilization or Barbarism: An Authentic Anthropology*, trans. Yaa-Lengi Meema Ngemi (Chicago, Illinois: Chicago Review Press, 1991), 85.

[136] Diop, 85.

[137] Diop, 87.

[138] Diop, 91–92.

[139] H. Heras, "Anu in India and in Egypt," *Indian History Congress*, Proceedings of the Indian History Congress, 5 (1941): 93.

[140] Heras, 93–94.

[141] Massey, *The Natural Genesis*, 1:4.

[142] E. A. Wallis Budge, *The Gods of the Egyptians, Volume 1* (New York: Dover Publications, 2012), 95.

[143] Gerald Massey, *Ancient Egypt: The Light of the World [Two Volumes In One]* (Mansfield Centre, CT: Martino Publishing, 2014), 7.

[144] Marimba Ani, *Yurugu: An African-Centered Critique of European Cultural Thought and Behavior*, First Edition (Trenton, N.J: Africa World Press, 1994), 110.

[145] Ani, 117.

[146] Ani, 119.

[147] Ani, 120.

[148] Ani, 124–25.

[149] "Legends of the Gods, The Egyptian Texts: Legends of Egyptian Gods: The History of Creation--A.," accessed May 26, 2020, https://www.sacred-texts.com/egy/leg/leg13.htm.

326 Glimpses of Eternity

[150] Budge, *The Gods of the Egyptians, Volume 1*, 352.

[151] "Legends of the Gods, The Egyptian Texts: Legends of Egyptian Gods: The History of Creation--B.," accessed May 26, 2020, https://www.sacred-texts.com/egy/leg/leg14.htm.

[152] Eloise McKinney-Johnson, "Egypt's Isis: The Original Black Madonna," in *Black Women In Antiquity*, ed. Ivan Van Sertima (Brunswick, NJ: Transaction Publishers, 1995), 62.

[153] E. A. Wallis Budge, *The Gods of the Egyptians, Volume 2*, Revised ed. edition (New York: Dover Publications, 2013), 213–14; McKinney-Johnson, "Egypt's Isis: The Original Black Madonna," 64.

[154] Wallis Budge E.A., *Egyptian Book of the Dead: The Papyrus of Ani* (Dover Publications, 1999), 1iii–11iv.

[155] E. A. Wallis Budge, *Legends of the Egyptian Gods: Hieroglyphic Texts and Translations*, Reprint edition (New York: Dover Publications, 1994), 1xxx–1xxxi.

[156] Budge, 1xxxii.

[157] Budge, 1xxxiii.

[158] Budge, *The Gods of the Egyptians, Volume 2*, 216–21.

[159] Budge, *The Gods of the Egyptians, Volume 1*.

[160] Raymond Faulkner, Ogden Goelet, and Carol Andrews, *Egyptian Book of the Dead: The Book of Going Forth by Day* (San Francisco: Chronicle Books, LLC, 1994), Plate 3-4.

[161] Acharya S, *The Christ Conspiracy: The Greatest Story Ever Sold* (Kempton, Illinois: Adventures Unlimited Press, 1999), 149–50.

[162] Acharya S, 150.

[163] Manly P. Hall, *The Secret Teachings of All Ages: An Encyclopedic Outline of Masonic, Hermetic, Qabbalistic and Rosicrucian Symbolical Philosophy*, Reprint edition (Seattle, WA: Pacific Publishing Studio, 2011), 40.

[164] Acharya S, *The Christ Conspiracy: The Greatest Story Ever Sold*, 184–214.

[165] Acharya S, 192.

[166] Acharya S, 191.

[167] Acharya S, 211.

[168] Acharya S, 152–53; John G. Jackson, *Christianity Before Christ* (Eastford, CT: Martino Publishing, 2015), 9.

[169] Churchward, *The Origins and Evolution of Religion*, 15–16.

[170] Churchward, 16.

[171] Churchward, 16.

[172] Churchward, 16.

[173] Jackson, *Christianity Before Christ*, 8.

[174] Doane, *Bible Myths and Their Parallels in Other Religions*, 289–304.

[175] Acharya S, *The Christ Conspiracy: The Greatest Story Ever Sold*, 340.
[176] Acharya S, 356.
[177] Acharya S, 356–58.
[178] Acharya S, 359.
[179] Michael Baigent, Richard Leigh, and Henry Lincoln, *The Messianic Legacy* (New York: Dell, 1989), 42.
[180] Eusebius, *Life of Constantine*, trans. Averil Cameron and Stuart Hall G., 1 edition (Oxford University Press, U.S.A., 1999), 152–53.
[181] "Serapis Religion," accessed April 16, 2020, http://platonism347.tripod.com/serapis_religion.htm.
[182] Doane, *Bible Myths and Their Parallels in Other Religions*, 527.
[183] Doane, 137.
[184] Aleister Crowley, S. L. MacGregor Mathers, and F. C. Conybear, *The Three Magical Books of Solomon: The Greater and Lesser Keys & The Testament of Solomon*, 1 edition (Mockingbird Press, 2017), 273.
[185] Crowley, Mathers, and Conybear, 275–76.
[186] Crowley, Mathers, and Conybear, 283.
[187] Franz Hartmann, *The Life and the Doctrines of Philippus Theophrastus Bombast of Hohenheim Known as Paracelsus* (Kessinger Publishing, LLC: Kessinger Publishing, LLC, 2010), 1–31.
[188] Hall, *The Secret Teachings of All Ages*, 113.
[189] Hall, 114.
[190] Hall, 114.
[191] Hall, 114.
[192] Hall, 114–15.
[193] Hall, 116.
[194] Hall, 117.
[195] The Three Initiates, *The Kybalion: A Study of The Hermetic Philosophy of Ancient Egypt and Greece: Three Initiates* (Mansfield Centre, CT: Martino Publishing, 2016), 22–27.
[196] The Three Initiates, 10–11.
[197] The Three Initiates, 11.
[198] The Three Initiates, 30.
[199] The Three Initiates, 52–54.
[200] The Three Initiates, 57.
[201] The Three Initiates, 57–58.
[202] The Three Initiates, 61.
[203] The Three Initiates, 65.
[204] The Three Initiates, 65.
[205] The Three Initiates, 66–67.

[206] The Three Initiates, 15.
[207] The Three Initiates, 72.
[208] The Three Initiates, 15.
[209] The Three Initiates, 72.
[210] The Three Initiates, 77.
[211] The Three Initiates, 79.
[212] The Three Initiates, 85–86.
[213] The Three Initiates, 10.
[214] George James, *Stolen Legacy: Greek Philosophy Is Stolen Egyptian Philosophy* (Independently published, 2019), chap. 3.
[215] James, chap. 3.
[216] James, In Notes Section.
[217] James, chap. 3.
[218] James, Appendix.
[219] The Three Initiates, *The Kybalion: A Study of The Hermetic Philosophy of Ancient Egypt and Greece: Three Initiates*, 5.
[220] The Three Initiates, 5.
[221] G. R. S. Mead, *Thrice-Greatest Hermes: Volumes I, II, III.* (Deuschland: Jazzybee Verlag, 2017), 23.
[222] Lydia Maria Francis 1802-1880 Child, *The Progress of Religious Ideas: Through Successive Ages; Volume 1* (Sydney: Wentworth Press, 2016), 173.
[223] Child, 174.
[224] Roelof van den Broeck and Cis van Heertum, *From Poimandres to Jacob Böhme: Gnosis, Hermetism and the Christian Tradition* (Leiden, Netherlands: BRILL, 2000), 48.
[225] Mead, *Thrice-Greatest Hermes*, 188.
[226] Edward Maitland and Anna Kingsford, trans., *The Virgin of the World* (Deutschland: Jazzybee Verlag, 2017), 39.
[227] Maitland and Kingsford, 38.
[228] Maitland and Kingsford, 38.
[229] Maitland and Kingsford, 38.
[230] Maitland and Kingsford, 18.
[231] Maitland and Kingsford, 21.
[232] Maitland and Kingsford, 20.
[233] Maitland and Kingsford, 10.
[234] Maitland and Kingsford, 10.
[235] Maitland and Kingsford, 11.
[236] Maitland and Kingsford, 11.
[237] Maitland and Kingsford, 11.

[238] Maitland and Kingsford, 30.

[239] Maitland and Kingsford, 30.

[240] Maitland and Kingsford, 14.

[241] Maitland and Kingsford, 14–15.

[242] Maitland and Kingsford, 13.

[243] Hermes Mecurius Trismegitus, *The Divine Pymander*, trans. John Everard (CreateSpace Independent Publishing Platform, 2015), bk. The Seventh Book, His Secret Sermon in the Mount of Regeneration, and the Profession of Science.

[244] Maitland and Kingsford, *The Virgin of the World*, 23.

[245] Maitland and Kingsford, 22.

[246] Charles Vail, *The Ancient Mysteries and Modern Masonry*, ed. Tarl Marwick, New (Independently published, 2019), 81.

[247] Vail, 15.

[248] Vail, 18.

[249] Vail, 16.

[250] Vail, 87.

[251] Vail, 15.

[252]Vail, 16.

[253] Vail, 81.

[254] Vail, 81.

[255] Vail, 81.

[256] Vail, 82.

[257] Vail, 82.

[258] Vail, 82.

[259] Vail, 83.

[260] Vail, 83.

[261] Vail, 84.

[262] Vail, 89.

[263] Vail, 91.

[264] Vail, 92.

[265] Vail, 93.

[266] W.Y. Evans-Wentz, *The Tibetan Book of the Dead: Or the After-Death Experiences on the Bardo Plane, According to Lama Kazi Dawa-Samdup's English Rendering* (Oxford: Oxford University Press, 2000), 111–12, https://www.amazon.com/gp/product/0195133129/ref=ppx_yo_dt_b_search_asin_image?ie=UTF8&psc=1.

[267] Evans-Wentz, 24.

[268] Evans-Wentz, 1xxiii.

[269] Evans-Wentz, 90.

[270] Evans-Wentz, 89–97.

[271] Evans-Wentz, 97–101.

[272] Evans-Wentz, 101–4.

[273] Evans-Wentz, 118–26.

[274] Evans-Wentz, 126–31.

[275] Evans-Wentz, 131–51.

[276] Evans-Wentz, 153–73.

[277] Evans-Wentz, 173–93.

[278] Evans-Wentz, x1.

[279] Max Guilmot, "The Initiatory Process in Ancient Egypt by Max Guilmot," AMORC, accessed June 2, 2020, https://www.rosicrucian.org/rosicrucian-books-the-initiatory-process-in-ancient-egypt.

[280] R.J. Rummel, "Definition of Democide (Genocide and Mass Murder)," accessed April 8, 2020, https://www.hawaii.edu/powerkills/DBG.CHAP2.HTM.

[281] R.J. Rummel, "20th Century Democide," accessed April 16, 2020, https://www.hawaii.edu/powerkills/20TH.HTM.

[282] R.J. Rummel, "Murder by Government--Democide," accessed April 8, 2020, https://www.hawaii.edu/powerkills/MURDER.HTM.

[283] Peter Brecke, "Data | Center for Global Economic History," accessed May 28, 2020, http://www.cgeh.nl/data#conflict.

[284] Maitland and Kingsford, *The Virgin of the World*, 28–29.

BIBLIOGRAPHY

Acharya S. *The Christ Conspiracy: The Greatest Story Ever Sold.* Kempton, Illinois: Adventures Unlimited Press, 1999.

Alabaster, Henry. *Wheel of the Law.* Reprint edition. Kila, MT: Kessinger Publishing, LLC, 1942.

Ani, Marimba. *Yurugu: An African-Centered Critique of European Cultural Thought and Behavior.* First Edition. Trenton, N.J: Africa World Press, 1994.

Asante, Molefi Kete. *Afrocentricity: Theory of Social Change.* Revised, Subsequent edition. Trenton, N.J: Africa World Press, 1988.

———. *Kemet, Afrocentricity and Knowledge.* Trenton, N.J: Africa World Press, 1990.

Baigent, Michael, Richard Leigh, and Henry Lincoln. *The Messianic Legacy.* New York: Dell, 1989.

Bernal, Martin. *Black Athena: The Afroasiatic Roots of Classical Civilization.* 1st edition. New Brunswick, N.J: Rutland Local History & Record Society, 1987.

Besant, Annie. *The Ancient Wisdom: An Outline of Theosophical Teachings.* Wheaton, Illinois: The Theosophical Publishing House, 1977.

BlackFacts.com. "(1909) Ida B. Wells, 'Lynching Our National Crime.'" Blackfacts.com. Accessed October 23, 2020. https://www.blackfacts.com/fact/1909-ida-b-wells-lynching-our-national-crime.

Blassingame, John W. *The Slave Community: Plantation Life in the Antebellum South.* Revised Edition. New York: Oxford University Press, 1979.

Bontemps, Arna. *Great Slave Narratives.* 2nd Printing Edition. Boston: Beacon Press, 1970.

Brecke, Peter. "Data | Center for Global Economic History." Accessed May 28, 2020. http://www.cgeh.nl/data#conflict.

Broeck, Roelof van den, and Cis van Heertum. *From Poimandres to Jacob Böhme: Gnosis, Hermetism and the Christian Tradition.* Leiden, Netherlands: BRILL, 2000.

"Buddha, The Word, The Eightfold Path (500BC)." Accessed September 12, 2020. http://www.columbia.edu/itc/ealac/moerman/fall2000/edit/pdfs/wk4/thewor.pdf.

Budge, E. A. Wallis. *Legends of the Egyptian Gods: Hieroglyphic Texts and Translations*. Reprint edition. New York: Dover Publications, 1994.

———. *The Gods of the Egyptians, Volume 1*. New York: Dover Publications, 2012.

———. *The Gods of the Egyptians, Volume 2*. Revised ed. edition. New York: Dover Publications, 2013.

Budge, Wallis, E.A. *Egyptian Book of the Dead: The Papyrus of Ani*. Dover Publications, 1999.

Carruthers, Jacob, H. "Science and Oppression." Chicago, IL: Kemetic Institute, 1991.

Carus, Paul. *The Gospel of Buddha*. Seattle, WA: Pacific Publishing Studio, 2011.

Child, Lydia Maria Francis 1802-1880. *The Progress of Religious Ideas: Through Successive Ages; Volume 1*. Sydney: Wentworth Press, 2016.

Childress, David Hatcher. *Technology of the Gods: The Incredible Sciences of the Ancients*. 1st Edition. Kempton, IL: Adventures Unlimited Press, 2000.

Church, A. M. E. "African Methodist Episcopal Church: Our History." AME Church. Accessed May 21, 2020. https://www.ame-church.com/our-church/our-history/.

Churchward, Albert. *The Origin and Evolution of Religion*. Brooklyn, NY: A&B Publishers Group, 1994.

Crowley, Aleister, S. L. MacGregor Mathers, and F. C. Conybear. *The Three Magical Books of Solomon: The Greater and Lesser Keys & The Testament of Solomon*. 1 edition. Mockingbird Press, 2017.

Däniken, Erich von. *Chariots of the Gods*. Translated by Michael Heron. New York: Berkley Books, 1999.

Diop, Cheikh Anta. *Civilization or Barbarism: An Authentic Anthropology*. Translated by Yaa-Lengi Meema Ngemi. Chicago, Illinois: Chicago Review Press, 1991.

———. *The African Origin of Civilization Myth or Reality*. New York: Lawrence Hill Books, 1974.

Dixon, Patricia. *African American Relationships, Marriages, and Families: An Introduction.* 2nd Edition. New York: Routledge, 2017.

Doane, T. W. *Bible Myths and Their Parallels in Other Religions.* Forgotten Books, 2012.

Du Bois, W. E. B. *The Philadelphia Negro: A Social Study.* New York: Schocken Books, 1967.

Digital Egypt for Universities. "Egyptian Chronology." Accessed May 27, 2020. https://www.ucl.ac.uk/museums-static/digitalegypt/chronology/index.html.

Eusebius. *Life of Constantine.* Translated by Averil Cameron and Stuart Hall G. 1 edition. Oxford University Press, U.S.A., 1999.

Evans-Wentz, W.Y. *The Tibetan Book of the Dead: Or the After-Death Experiences on the Bardo Plane, According to Lama Kazi Dawa-Samdup's English Rendering.* Oxford: Oxford University Press, 2000. https://www.amazon.com/gp/product/0195133129/ref=ppx_yo_dt_b_search_asin_image?ie=UTF8&psc=1.

Faulkner, Raymond, Ogden Goelet, and Carol Andrews. *Egyptian Book of the Dead: The Book of Going Forth by Day.* San Francisco: Chronicle Books, LLC, 1994.

FLH Testimony Before the Credentials Committee. Accessed October 23, 2020. https://www.youtube.com/watch?v=IRCUUzpfV7k&t=24s.

Franklin, Donna. *Ensuring Inequality.* Revised edition. New York, NY: Oxford University Press, 2015.

Franklin, John Hope, and August Meier, eds. *Black Leaders of the Twentieth Century.* Chicago, IL: University of Illinois press, 1982.

Giddings, Paula J. *When and Where I Enter: The Impact of Black Women on Race and Sex in America.* New York: W. Morrow, 1984.

Giles, J. A. *Hebrew and Christian Records: An Historical Enquiry Concerning the Age and Authorship of the Old and New Testaments;* London: Thubner & Col, Ludgate Hill, 1877.

Greene, John C. *The Death of Adam: Evolution and Its Impact on Western Thought.* New York: The New American Library of World Literature, Inc., 1961.

Guilmot, Max. "The Initiatory Process in Ancient Egypt by Max Guilmot." AMORC. Accessed June 2, 2020. https://www.rosicrucian.org/rosicrucian-books-the-initiatory-process-in-ancient-egypt.

"H. Rap Brown - 'Violence Is As American As Cherry Pie' - YouTube." Accessed May 26, 2020. https://www.youtube.com/watch?v=8WFFDm-Wyvw.

Hall, Manly P. *The Secret Teachings of All Ages: An Encyclopedic Outline of Masonic, Hermetic, Qabbalistic and Rosicrucian Symbolical Philosophy*. Reprint edition. Seattle, WA: Pacific Publishing Studio, 2011.

Hartmann, Franz. *The Life and the Doctrines of Philippus Theophrastus Bombast of Hohenheim Known as Paracelsus*. Kessinger Publishing, LLC: Kessinger Publishing, LLC, 2010.

Heras, H. "Anu in India and in Egypt." *Indian History Congress*, Proceedings of the Indian History Congress, 5 (1941): 92–101.

"Ida B. Wells-Barnett (1862-1931) and Her Passion for Justice, Black Women, African American Women, Suffrage, Women's Movement, Civil Rights Leaders." Accessed October 23, 2020. http://people.duke.edu/~ldbaker/classes/aaih/caaih/ibwells/ibwbkgrd.html.

Jackson, John G. *Christianity Before Christ*. Eastford, CT: Martino Publishing, 2015.

James, George. *Stolen Legacy: Greek Philosophy Is Stolen Egyptian Philosophy*. Independently published, 2019.

Jarvis, Malcolm. Interview with Malcolm "Shorty" Jarvis, 1994.

Jean, Clinton M. *Behind the Eurocentric Veils: The Search for African Realities*. Amherst: University of Massachusetts Press, 1992.

Journey to Enlightenment | THE RABBIT HOLE with Deepak Chopra, 2013. https://www.youtube.com/watch?v=NYi4hqjFfuc.

Karenga, Maulana. *Introduction to Black Studies*. 2nd Edition. University of Sankore Press, 1993.

Keto, C. Tsehloane. *Introduction to the Africa Centered Perspective of History*. London: Research Associates School Times Publications, 1999.

"Legends of the Gods, The Egyptian Texts: Legends of Egyptian Gods: The History of Creation--A." Accessed May 26, 2020. https://www.sacred-texts.com/egy/leg/leg13.htm.

"Legends of the Gods, The Egyptian Texts: Legends of Egyptian Gods: The History of Creation--B." Accessed May 26, 2020. https://www.sacred-texts.com/egy/leg/leg14.htm.

Lerner, Gerda, ed. *Black Women in White America*. New York: Vintage Books, n.d.

Libcom.org. "A Short History of Colonialism in Congo, 1885-1997." Accessed May 26, 2020. http://libcom.org/history/short-history-colonialism-congo-1885-1997

Lincoln, C. Eric. "The Black Church Since Frazier." In *The Negro Church in America/The Black Church Since Frazier*, edited by E. Franklin Frazier and C. Eric Lincoln. New York: Schocken, 1974.

Lincoln, C. Eric, and Lawrence H. Mamiya. *The Black Church in the African American Experience*. Duke University Press Books, 1990.

"List of Rulers of Ancient Egypt and Nubia | Lists of Rulers | Heilbrunn Timeline of Art History | The Metropolitan Museum of Art." Accessed May 27, 2020. https://www.metmuseum.org/toah/hd/phar/hd_phar.htm.

Lynchings by State and Race. "Lynching Statistics." Accessed May 25, 2020. http://law2.umkc.edu/faculty/projects/ftrials/shipp/lynchingsstate.html.

Maccoby, Hyam. *The Mythmaker: Paul and the Invention of Christianity*. Seventh Printing. edition. New York: Barnes & Noble Books, 1998.

Maitland, Edward, and Anna Kingsford, trans. *The Virgin of the World*. Deutschland: Jazzybee Verlag, 2017.

Massey, Gerald. *Ancient Egypt: The Light of the World [Two Volumes In One]*. Mansfield Centre, CT: Martino Publishing, 2014.

———. *The Natural Genesis*. Vol. 1. Baltimore, MD: Black Classic Press, 1998.

McCloud, Aminah, Beverly. *African American Islam*. 1 edition. London: Routledge, 2014.

McKinney-Johnson, Eloise. "Egypt's Isis: The Original Black Madonna." In *Black Women In Antiquity*, edited by Ivan Van Sertima. Brunswick, NJ: Transaction Publishers, 1995.

Mead, G. R. S. *Thrice-Greatest Hermes: Volumes I, II, III.* Deuschland: Jazzybee Verlag, 2017.

"Mob Violence and Anti-Lynching Campaign - A Voice for Justice - The University of Chicago Library." Accessed October 23, 2020. https://www.lib.uchicago.edu/collex/exhibits/voice-for-justice-life-and-legacy-ida-b-wells/mob-violence-and-anti-lynching-campaign/.

Muhammad, Nafeesa. "The Nation of Islam's Economic Program, 1934-1975," April 2, 2020. https://www.blackpast.org/african-american-history/the-nation-of-islams-economic-program-1934-1975/.

Pagels, Elaine. *The Gnostic Gospels*. Reissue edition. New York: Vintage, 1989.

Prabhupada, A. C. Bhaktivedanta Swami. *Bhagavad-Gita As It Is*. Los Angeles, California: The Bhaktivedanta Book Trust, 2001.

Richards, Dona. "African American Spirituality." In *African Culture: The Rhythms of Unity*, edited by Asante Molefi Kete and Kariamu Asante Welsh. Trenton, NJ: Africa World Press, 1989.

Robinson, Randall. *The Debt: What America Owes to Blacks*. Reprint edition. New York: Plume, 2001.

Roboteau, Albert, J. *Slave Religion: The "Invisible Institution" in the Antebellum South*. New edition. Oxford: Oxford University Press, 1980.

Rummel, R.J. "20th Century Democide." Accessed April 16, 2020. https://www.hawaii.edu/powerkills/20TH.HTM.

———. "Definition of Democide (Genocide and Mass Murder)." Accessed April 8, 2020. https://www.hawaii.edu/power-kills/DBG.CHAP2.HTM.

———. "Murder by Government--Democide." Accessed April 8, 2020. https://www.hawaii.edu/powerkills/MURDER.HTM.

Schuler, Timothy. "Mapping One of the World's Largest Landowners." Curbed, October 18, 2017. https://www.curbed.com/2017/10/18/16483194/catholic-church-gis-goodlands-esri-molly-burhans.

"Serapis Religion." Accessed April 16, 2020. http://platonism347.tri-pod.com/serapis_religion.htm.

Sitchin, Zecharia. *Twelfth Planet: Book I of the Earth Chronicles.* Reprint edition. New York, New York: Harper, 2007.

Slater, Philip. *The Pursuit of Loneliness: America's Discontent and the Search for a New Democratic Ideal.* 3rd edition. Beacon Press, 2016. https://www.amazon.com/Pursuit-Loneliness-Americas-Discontent-Democratic-ebook-dp-B01AEPR4DQ/dp/B01AEPR4DQ/ref=mt_other?_encod-ing=UTF8&me=&qid=1596491404.

"The Daily Star - Google News Archive Search." Accessed October 23, 2020. https://news.google.com/newspa-pers?nid=1297&dat=19090602&id=4PRNAAAAI-BAJ&sjid=sIoDAAAAIBAJ&pg=3567,2905466.

The Three Initiates. *The Kybalion: A Study of The Hermetic Philoso-phy of Ancient Egypt and Greece: Three Initiates.* Mansfield Centre, CT: Martino Publishing, 2016.

Trismegitus, Hermes Mecurius. *The Divine Pymander.* Translated by John Everard. CreateSpace Independent Publishing Platform, 2015.

Vail, Charles. *The Ancient Mysteries and Modern Masonry.* Edited by Tarl Marwick. New. Independently published, 2019.

Volney, C.F. *The Ruins of Empires.* Baltimore, MD: Black Classic Press, 1991.

Williams, Chancellor. *Destruction of Black Civilization: Great Is-sues of a Race from 4500 B.C. to 2000 A.D.* 3rd Revised Edi-tion. Chicago: Third World Press, 1992.

Williams, Robert, L. "The Death of White Research in the Black Community." *Journal of Non-White Concerns* 2, no. 3 (April 1974): 116–32.

York, Malachi. *The Holy Tablets.* 1st Edition. Holy Tabernacle Min-istries, 1996.

www.ingramcontent.com/pod-product-compliance
Lightning Source LLC
Chambersburg PA
CBHW030235030426
42336CB00009B/112